From These Beginnings

VOLUME TWO 2

From These Beginnings

A Biographical Approach to American History

Sixth Edition

Roderick Nash and Gregory Graves
University of California, Santa Barbara

 LONGMAN

An imprint of Addison Wesley Longman, Inc.

New York • Reading, Massachusetts • Menlo Park, California • Harlow, England
Don Mills, Ontario • Sydney • Mexico City • Madrid • Amsterdam

Editor-in-Chief: Priscilla McGeehon
Acquisitions Editor: Jay O'Callaghan
Executive Marketing Manager: Sue Westmoreland
Full Service Production Manager: Patti Brecht
Project Coordination, Text Design, and
Electronic Page Makeup: UG / GGS Information Services, Inc.
Cover Designer/Manager: Nancy Danahy
Cover Illustration: William Adelbert Dolwick. "Early Hobart" (mural study of
Hobart, Indiana Post Office), 1938. National Museum of American Art,
Smithsonian Institution, Washington, DC/Art Resource, NY.
Photo Research: Photosearch, Inc.
Senior Print Buyer: Hugh Crawford
Printer and Binder: The Maple-Vail Book Manufacturing Group
Cover Printer: Coral Graphic Services, Inc.

For permission to use copyrighted material, grateful acknowledgment is made to
the copyright holders on pp. 325–326, which are hereby made part of this
copyright page.

Library of Congress Cataloging-in-Publication Data

Nash, Roderick.
    From these beginnings : a biographical approach to American
history / Roderick Nash and Gregory Graves. — 6th ed.
        p.   cm.
    Includes bibliographical references and indexes.
    ISBN 0-321-00295-4 (v. 1). — ISBN 0-321-00315-2 (v. 2)
    1. United States—History.   2. United States Biography.
I. Graves, Gregory.   II. Title.
E178.N18   1999
973'.099—dc21   99-16632
                                                                      CIP

Please visit our website at http://www.awlonline.com

ISBN 0-321-00315-2

2345678910—MA—020100

Contents

Preface

There is properly no history; only biography.
—Ralph Waldo Emerson

That *From These Beginnings: A Biographical Approach to American History* has gone to a sixth edition provides continuing evidence for the old adage that the proper study of people is people. Certainly the proper study of the historian is humanity more than laws, treaties, elections, or eras. History is about people who loved, hated, achieved, failed, and shared with us a fascinating complexity of thought and feeling. Like its predecessors, this sixth edition is dedicated to the proposition that teaching and learning about history lose significance and fun when they are divorced from human beings.

The biographical approach is one way to enliven the study of history. The logic behind this choice is obvious: people are interested in people. History concerns, or should concern, people. Historical writing can be made as exciting as life itself if we think of it as a series of biographies. These assumptions underlie the novel structure of this book.

This is hardly a radical approach. Much of our best historical writing is in the form of biography or family history. In January 1977, record numbers of viewers watched *Roots*—and unknowingly and painlessly learned a great deal about the African-American experience. More recently, successful motion pictures have centered on Malcolm X, Jimmy Hoffa, Harry Truman, Richard Nixon, Janis Joplin, and Elvis Presley. Documentary-style biographies are regularly broadcast on television, and some cable networks specialize in weekly biographies. The success of all these ventures serves as a challenge to professional historians. Why should history be as "dry as dust"? Why shouldn't history have all the drama of life itself, which, after all, is what it is? Yet, surprisingly, no textbook used a biographical form of organization before the first edition of *From These Beginnings* (1973).

It has been our experience in teaching undergraduate history at several universities that biography is an effective lecturing tool. Whether in short vignettes or hour-long lectures, telling the story of people who affected and were affected by their times remains a reliable way of maintaining student interest. The standard textbook method of dividing the past into periods, eras, or ages has been discarded in *From These Beginnings*. Eighteen often overlapping lives provide the organizational framework, and the larger story of the American experience is woven around these lives. In this way, broad concepts are tied to specific examples. The frontier, slavery, and industrialization, for instance, acquire a sharper focus when viewed from the perspective of a pioneer, a slave, and an industrialist. At the same time, the narrative of national events deepens one's understanding of the eighteen individuals profiled.

The greatest problem in using a biographical approach is finding a happy compromise between "straight" biography and "straight" American history. This is not difficult, of course, when an individual life impinges directly on the course of national events. Thomas Jefferson writing the Declaration of Independence, Henry Ford revolutionizing transportation, and Martin Luther King, Jr., leading the civil rights movement are good examples. But frequently even a famous person sinks back into the general citizenry; the life becomes typical rather than unusual. On such occasions we have used a life-and-times approach consisting of a description of the historical context surrounding the individual. The technique is justifiable, we believe, on the grounds that any life is in large part shaped by the stream of events in which it floats.

Given the success of the fifth edition, biography replacements proved to be a challenge. For months we discussed who and why between ourselves and among our friends, colleagues, students, and families. Our decision to add a new biography of the "King of Rock and Roll," Elvis Presley, was done in the hope of providing better coverage of post-World War II American society. The Presley reading and all the existing biographies reflect many of the new historical interpretations regarding the person and the period. The most extensive additions to the existing biographies come in Christopher Columbus, Benjamin Franklin, and Jim Bridger in Volume 1, and in Gloria Steinem in Volume 2. The sixth edition also contains a new "For Consideration" section at the end of each biography. "For Consideration" challenges readers to analyze the person in his or her historical context.

While none of these eighteen individuals is completely satisfactory as the subject for a chapter in a book, there is some comfort in the realization that the choice is not all-important. A surprising amount of information about the course of national events can be tied to *any* American life. Try it, for example, with your own. *From These Beginnings* could feature any of the approximately half billion people who have called themselves Americans. As Americans, they have all affected, and have been affected by, American history.

We would like to acknowledge the help of our reviewers and thank them for their efforts: Brenda K. Jackson, San Jose State University; Joseph C. Thompson, Santa Fe Community College; Beatrix Hoffman, Northern Illinois University; James O. Breeden, Southern Methodist University; Steven Bucklin, University of South Dakota.

Roderick Nash
Gregory Graves

From These Beginnings

ONE 1

Mark Twain

The young reporter with the slow Missouri drawl stamped the cold of the high Nevada desert out of his feet as he entered the offices of the Virginia City Territorial Enterprise. It was early in 1863. The newspaper's editor, Joseph T. Goodman, looked puzzled at seeing his Carson City correspondent in the home office, but Samuel Clemens came right to the point: "Joe, I want to sign my articles. I want to be identified to a wider audience." The editor, already impressed with his colleague of six months, readily agreed. Then came the question of a pen name, since few aspiring writers of the time used their legal names. Clemens had something in mind: "I want to sign them 'Mark Twain,'" he declared. "It is an old river term, a leads-man's call, signifying two fathoms—twelve feet. It has a richness about it; it was always a pleasant sound for a pilot to hear on a dark night; it meant safe water."

For Samuel Clemens, the whole experience of growing up on the Mississippi River had "a richness about it." The flavor of that experience pervaded his best writing and happiest memories. But more and more, the author wrote about a myth. The river, the nation, and Twain himself changed radically during his lifetime, and much of the old magic rubbed off. One factor was their passage through the searing fire of civil war into an often sordid and ugly Gilded Age of industrialization and urbanization. There was also an experiment with imperialism. By that time the frontier, which had been close to Twain's Missouri boyhood in the 1830s, had retreated to the far corners of the continent. In many ways Mark Twain and the United States grew up together—and neither aged gracefully. Gradually the sunny humor left Twain's writing as he grew bitter and pessimistic about his country and his compatriots.

Mark Twain was fond of tracing his ancestry to one Flavius Clemens, a literary character noted for his "want of energy." In reality, his roots ran back to a Gregory Clemens, whose excessive energy on behalf of Oliver Cromwell in the English uprisings of the 1640s earned his severed head a place on a pole atop London's Westminster Hall. Gregory's family, however, escaped to the American colonies. Twain's grandfather had owned property in Virginia, but his father, in characteristic American fashion, had sought fresher fields over the mountains in Kentucky and Tennessee. Wealthy enough to own a few slaves and study law, John Clemens steadfastly pursued the material success that was the surest definition of status in the new society. In 1823, he married Jane Lampton. Twain's mother was descended from a long line of Kentucky pioneers, some of whom had followed Daniel Boone through the Cumberland Gap in 1767 and had remained to contest the ownership of the rich bluegrass country with bears and Indians.

For twelve years John and Jane Clemens followed a common frontier pattern. There were children, frequent moves from one small town to another, and always the gnawing hunger for fame and fortune that Jacksonian America easily aroused but only grudgingly satisfied. For a time John Clemens pursued a law career. But the mountain people frequently turned to more direct methods of settling their differences, so Clemens added storekeeping to his professions. And like almost all frontiersmen, Clemens dabbled in land—75,000 acres of it, in fact, which he bought in eastern Tennessee about 1826 for an incredible $400. Even this price was high for the struggling Clemenses, but they fully expected the investment to pay off a thousandfold. Young Samuel Clemens's first memories were of stories of the magical Tennessee land. By virtue of possessing so much land, John Clemens entered the social aristocracy of the Appalachian frontier. He bore the title "Squire" with a relish that seems surprising only to those who believe antebellum Americans more democratic than in fact they were. Provided there was equality of opportunity, many Americans had no reservations about accepting the trappings of Old World social differentiation.

John Clemens was among thousands of frontier entrepreneurs who rose and fell with the volatile national economy of the 1820s and 1830s. As a casualty of the downturn of the early 1830s, John Clemens looked for a new place to pursue his dreams. His choice meant that Samuel would come in contact with the Mississippi. The Clemenses' decision to go west—those seeking to improve their position in this period hardly ever considered going east—was made in 1835, the year of Samuel Langhorne's birth. The destination was Florida, Missouri, a frontier town at the fork of the Salt River. Some of Jane Clemens's relatives had settled the town a few years previously and, in the best booster tradition, urged everyone to come and share a glorious future. Realism suggested that such confidence was badly misplaced. Florida, Missouri, was in the middle of nowhere and, in Mark Twain's words, "nearly invisible." It consisted, in fact, of seventeen log and four frame houses, a long church that doubled as a school, two stores, and about 300 people. But fifty miles down the Salt River lay the Mississippi, an established highway of empire and potentially one of commerce as well. The first article of faith in Florida was that the town's proximity to the great river was a guarantee of prosperity. Dams and locks would make the stream navigable by steamboat. This meant direct water communication with commercial centers like Saint Louis, Cincinnati, and New Orleans. Beyond lay the world, and from the dirt streets of rural Missouri, dreams spiraled upward and outward.

It was the same throughout the trans-Appalachian West. Every village fully expected that the magic of internal improvements would make it a major city. Navigational aids and canals figured in the first wave of hope. Florida, Missouri, for example, anticipated transforming the shallow Salt River into an all-season, deep-water highway. Samuel's father headed a navigation company that obtained incorporation papers from the Missouri legislature. It built a dock and a small boat—which never sailed. Missouri provided no help in building the costly locks, and Andrew Jackson, in his 1830 veto of federal aid to Kentucky's Maysville Road, closed the federal treasury to local improvement projects. But it was a revolutionary new form of transportation, railroads, that struck the final blow at Florida's dreams.

Trains could run almost anywhere, at any season, and were less expensive than a canal-lock-dam system. Between 1830 and 1860 railroads came to dominate American transportation, and tiny Florida did not become part of the network of rails.

With five children now dependent on him, John Clemens struggled to make ends meet. He continued storekeeping and practiced law, but economic survival was a battle. In 1837 tightening credit and a drop in land sales produced a panic that led to one of the worst depressions in American history. Not until the mid-1840s did the economy turn upward again.

The Clemenses responded to the renewal of hard times by moving once again. This time they went to Hannibal, Missouri, the town identified with Mark Twain's youth, his fondest memories, and his best writing. Hannibal had one distinct advantage over Florida and the Tennessee hamlets. It was directly on the Mississippi, 100 miles north of Saint Louis. Mark Twain always remembered it as "a heavenly place for a boy," a "white town drowsing in the sunshine of a summer's morning; . . . the great Mississippi, the majestic, the magnificent Mississippi, rolling its mile-wide tide along, shining in the sun; the dense forest away on the other side." There were unlimited places to roam—woods and field and, if one dared, caves—and there was the river. After several narrow escapes from drowning, Clemens mastered swimming. Thereafter there was no containing him. In company with a gang of contemporaries, many of whom made their way directly into *The Adventures of Tom Sawyer* and *The Adventures of Huckleberry Finn*, Clemens turned the Mississippi into a giant playground. His days consisted of fishing, swimming, exploring islands, or sneaking a ride on a raft or steamboat. School was only a temporary and distasteful interruption.

There was, to be sure, the seamier side of frontier life. The young Samuel Clemens saw an old man shot down on Hannibal's main street at high noon. He was present when a drunk stabbed an immigrant with a bowie knife, and then remarked on the way the blood spurted from the wound in powerful jets. Cowering in the bushes, Clemens watched a widow mow down a local ruffian who had designs on her daughter. Fights and whippings were standard fare on the frontier, and Clemens never seemed to be far from the center of action. On numerous occasions he stumbled over corpses in his rambles along the river. And there was the fact of slavery.

The Clemenses had owned a few slaves in Tennessee and, as a result of the Compromise of 1820, were able to take them to their new home in Missouri. Like the family's fancy two-horse carriage, slaves were both practical and an indication of status. A black house girl enabled Jane Clemens to at least approach the southern ideal of ladyhood. A field hand allowed "Squire" Clemens to regard himself as something more than a storekeeper or farmer. Slaveholding, in sum, linked the Clemenses to the great planters whose dozens, and, in a few cases, even several hundred slaves actually provided the life of genteel ease that was the intellectual and emotional lifeblood of the antebellum South. To be sure, these big planters constituted only a small fragment of southern society. Over half the slaveowners had fewer than five slaves, which was about the number John Clemens owned in good times. To own more than twenty slaves was exceptional and a mark of high standing. And the really large slaveholders, whose holdings in human property ran to 100 or more, could have met together in a single hall. Yet it was this elite that dominated the South's economic and political life and set the social standards to which the humbler people aspired. Significantly, of the South's total white population of six million on the eve of the Civil War, fewer than 400,000 owned slaves. But such was the hold of the planter ideal on the mind and institutions of the South that the tail wagged the dog. And a civil war in defense of an institution that only a minority enjoyed was one result.

In time, Samuel Clemens came to understand and despise slavery, but in his youth slaves were an accepted part of life. Jennie, the Clemenses' house girl, was a second mother to Twain, and the slave children were his playmates. On winter evenings the whole family, black and white, would gather in front of an open fire to hear Uncle Ned, a slave, tell weird and wonderful stories about ghosts, spells, charms, and other manifestations of the supernatural. On at least one occasion a slave saved Samuel from drowning. Such human relationships with blacks were the source of Twain's tender account of Huckleberry Finn and the runaway slave Jim on their Mississippi raft. There is little doubt that Huck and, by implication, the young Clemens found more genuine affection and fatherly guidance in black men than he ever did in whites. The busy, cold John Clemens, in particular, was never close to his children. He died when Samuel was twelve.

Still, at an early age Samuel came to appreciate the significance of the color line. The boy learned that blacks, unlike other people, could be bought and sold. They were property in a frighteningly absolute sense. For instance, during a trip in 1842, John Clemens wrote the family an account of the difficulties he was experiencing in selling one "Charlie." "The highest price I had offered for him in New Orleans was $50, in Vicksburg $40. After performing the journey to Tennessee, I expect to sell him for whatever he will bring." For Clemens, the sale was just a livestock transaction.

On another occasion the house girl snatched a whip from the upraised hand of Jane Clemens. This challenge to authority produced an immediate and violent response. John Clemens tied Jennie's wrists and lashed her shoulders with rawhide. Confused and afraid, Samuel watched in silence. He also saw a runaway slave cornered and beaten by six whites. He saw a slave killed with a rock for a trifling offense. He was present when a Hannibal mob attacked and almost lynched an abolitionist. The man was spared only through the efforts of a minister who convinced the mob that the intended victim was insane rather than serious. As for slave auctions, the raw nerve ending of the institution, Twain's boyhood recollection is hazy. But he did "vividly remember," he later wrote, "seeing a dozen black men and women chained together lying in a group on the pavement, waiting shipment to a southern slave-market. They had the saddest faces I ever saw."

After his father's death in 1847, Samuel abandoned forever his career as a reluctant schoolboy and apprenticed himself to a Hannibal printer. The pay was in the usual form of board and clothes—"more board than clothes, and not much of either," he recollected. But the printing job opened Clemens's eyes, as it had Benjamin Franklin's, to the larger world. In time, he wanted to see it for himself, and, like Franklin, he left the printing shop to try his fortune in New York and Philadelphia. In 1853, Clemens stood before the grave of the famous Philadelphian. The young man recorded the event, without comment, in a letter home. He was more impressed by the size and pace of urban life. In awed tones, the country boy described New York's Crystal Palace Fair, which every day had 6,000 visitors—double Hannibal's entire population. New York itself contained an incredible 400,000 people and hummed with commercial activity.

It was during his year and a half in the East that Clemens first became aware that the slaves who had been an accepted part of his Missouri boyhood were the subject of a national controversy of growing intensity. The newspaper offices in which he worked fairly buzzed with discussion of the Compromise of 1850, especially its Fugitive Slave Law. The effort by the Free-Soil party, organized in 1848, to exclude slaves from the western territories was highly controversial. For the first time Clemens encountered widespread, vigorous abolitionism. Harriet Beecher Stowe's *Uncle Tom's Cabin* was the best-selling novel of the day, and the Missourian must have discussed it frequently. In Clemens's small-farming upper South, the pictures Stowe painted of huge plantations and brutal overseers did not ring true. But her charges were undoubtedly the basis of a certain amount of harassment of Clemens by his northern colleagues in the newspaper offices. On November 28, 1853, for example, Samuel wrote to his brother Orion, "How do you like 'free soil'?—I would like amazingly to see a good old-fashioned negro." But the problem refused to disappear. Abolitionists like Stowe and such blacks as Frederick Douglass who refused to be "old-fashioned" gave Clemens's and the nation's conscience little rest.

Late in 1854, having proved his independence and obtained a not altogether pleasing taste of the outside world, Clemens returned to his beloved Mississippi Valley. But the slavery controversy followed him west. By the fall of 1854 it was gnawing at the western edge of his home state. Missourians, in fact, played a major role in escalating the Kansas–Nebraska issue into a preview of the Civil War. Intensely proslave "border ruffians" from Missouri swarmed into neighboring Kansas to vote and, after 1855, to fight the advocates of free soil.

On the great river to the east of "bleeding Kansas," however, the pace of life was still measured. Clemens pursued his calling as a printer in several locations and found time to dream of going to South America and making a fortune on the upper Amazon. But in the spring of 1857 he turned to an even older dream: steamboating. His chance came when a veteran river pilot, Horace Bixby, agreed to take him on as an apprentice, or "cub." The next step was to "learn the river" upstream and down, day and night, high water and low. After eighteen months Clemens qualified as a pilot. The next two years were unquestionably the happiest of his life. He reveled in the glamour and excitement that came with being a star performer in the golden age of American steamboating. In peak periods there was a solid mile of the big black-stacked, triple-decked boats tied to the wharves of Cincinnati or Saint Louis or New Orleans. Piles of produce lined the docks, and the waterfronts seethed with activity. There was power and growth in these scenes, and at least in the 1850s Twain was proud to be a part of them. He also loved the quiet moments when, high in his glass-walled pilothouse, the beauty of the river was overwhelming. He poured the magic of these moments into the best descriptive passages of *Huckleberry Finn*.

For the United States as well as for Samuel Clemens, the decades immediately preceding the Civil War were, on the whole, a time of confidence. To be sure, the

Western Steamboat, with full cargo.

Engineer on duty : two feet water on lower deck.

A Hot Boat.—Ten 56lbs. weights on safety-valve.

Pittsburgh on a clear morning.

Running on a Bank.

Going over Falls of Ohio.—[Not exaggerated.]

Harper's Monthly, a leading American magazine, printed these impressions of travel on the Ohio and Mississippi rivers in its December 1858 issue. Mark Twain was piloting steamboats at this time and undoubtedly witnessed most of these scenes. The "hot boat" resulted from a captain's desire for maximum speed. The inoperative safety valve sometimes produced colossal explosions such as the one that killed Twain's brother.

rumblings of the sectional controversy were disturbing, but few before 1860 interpreted them as harbingers of real war. The nation's future appeared bright. The
anxious, uncertain years after independence were well behind, and the continuing
growth of capitalism, combined with the natural abundance of the continent,
promised unceasing prosperity. God, nature, and the course of history were on the
nation's side. Reformers would take care of any problems that rapid growth might
bring; progress, it appeared, was inevitable. Walt Whitman sensed this at his editor's desk in Brooklyn when he boasted in 1846 that "thirty years from this date,
America will be confessed the first nation on earth." And Henry Adams, in his
measured manner, recalled that as a young man in Massachusetts he, too, had subscribed to the faith that held the world to be simple, moral, well ordered, and secure. Clemens agreed. His pilot's view of the world bred confidence. Within a quarter of a century all three men would come to hold radically different opinions, but
in the halcyon antebellum years there was little reason to question humanity's
goodness or the nation's greatness.

Samuel Clemens had his first doubts about this idyllic world in June 1858. At
the time he belonged to the crew of the sleek new *Pennsylvania*, a steamboat sufficiently fast to make the round trip between Saint Louis and New Orleans in thirty-
five days. Through his connections he had obtained a clerkship on the *Pennsylvania*
for his younger brother, Henry. Then disaster struck. While taking on wood from a
flatboat sixty miles below Memphis, the *Pennsylvania*, for no apparent reason, exploded. The entire forward half of the boat blew out, and scalding clouds of steam
from the ship's boilers enveloped the trapped passengers and crew. By a quirk of fate
Samuel was not among them. A quarrel with another pilot on the *Pennsylvania* had
caused him to hire on a different boat and miss the ill-fated run. But Henry was present and horribly injured. Samuel rushed to his bedside, only to watch him die.

The personal loss was devastating for Clemens, but as he reflected on the explosion of the *Pennsylvania*, he perceived a level of tragedy at once broader and
deeper. Technology, which the steamboat symbolized and which constituted so vital a part of the nineteenth-century American idea of progress, had betrayed its
worshipers. For a horrible moment the machine had turned on its maker. The lesson was there for those who dared read it: The best condition for humanity might
well be the unmechanized past and not the technological future. Of course, neither
Clemens nor the United States gave up on mechanization because of incidents like
the *Pennsylvania* explosion. They could always be thought of as aberrations, temporary problems that a higher technology would surely solve. On the other hand, the
seeds of a later and deeper disillusionment were planted in his discovery of tragedy
on the shining Mississippi.

The second shock to Clemens's confidence in his nation was, of course, the
Civil War. Few Americans who lived through that cataclysm were unaffected. In
the first place, there was the spectacle of the vaunted democratic process shattering
completely on the rocks of the slavery controversy. The Compromise of 1850,
which many had expected to be a final settlement of the sectional differences,
proved only a temporary check. Westward expansion kept the old wounds open.
Only three years after the compromise, Clemens found "free soil" as burning an issue as ever, and as a states' rights southerner, he opposed the strengthening move-

ment. He also found American statesmen helpless in responding to it effectively. Franklin Pierce, a Democrat elected president in 1852, displayed an extraordinary lack of leadership during the Kansas–Nebraska controversy. His successor, James Buchanan, also proved adept in sidestepping the main issues. The best politician of the era, Senator Stephen A. Douglas of Illinois, could only devise a formula (popular sovereignty) that shifted the battlefield from the federal to the state and local level. By 1860, when the Republican Abraham Lincoln was elected without a single electoral vote from a slave state, it was clear that the national government was more a bone of contention than an agent of cohesion. Yet, in fairness to the politicians of the time, they faced the difficult—perhaps the impossible—problem of governing a house divided.

Samuel Clemens supported John Bell of Tennessee and his Constitutional Union party in the four-man election of 1860. It was the best of a poor slate for old-line Whigs like the Clemenses. But Bell, with his condemnation of sectional parties and loyalty to the Constitution and the Union, carried only three states, all in the upper South. Missouri, thoroughly divided, gave its nine electoral votes to the northern Democrat Stephen A. Douglas. After the election Clemens watched, only half believing, as the secession process gained momentum. Along with most of his contemporaries, he fully expected that the nation would come to its senses long before it came to blows. Yet another compromiser would appear. But the firing on Fort Sumter, South Carolina, on April 12, 1861, and its surrender two days later ended all illusions. On the Mississippi River people began to take sides. Clemens's instructor in piloting, Horace Bixby, went with the North and eventually rose to chief of the Union River Service. Clemens cast his lot with the Confederacy. But he and his associates were not radical; for a time, they saw validity in both positions. Moreover, the rivermen were, in a sense, men without a section. Their business was intersectional, and they thought in terms of long-distance trade and communication.

Gradually, however, attitudes hardened. On his last run up the Mississippi in April 1861, Clemens heard plenty of war talk and saw men seriously preparing to fight. At Memphis he and a companion were in the pilothouse when a cannon roared on the shore. Ignorant of its meaning, they steamed on. A second blast, this time no warning, sent a ball screaming into the deck immediately in front of the pilots. "Good Lord Almighty!" Clemens's friend gasped. "What do they mean by that?" Slowing and turning the boat toward shore, Clemens drawled, "I guess they want us to wait a minute." He was correct. After examination, the boat was allowed to pass. But it was the last steamboat to make the journey from New Orleans to Saint Louis, for war severed the natural artery of the river. It also ended Clemens's career as a riverman.

Undecided about his next step in a society crumbling before his eyes, Clemens went home to Hannibal. In this border state the claims of both the North and the South hung in the balance for most of the war. Governor Claiborne F. Jackson tried to lead Missouri out of the Union in March 1861 but failed to command the necessary legislative support. Yet Missouri was not prepared to side with the Union. When Lincoln asked the state for troops for the Union Army, he was bluntly refused. As a result of this ambivalence, the state began to experience its own civil war as neighbors took up arms against one another. Still, in the beginning, it was all very amusing and terribly romantic. Clemens recalled how companies of soldiers formed in and around Hannibal without the slightest idea of the nature of their cause or the identity of their enemy. It was a gay military lark, with the bonus of kissing one's sweetheart good-bye before marching off to war. Clemens himself went through this ritual after deciding, like Robert E. Lee, that he would defend his state from the northern invaders. His older brother, Orion, however, became a Union sympathizer, a Lincoln Republican, and an abolitionist.

As a Confederate soldier Samuel Clemens joined 30,000 other Missourians, but 109,000 men in that state eventually fought for the Union. Missouri as a whole never chose sides, remaining, along with Kentucky, Maryland, and Delaware, a slave state that did not join the Confederacy. Lincoln obviously wanted to preserve this indecision on the part of the border states and took every step, including some clearly illegal ones, to ensure the continuance of their neutrality. His success was a major factor in the Union's victory.

For the first few weeks, Clemens's military endeavors were only slightly more sophisticated than the games of war he had played as a child. The major armies had the same experience. Men dashed off to the First Battle of Bull Run, Virginia, in July 1861 in a holiday mood. No one expected the fighting to last more than a few months, but gradually the full meaning of civil war became apparent to Clemens and to the nation. After Union troops invaded Missouri in July 1861, Clemens and fourteen adventure-seeking friends swore vengeance on the invaders. Only a few years before, the Marion Rangers, as they called themselves, had organized as pirates. Now, without uniforms and with borrowed shotguns, they prepared to go to war. After the exciting farewells, the Marion Rangers settled into an uncomfortable camp life from which all traces of grandeur quickly vanished. There were ludicrous blunders—a Ranger shot his horse as it approached him in the dark—and there was the genuine fear of actually encountering the enemy. But what finally soured Clemens on the war was his recognition that its essence was organized killing.

He expressed his feelings in a short story centering on the panic murder by the Rangers of an unarmed stranger who innocently rode through their camp one night. The incident was fictitious, but without any doubt Clemens felt it was possible, and the thought made him sick. Also distressing were the accounts of warfare in the East. At Bull Run troops only slightly better trained than the Marion Rangers engaged in a wild medley of mistakes that would have been funny if the costs were not calculated in lives. And the slaughter had only just begun. Clemens, however, had seen enough. He had no personal stake in slavery and did not sympathize with the political and social philosophies he was allegedly defending. It was therefore with little regret that Second Lieutenant Clemens allowed a sprained ankle to force him out of the war.

Quitting the war with a curse for both belligerents, Samuel traveled to Iowa to join Orion Clemens. The disillusioned soldier found his brother in a frenzy of excitement. A friend in the Lincoln administration had just secured an appointment for him as secretary to the territorial governor of Nevada. Orion, in turn, needed an assistant, and Samuel did not hesitate to offer his services. Disgusted with the war that had transformed the happy valley of his youth into a nightmare, he was fully prepared to exercise the option he later extended to Huckleberry Finn and "light out for the Territory ahead of the rest." At the same time, he intended to catch up to the rapidly retreating American frontier that had been so intrinsic to antebellum Hannibal's appeal.

On July 26, 1861, the Clemens brothers boarded a sixteen-horse stagecoach of the recently formed Butterfield Overland Mail Company at Saint Joseph, Missouri. Nineteen days and 1,700 miles later they arrived in Carson City, Nevada. It was a glorious trip, really an escape. There were just enough outlaws and Indians to lend excitement without creating serious danger. Mark Twain, the author, described his feelings a decade later in *Roughing It*: "Even at this day it thrills me through and through to think of the life, the gladness, and the wild sense of freedom that used to make the blood dance in my face on those fine Overland mornings." The stage followed the South Pass route that Jim Bridger had pioneered a quarter century earlier and rumbled past Fort Bridger, which the old mountain man had operated until the Mormons bought him out in 1853. Clemens enjoyed a few days of rest in Salt Lake City and later delighted in poking fun at the Mormon residents of that city. But Nevada was his goal, and soon the rejuvenated horses were racing across the Great Basin to the territorial capital on the eastern flanks of the Sierra.

When the Clemens brothers descended from the hot, dusty stagecoach in August 1861, they entered an extraordinary world. Only two years before, Henry T. P. Comstock and several colleagues had struck rich veins of gold and silver directly across the Sierra from the California strikes of 1849 that had launched the mining boom. By the time of their arrival, the frantic heart of the bonanza had shifted from California and Colorado to Nevada. A hoard of "fifty-niners" rushed to the region to find one of the richest single deposits, the Comstock Lode, which yielded $350 million between 1859 and 1879. To harvest the wealth, cities appeared in the wilderness almost overnight. They were raw and violent. Virginia City's first twenty-six graves were those of murdered men. Samuel Clemens was impressed by the entire spectacle. "The country is fabulously rich," he wrote back home, "in gold, silver, copper, lead . . . thieves, murderers, desperadoes, ladies . . . lawyers, Christians, Indians, Chinamen, Spaniards, gamblers, sharpers, coyotes . . . poets, preachers, and jackass rabbits." The desert environment, of course, was new and shocking for the man from well-watered Missouri. "The birds that fly over the land carry their provisions with them," he remarked with characteristic wit.

Samuel Clemens originally intended to stay in the West a few months; instead he remained five and a half years. The principal reason was his enchantment with the region, which is apparent in his account of his first visit to Lake Tahoe. With another uprooted midwesterner, Samuel hiked from Carson City to the lake soon after his arrival in Nevada. Deep blue and fully twenty miles long, Tahoe sits on the Sierra slope at 6,300 feet. The surrounding snowcapped peaks rise several thousand feet higher. Clemens was stunned by his first view: "As it lay there with the shadows of the mountains brilliantly photographed upon its surface I thought it must surely be the fairest picture the whole world affords." Clemens and his friend had utilitarian reasons for coming to Tahoe. They intended to stake claims to several hundred acres of yellow pine forest on the lake shore. But the beauty and peacefulness of the

Travel in Mark Twain's day could be just as dangerous as on today's freeways. The cause of this 1856 accident was probably a front wheel's catching on the logs of the bridge and snapping off. Twain went to Nevada in 1861 in a larger coach pulled by sixteen horses.

In 1859 Henry Comstock (left) staked the first claim on one of the world's most concentrated deposits of gold and silver ore. It soon acquired the name Comstock Lode. At this time, wild game (foreground) was still plentiful, but by 1861, when Twain arrived, miners were obliged to pay grossly inflated prices for provisions.

Virginia City, perched on the side of a mountain in western Nevada, was Mark Twain's home from 1862 to 1864. The town literally rested on some of the world's richest gold and silver deposits.

location diminished their acquisitiveness. Drifting in a borrowed rowboat, much as Clemens had drifted on the Mississippi, they joked, and smoked, and counted the massive trout plainly visible in a hundred feet of crystal water. Clemens had indeed recaptured the magic of his Missouri boyhood. His happiness was nearly perfect. "Three months of camp life on Lake Tahoe," he wrote in *Roughing It*, "would restore an Egyptian mummy to his pristine vigor, and give him an appetite like an alligator." The only discordant note was a forest fire that their camp fire ignited, but "conservation" was not yet in the American vocabulary, and the sight of bright flames licking up the hillsides struck Clemens as a spectacle worthy of Tahoe's beauty.

While one part of Clemens's mind responded to the solitude and natural beauty of Tahoe, another part was infected by the get-rich-quick frenzy that had seized western Nevada. In this ambivalence he was representative of American society in the middle decades of the nineteenth century: Here was the frequently contradictory attraction to an older, simpler pastoralism and a future that was complex and increasingly urban. For Clemens the call of the civilized sounded with a vengeance just after his return from Tahoe. By early 1862 he was fully engrossed in the silver fever. Racing from strike to strike, frantically laying out claims and abandoning them just as impulsively, he became part of a money-crazed society. Taking for granted that he would become a millionaire before the year was out, Clemens used his fertile imagination to dwell on the lifestyle such affluence would permit: "San Francisco . . . , Brown stone front—French plate glass—billiard-room off the dining-room—statuary and paintings—shrubbery and two-acre grass plot—green-house—iron dog on the front stoop—gray horses—landau, and a coachman with a bug on his hat!" It was a far cry from Hannibal or Tahoe, and Clemens was also capable of bitterly attacking such materialism. But in this indecisiveness he expressed quite accurately the American dilemma regarding progress.

For Clemens, as for so many other actors in the drama of bonanza mining, success always remained just out of reach. But after several rounds of near misses, Clemens gave up on precious metals and turned to the pursuit of his real bonanza: writing. This quest took him first, in August 1862, to the *Territorial Enterprise* of Virginia City, Nevada, in the heart of the Comstock Lode. The printer-riverman-secretary-miner fitted perfectly into the staff of the newspaper. All the reporters relied on a brand of irreverent humor that Samuel Clemens, who here began using his famous pen name, Mark Twain, soon made his forte.

In Virginia City, where Clemens wrote until 1864, and then in San Francisco, the California mining camps, and, briefly, the Hawaiian Islands, the young author perfected his art. He learned much in these years from contact with Artemus Ward, the dean of American humorists, and Bret Harte, then an aspiring local-color writer. In 1865, Clemens took a giant step toward literary recognition with the publication of "The Celebrated Jumping Frog of Calaveras County." Short, funny, and somewhat sadistic (the story concerned a live frog filled so completely with lead pellets that it could not jump), the tale was carefully constructed and used dialect adroitly. Widely circulated in the East, "The Celebrated Jumping Frog" made Samuel Clemens, known thereafter as Mark Twain, a shining new talent in the literary world.

While Mark Twain experienced the West, the Civil War raged east of the Mississippi River. Twain's early pro-Confederate views prevailed for a time. But his "de-Southernizing," as a friend described it, came in Virginia City. His early writings for the *Territorial Enterprise* had been intensely pro-South. Still associating himself with the old cavalier ideals, he was, in his own words, "the most conceited ass in the Territory." On one occasion he disparaged a dance staged in Carson City as a benefit for the Sanitary Commission (a kind of Red Cross organized by the Union), writing that it was a scheme to promote miscegenation. Several outraged readers immediately challenged him to duels. Ordinarily a southern gentleman would have debated only the choice of weapons, but the challenges caused the former Confederate soldier to debate in his own mind the whole rationale of the southern way of life. Always frank, he concluded there wasn't much in it worth dueling about. The easiest way out of his predicament was to run away, and this he did, leaving Nevada for California in 1864. He did this not because he was afraid, but because he simply was no longer committed to the southern cause.

The California Mark Twain entered in 1864 was alive with activity. Since the discovery of gold at Sutter's Mill in 1848, frenzied prospectors had changed the landscape. The lure of gold nuggets the size of hen's eggs remained a magnet for fortune hunters, as rough-and-tumble mining towns dotted the Sacramento River valley; San Francisco, which had become an overnight city after the Mexican War, became a ghost town just as quickly when most of the population scurried to the gold fields. By 1850, California had over 100,000 people and skipped the usual territorial phase, moving directly to statehood. By the 1860s gold had made San Francisco and Sacramento the two wealthiest towns in the West, and four entrepreneurial shopkeepers dreamed of connecting California to the East by rail. With the establishment of the Central Pacific Railroad Company, Leland Stanford, Charles Crocker, Collis Huntington, and Mark Hopkins, better known as the Big Four, laid the foundations for the first transcontinental rail line. While Mark Twain was in California, the Southern Pacific pushed eastward into the Sierra Nevada toward an 1869 rendezvous with the Union Pacific Railroad at Promontory Point, Utah.

After witnessing the dramatic changes taking place in the West, Mark Twain returned to the East early in 1867. At once he sensed that his western sojourn, which had spared him a confrontation with the full meaning of the Civil War, had made him an exception. The bulk of his compatriots knew that the war had set them apart from earlier generations. A new mood prevailed. People had been forced to understand that, for all the country's pretensions to being a model society, a new Eden, the nation was not to be exempt from tragedy and suffering. The optimistic, innocent expectations of progress, even of perfection, that had characterized the prewar decades seemed a mockery after four bloody years. And the deaths of 600,000 Americans in vicious combat mocked the vaunted democratic process itself. Where was the substance for the belief that majority rule was the key to future harmony? The war and the shocking assassination of Abraham Lincoln in its aftermath on April 15, 1865, had left Americans with little choice but to accept the fact that force superseded reason and morality as a prime mover in human affairs. Perhaps, as the English biologist Charles Darwin argued in his 1859 *Origin of Species*, life on earth was best understood in terms of a struggle for existence in which only the fittest survived. Perhaps people were merely pawns in the hands of forces beyond their control and even beyond their comprehension. Some said the nation had grown up in the Civil War years; others felt it had begun to die. But no one disputed that it had become sadder, wiser, and less certain about the future.

Twain could read the new mood in the faces he encountered after his return from California. He also found it in the awkward silence that followed his inquiry about old friends along the Mississippi. "The eight years in America from 1860 to 1868," Twain concluded, "uprooted institutions that were centuries old, changed the politics of a people, transformed the social life of half the country, and wrought so profoundly upon the entire national character that the influence cannot be measured short of two or three generations."

Twain's shock in discovering the profound impact of the Civil War after his lark on the frontier certainly influenced his decision to leave the United States once again—this time on one of the first organized pleasure cruises in maritime history. The *Quaker City* left New York on June 8, 1867, for the Mediterranean. Twain sailed as a correspondent for the San Francisco *Alta California*, and his reaction to the Old World was thoroughly western. Confident in himself and in his country, Twain irreverently scoffed at the cultural treasures of Europe. Gone from his atti-

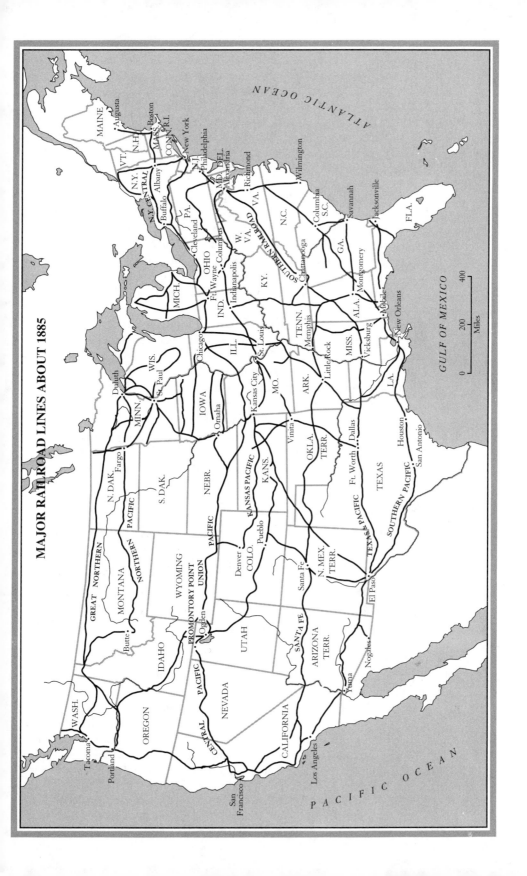

MAJOR RAILROAD LINES ABOUT 1885

ATLANTIC OCEAN

GULF OF MEXICO

PACIFIC OCEAN

Miles
0   200   400

MAINE
Augusta
VT.
N.H.
MASS. Boston
CONN. R.I.
New York
N.Y.
N.Y. CENTRAL
Albany
Buffalo
PA.
Philadelphia
N.J.
MD. DEL.
Alexandria
Richmond
VA.
Cleveland
W. VA.
N.C.
Wilmington
OHIO
Columbus
Ft. Wayne
IND.
Indianapolis
KY.
SOUTHERN RAILROAD
Chattanooga
Columbia
S.C.
Savannah
Jacksonville
FLA.
GA.
Montgomery
ALA.
Mobile
New Orleans
MICH.
Chicago
ILL.
St. Louis
TENN.
Memphis
MISS.
Vicksburg
Little Rock
ARK.
LA.
WIS.
Duluth
St. Paul
MINN.
IOWA
Omaha
MO.
Kansas City
OKLA. TERR.
Ft. Worth
Dallas
Houston
San Antonio
Vinita
N. DAK.
Fargo
NORTHERN PACIFIC
S. DAK.
NEBR.
PACIFIC
KANSAS PACIFIC
KANS.
Pueblo
COLO.
Denver
Santa Fe
N. MEX. TERR.
El Paso
TEXAS
TEXAS & PACIFIC
SOUTHERN PACIFIC
GREAT NORTHERN
MONTANA
Butte
WYOMING
PROMONTORY POINT
Ogden
UNION
IDAHO
UTAH
SANTA FE
ARIZONA TERR.
Nogales
Yuma
WASH.
Tacoma
Portland
OREGON
CENTRAL PACIFIC
NEVADA
CALIFORNIA
San Francisco
Los Angeles

tude was the embarrassed provincialism that had caused earlier generations of Americans to disparage their native culture and slavishly imitate European social and aesthetic taste. Poking fun at the cult of Michelangelo that he encountered in Italy, Twain remarked that "the Creator made Italy from designs by Michelangelo." And his impressions on seeing the czar of Russia were straight from the American frontier; this great personage was merely a man, and "if I chose I could knock him down."

Twain's patriotism is constantly on display in *Innocents Abroad*, the book that appeared in 1869 and described his tour. On one occasion in the Straits of Gibraltar, the *Quaker City* crossed the path of a strange sailing vessel. "She was one towering mass of bellying sail," Twain exulted, but when the ship displayed the American flag, his excitement knew no bounds: "She was beautiful before—she was radiant now." Then Twain philosophized on the meaning of the flag in a foreign locale: "To see it is to see a vision of home itself and its idols, and feel a thrill that would stir a very river of sluggish blood."

As Mark Twain gradually discovered after his return to New York in November 1867, it was easier to love the United States at a distance than up close. An era Twain later named "The Gilded Age" was already in full swing. As the Missourian began to fathom its ends and means, his disenchantment increased sharply. The vantage point for his initial investigations could not have been better. Before the *Quaker City* landed, Twain had accepted a position in Washington as private secretary to Senator William M. Stewart of Nevada. The job was a complete sinecure and allowed Twain plenty of time to examine the quality of national politics and politicians. His notebooks recorded his findings. "Whiskey is taken into the committee rooms in demijohns," Twain reported, "and carried out in demagogues." Government, he discovered, was a business. Everyone was out to enrich himself, and corruption was the standard means. The openness with which bribery, graft, and influence peddling occurred shocked Twain. There seemed to be no checks on immorality. As Senator Roscoe Conkling of New York put it, "Nothing counts except to win." And winning was defined in strictly material terms. Watching the impeachment and near removal of President Andrew Johnson play out its ludicrous course, Twain lost respect for the whole political process. When he wrote "There are some pitiful intellects in this Congress," he very likely understated his feelings.

Twain left Washington in disgust in 1868 to pursue a literary life, but the spoilsmen were just warming up. Under Ulysses S. Grant, who was elected president in 1868 and again in 1872, corrupt government flourished. The Civil War hero was not personally involved, but he failed to maintain integrity in his administration. With no experience in civilian affairs, he let his administration become the tool of smarter but less principled men. For Twain, who had met Grant early in 1868 and greatly admired him as a soldier, it was particularly painful to see the way the president allowed unscrupulous financial manipulators like Jim Fisk and Jay Gould to enjoy the protection of his friendship. Following close on the heels of Fisk's and Gould's attempts to corner the gold and stock markets in 1869 were scandals involving railroad contractors, whiskey distillers, and Indian traders. The threads of guilt in these cases ran through the House and Senate to the Cabinet and even as far as the vice presidency. Still, in Twain's mind, Grant was untouchable, a rock of integrity in a sea of spoils. Henry Adams, who was also observing Washington in the late 1860s, was not as charitable. The succession of presidents from his great-grandfather to Grant, he thought, was evidence enough to destroy Darwin's argument for evolution. Grant, in Adams's opinion, was a Stone Age president.

Although the Washington scandals were disturbing, the greatest moral explosion of the postwar decade for Mark Twain and many of his contemporaries involved a religious rather than a political figure. Henry Ward Beecher was the foremost clergyman of his time. Before the Civil War he had led a host of reform crusades, most prominently that of antislavery. In fact, the guns shipped to Kansas in the 1850s to defend Free-Soil principles were popularly known as "Beecher's Bibles." The minister's sister was none other than the author of *Uncle Tom's Cabin*, Harriet Beecher Stowe. Striking in appearance and a master of eloquent expression, Beecher seemed to be the embodiment of morality and idealism. His writings, sermons, and lectures inspired millions of Americans with confidence that a human being could transcend base urges and that, in the words of Ralph Waldo Emerson, one could "hitch your wagon to a star."

Mark Twain had known and admired Henry Ward Beecher since 1867, when the celebrated clergyman had played a leading role in organizing the *Quaker City* tour. At the last minute Beecher found it impossible to join the cruise, but many members of his congregation did, and at its conclusion he entertained Twain at a dinner party. A brother of Henry Ward Beecher performed the wedding ceremony between Twain and his bride, Olivia Langdon, early in 1870. When the couple settled in the fashionable Nook Farm area near Hartford, Connecticut, they became neighbors and friends of still more Beechers. Then the bomb dropped. In 1871, stories began to circulate in New York linking the Reverend Beecher in an adulterous relationship with Mrs. Elizabeth Tilton. Twain was outraged by what he considered a cruel slander of the magnificent Beecher. But the stories continued and, through the efforts of the militant feminist Victoria Woodhull, even appeared in print.

Twain denounced them. Beecher was vitally important to him and to his time as a bastion of order and decency, an assurance that the nation had not lost its moral compass in a wilderness of materialism. Gradually, however, Twain's eyes were forced open. Beecher's own sister declared that he was guilty of adultery. And Mrs. Tilton, who, along with her husband, was a member of Beecher's congregation, quietly admitted being a party to the illicit relationship. Beecher even wrote a letter of apology to Mr. Tilton. Unsatisfied, Tilton brought an alienation of affections suit against Beecher in 1874. The subsequent trial made headlines throughout the nation. Twain was, in the words of a friend, "tremendously worked up" by the Beecher–Tilton affair and even attended a few of the court sessions. The ultimate inability or unwillingness of the jury to pin blame on Beecher was not really a relief. The whole business left a bad taste in Twain's mouth. Had considerations of right and wrong become so obscured or irrelevant that even the nation's foremost religious leader could ignore them? Was force—in this case, lust—more powerful than reason and morality? For Twain, the Beecher–Tilton affair, like the explosion of the *Pennsylvania* and the Civil War, was a shock that cast shadows of doubt over the future of the United States. Antebellum expectations, at any rate, now appeared innocent, naive, and unfounded.

Early in 1873 Mark Twain struck back at what he called the "moral ulcers" of his age with the best weapon he could muster: a book. The idea for *The Gilded Age* began at a dinner party at which Twain and his guest, Charles Dudley Warner, accepted a challenge from their wives to write a better novel than the current crop of bestsellers. The coauthors also intended to write a "truer" novel. The resulting manuscript, completed in three months of intense work, was a searing indictment of the social, economic, and political fabric of American life after the Civil War. Many of its characters and incidents came directly from the lives of Warner and Twain. There were the vote-buying congressmen, the pretentious and hollow society ladies, the attractive younger ladies who parlayed their sexual favors into wealth and prominence, and a succession of various confidence men, frauds, and crooks. The protagonist of *The Gilded Age*, Harry Brierly, is a young idealist with plans for internal improvements in a middle western town strongly reminiscent of Twain's native Florida, Missouri. In the course of the novel Brierly learns the price of obtaining an appropriation from Congress. A series of bribes distributed to secure the grant finally leaves no funds to be used for the intended purposes. When he discovers this in the plush office of the bogus Columbia River Slackwater Navigation Company, Brierly's disillusionment and disgust are complete.

While satire like *The Gilded Age* was one outlet for Twain's anger about the moral corruption of the 1870s, the resurrection of earlier and allegedly better times was another. In the years after the Civil War, Twain found his thoughts straying back more and more to antebellum Hannibal and his boyhood on the river. In part, this was a form of escape, just as the trip to Nevada had been. Old times on the Mississippi were a pleasant subject to contemplate compared with the "moral ulcers" of the postbellum United States. Moreover, in Twain's hands, nostalgia produced good literature. *The Adventures of Tom Sawyer*, which appeared in 1876, was the result of happy summer hours recollecting happy summer hours thirty years before. The book was, in large part, pure evocative writing, a thinly disguised autobiography. But just beneath the surface Twain snapped and snarled at the business-minded society in which he lived. *Tom Sawyer* is a paean to irresponsibility. The Franklinesque virtues of discipline, hard work, and material success are deliberately juxtaposed to the happy idleness and nonsense of boyhood on the river. At the root of this juxtaposition are disturbing questions about traditional American definitions of prosperity and progress.

Twain continued his oblique attack on the established national creed in a series of clever essays. In "Advice to Youth" he appeared to agree with Franklin in advising aspiring boys to get up with the birds, provided the birds slept until half past nine. In "Autobiography of a Damned Fool" Twain parodied Franklin's famous autobiography by showing how the recommended cold swim every morning resulted in stolen clothing and death by exposure. Twain made his point explicit in two essays written about 1875. "The Story of the Bad Little Boy" and "The Story of the Good Little Boy" show that, in terms of success, at least, wrong is right. The essays raised questions about ethical criteria as well as about success, and they presaged Huckleberry Finn's "wrong" decision with regard to his black rafting companion, Jim (see pages 22–23). But at the same time Twain was challenging the validity of American values, most of his compatriots were cheering them. Horatio Alger's 119 books, beginning in 1868 with *Ragged Dick*, almost all dwelt on the theme of rising from rags to riches by dint of hard work, ability, and good luck. Expressing the heart of the American dream, Alger's books sold by the millions. Indeed, by the end of the century he was the only American writer who enjoyed the same level of public recognition as Mark Twain.

While Twain might question Alger's easy acceptance of Franklinesque virtues, he could not deny that it was the Benjamin Franklins, not the Tom Sawyers, who dominated the nation in the Gilded Age. Awakened in the 1830s by the Jacksonian policy of liberating capitalism, the national economy survived the depressions that had dashed John Clemens's hopes and, after 1843, entered a period of extraordinary expansion. The Civil War certainly slowed the economic growth rate, but the war also created opportunities. Moreover, the Union victory placed the federal government in the hands of those who believed that the business of America was business. Industrial expansion became a major objective of wartime and postwar politics. With the South eliminated as a factor in national decision making, there were few obstacles on the way to wealth.

The results of an accelerating economy boggled the mind of a small-town boy like Mark Twain. Between 1860 and 1900 the United States grew from a second-rate industrial power to the world's leader. After the tremendous success of the first transcontinental railroad in 1869, five more east–west lines crisscrossed the country during the next three decades. Railroad securities essentially created the New York Stock Exchange, and the railroads themselves dominated American economic and social life. Other large industries arose to take advantage of the railroad network. The value of American manufactured goods almost equaled the total production of the three former leaders combined. New England alone produced more goods per capita than any country in the world. The most intense economic surge occurred between 1877 and 1893. In these sixteen years the national output of copper increased seven times, crude oil four times, and manufacturing as a whole two-and-one-half times. The electric power industry, which had not even existed in 1877, was a $23-million business by 1893, providing electricity for inventions like the telephone, phonograph, microphone, kinetoscope (movie projector), and the incandescent light bulb. By that time the United States had no equal in the timber, steel, oil, meatpacking, coal, iron, and telephone industries. American locomotives and pianos were the best in the world.

The men who made this industrial bonanza possible were systems builders. They possessed the ability and accumulated the resources to order and integrate huge sectors of the American economy. Pragmatic, efficient, and extremely ambitious, they became the winners in the intense, wide-open competition that characterized the heyday of capitalism. Consider Andrew Carnegie, a man Mark Twain knew and always regarded as the epitome of the self-made captain of industry. "Saint Andrew," Twain called the steel king and, naturally, received the appellation "Saint Mark" in return. Carnegie, like Twain, had been born in 1835 in a small village, but the country was Scotland. When he was thirteen Carnegie came to the United States, settled with his impoverished parents in Pennsylvania, and began work as a bobbin boy in a cotton factory at a salary of $1.20 a *week*. Instead of being discouraged, Carnegie was thrilled by the prospect of being on the capitalistic ladder. In the next ten years he climbed it with astonishing speed. First railroads, then bridges, and finally steel occupied his attention. The huge Homestead steel plant on the Monongahela River near Pittsburgh, Pennsylvania, was started in 1872. By the end of the century the Carnegie Steel Company had emerged the victor in a struggle for existence that initially involved hundreds of competitors. In the course of the battle Carnegie became one of the richest men in the United States. In 1900, the one-time bobbin boy enjoyed a yearly income of $25 million. The following year Carnegie sold his interests to the financier J. P. Morgan, the architect of an even larger conglomerate called United States Steel. The purchase price of the Carnegie Steel Company was nearly half a billion dollars.

They were controversial figures in their own time, and the verdict is still not in on Andrew Carnegie and his colleagues in industrial empire building. Mark Twain, for example, could not suppress a sense of awe in the presence of Carnegie and his accomplishments. In an acquisitive age, Carnegie was a god. But Twain could also turn bitterly against the acquisitive impulse. Once, according to Twain, Americans "desired money"; now they "fall down and worship it." The new gospel, he added, was "Get money. Get it quickly. Get it in abundance. Get it in prodigious abundance. Get it dishonestly if you can, honestly if you must." One of the problems Twain and his contemporaries encountered in evaluating industrialization as personified by a man like Carnegie was that the process involved new techniques of organization that seemed wrong only because they were strange. Early in his rise to prominence, for example, Carnegie discarded the old idea of small-unit competition—the free-for-all that characterized the Jacksonian economic ideal. The need for ordering giant, nationwide industries, Carnegie realized, simply could not be met by small companies. Their size did not permit the economies of scale that were the key to large-scale production. Nor could the small units possibly command sufficient capital to undertake such tasks as building a transcontinental railroad or moving a mountain of iron ore from northern Minnesota to Pittsburgh's steel furnaces.

The new economic units that Carnegie envisioned and developed were built around the principles of either vertical or horizontal integration. In the former, the firm controlled all the steps in producing and marketing its product. Thus the Carnegie Steel Company did everything from mining the ore to producing finished steel. John D. Rockefeller's Standard Oil Company owned not only the wells, but the ships, pipelines, refineries, distributorships, and even the barrel-manufacturing companies necessary to market oil products for a variety of uses—including fuel for the recently invented internal combustion engine.

Horizontal integration, on the other hand, meant controlling all the production at a particular stage in the industrial process—all barrel manufacturing in the nation, for instance. Two techniques of horizontal integration existed. The *pool* preserved scattered ownership but instituted corporate management, such as the integration of several once-competing railroad lines into a pool controlled by a parent company. The *trust*, pioneered by Rockefeller with his Standard Oil Trust in 1879, actually absorbed the participating units into a supercompany. Stockholders in individual corporations turned their shares over to trustees in exchange for shares of the trust. Thereafter, the trustees made most decisions, and gave the shareholders a portion of the profits. Standard Oil was therefore both horizontally and vertically integrated. Both pools and trusts, as well as the holding companies that used stock control to accomplish their ends, worked to limit competition in the interest of efficiency and profits.

Many in Mark Twain's generation suspected the new economic combinations of foul play. After 1882, when a vocal critic of Standard Oil named Henry Demarest Lloyd coined it, the label *robber barons* was frequently attached to men like Carnegie, Rockefeller, and Cornelius Vanderbilt. These men undeniably mowed down competitors with ruthless precision, but they also made possible remarkable industrial progress from which the nation as a whole benefited. "Did Vanderbilt keep any of you down," one industrialist asked a group of disgruntled citizens in 1886, "by saving you two dollars and seventy-five cents on a barrel of flour, while he was making fourteen cents?" Implicit in the statement was the idea that the large capitalists' achievement of greater efficiency should be a cause for national celebration. The defenders of the so-called industrial statesmen also pointed out that only the old, inefficient forms of competition had died. Newer and higher forms still held capitalism together. The market system still worked to punish errors in production and pricing. And competition still existed between *ways* of doing the same thing. The struggle between oil and electricity as a source of lighting is a case in point. Mark Twain would learn to his sorrow that real competition also existed between alternative approaches to the mechanization of typesetting in the printing industry. The man who built a better mousetrap still had an advantage.

Although Twain was highly critical of the modernization of the United States by machines and millionaires, a complete understanding of the man as well as his time demands a recognition of his concurrent zeal for money and mechanization. In a period of rapid change such as the late nineteenth century it was natural to find aspirations split between the future and the past. Twain demonstrated such an ambivalence when he alternated between being awed by Lake Tahoe's wild beauty and being delighted by the prospect of striking it rich on the Comstock Lode. After his entrance into the national literary limelight in the late 1860s, Twain continued shifting back and forth. While idealizing Tom Sawyer's barefoot days on the Mississippi, he maintained and delighted in a grandiose standard of living. Twain's expenditures for the single year 1881 amounted to more than $100,000. The money came from his writing and from lecturing, as well as from his wife's substantial estate. But Twain remained unsatisfied, and his pursuit of financial success led him into a series of unfortunate investments. Indeed, Twain was so fascinated by the new technology that he became known as an easy mark for inventors interested in raising capital. In the early 1880s he poured thousands of dollars into a steam generator, a steam pulley, a new kind of watch, a device for marine telegraphy, and a new engraving process. There were lesser projects, too, such as a hinged pants button, a self-pasting scrapbook, and a mechanical organ.

But Twain's most revealing and most disastrous speculation began innocuously enough when a Hartford jeweler cornered him in his billiard room and peddled $2,000 worth of stock in a typesetting machine invented by James W. Paige. Twain paid the money before even seeing the machine. A former printer, he knew the value of a device that could perform the most laborious task in the business. On seeing the typesetter in action, he immediately subscribed an additional $3,000. The machine seemed almost human to Twain, a triumph of applied technology. Of Paige he wrote, "He is the Shakespeare of mechanical invention. In all the ages he has no peer." Paige came to Twain for more money, and the writer obliged first with $30,000, then $80,000, and ultimately a total of almost $200,000. Of course Twain expected to realize millions. He envisaged himself a Carnegie of typesetting, a new star in the national industrial constellation. But as with the Nevada mines, success always remained just beyond his grasp. Paige was a perfectionist who tended to overrefine his inventions beyond the point of practicality. While he tinkered and spent Twain's money, simpler devices like the linotype, which Twain spurned when offered an interest, captured the market. Finally, in 1894, the Paige machine was pronounced a failure and abandoned. Twain never realized a penny on his investments; in fact, the machine dragged him into an ignominious bankruptcy that filled his later years with bitterness. Ruefully, he recalled a conversation with Carnegie in 1893. Twain had tried to interest the multimillionaire in the Paige typesetter, citing the old maxim about not putting all one's eggs in the same basket. Carnegie regarded him for a moment with his eyes half-closed; then he offered his own maxim: "Put all your eggs in one basket—and watch that basket."

In the 1880s, while the Paige debacle was in the making, Mark Twain wrote two of his most important books. Each contained an unfavorable commentary on progress and a critical assessment of the modern United States. Twain began *The Adventures of Huckleberry Finn* as a sequel to *The Adventures of Tom Sawyer*. When he started it in 1876, the pages flowed easily from his pen as they usually did when he wrote about his happy boyhood. Brilliantly using the vernacular style of an untutored boy, Twain described Huck's relationship to Saint Petersburg (Hannibal) and introduced him to the runaway slave Jim. In the next block of chapters Huck and Jim begin drifting down the Mississippi. "You feel mighty free and easy and comfortable on a raft," Huck declares, and the picture Twain describes is indeed idyllic. But then, in Chapter 16, the raft drifts past the mouth of the Ohio River in a fog. The Ohio was to have been Jim's escape route to the North and freedom, but now the Mississippi is carrying him farther and farther into the heart of the South. At this point in the narrative Huck and Mark Twain faced a dilemma. Jim is a fugitive from justice; Huck, in effect, is stealing him. To continue to protect him on the raft demands that Huck reject society and its institutions. As a white boy Huck feels the tug of duty, but as an individual he also feels strong affection for Jim, a surrogate father. What should he do? Twain's dilemma was somewhat larger. To have Huck support society and betray Jim would involve a judgment on the merits of that society, which Twain was not prepared to make. He therefore stopped writing. Before he could make Huck's decision, he had to make his own.

For six years Twain avoided the *Huckleberry Finn* manuscript except for the addition of a few chapters that did not bear on the dominant question of what to do about Jim. He even considered burning the entire manuscript. He continued, however, to gather impressions about his society pertinent to his impending judgment. Then, in 1882, he returned to the river and took a steamboat over the route he used to pilot. The changes astonished and depressed him. Civilization had caught up to the Mississippi. Fields had replaced the forest Twain had known in his youth; huge levees marred the view of the riverbanks, and factories rose above them; towns that had barely existed in Twain's day now boasted 50,000 people. And money domi-nated. Even steamboating had deteriorated from a romantic adventure to a crass business. "The world I knew in its blossoming youth," Twain wrote in his account of the 1882 trip, "is old and bowed and melancholy . . . the fire is gone out of its eyes. . . . In Hannibal the steamboatman is no longer a god." Part of the reason for Twain's disappointing reunion with the river was the fact that by 1882 he was no longer young. But neither was his country. Both had passed through a civil war and into an age of industrialization. The society he found, at any rate, seemed a far cry from the one he remembered and had written about in the first half of *Huckleberry Finn*. Instead of the peacefulness and innate decency he associated with the earlier time, he found petty materialism, depravity, and callous inhumanity.

Returning to his studio in Hartford, Twain was ready to make his judgment and complete his novel. The last half of *Huckleberry Finn* is a series of exposures of a squalid civilization. Huck and Jim witness families engaged in bloody, pointless feuds; they see townsmen cheering as a drunk dies in the street; they watch as confi-dence men brazenly dupe a public that itself is gullible, cowardly, and hypocritical. When an angry mob tar and feather the confidence men, Huck's verdict is also Twain's: "It was enough to make a body ashamed of the human race . . . I never seen anything so disgusting." Now it was easy to decide what to do about Jim. Huck would not betray him; the nation wasn't worthy of that decision. In a further ges-ture of rebellion, Huck heads west to the territories just as Twain had done in 1861. But for Twain in 1884, the year of *Huckleberry Finn*'s publication, there was little territory left as an escape avenue. Considerations of debt and family further re-stricted him. Obliged, as a consequence, to remain and further contemplate the maladies of civilization, Twain became increasingly bitter in his social criticism.

Particularly distressing to Twain and his Connecticut intellectual compatriots was the government's handling of the "Indian problem" in the West. By the 1860s the pressure of miners and railroad builders on the western Indians had precipitated a series of bloody clashes. The first occurred in Colorado in November 1864, when Colonel J. M. Chivington butchered a Cheyenne village. The army followed this Sand Creek Massacre with a campaign against the Sioux in northern Wyoming and southern Montana—the Powder River country. In 1866 Captain William J. Fetter-man and his eighty-one soldiers were surprised and killed. General warfare contin-ued on the western plains throughout the next decade. The climax came in June 1876 when Chiefs Sitting Bull and Crazy Horse killed General George A. Custer and all his 265 men in the Battle of the Little Bighorn.

The Indian victory over Custer only delayed the inevitable. Four months later General Alfred H. Terry forced the surrender of the bulk of the Sioux nation. This surrender broke the back of serious Indian resistance on the Great Plains. The year 1877 saw the extraordinary running fight of Chief Joseph, of the Oregon Nez Percé tribe, end in defeat only a few miles from sure sanctuary in Canada. Joseph was the last great patriot chief, a man noted for his knowledge of the land and how it might be put to militarily advantageous use. Thereafter, it was a mop-up operation. Indi-ans occasionally left their reservations on raids, but these were short-lived. It was not just that the army herded them back. The environmental basis that had made their culture possible was gone. The buffalo, for instance, was almost exterminated

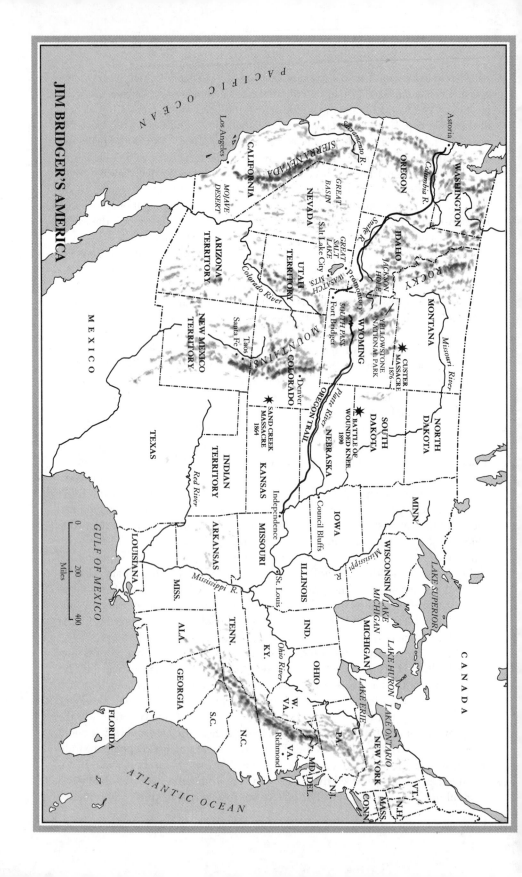

JIM BRIDGER'S AMERICA

in the 1800s. Less than a thousand animals remained of the millions that had once ranged from Kentucky to the Rockies. In one final shameful incident in 1890, Indian agents mistook the Sioux religious ghost dance for the precursor to an uprising in South Dakota. As a result, federal soldiers attacked the Sioux at Wounded Knee, killing more than 200 men, women, and children. For Twain, the government's Indian removal policy looked more like a plan of extermination.

With such atrocities in mind, Twain continued his scrutiny of modern America through writing. In A *Connecticut Yankee in King Arthur's Court*, published in 1889, he believed he was writing his literary farewell. Twain opened the tale by transporting a nineteenth-century Yankee from Connecticut, Hank Morgan, back to the sixth-century England of King Arthur. With Yankee ingenuity, Hank proceeds to transform Arthurian England (a place strikingly similar to antebellum Hannibal) into a replica of the United States in the 1880s, complete with democracy, universal education, and a sophisticated technology. For a while the book conceals its purpose; Twain seems proud of the shining machines and towering edifices that Hank's leadership makes possible. Perhaps progress is beneficent, humankind innately good. But there are hints of a darker perspective. "There are times," Hank admits, "when one would like to hang the whole human race and finish the farce." Yet Hank himself is a large part of the problem. His technological know-how makes possible not only schools, mines, factories, and labor-saving devices, but also revolvers, rifles, cannons, and huge bombs. Moreover, Hank's presence splits King Arthur's court into warring factions: the Yankees versus the knights. In the ensuing civil war, the new order wins, slavery is abolished, and, Hank feels, society is firmly directed toward progress and prosperity.

Ended at this juncture, A *Connecticut Yankee in King Arthur's Court* might have taken its place among the optimistic utopian novels of the time, such as Edward Bellamy's *Looking Backward, 2000–1887*. Bellamy confidently predicted a United States lifted to unprecedented heights by applied technology. His message captured the enthusiasm of millions of worried Americans. But Mark Twain was writing primarily for himself, and at the very time he wrote his book he was beginning to appreciate how misplaced was his confidence in James Paige (a technological genius comparable to Hank Morgan). So Twain prepared to give his own interpretation of the pursuit of progress. A new war breaks out in Arthurian England. Swarms of human "sheep" attack Hank and his elite corps of fifty-two boys armed with the latest weapons, including dynamite, Gatling guns, and electric fences. Their success in repelling the attack proves ironic. The stench from 25,000 rotting corpses pollutes Hank's stronghold and kills all the victors. Technology has turned against its creators; science is out of control; humanity's essential baseness has prevailed. In Mark Twain's opinion this was the way the world would end, and the United States in the nineteenth century was on the right track, going full speed ahead.

Twain's involvement in national politics after the Civil War offers another way of tracing his growing disillusion and pessimism. The election of 1876 pitted Democrat Samuel J. Tilden against Republican Rutherford B. Hayes. As governor of New York Tilden had won Twain's admiration by smashing the infamous Tweed ring of corrupt party hacks. On the financial front, Tilden was a "hard money" man, opposed to the expansion of currency (and consequent inflation) that the issuance of "soft," or paper, money encouraged. Hayes, the Republican, was a comparatively unknown Ohio governor, but he enjoyed a reputation for clean politics, and the famous novelist threw his considerable weight behind the Republican ticket.

In the election itself, one of the most extraordinary in American political history, Tilden, in the opinion of most observers then and now, was elected—but Hayes went to the White House. This curious phenomenon came about as the result of Republican tampering with twenty disputed votes in the electoral college. Nineteen of these were from southern states, where there was still military Reconstruction and, as a result, Republican control. Accusing the Democrats of intimidating black voters at the polls, Republican negotiators awarded all the contested votes and the election to Hayes. But the Democratic South exacted its price for allowing "His Fraudulency" to win. By the unwritten Compromise of 1877, Reconstruction ended, and control of the South returned to white southern Democrats.

Mark Twain's enthusiasm for Hayes did not last long. The Republican party, he discovered, stubbornly resisted permanent reform. Moreover, the Hayes administration did little about the strikes and unemployment that were by-products of industrialization. The human misery occasioned by this process troubled Twain deeply. To the consternation of his wealthy, conservative friends, he began openly sympathizing with the more militant labor organizations, such as the Knights of Labor and the Greenback Labor party. Twain also worried about the continuing influence in Republican circles of political spoilsman James G. Blaine, "the filthy Blaine" as Twain called him. Yet in the election of 1880 Twain supported Republican James G. Garfield over Winfield S. Hancock, the Democrat. His decision reflected less an admiration for Garfield and more a fear that a now solidly Democratic South might revive the old sectional partisanship. Twain joined Republican orators whose evocation of Civil War atrocities to unify the North behind their party was known as "waving the bloody shirt." By stooping so low and even trotting out General Grant for a speaking tour in which Mark Twain also participated, Republican leaders revealed their anxiety. In truth, their long hold on the presidency was nearing its end. Garfield squeezed by Hancock, however, and the Republicans had four more years in which to prove themselves.

The beginning of the Garfield administration was not auspicious from Twain's point of view. To his dismay, James G. Blaine became secretary of state. Then Garfield was assassinated on July 2, 1881, and succeeded by Vice President Chester A. Arthur, a former colleague of another spoilsman, Roscoe Conkling, in the domination of New York politics. But there were some encouraging signs. In 1881, the federal government succeeded in breaking Conkling's hold in New York and forcing his resignation from the Senate. Two years later the Pendleton Act created a bipartisan Civil Service Commission and instituted competitive exams for many government jobs. The act initially affected only one-tenth of the total federal work force, but it marked a watershed in the philosophy of government service.

The election of 1884 threw Mark Twain into a quandary, for the Republican nominee this time was Blaine. Deeply troubled, Twain and his fellow Connecticut intellectuals debated the question of party loyalty. Many bowed to the judgment of the smoke-filled rooms, but Twain remained true to his conscience. Throughout the fall of 1884 he tried to persuade Republicans to rise above orthodoxy and sup-

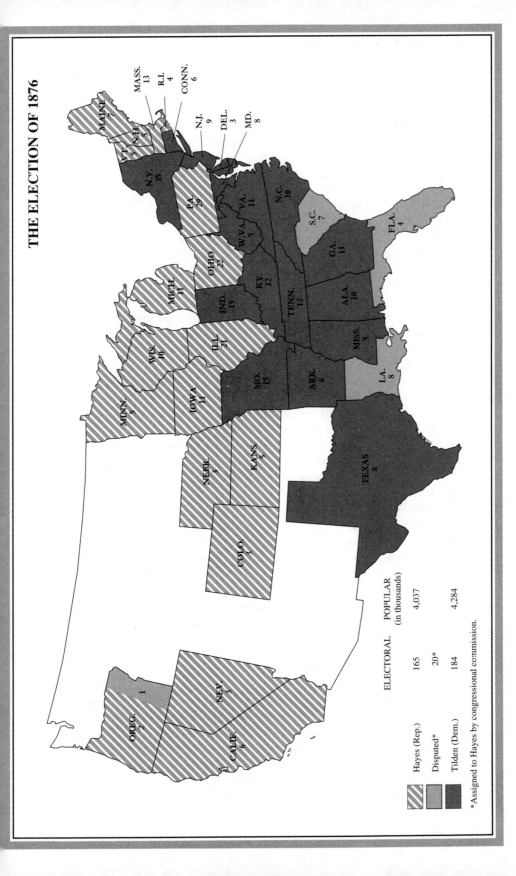

THE ELECTION OF 1876

	ELECTORAL	POPULAR (in thousands)
Hayes (Rep.)	165	4,037
Disputed*	20*	
Tilden (Dem.)	184	4,284

*Assigned to Hayes by congressional commission.

MAINE 7
VT. 5
N.H. 5
MASS. 13
R.I. 4
CONN. 6
N.Y. 35
N.J. 9
DEL. 3
MD. 8
PA. 29
W.VA. 5
VA. 11
N.C. 10
S.C. 7
FLA. 4
OHIO 22
KY. 12
TENN. 12
GA. 11
ALA. 10
MISS. 8
LA. 8
MICH. 11
IND. 15
ILL. 21
MO. 15
ARK. 6
WIS. 10
IOWA 11
MINN. 5
NEBR. 3
KANS. 5
COLO. 3
TEXAS 8
OREG. 3
NEV. 3
CALIF. 6

port the Democrat, Grover Cleveland. In this cause, which acquired the label *Mugwump*, Twain joined such well-known reformers as George William Curtis, E. L. Godkin, Carl Schurz, and Charles Francis Adams.

The Blaine–Cleveland campaign was one of the most bitter ever seen in the United States, and the political smear reached a new level of sophistication. Blaine's transgressions over the past decade received a full airing, and the Republicans countered with charges that the Democrats were the party of "Rum, Romanism, and Rebellion," a ploy that backfired in many quarters of America. But the major issue in the campaign involved the Republican charge that Cleveland had fathered an illegitimate child. When the Democratic nominee humbly acknowledged that as a young bachelor he and a consenting widow had indeed had an offspring but added that he had cared for the mother and the child ever since, public sympathy swung to his side.

Mark Twain was disgusted by the self-righteousness of Cleveland's detractors. They knew full well, Twain pointed out, "what the bachelor's other alternative was and . . . seem to prefer that to the widow." Then, in a statement suggestive of his growing misanthropy, Twain philosophized, "*Isn't* human nature the most consummate sham and lie that was ever invented? Isn't man a creature to be ashamed of in pretty much all his aspects? Is he really fit for anything but to be stood up on a street corner as a convenience for dogs?"

Having campaigned hard for Cleveland, Twain watched his ensuing administration with great interest. Made increasingly bitter by the hold of big business on American life, he applauded the passage in 1887 of the Interstate Commerce Act, which prohibited unreasonable, secret, and discriminatory railroad rates and practices. The act also created the Interstate Commerce Commission, the first federal agency authorized to regulate private enterprise. But intention was one matter, practice quite another. As Twain watched in disgust, railroad magnates, aided by a sympathetic Supreme Court and a lukewarm president, systematically evaded the spirit and the letter of the Interstate Commerce Act.

A similar fate befell the Sherman Antitrust Act, passed in 1890 under President Benjamin Harrison, a Republican who spoiled Cleveland's bid for reelection. The Sherman Act grew out of the fear that trusts and other business conglomerates were conspiring to restrict competition and fleece the public. But once again a conservative judiciary was unwilling to apply what few teeth the act possessed. In fact, in a classic distortion of purpose, the antitrust legislation was turned against the emerging labor unions as a consequence of the Supreme Court decision in *United States v. Debs* (1894). Like the Interstate Commerce Act, the Sherman Act proved effective mainly as a deterrent to truly meaningful reform.

From Mark Twain's perspective, the United States in the 1890s was a nation run by and for a wealthy, conservative elite. Benjamin Harrison's administration regularly favored the rich and powerful at the expense of farmers, laborers, small entreprenuers, and intellectuals like Twain. Monetary policy was a case in point. The Sherman Silver Purchase Act of 1890 did little to improve on the Bland-Allison Act passed twelve years previously. Neither really increased the amount of circulating currency or promoted inflation as critics of business had hoped. But when it came to the tariff, Congress and the president successfully enacted the highly protectionist (probusiness) McKinley Tariff of 1890.

Grover Cleveland was a personal friend of Mark Twain and entertained him frequently in the White House during his first administration. When Cleveland was elected to another term in 1892, Twain was pleased. He could not help noticing, however, that Cleveland's political and economic philosophy was strongly conservative and really differed little from that of the Republicans. Both camps were friendly to propertied interests and largely unsympathetic to the demands of the working people of the nation's farms and factories. Supporting Cleveland in this stance was a complex body of ideas about the nature of success in American history. In the first place, it was defined almost exclusively in material terms. The rich were generally conceded to be the top rung in society. Second, success was believed possible for anyone possessing the requisite talent and determination. As Horatio Alger and Andrew Carnegie had demonstrated in their separate ways, humble origin was not a handicap. This meant, in theory, that anyone could climb the magic ladder. But Mark Twain knew the facts. Even the most talented and energetic were often suppressed by the system. Yet insofar as Twain's contemporaries *believed* in the success myth, they proved willing to accept the prevailing social and economic framework. Rather than reform or abolish the free enterprise system, they hoped to become its beneficiaries by trying a little harder. The elegant mansion of a Vanderbilt or a Morgan was an object of envy and aspiration rather than a hated symbol of injustice and oppression. The bona fide rags-to-riches success of a few, like Franklin or Carnegie, proved a narcotic for millions.

The rich in Mark Twain's America resisted reform by parading the philosophy of social Darwinism and its conception of progress as something that stemmed from competition in which the unfit were weeded out from among the fit. A corollary was the idea that the government and the courts should leave free enterprise alone. Only in this way could the scythe of competition do its beneficial work. To aid the unfit, according to this perspective, was to impede evolution—to sustain dinosaurs and other losers in the natural selection sweepstakes. But the major bulwark of the propertied elite was the old Protestant idea that worldly success was both a sign of God's favor and a way of glorifying God. It followed that the rich could claim to be the beneficiaries of divine selection, too. As John D. Rockefeller said, "The good Lord gave me my money." Twain's old acquaintance Henry Ward Beecher added, "God has intended the great to be great and the little to be little." But the Reverend William Lawrence put it best when he wrote in 1901, "Godliness is in league with riches." Implied was the idea that those with superior character were rewarded with success; poverty was the product of sinfulness, a kind of punishment meted out by an angry God. Russell Conwell, one of the few rivals to Mark Twain as a lecturer in the late nineteenth century, argued in his stock speech, "Acres of Diamonds," that "ninety-eight out of one hundred of the rich men of America are honest. That is why they are rich."

Twain was not fully convinced. The entire gospel of wealth, including the argument that through their philanthropy the rich performed their obligation to society, seemed to him much like the confidence games he had written about in the second half of *Huckleberry Finn*. In company with Henry George, whose *Progress and Poverty* appeared in 1879, Twain understood that self-made wealth was as improbable as a self-laid egg. The success of individuals was the product of the growth of the whole economy. Moreover, Twain recognized that, while big business was applauding itself, the nation's morality and institutions were becoming so thread-bare that they were unable "to protect the body from winter, disease, and death." A partial reckoning would come in the Progressive years, but like Huck Finn, Mark Twain had seen enough. The failure of the Paige typesetter and Twain's consequent bankruptcy in 1894 were the last straws in his disenchantment with the cult of success.

Another shadow over Twain's last years was his country's entrance into the contest for international power and prestige called imperialism. Before the 1890s the nation had not been active in this endeavor. Mexico, to be sure, had been pushed out of the path of westward expansion in the 1840s, and in 1867 the United States had made one of the best real-estate deals in history by purchasing Alaska from Russia. But for the most part the development of the West and the economic colonization of the defeated South had kept the imperialist urge in check. By the 1890s, however, a growing nation was pushing at its geographic boundaries. The frontier had vanished, and American appetites, whetted by 250 years of expansion, sought new morsels across the seas. For those requiring philosophic justification there was Josiah Strong's *Our Country* (1885), with its vindication of a "divinely-commissioned" America assuming the role of its "brother's keeper." Strong also used the ideas of social Darwinism, arguing that in the worldwide competition of races it was either eat or be eaten. The United States needed to assert itself as a colonial force before the European powers carved up the rest of the world. Naval power advocate Alfred T. Mahan agreed completely.

One of the first opportunities for American expansion was provided by the Hawaiian Islands. Since Twain had visited there in 1865, a surge of sugar produc-tion had made Hawaii a primary target of American business and empire-building. The U.S. Navy maintained a base at Pearl Harbor on Oahu, the best natural harbor in the Pacific basin. The trouble began in 1891, when the McKinley Tariff imposed high duties on Hawaiian sugar and wrecked the islands' economy. Then King Kalakaua, who was friendly to Americans, died and was succeeded by Queen Lili-uokalani. Angry about the tariff and stridently anti-American, Liliukalani deter-mined to oust the Yankees from the islands. Before she could act, a group of Ameri-cans led by plantation owner Sanford Dole—and backed by U.S. Marines—stormed the royal palace, overthrew the government, jailed the queen, and declared a protectorate. Although the Marine participation was unofficial, the U.S. government did not denounce the action. Rather, in 1893, heavy pressure from President Harrison and Secretary of State Blaine forced Liliiukalani to capitu-late. Republicans hoped for quick annexation of the islands, but Cleveland's return to the White House delayed it for five years.

In other regions of the globe, the Democrats displayed their own brand of im-perialism. In 1895, Secretary of State Richard Olney revived the Monroe Doctrine of 1823 to assert America's virtual sovereignty in Latin America. The immediate target of Olney's warning was Great Britain, and many restless Americans hoped for a chance to back the secretary's words with bullets. Theodore Roosevelt, then pres-ident of the New York police commissioners, confessed, "I rather hope that the fight will come soon. . . . This country needs a war."

Roosevelt got his wish in 1898. Mark Twain was on a round-the-world debt-paying lecture tour when the fever of the new Manifest Destiny infected the nation and produced a war with Spain. The immediate cause was American disapproval of Spain's conduct in a war with its colony, Cuba. Dispassionate analysis indicates that atrocities occurred on both sides, but sensation-hungry American newspapers cast Spain in the villain's role. When the United States battleship *Maine* blew up in the harbor of Havana, Cuba, on February 15, 1898, with the loss of 260 lives, a declaration of war was only a matter of time. Evidence revealed later that an internal explosion—probably of a boiler—caused the *Maine* to sink, but the American presses blamed Spanish treachery. War came on April 25, and within four months the conflict was over. First Commodore George Dewey captured the Philippine Islands and broke Spain's naval power in the Pacific. Then a badly disorganized American force, which included Theodore Roosevelt and his Rough Rider colleagues, managed to defeat an even more mismanaged Spanish army defending Cuba. But the imperialists saw only stars and stripes. As Secretary of State John Hay said, it was "a splendid little war." Roosevelt simply called it "bully." Only 379 Americans died in combat, although disease, chiefly malaria, claimed more than 5,000.

By the terms of the Teller Amendment to the declaration of war with Spain, the United States forswore annexation of Cuba, even though American entrepre-

In the afternoon of February 15, 1898, one of America's mightiest battleships, the *Maine*, floated in the harbor of Havana, Cuba. The following morning, it looked like this. An explosion that was never fully explained had sunk the ship and claimed 260 lives. Public furor, goaded by hysterical press coverage, led directly to war with Spain.

neurs controlled 80 percent of the Cuban economy. But Guam, Puerto Rico, and the Philippines, all formerly Spanish, were a different matter. American hunger for empire led President William McKinley to support outright acquisition of these islands. The Philippines became the center of attention. Business interests, desirous of Pacific trade, and religious leaders trumpeting an "imperialism of righteousness" backed the administration. With money and God both on his side, McKinley rationalized that "duty determines destiny" and moved to annex the archipelago. The task proved considerably more difficult than defeating the Spanish. Philippine native leaders like Emilio Aguinaldo, whom the United States had supported in a mutual effort against Spain, resisted strenuously. They had expected the United States to grant freedom and independence to the islands at the conclusion of the war. When it appeared that McKinley intended to substitute one foreign regime for another, the natives grew restless. For most of 1899 fighting raged on the islands. Thereafter Aguinaldo took his remaining forces to the hills in guerrilla resistance. The Philippine Insurgency, lasting until 1902, cost 4,300 American lives. At least 50,000 Philipinos died in the conflict, although some estimates run much higher.

Back in the United States, meanwhile, a groundswell of opposition had arisen against imperialism and particularly against McKinley's policy in the Philippines. A substantial portion of the American people wanted no part of a colonial empire, on both idealistic and practical grounds. Even before the peace treaty with Spain was signed in December 1898, an Anti-Imperialism League had been organized and had attracted such diverse figures of national importance as Grover Cleveland, Andrew Carnegie, labor leader Samuel Gompers, Charles Eliot, the president of Harvard, and Mark Twain. Twain had disliked imperialism from the beginning because he saw through the hypocrisy of its pious pretensions to the underlying considerations of power, profit, and the national ego. His views are contained in a letter written late in 1899. According to Twain, the departing nineteenth century was bequeathing to the approaching twentieth a Christian civilization "bedraggled, besmirched, and dishonored from pirate raids" throughout the world. "Her soul," Twain bitterly continued, is "full of meanness, her pockets full of boodle, and her mouth full of pious hypocrisies. Give her soap and towel, but hide the looking-glass."

It was soon apparent that Mark Twain had just been sharpening his satirical guns against imperialism. His essay in the February 1901 *North American Review*, "To the Person Sitting in Darkness," was a devastating critique of the American foreign missions that carried civilization and the Gospel to allegedly backward peoples. The missions did their job, Twain explained, at the point of a bayonet. Those who really needed enlightenment, he continued, were the missionaries themselves. In another essay, Twain reviewed the whole history of American involvement in the Philippines. Of the $20 million given Spain for the islands by the treaty ending the war, he observed, "We bought some islands from a party which did not own them." Of Aguinaldo he wrote, "We went back on an honored guest of the Stars and Stripes when we had no further use for him and chased him to the mountains." Then the nation that had begun the era of colonial revolutions systematically crushed the natives by destroying their villages, burning their fields, and exiling their leaders. The remaining ten million had been subjugated, according to Twain, by "Benevolent Assimilation, which is the pious new name of the musket."

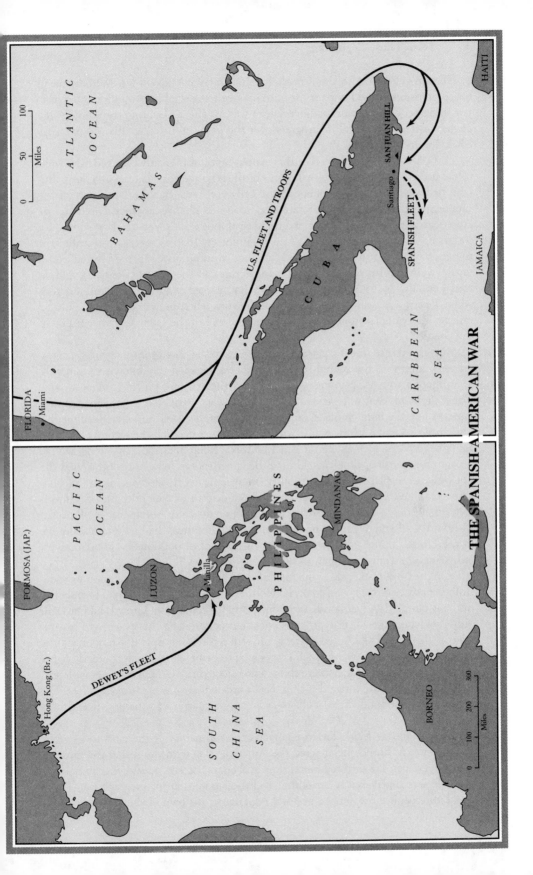

THE SPANISH-AMERICAN WAR

FLORIDA
Miami

ATLANTIC OCEAN

BAHAMAS

Miles
0   50   100

U.S. FLEET AND TROOPS

CUBA

Santiago SAN JUAN HILL

SPANISH FLEET

CARIBBEAN SEA

JAMAICA

HAITI

FORMOSA (JAP.)

PACIFIC OCEAN

Hong Kong (Br.)

DEWEY'S FLEET

LUZON

Manila

PHILIPPINES

MINDANAO

SOUTH CHINA SEA

BORNEO

Miles
0   100   200   300

Twain's essays on imperialism elicited a storm of public opinion. While some of his compatriots praised him for his frankness, others called him a traitor and worse. For these people, questioning imperialism was, in effect, doubting the whole value of the United States and its progress over the past century. Yet this was precisely Mark Twain's purpose.

By 1900, few could deny that the United States was greatly changed from what it had been at the time of Mark Twain's birth sixty-five years before. Of course, human history is not static; change is the only constant. But the latter part of the nineteenth century brought a rate and scope of change unprecedented in the American experience. Any one of a number of indexes is revealing. Population, for instance, had zoomed from about fifteen million in 1835 to seventy-five million at the end of the century. Steel, which was not even produced in the United States until Twain was twenty, was being manufactured at the rate of twenty-six million tons annually by 1900. Coal production had surged from fourteen million tons when Twain was twenty-five to 257 million tons when he was sixty-five. Railroad mileage had jumped from 30,000 miles on the eve of the Civil War to 193,000 at the century's end.

It is possible to find a spectrum of responses to the changes these figures suggest. At one extreme is the school of thought that applauded the differences. Growth, according to this perspective, was good, and the nation's progress unquestioned. Those problems that were acknowledged at all were attributed to un-American influences like the immigrants. As for the United States itself, this cheerleading philosophy could find nothing wrong with God's chosen people. The second broad category of response to a changing America was a frank admission that progress had brought some serious problems. Unlike the cheerleaders, adherents of this view did not hesitate to place the responsibility on Americans themselves instead of on a scapegoat like the immigrant. But they did not despair in their criticism. Optimistically, they sought means whereby the nation could enjoy the blessings of growth without the blight. With the proper controls and reforms, the high promises of life in the United States could be realized. This school of opinion was constructively critical and forward-looking in its reform endeavors.

On the pessimistic side of the turn-of-the-century spectrum of opinion were destructive critics or backward-looking reformers. They held that life had been better in the good old days before urbanization and industrialization. Growth had brought only problems. Indeed, true progress consisted of restoring the values and institutions of the past. The United States could still reform, but only if it renounced the technological future toward which it appeared to be heading. Finally, directly opposite the roseate cheerleaders were those who rejected the United States completely. Reform, of either the forward- or the backward-looking variety, was hopeless. The nation was moribund. Total collapse was only a matter of time and would be a blessing.

In his lifetime Mark Twain embraced the full gamut of these attitudes. As a young writer in Europe he cheered the American flag with the zeal of the most ardent imperialist. He devoted much time and energy to the pursuit of material success. He was captivated by machines and their potential for progress. But Twain could also idealize the simple, pastoral America of his own boyhood and viciously attack the Gilded Age. By 1894, when he published *Pudd'nhead Wilson*, Twain was prepared to take the final step into despair.

"Whoever has lived long enough to find out what life is," Twain wrote in a *Pudd'nhead Wilson* chapter heading, "knows what a deep debt of gratitude we owe to Adam, the first great benefactor of our race. He brought death into the world." Most of the book follows a similar vein. In commenting on the anniversary of Columbus's discovery of America, Twain declared, "It was wonderful to find America but it would have been more wonderful to miss it." Only twenty-seven years before, Twain had stood with the crowd at the rail of the *Quaker City* and cheered wildly as a passing ship displayed the American flag. The mood of these two passages from *Pudd'nhead Wilson* could not be more despairing nor the destruction of the American dream more complete in Twain's view. But his misanthropy transcended the United States. In his later years he toyed with the prospect of shutting off the earth's oxygen supply for two minutes and enjoyed contemplating the course of history if Noah had missed the sailing of the Ark.

It remained for *The Mysterious Stranger* (written in stages from about 1898 to 1905 and published posthumously in 1916) to summarize the mature and final version of Twain's desperation. The setting is once again a town beside a river, but now the locale is Austria (Twain and his family were living in Vienna in 1898), and the time the sixteenth century. In the course of the novel a mysterious stranger conducts a young boy (the Austrian equivalent of Tom Sawyer or Huck Finn) on a tour of the chamber of horrors that was and is human civilization. The revelations of cruelty, sadism, and suffering leave the boy with nothing but shame and contempt for the human race. He realizes that the ideals of his childhood are naive dreams and that the only hope for humanity is early death or insanity. Civilization, Christianity, and material progress have left depravity and desolation in their wake. Progress is a myth. The future is revealed to be only a continuation of the errors of the past, now multiplied by technology. The torture rack and wheel are replaced by bombs that kill thousands. Human life is as meaningless, Twain decided, as that of the miniature race the mysterious stranger eliminates with the comment that "man is a museum of diseases, a home of impurities; he comes to-day and is gone tomorrow; he begins as dirt and departs as stench." Finally, at the end of *The Mysterious Stranger*, the boy is told, "There is no God, no universe, no human race, no earthly life, no heaven, no hell. It is all a dream—a grotesque dream. Nothing exists but you. And you are but a *thought*—a vagrant thought, a useless thought, a homeless thought, wandering forlorn among the empty eternities!"

The intense pessimism expressed in *The Mysterious Stranger* is equaled, even exceeded, in Twain's bitter indictment of war, "The War Prayer" (1905). As a pastor and congregation pray for military victory during wartime, an old man dressed in a white robe appears in the sanctuary of the country church. As a messenger from God, he has come to answer their prayer, but first he tells the congregation what this means for their enemy. In the "unuttered prayer" that follows, the old man graphically details what the congregation has asked God to do to their enemy. "O Lord, our God," he shouts, "help us to tear their soldiers to bloody shreds with our shells ... help us to lay waste to their humble homes with a hurricane of fire. . . . Amen." After a pause the old man glowers at the churchgoers and says, "Ye have prayed it; if ye still desire it, speak." Twain ends the story with supreme irony. The old man is dismissed by the congregation as a lunatic—for nothing he said made any sense.

Mark Twain's bleak appraisals of the human race coincided with his own personal tragedies. *The Mysterious Stranger* and "The War Prayer" were completed during the time when his wife, Olivia, was succumbing to an agonizing terminal illness. From 1902 until her death in June 1904 she lay bedridden, and the sight of her wasting away was even more difficult for Twain to bear than had been the loss of his daughter, Susy, to spinal meningitis eight years earlier. After Olivia's death, Twain's life was empty, and his own health declined rapidly. He continued to write but refused to publish most of this work, including *The Mysterious Stranger* and "The War Prayer." For Twain, such works were truth, and, in his view, "Only dead men can tell the truth in this world."

The dead, Twain concluded, were lucky. In 1910, he joined their ranks. He would no doubt have been astonished by the eulogies written in his honor, essays in which he was portrayed as America's happy humorist and an important source of national pride. The popular image of him is still that of a Tom Sawyer or a cracker-barrel storyteller. Yet perhaps Twain would not have been surprised at all by this distortion of the truth; for him it would have been just one more instance of the gullibility of what he called "the damned human race."

SELECTED READINGS
The Person

Benson, Ivan: *Mark Twain's Western Years* (1966). The best history of Twain between 1861 and 1866.

Bridgman, Richard: *Traveling in Mark Twain* (1987). A study of the influence of personal travels in Twain's writing based substantially on Mark Twain's papers.

*Brooks, Van Wyck: *The Ordeal of Mark Twain* (1920). The dark, pessimistic side of Twain's later life.

*De Voto, Bernard: *Mark Twain's America* (1932). A rebuttal of the Brooks interpretation (see above).

Emerson, Everett: *Mark Twain: A Literary Biography of Samuel L. Clemens* (1984). An effective and extensive biography interweaving many of Twain's works.

Foner, Philip S.: *Mark Twain: Social Critic* (1958). A compelling analysis of Twain's views on politics, religion, economics, war, and peace.

Hoffman, Andrew: *Inventing Mark Twain: The Lives of Samuel Langhorn Clemens* (1997). A thorough biography reflecting recent scholarship.

Hoffman, Andrew Jay: *Twain's Heroes, Twain's Worlds* (1988). Explores the personalities of the heroes Huckleberry Finn, Hank Morgan (the Connecticut Yankee), and David (Pudd'nhead) Wilson.

*Available in paperback.

Kaplan, *Justice: Mr. Clemens and Mark Twain* (1966). A biography that sees Twain as divided between love and hate of success.

Lynn, Kenneth S.: *Mark Twain and Southwestern Humor* (1959). Valuable for its insights into the relationship between Twain's life and his writings.

Paine, Albert Bigelow: *Mark Twain: A Biography* (4 vols., 1912). A detailed but laudatory account.

Rasmussen, R. Kent: *Mark Twain A to Z: The Essential Reference to His Life and Writings* (1996). Alphabetical encyclopedia of facts and events.

*Smith, Henry Nash: *Mark Twain: The Development of a Writer* (1962). A study of Twain's literary craftsmanship.

Twain, Mark: *Mark Twain's Autobiography* (2 vols., 1924). Part of *The Complete Works of Mark Twain*, the autobiography is neither complete nor entirely accurate.

The Period

*Callow, Alexander B., Jr.: *The Tweed Ring* (1966). An examination of the classic political machine of the Gilded Age in its New York City setting.

*Cash, W. J.: *The Mind of the South* (1941). Important for its insights into the southern character and tradition.

Fishkin, Shelley Fisher: *Lighting Out for the Territory: Reflections on Mark Twain and American Culture* (1997). A broad look at Twain's lasting impact on the American mindset.

Keller, Morton: *Affairs of State: Public Life in Late-Nineteenth-Century America* (1977). Examines the relationship between social and economic change and American politics.

*Lafeber, Walter: *The New Empire: An Interpretation of American Expansion, 1860–1898* (1963). The background of the controversy over American imperialism.

McKelvey, Blake: *The Urbanization of America, 1860–1915* (1963). A discussion of one of the main forces of change in Twain's America.

Morgan, H. Wayne: *The Gilded Age: A Reappraisal* (1963). A revisionist assessment that makes the late nineteenth century seem more constructive than it seemed to Twain. See also Morgan (ed.), *The Gilded Age* (1970).

*Paul, Rodman W.: *Mining Frontiers of the Far West, 1848–1880* (1963). The authoritative account of bonanza mining.

*Pratt, Julius: *Expansionists of 1898* (1964). An interpretation of the Spanish–American War.

Sproat, John: *The Best Men: Liberal Reformers of the Gilded Age* (1968). Unlike Twain, some Americans tried to reform what they did not like about the United States after the Civil War.

FOR CONSIDERATION

1. Explore young Mark Twain's transformation from a proslavery Southerner to a staunch unionist. How did Twain view the Civil War?

---

*Available in paperback.

2. The optimism in Mark Twain's early literature gradually turned bitter and pessimistic. Discuss some of the blows to Twain's optimistic view of things between the publication of *The Adventures of Tom Sawyer* and *The Adventures of Huckleberry Finn*.

3. With regard to material gain and wealth, Mark Twain epitomized the ambivalence of the Gilded Age. Explain his feelings about the great industrialists of the day, and discuss some of his own attempts to gain financial fortune.

4. By the late 1890s, Twain had become an outspoken critic of American overseas expansion. Which actions did he find particularly distasteful?

5. How does the happy, carefree, and optimistic image of Twain's writing square with the reality of his literary life?

TWO

Jane Addams

*W*ithout knowing why, Jane Addams opened her eyes. It was pitch-black in her bed-room, and at first she heard nothing more than the muted night noises of the Chicago streets surrounding Hull House. Then she saw what had disturbed her sleep. A burglar had pried open the second-story window and was rifling her bureau drawers. Jane spoke quietly, "Don't make a noise." The man whirled around, then prepared to leap out the window. "You'll be hurt if you go that way," Jane calmly observed. A conversation ensued in the darkness. Addams learned that the intruder was not a professional thief, but simply a desperate man who could find no employment that winter of 1890 and had turned to crime to survive. Hull House had been founded the previous fall as a social "settlement" to serve just such people. It testified to Jane Addams's belief that only unfavorable circumstances stood between the innate dignity and worth of every individual and their realization. Moreover, Addams believed that as a well-to-do, cultivated lady she had a special responsibility for alleviating the social ills accompanying the nation's growth. So she was in earnest when she promised her unexpected visitor that if he would come back the next morning, she would try to help. The burglar agreed, walked down the main stairs, and left by the front door. At 9 A.M. he returned to learn that Jane Addams had found him a job.

In contrast to most of those whom she helped in Chicago's slums, Jane Addams was a fifth-generation American. Her mother's roots ran back to a German immigrant who had arrived in Philadelphia in 1727. John Huy Addams, her father, traced his ancestry to an Englishman who in 1681 had received a grant of 500 choice Pennsylvania acres from William Penn himself. John Addams also had an eye for good land, and in 1844, at the age of twenty-two, he had moved with his family to northern Illinois. The region was barely settled, and the Addamses found an excellent location on Cedar Creek in the rural hamlet of Cedarville. A mill, a bank, a shrewdness about the value of land, and an unbending morality soon lifted John Addams to a position of prominence in the financial, political, and cultural life of his community. In 1847, he helped start the first subscription library, a sure sign that the area was no longer pioneer territory. Seven years later Addams went to the Illinois state senate. At the time, he was a Whig in politics, but by the mid-1850s he had grown unhappy with this affiliation. The Whig party was torn with dissension. Northern, or "conscience," Whigs like Addams wanted nothing to do with southern Whigs and their proslavery dogma. In 1854 in Ripon, Wisconsin, men of this persuasion founded the Republican party.

The following year John Addams helped extend Republicanism to Illinois. Leadership of the new party had fallen to a Springfield lawyer-politician named Abraham Lincoln. Addams knew Lincoln well and treasured the letters beginning "My dear Doubled-D'ed Addams." Lincoln and Addams agreed that slavery was wrong, that its extension should not be tolerated, and that Americans had a moral responsibility to face and solve the slave problem. It was precisely this kind of driving conscience that led Jane Addams to attack the social evils of a later era.

Jane Addams's birth in Cedarville on September 6, 1860, came during one of the most tense periods of American history. The dissolution of the national Whig organization, followed by the divorce of northern and southern Democrats, had cleared the way for the election to the presidency of Abraham Lincoln. Five months later the nation plunged into civil war. John Addams did his part by recruiting and financing a company of Union soldiers, the Addams Guard, and Jane's girlhood was filled with stories of men risking their lives in the service of what they believed to be right. In later years she remembered standing on a thick dictionary and the family Bible to reach the plaque, crowned by an eagle, on which the names of the Guard were inscribed. She also recalled carefully putting the dictionary over the Bible so as not to profane that book with her feet!

The death of her mother when Jane was a baby increased the influence of her father in her life to the point of obsession. Her affection for him was, by her own admission, "doglike," and she lived constantly in the shadow of the ideals of conscience, integrity, and charity he set before her. Feelings of inadequacy quite understandably plagued Jane's early years. Her autobiography contains a characterization of herself as an "ugly, pigeon-toed little girl, whose crooked back obliged her to walk with her head held very much upon one side," and who lived in constant fear of being recognized as the child of her handsome, respected father.

Next to her father, the greatest influence on Jane's youth was Abraham Lincoln. Although only four at the time of his assassination in 1865, she distinctly recalled the American flags draped in black, the strange hush, and the tears of her father. Later she asserted that the memory—even the name—of Lincoln was "like a fresh breeze from off the prairie." He was the man who "cleared the title to our democracy" and confirmed the fact that democratic government was "the most valuable contribution America has made to the moral life of the world." For Jane Addams, Lincoln always remained "the greatest American." Many in her generation agreed.

After an indifferent education in the village school at Cedarville, Jane Addams, aged seventeen, contemplated college. The fact that such an option even existed for her testified to the emerging recognition of women's rights in the United States. But the movement was neither old nor well supported in the 1870s. Jane Addams and her contemporaries were expected to be demure and genteel—the custodians of morals and aesthetics who freed men to concentrate on politics, power, and making money. In the sweep of Western history this had not always been the case. After the Reformation in Europe, women could vote and hold property, and the law recognized their rights. Gradually, however, they lost this parity with men and became legal shadows of their fathers or husbands. Even in the New World, where pioneering women often did what might have been considered a man's work, the pall of Victorian morality gradually settled over women's lives. Their spheres of influence were limited to the home. Social approval of a career began and ended with marriage. Women had no vote in federal (and most state) elections. Married women in most states could not manage property or serve as witnesses at a trial. They were, in short, legal minors, second-class citizens. After 1870, when ratification of the Fifteenth Amendment guaranteed the right of blacks (men only, of course) to vote, women fell to the bottom rung of the American social ladder.

The movement for women's rights had its roots in the Enlightenment concept of the dignity and capability of every human being and the Enlightenment ideal of human freedom. The Industrial Revolution helped, too, with its creation of job opportunities for women. In the United States women also benefited from the growth of the influence of the frontier. The attitudes and institutions that emerged from the successive series of American "Wests" favored equality of opportunity. It was no accident that the new territories and states of the West granted women the vote long before the older eastern regions. Another factor in the rise of the American woman was the ferment of social reform that gripped the nation in the mid-nineteenth century. This revolution of rising expectations could not be segregated by sex. In 1848, the first women's rights convention, with Lucretia Mott and Elizabeth Cady Stanton presiding, took place at Seneca Falls, New York. The presence of Frederick Douglass at the meeting linked the cause of blacks and women.

Male response to the Seneca Falls meeting was disappointing, but by the time Jane Addams was born, the continued efforts of feminists such as Susan B. Anthony had at least made women's rights a serious issue. The Civil War provided additional impetus. Women were needed as teachers, clerks, and nurses. In the absence of men, many served as farmers and mechanics. Some, particularly the nurse Clara Barton, won national acclaim for heroism on the battlefield. Older leaders like Stanton and Anthony raised money for the war effort through the National Women's Loyal League. But in the aftermath of the war, women anxious to collect a toll of respect from a grateful nation were put down with the admonition that it was "the Negro's hour." Indignantly, in 1869 Stanton and Anthony organized the National Woman's Suffrage Association (NWSA) in New York. It demanded immediate suffrage for women and called for radical modification of the institution of marriage. A rival organization that focused more narrowly on suffrage, the American Women's Suffrage Association, formed in Boston the same year under Lucy Stone and Julia Ward Howe. This group moved to leadership of the women's movement in the mid-1870s, when the NWSA became associated in the public mind with the free-love and birth-control ideas of Victoria Woodhull. In 1890, the two groups merged to form the National American Women's Suffrage Association with the primary emphasis on obtaining the vote at all electoral levels.

While feminists were making headlines and raising eyebrows, other women worked quietly in the crucial field of education. The problem here was to overcome the belief that, beyond the primary-school rudiments, education was for males, that women's minds were incapable of being educated at the higher levels, and that what advanced training ladies received should be restricted to such pursuits as embroidery, painting, French, singing, and playing the piano.

One of the first Americans to challenge this pattern was Mary Lyon, the founder, in 1837, of Mount Holyoke Seminary in South Hadley, Massachusetts. In a way that anticipated the career of Jane Addams, Mary Lyon rebelled against what she called the "genteel nothingness" that condemned women to protected, ineffective lives. Mount Holyoke was bold to offer a curriculum equal in content and rigor to the best men's colleges of the period. Oberlin College in Ohio went a step further in 1841 by graduating the first women from a coeducational college. In 1865, women's higher education achieved real distinction when the philanthropy of a brewer named Matthew Vassar enabled a women's college to open in Poughkeepsie, New York, with a physical plant and a faculty that most men's colleges could only envy. Vassar's most distinguished professor was a woman, the internationally acclaimed astronomer Maria Mitchell. Large-scale philanthropy also enabled Smith and Wellesley colleges to open in 1875. Four years later Harvard blessed the beginnings of a women's annex that evolved into Radcliffe College.

Jane Addams wanted to attend Smith and even made the long journey to Northampton, Massachusetts, to take and pass the entrance examinations in the summer of 1877. But her father was adamant: Jane would attend the Rockford Female Seminary in Rockford, Illinois. Questioning her revered father never even occurred to the young woman, and in the fall she dutifully, if unenthusiastically, packed her bags for "The Mount Holyoke of the West." The intellectual atmosphere at Rockford was intensely religious. Jane and many of her classmates chafed under the rigid discipline and the evangelical emphasis. Once Jane went for three months without praying and confessed she felt none the worse for the experience. She responded more positively to the doctrine of Christian usefulness, with its stress on taking religion out of the church and into society. Her sense of social responsibility was heightened by reading the works of English social thinkers such as Thomas Carlyle and John Ruskin. Ruskin particularly interested Jane because of his exposure of the injustices inherent in industrialism. At Rockford, Jane also studied Latin, Greek, French, natural science, ancient history, and moral philosophy. She was active in debate, edited the seminary magazine, and graduated in 1881 with the highest standing in her class.

For four years college had filled Jane Addams's life, but after graduation she stepped into a world that had little interest in or use for a college-educated woman. Adding immeasurably to her bewilderment was the death of John Addams in August 1881. Deprived of his moral guidance and inspiration, Jane felt completely adrift. As if this were not enough, a spinal operation cut short her study of medicine at the Woman's Medical College in Philadelphia and left her incapable of having children. After recovering from her illness, Addams immersed herself in culture. To that end, Jane Addams, her stepmother, and four other women toured England and the Continent for more than two years beginning in 1883. The group took language lessons, heard concerts and operas, and went to art galleries. But as for defining a purpose for her life, she was, by her own admission, "absolutely at sea." The pursuit of culture for its own sake seemed pointless, especially in view of the social problems that remained unsolved. Equally unappealing to Addams was the sheltered life of a gentlewoman-housewife, and because of her illness, motherhood was an impossibility. So she traveled idly, yearning for usefulness and hoping to break free of the trap of endless "preparation" and "construct the world anew."

At this low point in her life, Jane Addams happened to glimpse the grinding poverty and depravity that existed beneath the polished surface of Europe's cities. The most significant moment of awakening came in April 1888 in Madrid, Spain, on her second trip abroad. Addams and her traveling companions attended a bull-fight. As the bloody spectacle built to a climax, her friends, nauseated, excused themselves. Addams lingered on, delighting in the pageantry and its overtones of ancient gladiatorial combat. Later that evening, stung by the reprimands of her friends, she experienced "deep chagrin." She realized that by allowing cruelty to serve her personal pleasure, she had indirectly countenanced the whole system of exploitation that stripped many lives of dignity so that a few might flourish in luxury. After a restless night in Madrid, Addams arose determined to crystallize her vague ideals of social service into meaningful action. She began by describing to Ellen Gates Starr, a college friend and fellow traveler, a plan to rent a house in the most squalid section of an American city. There educated women could both learn about and serve the real needs of the oppressed. London's Toynbee Hall offered a model of such a "settlement," and Addams used the remainder of her trip abroad to study it. The art galleries and operas were forgotten. After eight years of drifting, Jane Addams had found a career.

In June 1888, she returned to the United States eager to implement her ideas. The time was ripe for them. As urbanization and industrialization had accelerated through the nineteenth century, they had left in their wake social problems of unprecedented breadth and intensity. The abundance and opportunity that had always seemed a part of the United States simply had not materialized for millions of Americans. Mired in poverty and obliged to live in the slums of the larger cities, they lived lives that were a nightmare of hard labor, poor health, and early death.

Although immigrants had not *caused* the slums, as some self-righteous "native" Americans maintained, they constituted an inordinate proportion of slum dwellers. And in the decades immediately preceding the beginning of Jane Addams's "settlement" in 1889, the stream of immigration had increased to a flood. From 1850 to 1880 about 2.5 million foreign-born people arrived in the United States each decade; in the 1880s, the figure leapt to 5.5 million. In the year after Jane Addams graduated from college (1882), almost 800,000 immigrants reached the New World. By 1890, approximately one-third of the population of Chicago was foreign-born. In the eastern seaboard cities the percentage was even higher. Because many newcomers had spent their last money to reach the United States, they usually remained trapped in their port of entry. There were more Italians in Brooklyn (a borough of New York City) by 1900 than in Naples, Italy; three times as many Irish lived in New York as in Dublin. By 1900, of the seventy-five million Americans, ten million were foreign-born and twenty-six million of foreign-born parentage.

Between Jane Addams's birth in 1860 and the founding of Hull House in 1889, the total population of the United States doubled. This was not as great a rate of increase as had occurred in the early nineteenth century, but in effect the nation became more crowded. The explanation lies in urbanization. In 1830, only 1 in 15 Americans lived in a city (a community of over 800 persons). In 1860, the ratio was 1 in 6; in 1900, 1 in 3. By 1910, nearly half of all Americans were city dwellers.

SOURCES OF IMMIGRATION INTO THE UNITED STATES: 1871–1910

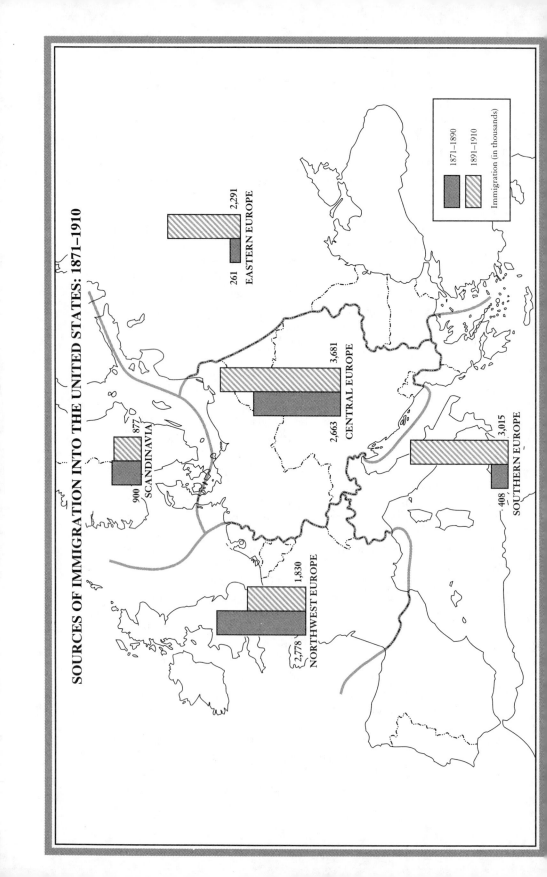

Viewed another way, there were 141 cities (by the same definition) in 1860, and 778 in 1910. The impact of this change on American thought and institutions was profound. Before Jane Addams's generation the nation had been, and had enjoyed thinking of itself as, a rural society of pioneers and yeoman farmers with a scattering of village blacksmiths plying their trade under the spreading trees of small towns. Cities were suspect. The popular mind saw them as dens of aristocracy and iniquity, where rosy-cheeked farmers' daughters became painted and fallen women. Yet the bright lights fascinated another corner of the American mind. The cities were a new frontier where "pioneering" lads like Horatio Alger's dime-novel heroes could climb the ladder from rags to riches. Feeding this dream of success were the palatial townhouses of the elite and the life of idle elegance lived within them. Very few Americans had the courage to confront the gulf between this lifestyle and that of the urban poor. Fewer still protested the fact that 1 percent of the population controlled the vast majority of the nation's wealth. But a few dared to ask the embarrassing questions. Jacob Riis, who published a blistering study of New York's slums in 1890 under the title *How the Other Half Lives*, was one. Jane Addams was another.

The meaning of industrialization, urbanization, and their attendant social frictions forced its way into the American consciousness with several headline-making events in the last quarter of the nineteenth century. Jane Addams was traveling to Smith College for an entrance exam when the first shock occurred in the summer of 1877. The weather was especially hot, and on the network of America's railroads the discontent of sweltering workingmen approached the breaking point. Railroad owners, playing free enterprise for all it was worth, had pared wages to the bone. The absence of safety features and employment compensation for injury was a further source of complaint. In July the railroads exploded in violence. A nationwide strike, the first in U.S. history, paralyzed transportation. Mobs of workers derailed and burned trains. Beatings, stonings, and shootings were commonplace. In the case of the Baltimore and Ohio Railroad, federal troops crushed the protesters. But the Pennsylvania Railroad management found itself opposed by virtually the entire community of Pittsburgh. Company property amounting to $5 million was destroyed, and a heavy loss of life was sustained by both parties in the dispute. Similar violence flared in Chicago, Saint Louis, and San Francisco. The U.S. Army finally came in to run the trains and halt the strike, but disturbing questions about capitalism and society arose in its aftermath. And Jane Addams, wondering if the disrupted railroads would permit her to return to Rockford after her exam, had her first encounter with the social ills that would be the object of her later reform endeavors.

The second major shock of the late nineteenth century occurred in 1886, when Jane Addams was between European trips and struggling unhappily with the question of a useful career. The locale was Chicago, and that fact may well have directed Jane's attention to this city as the subsequent site of her settlement. The background of the Haymarket Riot was widespread unemployment and unrest in the nation's industrial empire; the immediate cause was a clash between striking workers and police at the McCormick farm machinery factory. On the evening of May 4 some 1,400 men gathered in Haymarket Square to hear labor leaders defend the eight-hour day. Just as the meeting began, a squad of 180 policemen entered the square and ordered the crowd to disperse. At that moment a blinding flash and deafening roar came from the midst of the policemen. Someone (the subsequent trial never ascertained who) had tossed a powerful bomb into the ranks of the police. The explosion killed seven and injured scores. The surviving police began firing into the mob, killing four more. As news of the Haymarket Riot spread over the nation, Jane Addams and her contemporaries were horrified. Such social violence might be the norm in Europe, but in the New World of democracy and opportunity it seemed incongruous indeed. The bright future of an industrializing America suddenly seemed clouded.

The third blow to American expectations took place in the countryside and, initially at least, involved natural rather than human violence. Beginning in 1880 the trans-Mississippi West had a series of abnormally wet years. Coupled with the rapid disappearance of unclaimed farmland farther east, the weather reports tempted farmers into regions only marginally suited to agriculture. The propaganda of railroad and land developers spurred the westward push with promises of bumper crops and easy profits. Rain, it was illogically argued, followed the plow. In response, hopeful people mortgaged everything to get a start in farming and ranching. The "garden" of the American West, they believed, would provide a safety valve for the nation's social troubles; the unemployed and discontented could go west to a cornucopia of plenty. The inevitable confrontation with reality came in the late 1880s. The climate reverted to its normal pattern, and the fields turned to dust. Insects and lending institutions took care of whatever the fierce western sun spared. On top of this, howling blizzards in the winter of 1886–1887, the worst in the history of trans-Mississippi agriculture, decimated livestock. These bitter Americans who had paid the price searched for an explanation. Unwilling to blame themselves or nature, they turned on the political and economic establishment. Many of the alienated drifted back to the urban slums to provide additional subjects for reformers like Jane Addams.

In general, Americans responded to social problems in two ways. The first response simply denied that problems existed or blamed them on scapegoats. The high priest of this point of view, which was common in the ranks of the successful and powerful, was a Yale professor named William Graham Sumner. Its most visible exponent was the "self-made" Scottish immigrant named Andrew Carnegie. Sumner and Carnegie were social Darwinists. Drawing on the evolutionary thinking of Charles Darwin and Herbert Spencer, they argued that the concept of "survival of the fittest" could be applied to contemporary society. And as Sumner and Carnegie saw it, wealth demarcated ability: The richest were the fittest. The successful had emerged the winners in the social and economic sweepstakes; the poor deserved their fate. If poor people had possessed the requisite ability and determination, the social Darwinists contended, they would not be poor. Carnegie habitually quoted Shakespeare in reply to letters from impoverished acquaintances pleading hard times: "The fault, dear Brutus, is not in our stars, but in ourselves, that we are underlings." It followed from this view that the competitive free-enterprise system must be allowed to spin freely, rewarding talent with success and punishing incompetence with failure. Sumner, Carnegie, and their colleagues believed that the progress of the race depended on the inexorable workings of this "natural law." Neither the government nor private philanthropists should meddle in the struggle for existence that was nineteenth-century American capitalism. To help the poor, the social Darwinists maintained, was like trying to save the dinosaurs. Both were unfit to survive.

The second response to social problems, the one to which Jane Addams subscribed, broke sharply with the diagnosis and remedy offered by the social Darwinists. It regarded much about American life in the late nineteenth century as neither desirable nor inevitable. While freely admitting that urbanization and industrialization had made great achievements possible, people of this persuasion recognized that the changes had also created gross wrongs that should be remedied. Underlying this position was a basic respect for the dignity of the individual regardless of his or her social and economic status, as well as the assumption that progress resulted from a planned, cooperative attack on problems rather than from the inevitable working of the grindstone of competition.

Foremost among the advocates of this reform philosophy in Jane Addams's youth were Lester Frank Ward, Henry George, and Edward Bellamy. Ward's *Dynamic Sociology* of 1883 excited Addams and other critics of the status quo with its argument that government must interpose itself between the strong and the weak, the privileged and the underprivileged, to ensure equality of opportunity, economic security, and a minimum standard of human dignity. Arguing that human beings could exert a creative, shaping force on evolution, Ward refused to accept the conservative Darwinists' conception of human beings as helpless chips floating on the stream of time. Henry George and Edward Bellamy attracted widespread attention with specific proposals for alleviating the nation's social and economic ills. A world traveler, George had long been troubled by the coexistence of progress and poverty in the industrializing nations. He was especially critical of the system of private land ownership that allowed a fortunate few to profit from the growth of society as a whole. In 1879, George published his ideas on the problem in *Progress and Poverty*. The book called for the abolition of all taxes except a massive single tax on real estate. Although not avowedly socialistic, the "single taxers" were clearly in revolt against many of capitalism's fundamental principles. The same was true of the followers of Edward Bellamy's "nationalism." The point of his *Looking Backward, 2000–1887* (1888) was to demonstrate that the unregulated, competitive profit system was an obstacle to human happiness and the true progress of the race. In Bellamy's America in the year 2000, an all-powerful but beneficent state has "nationalized" every aspect of the economy and thereby secured social justice. Every citizen in Bellamy's utopia lives an efficient, dignified, and enlightened life. The benefits of technological progress have been realized and the social liabilities left behind. It was a dream that inspired many of the reformers of Jane Addams's generation.

Social feminism was another expression of the concern that motivated Ward, George, and Bellamy. Beginning in the late 1870s a number of American women turned from agitating for the vote to various forms of social service and philanthropy. At first, their activities centered on the church and the Sunday school and consisted of aiding indigent mothers and children. Later, the effectiveness and scope of the women's organizations broadened to the point of launching campaigns to eliminate or regulate prostitution, to abolish alcohol (the Women's Christian Temperance Union was formed in 1874), and to advance the general level of national morality (through the Social Purity League). In addition, many middle- and upper-class women joined local associations aimed at improving both themselves and their society. National leadership came from the General Federation of Women's Clubs (1890) and the Junior League (1901). But the high point of social feminism was the "settlement," and its showcase was Jane Addams's Hull House.

When Addams returned from Europe in 1888 she had a cause, a plan of attack, an income that permitted its implementation, and the energy born of almost thirty years of what she considered a useless life. January 1889 found her and Ellen Starr in Chicago, a city that the author Lincoln Steffens later described as "first in violence, deepest in dirt; loud, lawless, unlovely, ill-smelling, new; an overgrown gawk of a village, the teeming tough among cities." Of course it was this condition that attracted Jane Addams, and once in Chicago she deliberately searched out the rawest and most impoverished sections for a base of operations. Hull House at 800 South Halsted Street was ideal. Built in 1856 as a country home for a wealthy businessman, it stood thirty years later in the center of a squalid wilderness of tenements and factories populated largely by desperately poor immigrants. There were 7 churches and 255 saloons in the neighborhood. Mr. Hull, needless to say, had long since moved to greener fields beyond the sprawl of metropolitan Chicago, and Jane Addams was able to rent his mansion. On September 18, 1889, she moved in and, in company with a few other educated women of conscience and leisure, began a comprehensive assault on human degradation.

After a short period of hesitance and mistrust, Jane Addams's new neighbors accepted her experiment with enthusiasm. Some 2,000 people a week poured through the doors on Halsted Street. They received everything from hot lunches and child care services to instruction in English and lectures on art and philosophy. There was something for every age and interest. Jane Addams was convinced that the only way to reduce the influence of saloons, dance halls, and delinquency was to provide wholesome alternatives in the way of entertainment. Hull House therefore also organized parties and games at every opportunity to offer the hopeless something for which to live. Officially, according to its charter, Hull House existed "to provide a center for a higher civic and social life; to institute and maintain educational and philanthropic enterprises, and to investigate and improve the conditions in the industrial districts of Chicago." But for thousands of slum dwellers, the settlement simply meant that someone cared.

Alleviating human misery on a day-to-day, personal basis was only the start of Hull House's mission. Jane Addams was dedicated to making permanent improvements in the urban environment. To this end she campaigned for more effective garbage collection, won appointment as garbage inspector for her neighborhood, and in this capacity personally followed the wagons at six o'clock every morning. Encouraging her in these efforts was evidence that cleaner streets meant a greatly reduced death rate. On other occasions Addams organized a community improvement association that persuaded the city government to pave the streets, construct public baths, and build parks and playgrounds. People, she constantly insisted, were not machines, not objects of exploitation. They needed such things as playgrounds and baths and settlement houses to sustain a spark of joy and of hope. On another front Jane Addams took the lead in forming consumer cooperatives that secured better prices and higher quality in commodities such as coal and milk. Schools, in her estimation, were vital elements in long-range reform. Elected to the Chicago Board of Education, she pressed for reforms that made the schools better able to prevent delinquency and to prepare students for useful lives. As in the case of Hull House, her philosophy centered on stimulating rather than disciplining people.

Much of the activity at Hull House in the first decade of its existence had a close parallel in the Social Gospel movement. This attempt to make Christianity, particularly Protestantism, more useful in solving the problems of an industrial age took religion out of the churches and into society on a seven-day-a-week basis. Like Jane Addams, the Social Gospelers were not afraid to plunge into the heart of the ugliest parts of their social and physical environment. In Columbus, Ohio, Washington Gladden used his pulpit as a platform from which to negotiate a Christian solution to industrial strikes. Gladden's book, *Applied Christianity* (1886), was a defense of the new emphases. And by this time the Salvation Army, founded in London in 1878, had reached the United States. Its original intent had been to save the souls of the urban poor, and its uniformed soldiers of both sexes had leaned heavily on brass bands and similar revivalist techniques. But by the 1890s, the Salvation Army had joined forces with settlements like Hull House in offering slum people ways to improve their condition short of the pearly gates. Social service brigades went into the ghettos with relief and self-betterment programs.

Jane Addams's experiment on Halsted Street attracted many of the leading exponents of the Social Gospel. George Herron lectured there to overflow audiences on the incompatibility of modern capitalism and traditional Christianity. American society, he maintained, was on the verge of degenerating into atomized chaos. Herron called for a social ethic and a sense of community responsibility that would replace the dog-eat-dog relationships of free enterprise. William T. Stead also frequented Hull House. His biting indictment, *If Christ Came to Chicago*, published in 1894, appealed to the conscience of the city. Stead was especially anxious to stop Chicago's flourishing white slave trade. Working closely with Jane Addams and other reformers, Stead managed to find homes and legitimate employment for some of the prostitutes. The greatest Social Gospeler of them all, however, was Charles M. Sheldon, whose book *In His Steps* (1897) eventually sold twenty-three million copies. Sheldon told the story of a town that decided to approach all questions of policy by asking, "What would Jesus have done?"

In real life, however, social problems proved less susceptible to reform; indeed, they seemed to grow in scope and intensity as the nineteenth century drew to a close. Hull House was only three years old when a depression of unprecedented severity paralyzed the economy. The poor, of course, suffered most. In the disastrous year of 1893, railroads, mills, factories, and mines went bankrupt and closed their doors. Dazed legions of unemployed walked the streets of the major cities. There was a shocking and ironic contrast between Chicago's Columbian Exposition, a world's fair in praise of technological progress, and the thousands of homeless people sleeping on its outskirts. Four hundred years after its discovery, the New World seemed to have fallen far short of the promise of its beginnings.

Jane Addams did her best. Hull House strained its resources in an effort to alleviate the social consequences of the Depression of 1893, but it hardly made a dent in the misery of a single city. Thinking bigger, Jacob S. Coxey proposed a massive federal work-relief program centered on the idea of building good roads. When a conservative, business-oriented Congress rejected the idea, Coxey vowed to "send a petition to Washington with boots on." On Easter Sunday 1894, Coxey and his followers left Mission, Ohio, and walked to the capital. On the way they recruited jobless workers in Pittsburgh, chiefly among the bitter losers of an 1892 strike at Andrew Carnegie's Homestead steel plant. When "Coxey's Army" reached Washington, their spirits were high; surely a democratic government would respond to the genuine needs of so many of its citizens. But the Grover Cleveland administration regarded the march as a form of rebellion and met it with fixed bayonets, arrests, beatings, and even killing. Thoughtful Americans joined Jane Addams in taking a hard look at what they had assumed were established American rights and principles. Popular confidence in the government was further shaken when an 1895 ruling by the Supreme Court declared a modest 2 percent tax on incomes over $4,000 unconstitutional. The wealthy, it appeared, were beyond challenge, and the election of 1896, in which the conservative Republican William McKinley defeated William Jennings Bryan despite the support Bryan had received from most lower-income Americans, confirmed this impression.

For Jane Addams, the single most disturbing event of the 1890s was the Pullman strike. Not only did it raise disconcerting questions about the beneficence of capitalism and the federal government, but it took place just a few miles from Hull House in the Chicago suburb of Pullman, which George M. Pullman had created as a setting for his railroad car factory. Jane knew Pullman personally. She sat on the Citizens Arbitration Committee that made a futile endeavor to settle the strike.

For Addams and most of her contemporaries the most shocking thing about the Pullman strike was the fact that Pullman, Illinois, had been widely heralded as a model of enlightened labor–management relations. Although a company town, it was carefully planned, with neat, comfortable housing, ample recreational facilities, beautiful parks, and excellent schools. Pullman seemed to prove that capitalism could benefit all parties—to dispel the gloom cast by Homestead, Haymarket, and the great railroad strike of 1877. George Pullman had apparently shown that the nation could advance peacefully into a future that was at once industrialized and just.

The Depression of 1893 gave the lie to such expectations. As Pullman's profits declined, management lowered wages again and again—a total of five times by the summer of 1894. Rents and food prices in the company town, however, remained at the predepression level. And George Pullman, standing firmly on the doctrine of benevolent paternalism, refused to hear his laborers' complaints or to submit them to arbitration. In June 1894, rising tensions exploded in a massive strike. The newly organized American Railway Union, under the leadership of Eugene V. Debs, voted to refuse service to all Pullman cars on America's railroads. Management responded by asking President Grover Cleveland to use the armed forces to invade the town of Pullman and end the strike. The president and his attorney general, Richard Olney, were more than agreeable. Ignoring the protests of Illinois Governor John P. Altgeld, the Cleveland administration secured an injunction from a federal court and ordered 2,000 troops to Pullman on July 4, 1894. Their arrival triggered a full-scale riot. Neither the union nor the army could preserve order. Mobs ranged the streets of Pullman. Before the troops prevailed, twelve men lay dead and millions of dollars worth of property was reduced to smoldering rubble.

The emotional currents generated by the Pullman strike swirled around Hull House, and Jane Addams became deeply troubled by what she called "the growth of class bitterness." On the one hand were the unemployed workers, wearing the white ribbons of the strikers, who told her about the perfidy of Pullman. Beneath the guise of benevolent paternalism, they charged, George Pullman was a tyrant, and his philosophy of labor–management relations little better than slavery. On the other hand, Jane Addams was a lady of wealth and breeding whose circle of friendships included capitalists. One acquaintance, who had lost thousands of dollars as a result of the strike, told Addams, "The strikers ought all to be shot."

Sifting these competing claims in her own mind, Jane Addams wrote "A Modern Lear." The point of the essay was that George Pullman, like Shakespeare's King Lear, had reaped ingratitude as the result of his peculiar form of dictatorial benevolence. In Addams's opinion, true friendship stemmed from genuine, unsolicited, and mutual respect. The Pullman Palace Car Company was, in the last analysis, a commercial operation. When pressed, it put commercial considerations before those of social welfare. Like Lear, Pullman affected kindliness only when it served his interests; his employees actually had no social identity save that of well-tended machines. The Pullman affair taught Jane Addams that, if a capitalist was really interested in effective reform, he had to consult and, if necessary, compromise with the desires of the workers, even if this meant departing on occasion from strictly commercial criteria. Social progress, she concluded, "is not the result of [the capitalist's] individual striving, as a solitary mountain climber beyond sight of the valley multitude." Instead, progress should be "lateral." The rise of the entire society, Jane Addams believed, constituted the only legitimate definition of progress.

The aftermath of the Pullman strike found Jane Addams and her contemporaries doubtful about the susceptibility of American capitalism to reform. Perhaps there was an inherent incompatibility between the profit motive and social justice. Perhaps Hull House was only painkilling ointment for a chronic, deep-rooted disease. In this frame of mind she began to listen to the arguments of socialists, who proposed an alternative socioeconomic system based on mutual assistance rather than individual accumulation. The roots of this idea ran back half a century in the American context. The many utopian communities born of the great reform wave of the 1820s, 1830s, and 1840s had operated on social and communal principles even before Karl Marx published his *Communist Manifesto* in 1848. In 1825, at a place significantly named New Harmony, Robert Owen organized a commune based on the principles of cooperative labor and collective property ownership. The harmony at New Harmony was short-lived, but people continued to dream. Albert Brisbane revived communalism in the 1840s with the aid of the ideas of the French social thinker Charles Fourier. Brisbane's idea of economically efficient living units (he called them "phalanxes") inspired other undertakings, notably the Transcendentalists' Brook Farm. Perhaps the most visible of all the utopian communities was

Leo, shown at his job in a textile mill in Fayetteville, Tennessee, was eight years old in this photograph. He earned fifteen cents a day. Jane Addams campaigned for laws prohibiting such exploitation of children.

the one John Humphrey Noyes founded at Oneida, New York, in 1848. The Oneida perfectionists even extended their criticism of private property to a condemnation of the institution of marriage. In addition, there were various religious groups—the Shakers and the Mormons in particular—who successfully practiced forms of cooperative living.

After the Civil War the social abuses that came with the rapid growth and transformation of the American economy spurred renewed interest in socialism. Jane Addams was among those Americans who gave it serious consideration, and Hull House became a mecca for radical social thought. In 1890, its members formed the Working People's Social Science Club to discuss the various ways of organizing society. Marxist doctrine received considerable attention, and so did the American varieties of socialism propounded by Henry George and Edward Bellamy. A few years after his spectacular but unsuccessful campaign for the mayoralty of New York City, George personally addressed a Hull House audience. According to Jane Addams, this "great leader" received an ovation that rocked the building. On the whole, she welcomed such displays. "A Settlement," she wrote, "is above all a place for enthusiasms, a spot to which those who have a passion for the equalization of human joys and opportunities are early attracted."

Pursuing her personal exploration of alternatives to capitalism, Jane Addams journeyed to Russia in 1896 to study the life and thought of Count Leo Tolstoy. A

Jane Addams deliberately located her social settlement, Hull House, in a slum neighborhood such as this one. Although the street shown has lighting, sidewalks, and cobblestone paving, it was far above average for American cities. And even this street appears to lack an effective garbage collection system (note the dead horse) and sewage system (the open gutters, left, carry the waste).

disciple of Marx, Tolstoy had renounced his comfortable way of life to live communally with poor peasants in a remote village. Addams seemed to sense the similarities between Tolstoy's upbringing and her own. Perhaps, she reasoned, the Russian's refusal to live off the work of others' hands was the key to social justice. She therefore awaited her interview with great eagerness. But the meeting between the two reformers was short and to the point. Tolstoy had been working in the fields in his simple peasant garb. On seeing Jane Addams's elaborate dress, he remarked that it contained enough material in a single sleeve to make several peasant frocks. Didn't she find such clothes a barrier between herself and those she desired to help? Tolstoy demanded. His next questions concerned where Jane Addams's food and income came from. Mortified that she did not till the soil, the American returned to Chicago resolved to purify herself with humble work. Yet after a brief stint at bread baking in Hull House's kitchen, Jane abandoned Tolstoy's plan as "more logical than life warrants." The service of the poor, she concluded, could not be "pushed aside . . . while I saved my soul by . . . baking bread." The decision showed her commitment to reform within the capitalistic framework; she would elevate the underprivileged rather than join them.

Another indication of Addams's position was her relationship with the movement for organized socialism that gathered strength in the United States in the 1890s. On the one hand, she admired the sincerity and the intensity of the socialist attack on human degradation. Few Americans, she realized, were doing more to fulfill the ideals to which she subscribed than Eugene V. Debs, Victor Berger, and their colleagues. Yet the socialists demanded a degree of intellectual conformity that repelled Jane Addams. "I should have been glad," she remarked, "to have had the comradeship of that gallant company had they not firmly insisted that fellowship depends upon identity of creed." On another occasion, at a street corner rally, she angrily told an unruly crowd of laborers that she intended to resist the bullying of both millionaires and socialists. If democratic institutions were to endure, she believed, the tyranny of both ends of the political spectrum had to be resisted.

Having thus rejected the alternative of dismantling the capitalistic system, Jane Addams directed her energies toward its improvement. One of the first fronts she attacked was the labor problem. Her neighbors around Hull House provided ample evidence of the depths of misery possible under the unregulated profit system. Wage slavery had a vivid meaning for Jane Addams. Most of her neighbors worked in Chicago's sweatshops making clothing, glass, and other products. Their hours were long—fourteen a day was the norm—and their wages so low as to necessitate the labor of the entire family. Children were not exempt. Jane Addams reported one case of a "little girl of four who pulled out basting threads hour after hour, sitting on a stool at the feet of her Bohemian mother, a little bunch of human misery." For Americans with social consciences, such a situation was intolerable.

Given the unwillingness of employers to alter a profitable system, two remedies seemed possible to Jane Addams. The first involved the organization of laboring people in their own behalf. The first such attempts in the United States came before the Civil War and involved skilled craftsmen such as machinists and carpenters. These craft unions managed to wring some concessions from employers dependent on their skills, but they did nothing for the great mass of unskilled workers. In 1869, Uriah Stephens attempted to organize this group in the Noble Order of the Knights of Labor. All workers except gamblers and bartenders were welcome, and under the leadership of Stephens and later of Terence V. Powderly, the Knights of Labor grew prodigiously. But Powderly's call for a cooperative working commonwealth with no distinction between labor and capital raised suspicions among owners. After the Haymarket Riot of 1886, which many attributed to labor agitation, the Knights lost most of its membership. As the Knights fell, a new national union, the American Federation of Labor (AFL), rose. Organized in 1881, the AFL returned to the principle of skilled-craft unionism. Samuel Gompers, a cigar maker, provided the leadership that brought a million workers into the union fold by 1895. In contrast to the Knights, the AFL focused on short-term economic gains such as increased wages, shorter work days, and improved working conditions.

Jane Addams made Hull House a center of union activities in the Chicago area. She believed that unions offered a means of constructive social change. Until the public and its government recognized and protected the rights of working people, unions had to fill the breach as best they could. Under AFL auspices, bookbinders, shirtmakers, and glass processors organized at Hull House. So did various local unions and workers' clubs. For many of the participants, union activity marked the first faint stirrings of hope—the first light in dark and bewildered lives. Jane Addams stirred these sparks. She took special pleasure in the Jane Club, a cooperative living arrangement for working girls. Here was a demonstration of an alternative to the dog-eat-dog competition she saw at the root of so many of her nation's social and economic ills.

Although labor unions were an important forward step, Jane Addams recognized their limitations. Employers could, and customarily did, ignore their demands. It was a simple matter in the 1890s to fire "troublemaking" union workers and hire replacements from the masses of desperately poor immigrants. As for strikes like that at Pullman in 1894, Jane Addams saw them as little better than extensions of the old, unregulated competition on the part of both labor and management. What was needed, she felt, was the substitution of the rule of law for that of force in industrial relations. The government, in her opinion, had to be more than an observer at a prize fight. It had to make and enforce the rules that would ensure that the fight would be fought fairly and with dignity for all concerned.

This position gave rise to Jane Addams's interest in labor legislation. As early as 1891, the Hull House women helped push through the Illinois legislature a law limiting factory labor to persons older than thirteen. But the law proved ineffective. Employers simply ignored it, and—to Jane Addams's surprise—so did the impoverished parents of working children. Regarding the latter as victims of the system, she persisted in her belief that child labor was a social evil. In 1893, she had the satisfaction of seeing a Hull House campaign result in tighter labor laws, including an unprecedented eight-hour maximum day for working women. At the same time a Hull House resident, Florence Kelley, was appointed by prolabor governor John P. Altgeld to inspect state factories, with the responsibility of reporting infractions. The honeymoon ended abruptly, however, in 1896, at the expiration of Altgeld's term. The new governor replaced Kelley with a factory owner. Moreover, the Illinois Supreme Court declared the eight-hour legislation unconstitutional on the grounds that women who wanted to should be allowed to work more than a third of a day. Embittered by what they considered a travesty of the concept of individual freedom, Hull House workers launched a vigorous campaign for new legislation. The Chicago business community chastised Jane Addams and her friends, labeled them flaming radicals, and finally offered them $30,000 to "keep quiet." Goaded by these insults, the women battled even harder. In 1903, they had the satisfaction of witnessing the passage of a second children's wages-and-hours act.

After 1903 the fight for labor legislation shifted from the state to the federal level. At first, the U.S. Supreme Court ruled (*Lochner v. New York*, 1905) that acts limiting working hours were invalid, but a breakthrough came in 1908 in the case of *Muller v. Oregon*. The Supreme Court had been asked to rule on an Oregon statute limiting the hours of laundresses. Realizing that the verdict would affect Illinois legislation as well, Jane Addams followed the proceedings closely. Florence Kelley even helped secure the services of the brilliant lawyer (and later Supreme Court Justice) Louis Brandeis. In a famous legal brief, Brandeis dismissed precedent and the free enterprise system in two pages. He devoted the next hundred to a detailed examination of the harmful effects of unlimited working hours on society. This sociological approach convinced a majority of justices, and the Oregon law was upheld. Jane Addams breathed a sigh of relief. Perhaps, if pushed hard enough and long enough, capitalism was capable of self-reform.

Political corruption also drew Jane Addams's fire in the late nineteenth and early twentieth centuries. Chicago provided a large target for her crusading zeal. In the 1890s she estimated that of the sixty-eight aldermen on the city council, fifty-seven were corrupt. Bribes and graft were their way of life. One of the worst aldermen represented Hull House's district. Three times the settlement campaigned to unseat him, and three times he triumphed with surprising ease. The reason, Jane Addams discovered, was that many voters were directly obligated to this political boss and his political machine for jobs, favors, and protection. Continuing her analysis of the urban political situation, Addams came to understand that corrupt as he was, the boss was also a beneficial force in the community. With the exception of settlement workers like herself, he was the slum dwellers' only friend. The boss, for example, might put a needy person on his payroll, or release someone from jail, or send medicine to a sick family, or pay the costs of a funeral. The Hull House alderman distributed ten tons of turkey during the Christmas season in 1897. Needy recipients did not forget such kindnesses, and the politicos made certain that their memories were fresh on election day.

For the immigrants, there was little need for reminders. The political boss was understood as the American equivalent of the European nobleman or feudal lord. He was a benevolent authority figure to be feared and revered. Of course his concern for the poor was insincere; votes and continued power were his real object. But the corrupt political system indisputably worked to alleviate some of the miseries of life in the ghetto. In this sense, Jane Addams realized, the boss was her colleague. Urban politics was an informal welfare agency. The boss raised funds from the wealthy and distributed them among the urban poor, whose votes were vital to his political existence.

Although Jane Addams came to appreciate the social function of the city bosses, she understood them as a poor substitute for sincere concern for the welfare of the urban masses. The real need was for honest, efficient, and democratic government that addressed the causes, rather than the symptoms, of human suffering. In this concern she had substantial help. "Good government" reformers had been at work since the 1870s. On the federal level the Pendleton Act of 1883, creating a civil service system, marked a major triumph over the spoilsmen. But the state and especially the local "rings" of corrupt politicians were harder to dislodge. In New York City, for instance, Boss William M. Tweed and his successors in Tammany Hall simply laughed at civil service and continued to surround themselves with partners in plundering the public. Beginning with a series of articles in *McClure's* magazine in 1902, Lincoln Steffens gave Americans a frank look at their local governments. But his bitter exposé, collected under the title *The Shame of the Cities*, made it clear that the ultimate blame rested with the American people. Their apathy made the system of boss rule possible. Jane Addams agreed heartily. She took every opportunity to arouse the public in support of reform candidates throughout the nation. Samuel M. "Golden Rule" Jones, the mayor who had cleaned up politics in the city of Toledo, Ohio, was a favorite speaker at Hull House. So was Hazen S. Pingree, who had done the same for Detroit and later, as governor, for Michigan.

Perhaps the most visible reformer on the state level was Robert M. "Fighting Bob" La Follette, the Wisconsin governor (1900) and U.S. senator (1906). Jane

Addams applauded his success in instituting civil service reform, direct primaries, lobbying regulations, popular referendums, and the first state income tax. She also thought well of Governors Hiram Johnson of California and Woodrow Wilson of New Jersey. As for her home state, she became one of the leaders of the Civic Federation and the Municipal Voters' League, which helped Mayor Carter Harrison make a dent in the multilayered corruption of Chicago. Other cities rejected mayors altogether in favor of government by a commission of experts or by an impartial city manager whose position was not dependent on elections. Those communities that retained elected officials made them more responsive to their electorates through the adoption of new political devices such as the initiative, the referendum, and recall.

In her role as reformer after the turn of the century, Jane Addams found herself in the company of a loosely knit band of fellow crusaders who assumed the label *Progressives*. More a mood than an organized movement, progressivism was characterized by confidence in human efforts to improve the quality of American life. Progressives like Jane Addams followed Lester Frank Ward and the reform Darwinists in rejecting the belief that humans were pawns in the hands of deterministic forces beyond their control. The future, as Herbert Croly put it, would *not* take care of itself. Mastery and control, Walter Lippmann added, should replace passivity and drift. The Progressives also agreed with John Dewey and the pragmatists that traditional ideas and institutions should be tested for their effectiveness in meeting current needs and, when ineffective, discarded. Most Progressives could agree on the matter of goals: justice in social relations, democracy in politics, and equal opportunity in business. The umbrella for all these was the goal of orderly, efficient progress toward the millennium that most Progressives believed lay at the end of the rainbow of reform.

Jane Addams was in complete accord with Progressive ideology, and she exemplified the social-consciousness aspect of the crusade. She also personified the average Progressive. Differing sharply from the Populists of the 1890s, the Progressives were, on the whole, middle and upper class, urban, and comfortably wealthy. In fact, most of the Progressives had voted in 1896 for William McKinley and against the Populist champion William Jennings Bryan. The typical Progressives felt threatened on several fronts. They feared, and to some extent envied, the growing might of big business and its affluent owners. Statistical compilations such as that of 1902, which revealed no less than 3,561 millionaires in the United States, disturbed the Progressive mind. But so did the rising power of labor and immigrant groups. Blue-collar radicalism, Progressives believed, was as dangerous as concentrated wealth. As descendants, more often than not, of old American families once accustomed to social dominance, Progressives took for granted their right—indeed, their duty—to lead their country out of the morass. Moreover, they saw in this leadership an opportunity to halt the slippage in their own status, and to give themselves an active role along with the new rich and the organized poor. Reform appealed, then, not only as a remedy for external evils, but as a means of personal reassertion.

In Jane Addams's case, this self-interest was clearly evident and, to her credit, frankly admitted. Social work had been her salvation. Her early life had consisted of a frustrating pursuit of genteel culture; founding Hull House had given her a purpose and, in time, an international reputation. It had given her the contact with reality she craved. In 1892, in the course of a lecture on "The Subjective Necessity for Social Settlements," Jane confessed that Hull House existed as much for frustrated college-educated upper-class women as it did for the immigrants and the urban poor. The "undirected" lives of the women, she declared, seemed "as pitiful as the other great mass of destitute lives." Later in the same address she referred to the "joys of self-sacrifice," not the least of which was "a love of approbation so vast that it is not content with the treble clapping of delicate hands, but wishes also to hear the brass notes from toughened palms." The Jane Club and Addams's willingness to be called "Saint Jane" by the Hull House community support this analysis. But Jane Addams was not saying anything new about human nature; she only called a spade a spade. And if egoism could be channeled into constructive social purposes, who was to deny its value? Reform, in sum, had clearly helped Jane Addams; but Jane Addams had unquestionably advanced reform.

By 1910 Jane Addams was famous. Her work at Hull House and her numerous writings, particularly *Twenty Years at Hull House* (1910), in a field one would now call sociology, were known all over the world. In some quarters, to be sure, she was considered a radical and a crank, but in others she was seen as the first lady of American reform and one of progressivism's brightest lights. As such, she occupied a position of influence in national politics. Her first venture into this arena was in 1912, when she threw her weight behind the new Progressive party. This organization had taken shape in the last year of William Howard Taft's administration as a protest against his apparent indifference to the reform policies of his predecessor, Theodore Roosevelt. At first the dissatisfied Republicans rallied around Senator Robert La Follette, but early in 1912 Roosevelt, refreshed after an African safari, expressed an interest in opposing Taft. The organizers of the Roosevelt-for-President boom that immediately developed set their sights on the Republican National Convention scheduled for June 18 in Chicago. Jane Addams traveled uptown to attend. Her reputation got her a hearing before the Republican Platform Committee, and she used the opportunity to advocate the adoption of a plank favoring women's suffrage. But when the platform appeared, there was no reference to women and the vote. Addams had companions in frustration, for the Roosevelt supporters, too, had been thwarted by the Taft-controlled Republican Central Committee. After Taft received the party's nomination on June 22, the Roosevelt supporters reconvened in another part of town to form a new party. A personal friend of Roosevelt, Addams decided to attend. When the Progressive, or Bull Moose, party endorsed women's suffrage as well as advanced reform measures on labor, health, and justice, she decided to join.

Theodore Roosevelt became the Progressive party's standard-bearer; Jane Addams seconded his nomination. In doing so, she forced herself to swallow two unpalatable policies. One was Theodore Roosevelt's militarism, and the other the Progressive party's deliberate silence on the problems of black Americans. Jane Addams rationalized the first with the fact that more people were killed or injured in industrial accidents than in war. The Progressives' proposals for reform in this area made their endorsement of war bearable. As for blacks, she offered the explanation that her party's silence was preferable to the Republicans' hypocrisy. In time, when white southerners were better prepared to cooperate, the Progressives would help blacks. If such reasoning satisfied Jane Addams, it left many of her supporters deeply disturbed. A group from Hull House gathered outside her hotel room door and wept throughout the night.

Nevertheless Jane Addams took to the campaign trail, lecturing throughout the nation for Roosevelt and his running mate, Hiram Johnson of California. It was an uphill battle. The nation's Republicans were sharply divided. The more liberal were willing to bolt for Roosevelt; the rich and powerful felt that the twin pillars of the establishment—the sanctity of private property and the autonomy of business—were safer in the hands of Taft. Woodrow Wilson, reform governor of New Jersey and the Democrats' nominee, offered another alternative. At the core of Wilson's "New Freedom" was the belief that an economy based on freely competing small units would restore equal opportunity. Completing the slate for the election of 1912 was Eugene V. Debs, the nominee of the rapidly growing Socialist party.

Given these options, the election results were easy to explain. With the Republicans disunited, Woodrow Wilson won easily. Roosevelt ran second, Taft third, and Debs a respectable fourth (see also Chapter 3). Undiscouraged, Jane Addams felt that the Progressive effort had at least blocked the reelection of Taft. And "new parties," as she put it, "ultimately write the platforms for all parties." Moreover, Woodrow Wilson gave promise of continuing the age of reform. The next few years fulfilled many of her expectations. Two constitutional amendments, the Sixteenth (a personal income tax) and the Seventeenth (direct popular election of U.S. senators), instituted reforms Jane Addams had long favored. She also applauded the passage in 1914 of acts creating the Federal Trade Commission and establishing a stricter antitrust policy (the Clayton Act). Wilson also helped labor with more favorable wages-and-hours legislation, although, in truth, the main thrust of reform in this area was carried by Henry Ford (see pages 116–117). Finally, all Progressives were heartened by Wilson's 1916 appointment of Louis Brandeis to the Supreme Court.

While pleased enough by the record of Wilson's first administration to support him in the election of 1916, Jane Addams believed that progressivism could best be furthered by extending the vote to American women. Her argument was straightforward. Women were the traditional custodians of morality; they knew the value of the life they brought into the world better than did men. They would therefore be more responsive to problems such as child labor, prostitution, political corruption, and health. As women had disciplined families for generations, so they would discipline the nation. Their participation in elections could not fail to advance reform.

The roots of Jane Addams's interest in women's suffrage lay in her father's support of the policy. By the time she had graduated from college in 1881, she was an enthusiastic suffragist, but her interest in the movement faded as she became engrossed in the settlement idea. Jane Addams decided she was more concerned about alleviating misery in the ghettos than about women's rights. But after Hull House was well established, she turned once more to the suffrage crusade. As historian Glenna Matthews has observed, Addams was at the forefront of those who believed

These early feminists were assembled for the first International Convention of Women, held in Washington, DC, in 1888. Only a few can be identified for sure. Front row: third from left, Susan B. Anthony; fourth from right, Elizabeth Cady Stanton; third from right, Matilda J. Gage, a Civil War researcher and writer. Second row: third from left, Frances Willard, Women's Christian Temperance Union; fourth from left, Lillie Devereux Black (nicknamed Tiger Lillie), author of "Fettered for Life."

Jane Addams (right), here demonstrating with a friend, Mary McDowell, was a leading advocate of world peace all her adult life.

The European immigrants who thronged to the United States in the late nineteenth and early twentieth centuries were a major recipient of Jane Addams's social service. The group here is on a 1906 ocean liner.

that politics was essentially "national housekeeping," and that government currently lacked the "domestic" influence of women. Government, especially in blighted urban areas, operated poorly because women had no involvement. In 1907, Addams led more than a hundred Chicago area women's clubs in a campaign for political status in that city. By 1916, twelve states had granted women the vote, and Carrie Chapman Catt had revived the National American Woman's Suffrage Association as the spearhead in the campaign for a constitutional amendment. The first success came in the House of Representatives in 1918, but it was not until August 26, 1920, that the thirty-sixth state approved the Nineteenth Amendment. Exactly fifty years after white American males granted the vote to black males, they extended equal political rights to women. For Jane Addams, it was one of the triumphs of progressivism.

Peace rivaled social justice as an ideal in the mind of Jane Addams. True, her father had sponsored a company of soldiers during the Civil War, and the family had always admired the brave men who fought so that the slaves could be free. By the time Jane Addams founded Hull House, however, she was beginning to have doubts about war. For one thing, it was inefficient and wasteful, and like most Progressives, Jane Addams reserved special hatred for these qualities. Why fight, she asked, when the alternative of reasoning together existed? War, in her opinion, was a rejection of human intelligence as a shaping influence on progress, a throwback to the tooth-and-claw existence of the jungle. In practice, armed conflict was a failure; it created far more problems than it solved. Moreover, in Jane Addams's view, war diverted the nation's attention from much-needed social, political, and economic reforms. It was in this area, not in militarism, that she felt the nation's vigor could be both maintained and displayed. This was her answer to Theodore Roosevelt and the turn-of-the-century imperialists.

Another factor in Addams's pacifism and internationalism was her experience in the ghettos. Very different types of people, she became convinced, could coexist peacefully. If Chicago's immigrants, who constituted a microcosm of the Western world, could live together in a neighborhood, nations should be able to do the same. The end result would be a better life for all. Cooperation, not competition, held the answers to society's problems. On behalf of this belief, Jane Addams was willing to make pacifism aggressive. In 1907 she wrote that pacifists must renounce the "older dove-like ideal" and adopt a dynamic, forceful approach.

In that same year Jane Addams joined Samuel Gompers and William Jennings Bryan on the speakers' platform at the first National Peace Conference. The tone of this meeting and that of the following year was optimistic. "Physical force," as Jane Addams put it, "had ceased to be functional and would therefore disappear." It was the law of evolution. War was obsolete. Imagine, therefore, the shock of Jane Addams and other pacifists when, on June 28, 1914, the assassination of Archduke Francis Ferdinand, heir to the Austro-Hungarian throne, ignited a major war in Europe. Initially the United States had no part in the conflict, and many Americans retreated smugly behind three centuries of believing themselves God's chosen people and 3,000 miles of ocean. But for others, including Jane Addams, this position was extremely naive. She knew that the New World's immunity to European problems was not as complete as many of her contemporaries hoped. International trade and shipping linked the continents as did considerations of national security. There was also the sense of responsibility of many Americans for the kind of world in which they lived now and would in the future.

In 1914 and 1915, Jane Addams played a leading role in putting into practice President Wilson's request for neutrality in thought as well as in deed. But for her the real goal was permanent world peace, and it was to this end that she directed the bulk of her energies. In January 1915, she helped Carrie Chapman Catt found the Women's Peace party. At its first convention the party adopted a platform of eleven planks. Foremost among them was a proposal for a permanent neutral commission of international mediators to stop wars before they started. This harbinger of the League of Nations and the United Nations testified to the belief of Jane Addams and her colleagues that peace was a cause amenable to scientific solution.

Three months after setting forth this plan, Jane Addams was at The Hague in Holland presiding over the first congress of the Women's International League for Peace and Freedom. Twelve nations sent delegations, and the united body expressed its conviction that women's natural concern with the preservation of human life should be capitalized on in the interest of peace. The peace movement was allied with the suffrage movement. If women had the vote, it was implied, war would be less likely. At the conclusion of the Hague meeting, Addams toured the belligerent countries in the company of Dr. Aletta Jacobs, Holland's first female physician. They found the leaders of the warring nations receptive to their ideas, but reluctant to take a stand on peace for fear it would weaken their bargaining position with their enemies. Nonetheless, the press and the public in the various nations treated this visit as a hopeful sign.

On returning to the United States in July 1915, Jane Addams found a climate of opinion markedly different from that she had encountered in Europe. The majority of Americans and their newspapers ridiculed the pacifists. Typical was the remark of Theodore Roosevelt, who otherwise had the highest opinion of Jane Addams. "Pacifists," said the hero of the Spanish–American War, "are cowards." Several factors figured in this hostility. First, German submarines, or U-boats, were making an all-out attack on the blockading British navy. Neutral vessels were advised to remain clear of the North Atlantic in order to avoid unfortunate mistakes. Americans, however, insisted on their right to trade with whomever they pleased. Then the inevitable happened: An American ship, the *Gunfight*, was torpedoed. The country had scarcely absorbed this affront when news arrived that a German U-boat had sunk the British passenger liner *Lusitania* on May 7, 1915, with the loss of 1,198 lives, including 128 Americans. Woodrow Wilson still kept the United States out of war, but he found less and less support for his neutralism.

Added to the submarine issue was an economic one. American bankers were making heavy financial commitments to England and France. It followed that an Allied defeat would mean the loss of billions of dollars. Moreover, American manufacturers enjoyed a lucrative business supplying munitions and other war products to the Allies. To a considerable extent, the prosperity of the United States was entwined with Allied military fortunes. Finally, there was the matter of historical and cultural ties. Most Americans felt closer to England than they did to Germany.

American ideals, it was widely believed, were on the side of the Allies, and British propaganda skillfully nourished such thinking. In the public mind the Germans emerged as Stone Age barbarians bent on the rape and pillage of innocent peoples.

The growing mood of sympathy for England explained in large part the ridicule and outright abuse heaped on Jane Addams and other pacifists. The criticism centered on the peace ship that Henry Ford dispatched to Europe on December 4, 1915. Jane Addams helped plan the venture despite her reservations about its seriousness. A few days before the sailing she fell ill with a serious kidney disease and was hospitalized.* The Ford debacle was played out to its ineffective end without her.

Woodrow Wilson was reelected in 1916 on the campaign slogan "He Kept Us Out of War." The president personally hated war for many of the same reasons as Jane Addams, and he mounted a commendable struggle for peace and American noninvolvement. Twice he sent his top adviser, Colonel Edward M. House, to Europe in unsuccessful attempts to arrange peace negotiations. In December 1916, he tried once more to end the war by asking England and Germany to state their objectives as a prelude to compromise. But neither belligerent would give up the hope of a full-fledged victory. Even as Wilson urged "peace without victory," Germany was planning a total military effort. Wilson had no choice but to prepare for the possibility of American involvement in the war. In 1916, Congress voted to increase the size of the army and to construct new warships, and Wilson created a Council of National Defense to facilitate industrial production.

Preparedness seemed to make sense when Germany announced on January 31, 1917, that it was beginning unrestricted submarine warfare. All ships, those of neutral nations included, were henceforth subject to attack. Wilson responded by breaking diplomatic relations with Germany, but he hesitated to take the final step to war. Three developments in the spring of 1917 changed his mind. First, an intercepted communication from German foreign minister Alfred Zimmerman revealed his country's interest in allying with Mexico and conquering part of the United States. Second, a revolution against the Russian czar had removed the aristocracy in control of that country. Thus it now appeared that the Allies (England, France, Italy, and Russia) were united in carrying the banner of popular sovereignty against autocracy. Finally, between February 3 and April 1, 1917, German submarines sank eight American ships in the North Atlantic.

In spite of these provocations, the actual decision to intervene as a belligerent in the European conflict was agonizing, particularly for a progressive-minded president who believed in reason and Christian harmony. Given this belief, Wilson had to state the American war objectives in highly idealistic terms. "The world must be made safe for democracy," he told the Congress on April 2, 1917. "We have no selfish ends to serve." As the president conceived of it, the war was to be the greatest crusade of all; the goal was no less than freedom and justice for all humanity. On April 6, by a vast majority, Congress passed the war resolution.

*Ford's peace ship is further discussed on pages 120–121.

Wilson deliberately phrased his rationale for war in terms that would appeal to the Progressive mind, and many Progressives followed him in supporting American intervention in World War I. They argued that this would be a war to end all wars and that the federal government would begin assuming in wartime greater responsibility for the national welfare. John Dewey, Jane Addams's intellectual hero, defended the war as a practical step toward the advancement of permanent peace and liberal reform. But Addams was unconvinced. In her opinion, war, for any reason, was a disaster, an admission that reason had given way to violence. As for the domestic social advances that might be made during a war, she pointed out that many more might have been made if peace had prevailed.

In her opposition to World War I Jane Addams stood with some German-Americans and a handful of liberal intellectuals. But after April 6, 1917, most Americans regarded pacifists as traitors. Patriotism was easily warped into intolerance. George Creel's Committee on Public Information, created by the federal government to "sell the war to America," censored news, marshaled patriotic orators, and saturated the country with anti-German propaganda. A wave of bigotry resulted. Many schools stopped teaching German; a mob pulled a German orchestra conductor off his podium. Sauerkraut was renamed "liberty cabbage"; frankfurters, "liberty pups." Those who openly opposed the war were subjected to vigilante justice. Hull House itself was "watched" by superpatriots from Chicago's American Protective League. The Espionage Act (1917) and the Sedition Acts (1918) provided mechanisms for punishing dissent. Jane Addams escaped personal abuse largely because she discontinued her public pacifist activities. Instead, she tried to humanize the war as much as possible. She argued for the right of conscientious objection and opposed the draft. Under its head, Herbert Hoover, she served the U.S. Food Administration in an effort to promote food conservation and distribution to the needy. Occasionally, to be sure, she raised eyebrows by holding that hungry Germans should be fed as well as the citizens of the Allied nations. For Jane Addams, partisanship was inappropriate in the face of human suffering.

The armistice Jane Addams had so anxiously awaited came on November 11, 1918. Americans had played a major role in bringing it about. Their initial contribution was in the form of morale, for when the United States joined the war in April 1917, the Allied will to resist was at low ebb. The U-boat blockade of food and supplies had proved so successful that the English doubted they could hold out for more than a few months. Russia had lost a million men in 1916 alone and was preoccupied with a revolution at home. On the western front, France seemed about to collapse before the German onslaught. In this context, America's decision to intervene began to have an effect even before troops could be mobilized. The U.S. Navy immediately challenged the submarine menace with convoys and mines. Within six months losses to the U-boats had decreased sharply. On the home front, American industry and agriculture launched a massive effort to feed and equip the Allies, and in Europe American troops confronted the German armies. Some two million "doughboys," many recruited under the Selective Service Act of 1917, manned the trenches across the path of the German advance into France. At Château-Thierry, only fifty miles from Paris, and at the Argonne, the American Expeditionary Force under General John J. Pershing provided vital assistance in turning back the invasion. Then the Americans joined the counteroffensive that ended the war.

After the armistice Jane Addams resumed her fight for world peace. Her first duty was to call another meeting of the Women's International League for Peace and Freedom, the first since 1915. The site selected was Zurich, Switzerland—a neutral vantage point from which delegates from all concerned nations could follow the course of the official peace negotiations in Paris. At both meetings, discussion revolved around the Fourteen Points that Woodrow Wilson had set forth early in 1918 as a basis for a just and lasting peace. Eight of the points called for adjustments of European boundaries according to the principle of national self-determination. Five concerned guidelines for the conduct of nations, including the abolition of secret treaties and the freedom of the seas. The final point urged "a general association of nations . . . for the purpose of affording mutual guarantees of political independence and territorial integrity to great and small states alike." The Allied governments thought Wilson's formula too idealistic and too lenient with respect to Germany. In the course of the negotiations they gradually eroded the Wilsonian principles. When the final draft of the Treaty of Versailles was signed on June 28, 1919, Jane Addams joined Wilson in condemning it as punitive and calculated to increase, rather than lessen, the possibility of future war. Only the acceptance of the League of Nations idea, Wilson's fourteenth point, brightened the gloom.

Back in the United States, however, a quite different opinion of Wilson and the league was developing. Reacting against his crusading zeal, large segments of the people turned away from their president. His handling of the Paris negotiations created the impression that he was forcing his personal conception of world organization on the country. While such self-righteous leadership had its merits in beginning a war, it offended those seeking a return to normal conditions. In the congressional elections of 1918, voters returned Republican majorities to both houses of Congress.

After a sorrowful tour of the war-torn nations of Europe, Jane Addams returned to the United States to campaign for acceptance of the League of Nations. The Senate, which had to approve the Treaty of Versailles and the league, was sharply divided. Wilsonian Democrats favored ratification, but their number fell far short of the two-thirds needed for approval. Twelve to fifteen senators, the Irreconcilables, opposed the treaty absolutely. They especially objected to the league on the ground that its provisions for collective security would involve the United States in an endless series of overseas wars. According to this viewpoint, the United States had erred in entering World War I and should henceforth isolate itself from Europe's problems. The remainder of the Senate was willing to accept a revised treaty—in particular, one that accorded more respect to national sovereignty.

Had Wilson been less of a moral idealist, he might have accepted some revisions and thereby gained enough votes for ratification. But despite the pleas of his friends, Wilson chose not to compromise his principles. He was especially determined to resist the influence of Henry Cabot Lodge of Massachusetts, the prominent Republican chairman of the Senate Foreign Relations Committee and a bitter personal enemy. In September 1919, Wilson began an 8,000-mile speaking tour to take his cause to the people. In the midst of it he collapsed, the victim of a paralyz-

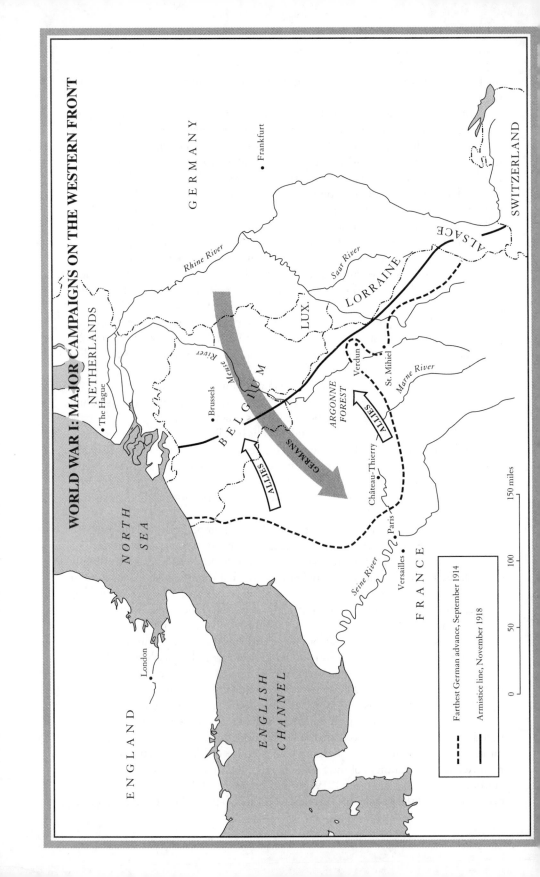

WORLD WAR I: MAJOR CAMPAIGNS ON THE WESTERN FRONT

ENGLAND

London

NORTH
SEA

ENGLISH
CHANNEL

NETHERLANDS

The Hague

GERMANY

Frankfurt

Rhine River

Saar River

Meuse River

Brussels

BELGIUM

LUX.

LORRAINE

ALSACE

SWITZERLAND

GERMANS

ALLIES

Verdun

St. Mihiel

Marne River

ARGONNE
FOREST

ALLIES

Château-Thierry

Paris

Versailles

Seine River

FRANCE

- - - - Farthest German advance, September 1914

———— Armistice line, November 1918

0   50   100   150 miles

ing stroke. But still he refused to compromise. When the election of 1920 resulted in the overwhelming defeat of the Democrats by Republican nominee and "normalcy" advocate Warren G. Harding, Wilson's last hopes died. The United States never joined the League of Nations and eventually made peace with Germany in a separate treaty.

Disillusioned as she was by these events, Jane Addams continued to make peace her overriding concern in the 1920s. Her most important contributions were writings analyzing why her compatriots were unable to enter into the cooperative internationalism on which world peace depended. The villain, she decided, was a virulent self-righteousness that deluded Americans into thinking they could best serve the world by looking after their own interests. The rejection of the League of Nations was clear evidence of this attitude. So, according to Addams, was American indifference to the spirit of the Washington Treaties of 1921–1922, which were an attempt to limit naval armaments and stabilize the situation in the Pacific. A similar insincerity marked American participation in the Kellogg-Briand Pact of 1928 outlawing war. Yet another instance of self-righteousness that troubled Jane Addams was the Red Scare of 1919, during which the government hounded thousands of alleged Communists. Jane Addams herself suffered verbal abuse from the American Legion, the Daughters of the American Revolution, and other strongly patriotic organizations because of her compassion for the peoples of Germany and Russia.

In Addams's estimation, the same ugly nationalism appeared in even grosser form in the trial of Nicola Sacco and Bartolomeo Vanzetti. These two Italian-Americans and admitted radicals were convicted, on inconclusive evidence, of a 1920 robbery and murder near Boston. Jane Addams was among the many liberal intellectuals who believed the men guilty only of being different. When Sacco and Vanzetti were electrocuted in 1927, she felt a part of American liberalism had died with them.

Another development that disturbed Jane Addams in the 1920s was the growing opposition to immigration. She had long felt that immigrants constituted a vital and valuable component of American society. Indeed, with the exception of the Indians, every American had immigrant ancestry. The immigrant "problem" in her estimation, stemmed less from the immigrants themselves than from the injustices of American social and economic life. Given a chance, the foreign-born could become excellent Americans. Hull House existed to further this process. But many of her contemporaries disagreed. In their eyes, immigrants, particularly the non-Aryans from southern and eastern Europe, were the cause of the nation's urban problems rather than their unfortunate victims.

The proponents of 100 percent Americanism gradually developed a case against immigration. One milestone was the forty-two-volume report of the U.S. Immigration Commission issued in 1910. It provided an elaborate, if heavily biased, correlation of immigration and vice, crime, poverty, and slums. Popular writing echoed these "conclusions." Madison Grant's The Passing of the Great Race (1916) argued that the "melting-pot" concept was a huge mistake. America could not continue to absorb undesirable racial elements and still maintain the "native" American type, characteristics, and institutions. "Maudlin sentimentalism" about the world's oppressed, Grant insisted, must be replaced with realism; the open door must be slammed shut. The *Saturday Evening Post* put it somewhat more bluntly: Unless action was taken, one of its authors warned, Americans would become "a hybrid race of people as worthless and futile as the good-for-nothing mongrels of Central America and Southeastern Europe." Labor unions took up the cry for exclusion on the grounds that an abundance of immigrants depressed wages. Employers, of course, welcomed immigrants for the same reason, but by the 1920s mechanization had decreased the demand for unskilled labor.

The urgency of the immigration question increased suddenly after World War I as millions sought a sanctuary in the New World. More than 800,000 foreigners arrived in 1921 alone. Frightened, Congress passed an emergency measure establishing frankly discriminatory quotas. English-speaking immigrants and Aryans from northern and central Europe were given preference, and the total number of newcomers permitted to enter the country each year was sharply reduced. The National Origin (Immigration) Act of 1924 lowered quotas even further. To Jane Addams's way of thinking the country had come to the sad and callous end of a three-century dream. The United States was no longer synonymous with opportunity and hope.

A heart attack in 1926 slowed Jane Addams down considerably, but she still maintained a keen interest in the American social scene and continued to write what ultimately amounted to over 500 books and papers. Reform also retained its interest for Jane Addams in the 1920s and early 1930s. Critical of the unimaginative conservatism of Republican Presidents Warren G. Harding and Calvin Coolidge, she voted in a losing cause for Eugene V. Debs, the Socialist, in the election of 1920, and for Robert La Follette, nominee of the revived Progressive party, in 1924. Of the latter and his accomplishments as governor and senator she wrote, "The political air of Wisconsin filled my lungs like a breath from the mountain tops of the finest American tradition." Also encouraging was the organization in 1920 of the American Civil Liberties Union, which took its stand on the people's capacity for self-government. But on the whole she felt that the American people in the 1920s were afraid of reform. They had seen the Russian Revolution wipe out private property rights, and any governmental curbing of the individual freedoms of the privileged was suspect. From Jane Addams's perspective the period 1919–1929 was "inhibited" compared with the ten years preceding World War I.

Although Jane Addams voted for Herbert Hoover, a long-time personal friend, in the election of 1928 and again in that of 1932, she took considerable interest in the rising political star of Franklin D. Roosevelt. His concern for the masses, as opposed to the rich, powerful, and established, was in line with her own. And his willingness to use the power of the federal government to achieve social justice delighted her after the timidity of the 1920s. Although she died some months before it was enacted, the Social Security Act of August 8, 1935, was the kind of law she had long advocated. But in the last analysis she approved of Roosevelt because, even in the trying times created by the Great Depression, he avoided the extremes of communism on the one hand and totalitarianism on the other. Jane Addams agreed with such reforms to preserve the American system; for a half century she had worked to do the same.

SELECTED READINGS

The Person

*Addams, Jane: *Twenty Years at Hull House* (1910). Along with her *The Second Twenty Years at Hull House* (1930), the best source of Jane Addams's thought and of information about her life.

*Bryan, Mary Lynn McCree: *The Jane Addams Papers: A Comprehensive Guide* (1996). Gives subject and correspondent access to the 82-reel microfilm edition of the Addams papers.

Davis, Allen: *American Heroine: The Life and Legend of Jane Addams* (1973). The definitive biography.

Farrell, John C.: *Beloved Lady: A History of Jane Addams's Ideas on Reform and Peace* (1967). A summary of Addams's involvement in two of her major interests.

*Lasch, Christopher (ed.): *The Social Thought of Jane Addams* (1965). A useful selection of key articles by Jane Addams.

Levine, Daniel: *Jane Addams and the Liberal Tradition* (1971). The interrelation of a life and a political philosophy.

Linn, James Weber: *Jane Addams: A Biography* (1935). The first full-scale study.

The Period

*Bremer, Robert: *From the Depths: The Discovery of Poverty in the United States* (1964). The beginnings of the social welfare crusade.

Cott, Nancy: *The Grounding of Modern Feminism* (1988). Offers current scholarly thinking on the "New Women" of Jane Addams's era.

*Flexner, Eleanor: *Century of Struggle: The Women's Rights Movement in the United States* (1975). A reliable general survey.

*Graham, Otis L., Jr.: *The Great Campaigns: Reform and War in America, 1900–1928* (1971). National politics.

*Hofstadter, Richard: *The Age of Reform from Bryan to F.D.R.* (1960). A pioneering interpretation of the liberal impulse from Populism to the New Deal.

*Lasch, Christopher: *The New Radicalism in America, 1889–1963* (1965). An analysis of the intellectuals, including Jane Addams, who questioned values and institutions in the twentieth century.

*Link, Arthur: *Woodrow Wilson and the Progressive Era: 1910–1917* (1954). The best general survey by the author of a multivolume Wilson biography.

Matthews, Glenna: *Just a Housewife: The Rise and Fall of Domesticity in America* (1987). A compelling study of the changing roles of housewives as shapers of modern American society.

*Mowry, George: *The Era of Theodore Roosevelt and the Birth of Modern America* (1958). A broad look at the Progressive years.

*Stebner, Eleanor J.: *The Women of Hull House: A Study in Spirituality, Vocation, and Friendship* (1997). A group biography of women of all classes who worked in the Chicago settlement house.

---

*Available in paperback.

*White, Morton: *Social Thought in America: The Revolt against Formalism* (1957). Intellectual cross-currents of the late nineteenth and early twentieth centuries.

FOR CONSIDERATION

1. What were the career options for women of Jane Addams's social class during the latter 1800s?

2. Addams attended Rockford Female Seminary during the late 1870s. What lessons of Christianity did she take to heart that would later shape her future career?

3. Why did Jane Addams choose Chicago and Hull House to establish her settlement house?

4. Discuss the concept of "national housekeeping" with regard to the women's suffrage movement. How did the suffrage movement become part of the Progressive movement? What was the ultimate result?

5. Discuss Jane Addams's pacifism before, during, and after World War I.

---

*Available in paperback.

THREE

Gifford Pinchot

*I*n the fading light of a February afternoon in 1907 a solitary horseman moved slowly along a trail in Rock Creek Park in Washington, DC. Gifford Pinchot was mulling over an idea. As head of the young U.S. Forest Service, Pinchot had charge of administering the national forests. It was a big job, but he saw still larger horizons. Trees, after all, were only one natural resource. On that same day Pinchot had dealt with questions of stream flow, navigation, irrigation, flood control, waterpower, soil erosion, minerals, grassland, and wildlife. Yet these matters were pigeonholed in separate government bureaus, and that, Pinchot mused, was part of the problem. "Suddenly," in his words, "the idea flashed through my head that there was a unity in this complication." The "island" approach to environmental management was not compatible with the indivisibility of the environment.

For Pinchot, the revelation in Rock Creek Park "was a good deal like coming out of a dark tunnel." Now he saw the landscape as a whole and the need for an equally comprehensive, long-range administrative policy. A few days after the ride, in consultation with his associates in the Forest Service and with his close friend President Theodore Roosevelt, he coined the term *conservation*. During the next four decades he saw it become a household word as increasing numbers of Americans came to share his concern over environmental deterioration.

The young Gifford Pinchot had not seemed destined to be a reformer. His family had a firm position in the uppermost social and economic echelon of nineteenth-century America, a group for whom conservatism was a way of life. Grandfather Cyril Pinchot had fought with Napoleon. In 1816, after the restoration of the French monarchy, Cyril fled to the United States. Settling in Milford, Pennsylvania, near the Delaware River, he quickly established a prosperous dry goods and transportation business. His son and Gifford's father, James Pinchot, inherited the knack for success. After a decade of business in New York City, money was no longer a problem. The rich got richer in 1864, when James married Mary Jane Eno, the daughter of real estate mogul Amos Eno.

Gifford Pinchot was born August 11, 1865, at the elegant Connecticut estate of his maternal grandfather. His early life was typical of a small number of very rich Americans. There were tutors and governesses who shined and polished their little charges for parental audiences. Private preparatory schools and colleges—Phillips Exeter Academy and Yale in Pinchot's case—intensified the polishing. Summers were passed pleasantly at the shore or in the mountains. The former meant Newport, Rhode Island, a village on Narragansett Bay that the Pinchots, along with Ward McAllister and New York's socially prominent "Four Hundred," discovered after the Civil War. The inland alternative took the Pinchots to Upstate New York's Adirondack Mountains. There, in a comfortable sportsmen's lodge setting, Gifford acquired a love of hunting and especially of fishing that he never lost. For shorter vacations the Pinchots repaired to their manor house at Milford, Pennsylvania. Grey Towers, as it was called, had been designed by Richard Morris Hunt, architect to the affluent in the late nineteenth century. It was taken for granted that such houses would be in the European mold; America's gentry of this era still sought to reproduce the aura surrounding Europe's nobility. A half century elapsed before Frank Lloyd Wright and other architects of a native American style received recognition. With Wright's buildings, so sharply in contrast to the homes of the Pinchots, the nation finally dared to be itself.

Of course, the Pinchot family was well connected. In later years Gifford could state as a simple fact that he had known every president from Ulysses S. Grant to Harry S Truman. When such connections smoothed his way into Yale in 1885, it appeared he was well launched on a life of genteel ease. But the young man had a different orientation. Pinchot chafed at the uselessness of his situation. In a note written to a friend in 1914 during his campaign for the U.S. Senate, Pinchot said: "My own money came from the unearned increment on land in New York held by my grandfather. . . . Having got my wages in advance in that way, I am now trying to work them out." Comfort, in short, was no challenge to a person who had inherited $3 million in his twenties. In company with other overprivileged children (one thinks especially of Theodore Roosevelt), Pinchot felt compelled to strive, to excel, to lead. Public service of a reforming nature offered an outlet for these drives. Find a cause and become its champion—here was the formula for the genuine achievement that people like Roosevelt and Pinchot craved.

For social reformers, the human refuse of growth provided the opportunity to serve. Gifford Pinchot chose another victim of capitalistic exploitation: the American forest. James Pinchot had started his son's career when he suggested in 1885, on the eve of Gifford's departure for his freshman year at Yale, that forestry might be an exciting vocation. Certainly it would be new; the profession simply did not exist in the United States at that time. Gifford Pinchot recalled that, when his father made the suggestion, he had had "no more conception of what it meant to be a forester than the man in the moon." The only image the word conjured up was that of a man who "wore green cap and leather jerkin and shot cloth-yard arrows at the King's deer." But Gifford "loved the woods" and, with breadwinning beside the point, he was willing to experiment with his life.

In the 1880s neither Yale nor any other American college or university offered instruction in forestry. Pinchot therefore chose courses in biology, geology, meteorology, and astronomy. He also found time for participation in the activity of the clubs, teams, literary societies, and class "rushes" that were so much a part of collegiate life in that era. Tall, lean, and ruggedly handsome, Pinchot made friends easily and took keen pleasure in his college years. As commencement approached, a classmate asked him the inevitable question: "What are you going to do after graduation?" Be a forester, Pinchot replied. "What's that?" responded the friend. "That's why I am going to be a forester," Pinchot rejoined. Being one, however, demanded special training available only in Europe. In the Old World, where supplies of wood were limited, forests had long been regarded as crops and carefully managed so as to ensure a sustained yield of lumber. This, in fact, was the definition of forestry that Pinchot should have provided his inquiring classmate.

Gifford's first stops on his postgraduate tour were England and Germany, where he talked with the men responsible for introducing forestry to British India. From these interviews the trail led to France and the French Forest School at Nancy. Bilingual as a result of years of tutoring, Pinchot learned easily and eagerly. He was especially impressed by the seriousness of European forest management. The foresters in charge were powerful government officers, and the penalties for burning or illegally cutting trees were severe. Every scrap of wood, down to pencil-sized sticks, was carefully collected and used. The annual revenue of the forests of France and Germany astonished the young American, and he was amazed to learn that their level of productivity had remained constant since the time of Columbus. Here was sustained yield for sure!

In 1890, Pinchot returned to the United States. After making an extended tour of the West, he set up a forestry consultant service in New York City. One of his first clients was railroad magnate George Vanderbilt, who, under the direction of architect Frederick Law Olmsted, was building a palatial home near Asheville, North Carolina. The estate, called Biltmore, was to have a model farm, an arboretum, a game preserve, and a working forest. The sustained yield and sustained profits Pinchot extracted from Biltmore's hardwood stands persuaded the Vanderbilts to purchase 100,000 adjoining acres. Pinchot took charge and made western North Carolina the birthplace of forestry in the United States. Meanwhile, his forestry consulting service enjoyed a succession of private and state clients.

Despite these successes, Pinchot wanted more. He next set his sights on changing the nation's attitude toward the wasteful consumption of its forests. "So far as . . . natural resources were concerned," he observed, "we were still a nation of pioneers." With very few exceptions, Americans subscribed to the myth of inexhaustibility. The environment, they assumed, was a cornucopia from which could be wrung a never-ending bounty of raw materials. Attitudes had not changed appreciably since the seventeenth century. Progress was synonymous with exploitation; profit was good; and the environment's sole function was to line American pockets. Armed with such ideas and unrestrained by government regulation, Americans were plundering their land. In lumbering, a strip-and-run philosophy prevailed. Rather than harvesting timber on sustained-yield principles, as a crop, loggers clear-cut the forests, moving westward like a swarm of locusts. A scarcity of trees? Absurd! Over the next ridge there were more and more trees. Indeed, the problem was too many, not too few. The long-term interests of society made little difference to a people who measured their history in decades rather than millennia. What, the typical American demanded, did posterity ever do for me?

Bolstering the economic rationale for exploiting the environment was the assumption that undeveloped land was not only useless but evil. The first settlers carried from Europe, and particularly from the Christian tradition, the idea that a wilderness was a cursed place, the abode of Satan and lesser devils like the heathen Indians. The wilderness was feared and, whenever possible, avoided until its redemption by the twin forces of civilization and Christianity. It followed that the conquest of the land was the pioneer's special pride. Symbolic of that victory was the clearing of the land and the destruction of trees. The result, both literally and figuratively, was the substitution of light for darkness.

The pioneer situation was simply not conducive to conservation. Here, trees were enemies. When the land was covered with trees and settlements were specks in a vast wilderness, forest management was not even a consideration. The difficulty was that pioneer priorities remained long after true pioneer circumstances had vanished. This frontier hangover worked against every conservation effort.

Pinchot's postgraduate year in Europe made him keenly aware of the price Americans were paying for the lack of government regulation of the use of the environment. Government, indeed, seemed to be in league with the exploiters. For over a century the state and federal land agencies had diligently pursued a policy of selling the land to private owners at prices that could best be labeled handouts. North Carolina had sold some of the finest hardwood forest in the world at ten cents an acre. The federal government had bettered even this price by giving millions of acres free to mining and railroad interests. The Northern Pacific Railroad alone had received more land than the total area of Pennsylvania, New Jersey, and Rhode Island combined to build its transcontinental line. Under the Timber and Stone Act of 1878 a citizen could obtain up to 160 acres of forest land supposedly "unfit for cultivation" at a price of $2.50 per acre. In theory the act had been intended to help individual settlers, but in practice it had invited corruption. Lumber companies quickly lined up "dummies" whose "claims" soon became part of their sprawling empires. But such circumvention was not really necessary. Many companies operated on cut-out-and-get-out principles wherever they pleased—"stealing timber," as Pinchot put it, from the nation. Enforcement of the existing forest laws was out of the question in the vastness of the West. Moreover, the whole issue of federal land administration was, in Pinchot's words, "dripping with politics." According to Pinchot, the most unfortunate part of the disposal of the public domain was that, once the land left government ownership, so did all power to regulate its use. The sacred cows of individualism, free enterprise, and Anglo-American law combined to ensure that people could do as they pleased with the land they possessed. Ownership, for all intents and purposes, was absolute.

The forest fire question typified the American attitude toward resources in the late nineteenth century. Nobody cared. In 1891 alone, Pinchot estimated, at least twelve million acres of forest burned in the United States. The fact elicited only yawns. In Europe, by way of contrast, Pinchot found that a single fire of less than 6,000 acres was still lamented *ninety years* after it occurred. He concluded that the nation to which he had returned to practice forestry was "obsessed . . . by a fury of development. The American Colossus was fiercely intent on appropriating and exploiting the riches of the richest of all continents—grasping with both hands, reaping where he had not sown, wasting what he thought would last forever."

Gifford Pinchot obviously bucked the mainstream of environmental thinking in the 1890s, but he could find some reasons for optimism in the nation's past. As early as 1626 cracks had appeared in the illusion of inexhaustibility. After only six years of occupying the region, the colonists around the Plymouth settlement in Massachusetts found that convenient supplies of timber were disappearing. They

The opening of the last Indian territories in the West occasioned wild scrambles for land claims and signified the ending of the frontier. Here homestead claimants rush into Oklahoma's "Cherokee Strip" on September 16, 1893.

therefore passed a law regulating the cutting and sale of timber, the first conservation measure in American history. Thirteen years later Rhode Islanders looked at their shrinking meat supply and instituted a protective policy for deer for six months of the year. The first large-scale instance of enlightened environmental planning occurred in Pennsylvania in 1681. William Penn, the proprietor, decreed that "in clearing the ground, care be taken to leave an acre of trees for every five acres cleared." Penn even appointed a "woodsman" to supervise the cutting and took steps to eliminate forest fires. Over the next century and a half there were a number of similar responses to regional shortages of natural resources.

A new note sounded in the 1840s, however, with the emergence of the American sportsman. He was a gentleman hunter or fisherman who believed that game and fish had value other than as food. With his finely tooled shotgun and light bamboo fly rod, he elevated hunting and fishing to the level of sport. The sportsmen also launched a protest against the market hunters' wholesale slaughter, which threatened the end of the game supply. In 1850, the New York Game Protective Association became the nation's first private conservation organization. In the West the pioneer perspective held sway; it was the older states, where the first pinches of scarcity occurred, that were the first to respond. A social factor also figured in the emergence of a conservation mentality. Upper-class easterners, particularly those who lived in cities, did not have to wrest a living from the land. From the perspective of paved streets and townhouse libraries, nature took on quite a different meaning. Less a threat, the natural world could be appreciated and even protected. Pinchot illustrates the point: Had he been the son of a Minnesota lumberman instead of a Manhattan millionaire, it is doubtful that he would have become a champion of conservation.

As Pinchot reviewed the progress of environmental protection in his own lifetime, the work of several foresighted men gave him reason for encouragement. One was George Perkins Marsh, scientist, diplomat, and world traveler, whose book *Man and Nature* appeared in 1864. Pinchot had read the book as a student at Yale and found it exciting and inspiring. Marsh contended that the condition of the environment was as much a product of humans as of nature. The human power to transform the natural world should entail a commensurate sense of responsibility. That it did not, he warned, was one of the gravest threats to the welfare—and, indeed, to the survival—of civilization. Focusing most of his book on deforestation's disastrous consequences for the water supply, Marsh pointed to ancient empires around the Mediterranean Sea whose decline paralleled that of their woodlands. Specifically, he postulated that the fall of the Roman Empire had occurred in part because of forest depletion around the capital city. Would the United States follow the same suicidal course? In Marsh's opinion there were already strong indications that this would be the case. His book had been written to stem the tide of environmental destruction, and he called for immediate reforms in forest and watershed management. One sentence stuck in young Pinchot's mind: "Man has too long forgotten," Marsh wrote, "that the earth was given to him for usufruct alone, not for consumption, still less for profligate waste."

The second giant in early American conservation history was John Wesley Powell, a scientist-explorer whose loss of one arm in a Civil War battle did not prevent him from leading the first descent of the Colorado River in 1869. Powell subsequently conducted detailed investigations into the geography and hydrology of the Great Basin between the Rocky Mountains and California's Sierra Nevada. In 1878, he presented to Congress a *Report on the Lands of the Arid Region of the United States*, and three years later he assumed direction of the U.S. Geological Survey. Powell challenged traditional American ideas in three important ways. First, he showed the Great Basin to be neither an agrarian paradise nor a "Great American Desert," but a region suited to limited, carefully controlled agriculture. The second element of Powell's challenge was his insistence that the dams and irrigation projects necessary for agriculture in the Far West could not be built by private enterprise. Money and workers on a scale only the federal government could provide would be required for the reclamation of arid lands. Finally, Powell dared to question the beneficence of the widely heralded Homestead Act of 1862 and its 160-acre allotments of virtually free land. Beyond the 100th meridian of longitude, where the annual rainfall seldom exceeded twenty inches, Powell felt that 160 acres was an unworkable unit. It was much too small for grazing stock and much too large for intensive irrigation. The overall import of Powell's report was clear. Instead of allowing preconceived hopes and fears to determine environmental policy, Americans should base policy on a long, realistic look at their landed heritage and their future needs.

Another American who commanded Pinchot's respect was Carl Schurz. As secretary of the interior from 1877 to 1881 under President Rutherford B. Hayes, Schurz had brought the European perspective of his native Germany to the question of resource management in the United States. During his tenure as secretary he had called repeatedly for federal forest management. It was time, he believed, to stop selling the public domain to private exploiters; the land should be leased to responsible developers. In this way tight federal control could be maintained. In view of this stand, Pinchot correctly identified Schurz as the father of the national forests.

Marsh, Powell, and Schurz had led a small group of Americans bold enough to challenge the prevailing conception of the land's purpose and to expose inexhaustibility as a myth. They had also been prepared to question the free enterprise dogma that rejected the prospect of government regulation even in society's interest. In their lifetimes Marsh, Powell, and Schurz had been dismissed as hysterical alarmists and dangerous radicals. It would fall to Pinchot and other second-generation conservationists to implement their ideas in the federal government.

Utilitarianism was the primary defense for early conservation and the one that always made the most sense to Gifford Pinchot. Natural resources were useful, so they should be conserved. Economics explained everything. Forests, Pinchot had learned in Europe, must *pay*. But aesthetic considerations also had a place in the growing conservation movement. Those concerned with the preservation of beauty agreed with Ralph Waldo Emerson that nature could serve many purposes. A tree might be lumber; it might also be the inspiration for poetry and religion. The roots of the aesthetic appreciation of the American environment extended a century before Pinchot's birth to romantics like the Virginia country gentleman William Byrd, the botanist William Bartram, and the ornithologist John James Audubon. In the first half of the nineteenth century, painters like Thomas Cole, writers like James Fenimore Cooper, and poets like William Cullen Bryant had led the way. But the preeminent champion of the beauty and spirituality of unspoiled nature was Henry David Thoreau. Beginning in the late 1830s, Thoreau used the ideas of his fellow Transcendentalist Emerson to build a philosophy of the value of the wild. At its heart was the idea that nature reflected moral laws and spiritual truths. "In Wildness," he declared, "is the preservation of the World." Both physical and intellectual vigor depended on occasional contact with nature. Thoreau deplored the commercialism of the Age of Jackson. In 1845, he moved to an isolated cabin at Walden Pond to seek ways to simplify his existence and commune with nature.

For aesthetic conservationists like Thoreau, the preservation of unspoiled nature against the encroachments of American enterprise was imperative. The institutional embodiments of such thinking were national and state parks and forest preserves. The calls for wilderness protection that had begun with George Catlin in 1832 were climaxed exactly forty years later with the establishment of Yellowstone National Park. This designation of over two million acres in northwestern Wyoming as a "public park or pleasuring ground for the benefit and enjoyment of the people" marked the first instance in history of large-scale wilderness preservation in the public interest. The second milestone had been the establishment in 1885 of a state Forest Preserve in New York's Adirondack Mountains, and in 1890 naturalist John Muir had successfully persuaded Congress to designate 1,500 square miles of California's Sierra Nevada as Yosemite National Park.

Gifford Pinchot was skeptical about aesthetic conservation and national parks. He welcomed men like Muir as allies in the crusade against environmental exploitation, but as a professional forester accustomed to thinking of trees as a crop, he could not accept simple preservation. The science of forestry demanded the periodic cutting of selected mature trees. This was not the intent of those who established the early national parks. As a consequence, Pinchot and Muir were uneasy colleagues in the 1890s, uncertain of each other's ultimate intentions.

The Forest Reserve Act of 1891 increased the confusion. This law, which slipped through Congress almost unnoticed, gave the president power to withdraw from private sale and proclaim as a public reservation any forest land owned by the federal government. Within a month after its passage, President Benjamin Harrison designated thirteen million acres in various parts of the West as forest reserves. At the time, no one in the federal government had a clear idea of what to do with the land in question. John Muir, who founded the Sierra Club in 1892 as a defender of wilderness, hoped the reserves would be managed as national parks. Pinchot, on the other hand, assumed that the new reserves marked the beginning of federal involvement in sustained-yield forestry.

What to do with the forest reserves had never been resolved in the 1891 act, which simply allowed the president to withdraw certain forested lands from the public domain. Preservationists and utilitarians had found enough common ground to get the legislation passed, but whether the land would be used or preserved as wilderness remained an issue of debate. In 1896 Congress appointed a National Forestry Commission to make recommendations. Gifford Pinchot served on the commission, which spent the summer in the West. For part of the summer John Muir served as a guide for the commission. On one occasion in Arizona Territory, Muir and Pinchot were separated from the rest of the group and spent the night camped on the rim of the Grand Canyon. Pinchot was enchanted by Muir's storytelling but was a bit bemused when they came upon a tarantula. Pinchot wanted to kill it, but Muir prevented him, saying "it had as much right there as we did."

Despite his respect and admiration for Muir, Gifford Pinchot had no ambivalence in his utilitarian viewpoint. His tour of the West convinced him that local people resented the current law, which prevented them from even setting foot in the forest reserves. President Cleveland had hoped the commission would recommend a use plan so he could add more reserves, but its report was mired in controversy. Pinchot and the commission chairman, Harvard botanist Charles Sargent, disagreed so strongly that Sargent quit recognizing the impudent young forester in meetings. Sargent, of course, wanted current and future reserves to be free of all commercial use, and to serve as giant botanical laboratories. Pinchot and his single ally on the commission disagreed. As a result, Cleveland waited in vain.

The controversy came to a head when, on February 22, 1897, departing President Grover Cleveland created over twenty-one million acres of forest reserves in

THE DECLINE OF U.S. VIRGIN FORESTS

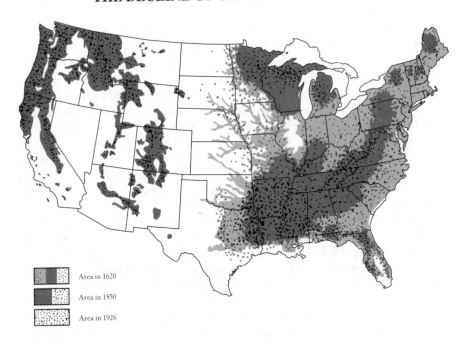

Area in 1620

Area in 1850

Area in 1926

the West without any plan for their use. The seventeen million acres that had already been reserved were in remote locations, but Cleveland's "midnight proclamations" on the eve of his leaving office were adjacent to populated areas of Washington, Montana, and California. Western congressmen and businessmen, by now fully aware of the Forest Reserve Act, howled in protest at Cleveland's "monstrous usurpations." In their opinion, the reserves "locked up" natural resources, and with them growth, jobs, and prosperity. Many called for their outright abolition.

As Congress debated the issue in the wake of the midnight proclamations, Pinchot defied Sargent's order to keep silent. He traveled to Washington armed with his own plan for the forest reserves and began discussing it with legislative friends and foes. Pinchot announced to the press, "The intention of the commission is to prepare and recommend a plan by which the whole value of the reserves may be used for the good of the people." While this falsification of the commission's intent enraged Sargent, Pinchot believed the stakes too high not to intervene. Congress was either going to pass a law that would ban commercial use, permit it, or abolish the reserves altogether; he intended to see that the second possibility came to pass.

On June 4, 1897, the Forest Management Act was passed, leaving no doubt that the reserves would be developed. Pinchot lobbied ambivalent western congressmen, testified, and essentially wrote the drafts of the law. According to the act, the primary purpose of the government forests was "to furnish a continuous supply of timber for the use and necessities of citizens of the United States." It also opened the reserves to mining and grazing. Pinchot's philosophy of environmental management had been vindicated; the forest reserves would remain, but they would be open to commercial use.

Gifford Pinchot's crusade benefited considerably during the 1890s from the impact of the closing of the frontier. In the beginning all America was a frontier, and the presence of virgin land to the west exerted an enormous influence on American life and thought. Indeed, Americans mistakenly assumed that the frontier, like natural resources, was inexhaustible. Westward expansion, however, went on at an accelerating pace. The frontier shifted decade by decade as a growing population carved out settlements in the wilderness. The inevitable end came, marked with terse, bureaucratic finality in the census of 1890: "Up to and including 1880 the country had a frontier of settlement, but at present the unsettled area has been so broken into by isolated bodies of settlement that there can hardly be said to be a frontier line. In the discussion of its extent, its westward movement, etc., it can not, therefore, any longer have a place in the census reports."

The shock prompted disbelief, but Americans were gradually forced to admit that the frontier had actually vanished. Pioneering was history. The historian Frederick Jackson Turner led the way in assessing the meaning of the vanished frontier. In 1893, three years after the census report, he published an essay entitled "The Significance of the Frontier in American History." Turner's ideas cut the channels in which a great deal of American thought on this subject subsequently flowed. The crux of his argument was the belief that the frontier had played the dominant role in shaping American character and institutions. Democracy, he contended, was a forest product. Individualism, self-reliance, respect for common people, and an urge to perfect society had emerged from the opportunities inherent in wilderness conditions. The New World, according to Turner, had been a clean slate on which idealists had drawn their dreams for a better life. By virtue of being exposed to the transforming influence of the frontier, Americans were better than Europeans. Although Turner occasionally recognized that frontier democracy had some liabilities, his attempts at scholarly impartiality only thinly masked a conviction of the superiority of democracy.

Even if we grant the oversimplifications in Turner's thesis, there was enough truth in his environmental explanation of American development to cause his contemporaries to think of the frontier as a valuable part of the national heritage. Concern over the disappearance of frontier conditions followed. Turner himself wondered whether American ideals "have acquired sufficient momentum to sustain themselves under conditions so radically unlike those in the days of their origin." The implication was that, with the passing of the frontier, the United States might have seen the passing of its greatest age. The course of the nation might now be a downhill slide.

By the turn of the century, many Americans had joined Turner in his uneasiness about the ending of the frontier. One did not have to read his essay to perceive that for two and half centuries the frontier had largely explained the remarkable material growth of the United States as well as many characteristics of its citizenry. One result of this frame of mind, and the one that helped Gifford Pinchot, was a tendency to be receptive to the conservation idea. It seemed logical that conservation would preserve the remainder of America's abundance, deny the chilling implications of the census pronouncement, and assuage anxiety over the nation's advancing age. Conservation, to be sure, was not the only beneficiary of turn-of-the-century anxieties. Imperialism, which in some eyes represented a search for new frontiers, also reflected the prevailing mood. But conservation had special appeal because it attacked the problem, which was basically environmental, directly. Conservation would be, in a sense, the new frontier, keeping the nation young, vigorous, prosperous, democratic, and wholesome. For a civilization that had begun to notice its first gray hairs, conservation was a welcome psychological as well as environmental tonic.

Gifford Pinchot used the changing attitudes to advance his cause. With the passage of the 1897 act, the secretary of the interior asked Pinchot to be a special agent for the General Land Office in managing the forest reserves. Pinchot declined for several reasons. First, he did not believe the management of the reserves should be in the land office because it had no trained foresters. Moreover, the land office had historically been in charge of selling off the public lands, not managing them. Finally, Pinchot believed the land office was corrupt and full of "worthless political rejects," and he wanted no part of it. Instead he began lobbying for the establishment of a federal forestry service outside the Department of the Interior.

In 1898, Pinchot was presented with a new opportunity. Bernhard E. Fernow resigned as head of the federal Division of Forestry, a small fact-finding office in the Department of Agriculture. Quickly, President William McKinley's secretary of agriculture offered Pinchot the job; just as quickly Pinchot accepted. At the time the division was little more than an information agency, a forestry organization without forests. But Pinchot was delighted to join the federal team. His vision was fixed not on what federal forestry was, but on what it might become. In particular, his hopes centered on the forest reserves and the possibility of consolidating their management under the direction of his office.

At this point in his career Gifford Pinchot and conservation became the beneficiaries of two significant national developments: the advent of progressivism and the succession to the presidency of Theodore Roosevelt. Historians have called 1890 to 1920 the Progressive Era because of widespread efforts to reverse the corruption, inequity, and inefficiency of Mark Twain's Gilded Age. Progressives, of course, believed in progress and the continuing existence of American greatness. Those who called themselves Progressives included wealthy elites like Pinchot, middle-class professionals, and reform-minded zealots. While their causes were diverse, their commonality lay in the view that society could be improved, even perfected, by human intervention. Their reform causes covered the spectrum of American life, ranging from temperance, to election reform, women's suffrage, workers' rights, the regulation of big business, and, of course, conservation.

One of the first major expressions of progressivism came during the 1890s with the Wisconsin Idea of gubernatorial candidate Robert M. La Follette. Using the name of Abraham Lincoln as a model, La Follette urged a return to democracy. Vowing an attack on the machine politics of Wisconsin, La Follette was elected governor in 1900. Under his watch the people of Wisconsin approved election reforms, railroad regulations, and forest management, making the state "a laboratory of democracy."

Progressivism came to the federal level in the person of Theodore Roosevelt, who succeeded to the nation's highest office on September 14, 1901. President William McKinley had died from an assassin's bullet fired a week earlier. Quite in character, the vice president had been on a mountain-climbing expedition when news of the shooting reached him. At forty-two he was the youngest chief executive in American history to that date. In background and character he closely resembled Pinchot. Roosevelt's family was equally wealthy and of the patrician class. His youth had been spent in private schools, on European tours, and in an Ivy League college: Harvard. After graduating in 1880, Roosevelt had faced the choice of a career with mixed emotions. His strong sense of personal morality and social consciousness, along with his distaste for the crass materialism of the newly rich, ruled out business. For a time he considered teaching and writing, and he actually published several creditable volumes of history, but a literary life left his passion for physical challenge and leadership unsatisfied. Being a gentleman-sportsman appealed to his obsession with virility and his love of outdoor adventure but did little for his sense of duty. So Roosevelt decided to become a politician and lead the nation to greatness.

With this decision behind him, he rose rapidly. He served as a New York state assemblyman, the police commissioner of New York City, assistant secretary of the navy, and governor of New York. In 1898, Roosevelt's participation in the Span-ish–American War gave him the national reputation he needed for federal office. Two years later the hero of San Juan Hill was elected vice president under McKin-

Along with Gifford Pinchot, Theodore Roosevelt (left) and John Muir (right) dominated the early American conserva-tion movement. Here they stand on the rim of Yosemite Valley, part of the national park Muir had played a major role in establishing. The year of the photograph is 1903.

ley. New York's political boss, Senator Thomas C. Platt, was delighted to see the unmanageable governor removed to the relatively innocuous pastures of the vice presidency. But many conservative Republican leaders had their doubts about the impetuous Roosevelt. Republican strategist Mark Hanna dourly warned, "There's only one life between this madman and the White House." But while Roosevelt's rhetoric and general aggressiveness gave a promise of radicalism, he had a self-confessed "horror of extremes." He preferred a compromising middle way that would champion reform and still preserve the best of the old order. He would act—but, as he told Mark Hanna, he would go slow.

The trails of Pinchot and Roosevelt had first crossed in 1894 when Pinchot was a consulting forester in New York. From their correspondence it appears that Pinchot had no difficulty convincing Roosevelt of the need for scientific forest management. In 1897 Roosevelt sponsored Pinchot's election to the Boone and Crockett Club, an elite group of trophy hunters. Two years later, when Roosevelt was governor, the relationship of the two men seems to have taken a more personal turn. Pinchot's autobiography notes that on one visit to the executive mansion, "T.R. and I did a little wrestling, at which he beat me; and some boxing, during which I had the honor of knocking the future President of the United States off his very solid pins." In later years in Washington, DC, the president and his chief forester expanded their activities to include hiking, riding, and a great deal of tennis. Indeed, Pinchot was in the circle of close Roosevelt friends, enjoying the kind of access to the president of which most bureaucrats only dream. Such personal contact goes a long way toward explaining the rise of the conservation movement in the early twentieth century.

When Roosevelt entered the White House to complete McKinley's term, the alleged abuses of big business were a leading national issue. Beginning in the 1890s a number of journalists threw off illusion and restraint in their anger over economic and political injustice. Their purpose was protest and, ultimately, reform; their target was the concentrated power of the nation's largest companies and corporations. Popular magazines provided the primary outlet for these exposés. Ida M. Tarbell continued Henry Demarest Lloyd's criticism of the oil industry in a series of bitter articles in McClure's magazine. Ray Stannard Baker used the same journal to lash out at the railroads. In the widely read pages of Everybody's and Cosmopolitan, Thomas W. Lawson and David Graham Phillips added fuel to the fire under high finance and high politics. Such articles obviously contained exaggeration as well as fact, but they influenced millions of readers. Novels also made a significant contribution. Theodore Dreiser, Frank Norris, and Jack London portrayed economic and social conditions in a way calculated to arouse the wrath of idealistic Americans.

Roosevelt was not sympathetic to such one-sided criticism. In fact, it was he who coined the deprecatory term muckraking to describe those writers who could see only the sordid. But while the muckrakers were clearly on the angry fringe of progressivism, they provided the vital spark that stimulated many of their more moderate compatriots to concern and action.

Criticism of the free enterprise system, with its unrestrained competition and resulting concentration of wealth and power, represented a considerable change for beneficiaries of that system such as Theodore Roosevelt and Gifford Pinchot. As an undergraduate at Yale in the 1880s, Pinchot had swallowed William Graham Sumner's brand of social Darwinism whole. When asked in an assignment to discuss the government regulation of railroad rates, Pinchot had responded as a conservative: "The railroads own the tracks and the cars, don't they? Then why shouldn't they charge what they please?" It was dog-eat-dog, and the victor deserved the spoils. But as he matured Pinchot began to see flaws in this philosophy. He noticed that unrestrained lumber companies left environmental chaos in their wake. And he saw how concentrated wealth could warp the purposes of laws. In time Pinchot became convinced that, despite its blessings, private enterprise sometimes thwarted the long-term public interest. He also came to see that the only organization strong enough to make business socially responsible was the federal government. With this perspective, Pinchot was well on his way to becoming a Progressive.

Theodore Roosevelt felt much the same way about big business. He admitted that "this is an age of combination," and he readily acknowledged the contributions that efficient, large-scale businesses made to American life. But he also understood that large corporations often acted without regard to the common good. The solution, as Roosevelt and Pinchot saw it, was for the federal government to control and regulate the giant trusts and corporations in the name of the people. They had no intention of destroying the basis of the free enterprise system, but they would use the state as a positive force to preserve fair play. This stewardship concept most nearly defined Roosevelt's and Pinchot's variety of progressivism.

Seeking tools to implement his reform philosophy, Roosevelt dusted off the Sherman Antitrust Act, which had been notoriously ineffective since its passage in 1890. His attorney general, Philander C. Knox, announced soon after Roosevelt became president that the federal government was planning a suit under the Sherman Act with the purpose of breaking up the Northern Securities Company, the huge financial conglomerate that had resulted from the merger of the railroads of James J. Hill and Edward H. Harriman. Since the names of Rockefeller and Morgan were also involved, the Northern Securities Company was the preeminent symbol in the public mind of consolidated, unprincipled wealth. Roosevelt's challenge to its legitimacy met with widespread approval. When, in 1903, a federal court order directed the company to dissolve and a year later the Supreme Court upheld the decision, the president became a shining knight to reformers. The cheers continued as the Roosevelt administration undertook the prosecution of forty-four more corporations in such industries as meat, tobacco, and oil.

The Roosevelt administration applied what the president called a "rule of reason" to corporate regulation. A corporation was reasonable if it did not subject consumers to monopolistic pricing; it was unreasonable if it did. A corporation's size did not necessarily render it unreasonable, but corporations that eliminated competition were. Roosevelt believed that monopolistic corporations were inefficient, a condition running counter to his progressive ethos of efficiency. Progressives of Roosevelt's ilk were almost obsessed with what historian Samuel Hays dubbed "the gospel of efficiency." In efficiency lay the keys to continued American greatness. In these people's personal lives, efficiency encompassed punctuality, including quick meals and quick baths. In the economic and social life of the country, efficiency meant businesses operating at their maximum output while competing fairly in the marketplace, and individuals working honestly for just wages and the good of the nation. In government, efficiency meant reform. Government must be modernized to perform its function of regulating the affairs of the expanding nation.

The Roosevelt system based on efficiency managed to satisfy a broad cross section of Americans. Even while developing a national reputation as a "trustbuster," Roosevelt assured capitalists that he was not their enemy. Big business quickly perceived that progressivism was its best protection against more radical proposals such as those of agrarian reformers known as the Populists, the labor organizations, and the Socialists. Roosevelt satisfied the public demand for reform, yet left the American economy essentially unchanged. He reformed in order to preserve, and in many cases he allowed the representatives of business to write and implement their own reform proposals. Only to those who accept the trustbusting myth is it surprising that the Morgans, the Rockefellers, and other captains of industry donated generously to Roosevelt's war chest in the 1904 presidential campaign.

After trouncing the Democrats, the Populists, and the Socialists in the election of 1904, Roosevelt and his colleagues pressed forward with what came to be known as the Square Deal. At the top of the program was the regulation of business in the public interest, and the business the Progressives most desired to regulate was the railroads. Despite previous attempts at reform, such as the Interstate Commerce Act (1887) and the Elkins Act (1903), the railroad companies continued to set rates and grant privileges that many citizens regarded as grossly unfair. Roosevelt's efforts to obtain an effective law were initially thwarted by strong opposition by congressional conservatives. Finally, after months of political haggling, the administration obtained passage of the Hepburn Act (1906).

The new legislation empowered the Interstate Commerce Commission to set and enforce railroad rates in response to shippers' demands. The railroads might protest through the courts, but meanwhile the altered rate schedule would be in effect. The Hepburn Act disappointed the more radical Progressives, particularly those who noticed the railroads' ability to infiltrate the regulating agency, but it greatly expanded the idea of federal control of business. Further control came in the wake of Upton Sinclair's classic muckraking novel, *The Jungle* (1906). Taking aim at the meat-packing industry of Chicago, Sinclair told of the deplorable conditions in which fetid, maggot-infested meat was shoveled from dirty floors and made into sausage. When Roosevelt read the novel, he refused to believe Sinclair. But surprise inspections confirmed these conditions. With the president's urging, Congress passed the Pure Food and Drug Act and the Meat Inspection Act in 1906. Such laws made it clear that not only interstate commerce but any industry directly affecting public health and safety was subject to federal regulatory control.

The Roosevelt administration's goal of creating efficient government agencies fit perfectly into Gifford Pinchot's conservation plans. Indeed, Pinchot had been pressing his cause since Roosevelt's succession to the presidency. The forester's first goal was securing the transfer of the forest reserves from the jurisdiction of the Department of the Interior to that of the Department of Agriculture, where they would be under the supervision of his division. Pinchot had been working toward the transfer since he became chief forester in 1898. By 1901, he had secured an elevated status for his agency, which was renamed the Bureau of Forestry. He had launched investigations which concluded that the Department of the Interior's management of the forest reserves was "a perfect farce." Pinchot knew that the growing assembly of scientifically trained foresters who came to work for him could do better, and he was determined to publicize that fact.

Pinchot's relationship with President Roosevelt was crucial to the advance of federal forestry and conservation. No bureau chief in history enjoyed such influence with a chief executive. Pinchot could literally walk into Roosevelt's office with an idea, to which the president normally gave an enthusiastic "bully." Each summer Pinchot would tour the West, riding on horseback through the vast public domain. On his return to Washington, he showed the president mapped tracts of potential forest reserves. Rarely doubting the judgment of his friend and chief forester, Roosevelt used the presidential proclamation provision of the 1891 act to add almost 150 million acres to the forest reserve system during his administration.

In 1905, Pinchot's wish to manage those reserves came true. After seven years of fieldwork on private land, a successful experiment in forestry on federal land in Minnesota, articles in forestry journals and the Department of Agriculture's *Yearbook*, and constant lobbying, Congress passed the Transfer Act, taking management of the reserves from the Department of the Interior and giving it to the Bureau of Forestry. With his "cup . . . full and brimming over," an eager Pinchot swung into action, securing a new name for his agency, the U.S. Forest Service, and a new name for the forest reserves, National Forests. Pinchot's foresters took to the woods, implementing their sustained-yield management policies learned in university forestry programs that the chief forester had endowed. The Transfer Act had given them the power to arrest those who violated regulations, and they saw to it that no young trees were harvested, that a percentage of trees were left standing, and that brush was gathered and burned carefully to prevent major forest fires. As his dedicated public servants brought their expertise to bear on improving society, Pinchot's Forest Service became a model agency of modern federal government. An unusual *esprit de corps* animated the members of Pinchot's team. Sensing from their chief and from the enthusiastic Theodore Roosevelt that theirs was a mission, not merely a job, they plunged into the task with astonishing zeal.

Pinchot's Forest Service began to flex its muscles just at a time when western muckrakers were uncovering enormous mineral and land frauds. Reporters operating out of San Francisco and Portland told stories of wealthy lumbermen from the Great Lakes states bringing "carloads of dummy entrymen" to file timber and homestead claims on unreserved public lands. The "dummies" then signed their deeds over to the "timber barons" in exchange for whiskey and cash. Meanwhile, mining and railroad syndicates were terrorizing small prospectors throughout the Pacific Northwest by jumping claims through the use of paid-off land officers and law officers—or even at gunpoint. Fraudulent entries into the public domain had yielded some individuals more than 500,000 acres of rich timberland, and total losses to the government ran well into the billions of acres. The 1907 exposé *Looters of the Public Domain*, written by a convicted timber speculator, described in lurid detail the methods of the lumbermen—and the frequent collusion of government officials. Determined to "remedy the evils" of land fraud, Gifford Pinchot sent his men out with strict orders to enforce the laws concerning the national forests.

Pinchot's mission to clean up abuses and bring laissez-faire land-use habits under federal control did not meet with universal approval. Those involved in large-scale land swindles, of course, lamented the federal foresters' arrival. But in the West, where the reality of a frontier died hard, unrestricted use of the public domain was considered a birthright. From the western point of view the chief forester was an obstacle to progress and prosperity, and his Forest Service personnel were an unwanted nuisance. As a rich and aristocratic easterner, it was said, Pinchot had no conception of the need for continued exploitation of undeveloped land. Easterners had no right to tell westerners what to do with the public domain. One western congressman spoke for his constituents when he complained of the "grinding injustice they have so long suffered from the East, who so patronizingly tell us what should and should not be done."

Try as he might to convince his critics that he, too, favored prosperity, but on a long-term basis, Pinchot nevertheless became a political target both in the West and among certain members of Congress who decried the system of "Pinchotism." "This enormous territory of the forest reserves," one detractor declared, "is an empire within a republic, ruled by a despot with as much power as the Czar of Russia. Who made this Pinchot Czar?" Partly in answer to such criticism, Pinchot decided to give conservation maximum publicity after he hit on the idea during that 1907 ride in Rock Creek Park. Writing and speaking constantly in the next few years, the chief forester sought to explain the utilitarian aspects of his brainchild, often to hostile audiences in the West. First of all, he explained, conservation involved the management of the total environment, not just the forests or grasslands or rivers. Second, "conservation is development, the use of the natural resources now existing on this continent for the benefit of the people who live here now." Obviously Pinchot intended this as an answer to those who took conservation to mean permanent preservation, the "lockup" idea so hateful to westerners. "All the national forests are for use," he declared again and again throughout the West, where rumblings of abolition of the forest system were often heard.

The third principle of conservation was the prevention of waste. Along with many Progressives, Pinchot deified scientific experts. Through scientific planning and applied technology, he believed, human beings had the ability to control every aspect of their existence. "Experts" held the keys to the millennium. Finally, Pinchot linked conservation to the mainstream of progressivism with his insistence that "natural resources must be developed and preserved for the benefit of the many, and not merely for the profit of a few." In this light, conservation was an extension of democracy, and Pinchot capitalized fully on the early-twentieth-century enthusiasm for this cause. At every opportunity he stressed the public's interest in and right to the environment and its resources. It was clever politics, for by implication it allied the opponents of conservation with self-seeking trusts, monopolies, and what Pinchot called "concentrated wealth."

The zenith of the progressive conservation drive was 1908. On February 26, the Inland Waterways Commission, which Roosevelt had appointed the previous year, submitted plans for multipurpose river development. Under the guidance of Pinchot and a talented protégé of Powell named William John McGee, the commission pioneered in treating rivers as a single unit from source to mouth. This kind of comprehensive environmental planning became the special province of the U.S. Reclamation Service (later Bureau of Reclamation). Implementing progressivism's faith in science, efficiency, and federal control, the Bureau of Reclamation's planners and engineers had twenty-five major water projects underway by 1908. Located for the most part in the arid West, the projects had as their goal the reclamation by irrigation of over two million acres.

In May 1908, a thousand national leaders, including the state governors, met at the White House at the president's invitation for a conference on conservation. Gifford Pinchot was the moving force behind the unprecedented gathering. He wrote several of the speeches the conferees heard and underwrote a large share of the conference expenses. President Roosevelt himself opened the meetings with a ringing plea for concern about "the weightiest problem now before the Nation." The rest of his speech reflected Pinchot's utilitarianism. Roosevelt called for the elimination of waste by more efficient methods of harvesting natural resources. The specter that haunted him and the other delegates was "running out" of vital raw materials. National prosperity and greatness were the ends to be served. Near the close of his address, Roosevelt lashed out at "unrestricted individualism." Previously, he thundered, "we have admitted the right of the individual to injure the future of the Republic for his own present profit. . . . The time has come for a change." Pinchot thought it had already occurred. In his opinion, the 1908 conference marked "a turning point in human history."

The White House Conservation Conference and the Pinchot-chaired commission that Roosevelt subsequently appointed to inventory the nation's natural resources helped to make conservation part of the American vocabulary. Pinchot had high hopes that the movement would spread throughout North America and then to the world. Along with Roosevelt he planned a series of international conferences. But Congress, the expected source of funds, was not impressed. Congressional leaders, in fact, actively resented the aggressive executive leadership that Roosevelt and Pinchot personified. The legislators were particularly unwilling to be swept off their feet by conservation in view of Roosevelt's announcement that he would not run for reelection in the fall of 1908. Added to these political problems were certain intellectual shortcomings of the conservation idea itself. Pinchot's neat formulas, such as his definition of conservation as "the greatest good to the greatest number for the longest time" and the multiple-use dogma, proved on close examination to be unsatisfactory guidelines for policymaking. Consensus could not often be reached on what in fact was the "greatest good," and the "greatest number" principle left no room for minority interests in the environment like those of wilderness preservationists. The multiple-use idea offered no means of adjudicating the claims of competing uses.

Some of these shortcomings became apparent after 1908 in the bitter battle over the Hetch Hetchy Valley in California's Yosemite National Park. The City of San Francisco, recovering from the devastating earthquake and fire of 1906, wanted Hetch Hetchy as the site for a municipal reservoir and hydropower station, and it applied to the federal government for permission to build a dam there. The friends of wilderness and parks leaped forward to oppose the dam and defend the national park concept. As "Mr. Conservation," Gifford Pinchot found his opinion on Hetch Hetchy eagerly sought. He had little difficulty making up his mind. Parks, in Pin-

Two newspaper cartoons of 1910 present the contrasting public images of Gifford Pinchot. Above, Pinchot is represented as the faithful watchdog guarding the nation's resources from Secretary of the Interior Richard A. Ballinger and other "wolfish" special interests. The sleeping shepherd, President William Howard Taft, has not maintained the corral constructed from "big sticks" by his predecessor Theodore Roosevelt.

THE WILD AND WOOLLY EAST.

This second cartoon unfavorably depicts Pinchot as the enemy of traditional pioneer ideals. Note Pinchot's attire, a reference to his eastern aristocratic background, which was widely condemned in the West.

chot's view, were nice, but they had to give way to the material needs of a large city. Explaining his reasoning to a congressional committee, Pinchot declared that "the fundamental principle of the whole conservation policy is that of use, to take every part of the land and its resources and put it to that use in which it will serve the most people." Pinchot's pragmatism stood in the way of his acceptance of wilderness as a legitimate use of public land. In his view, ample wild land still remained.

John Muir did not agree. Long hostile to Pinchot's utilitarianism, which he regarded as little better than that of the pioneers, Muir made the defense of Hetch Hetchy a personal challenge. A national park, he insisted, should be safe for all time from "ravaging commercialism." Otherwise the amenities were lost and life degenerated into a race for the feed trough. As for damming Hetch Hetchy, Muir was incredulous that anyone would even consider flooding a valley that in many ways was the scenic equal of the famous Yosemite just to the south. "Dam Hetch Hetchy!" Muir roared. "As well dam for water-tanks the people's cathedrals and churches, for no holier temple has ever been consecrated by the heart of man." Muir's point was that the use of the environment had to encompass aesthetic and spiritual as well as economic dimensions.

Because the multiple-use management philosophy was no help in solving the Hetch Hetchy problem (obviously the valley could not be *both* a wilderness and a hydropower development), the antagonists took their differences to higher authorities. Opinion there was also divided. Only after six years of nationwide controversy and three separate congressional hearings did a bill granting Hetch Hetchy to San Francisco become law in 1913. John Muir and most of his Sierra Club colleagues were deeply disappointed. Evil, in Muir's estimation, had triumphed over good; Americans had shown "a perfect contempt for Nature, and instead of lifting their eyes to the God of the Mountains, lift them to the Almighty Dollar."

Although those who held the aesthetic conservationist or preservationist position lost the Hetch Hetchy fight to defenders of Pinchot's "wise use" school of thought, there was an element of victory in their defeat. Indeed, the most significant thing about the Hetch Hetchy controversy was that it occurred at all. One hundred or even fifty years earlier, a similar proposal to dam a wild river would not have occasioned the slightest ripple of public protest. Traditional American assumptions about the use of undeveloped country did not include reserving it in national parks for its recreational and inspirational values. The emphasis was all the other way, on civilizing it in the name of progress and prosperity. Older generations conceived of the thrust of civilization into the wilderness as the working out of divine intentions. But Muir and his colleagues had been successful in generating widespread resistance to this very process. What had formerly been the subject of national celebration was made to appear in many eyes to be a national tragedy. Moreover, scattered sentiment for wilderness preservation had jelled in the course of the Hetch Hetchy controversy into the beginnings of a national movement. And in Hetch Hetchy, preservationists had a symbol that, like the *Maine*, would not easily be forgotten. In fact, in 1916 the passage of the National Park Service Act made economic development of the parks much less likely.

Another impetus to the preservation idea was the growth and refinement of an American cult of the primitive. With the closing of the frontier and the corresponding burst of urbanization, more and more upper- and-middle-class Americans had become enthusiastic about getting back to nature. They moved to the suburbs, planted gardens, joined country clubs, and vacationed in the nation's parks and wildernesses. The interest in preserving outdoor virtues and skills also accounts for the emergence of the Boy Scouts as the nation's most popular youth organization after 1910.

Literature also reflected the new taste for nature. After Owen Wister invented the "western" in 1902 with *The Virginian*, it became a staple in the literary diet of millions of Americans. Cowboys became national heroes. No one contributed more to this process in Gifford Pinchot's lifetime than Zane Grey. Endlessly riding the purple sage, Grey's characters reminded Americans of an older—and many were prepared to say a better—way of life. Other best-selling books, such as Jack London's *Call of the Wild* (1903) and Edgar Rice Burroughs's *Tarzan of the Apes* (1912), were even more explicit in their message that wildness—in humans as well as nature—could be an asset. Spurred by such writings and by the general sense of malaise that accompanied the beginning of the frontierless twentieth century, Americans began to consider the possibility that they might be overcivilized. The doubts about growth and prosperity implicit in such thinking were important reasons for the rise of aesthetic conservation and the wilderness preservation movement. The majority still clung to the traditional exploitive ethic, but as the Hetch Hetchy protest demonstrated, their views were no longer being unchallenged.

Before the battle over Hetch Hetchy grew to national prominence, Gifford Pinchot became embroiled in the biggest political controversy of the era. The roots of the Ballinger–Pinchot affair of 1909 and 1910 lay in the struggle over the issue of reform within the Republican party. When Theodore Roosevelt left office in the spring of 1909 and departed for an African safari, he had had the satisfaction of knowing that his secretary of war and hand-picked successor, William Howard Taft, would enter the White House. In the election of the previous fall, Taft had easily defeated the perennial Democratic loser William Jennings Bryan. But thereafter Republican fortunes declined. Even granting that Roosevelt was a tough act for anyone to follow, Taft's presidency was still not a success. Within a year after he took office, the unity that had elected four successive Republican presidents shattered into bitter factionalism. Taft, it quickly appeared, was not about to follow in Roosevelt's footsteps with respect to reform. As his administration began, he endorsed conservative speaker of the house Joseph Cannon in preference to reform-minded insurgents such as Representative George Norris. The president's support of the highly protective Payne-Aldrich Tariff of 1909 further angered Progressives, who expected lower rates. But the darkest cloud over Taft's term in office involved Gifford Pinchot.

Pinchot had doubted Taft's "conservation-mindedness" from the outset of the 1908 campaign. The president had made a pledge to Roosevelt and Pinchot regarding his support for conservation and other reforms, but during the campaign and after, he refused to use the speeches the forester had prepared for him. Pinchot found Taft lazy and unenthusiastic in comparison with the former president, and the forester soon lamented Roosevelt's firm refusal to run for a third term. Pinchot's own presidential aspirations were clearly damaged without Roosevelt paving the way for him in 1912. His suspicions about Taft were soon confirmed when Taft announced there would be "no more government by commission." Pinchot had served on all seven Roosevelt committees regarding land use and government efficiency.

Taft had retained Pinchot as forester only because of his influence with the liberal wing of the Republican party. The president confided to his brother that he considered Pinchot "a radical and a good deal of a crank." Taft cared little for the reformer's apocalyptic warnings that the nation was running out of natural resources. In contrast to Pinchot, Taft's other appointees represented the conservative interests of the party. Among those was his secretary of the interior, Richard Ballinger, a former mayor of Seattle and former director of the General Land Office.

Within a month after Roosevelt left Washington, Pinchot found the federal government "dead." "Listlessness pervaded it," he lamented. "Hardly anybody seemed to care about anything any more." The passage of time only deepened his disappointment. Roosevelt, in his view, had "made" Taft, and Taft had pledged his support of Roosevelt's policies. But Pinchot found little evidence of continuity between the two administrations. Overlooking the Taft administration's passage of the Mann-Elkins Act (1910), which tightened federal regulation of the railroads, and its institution of almost twice the number of antitrust suits as under Roosevelt, Pinchot saw only the growth in power of conservative Republicanism. The Old Guard and the special interests were back in the federal saddle at the expense of the public interest. Summarizing his impressions, Pinchot remarked that replacing Roosevelt with Taft was "as though a sharp sword was succeeded by a roll of paper, legal size." The government service that Pinchot so revered in Roosevelt's day was now "slumped down on its heels."

Symbolic of this change in Pinchot's eyes was the way Ballinger administered federal lands. Alaska was the focal point. In the summer of 1909, just when Pinchot's rage at Taft was at the boiling point over the latter's refusal to support Roosevelt's plans for a world conservation conference that fall, charges of the fraudulent federal sale of Alaskan coalfields reached his receptive ear. According to the informant, a young Department of the Interior land inspector named Louis R. Glavis, Ballinger had cleared the way for some of the nation's most powerful financial syndicates, including those of J. P. Morgan and Daniel Guggenheim, to acquire valuable public lands on what amounted to the nation's last frontier. Pinchot felt the public interest had been violated, Roosevelt repudiated, and the whole conservation movement ridiculed.

Seeing this as an opportunity to cast the Taft men "in their real light," Pinchot and his top assistants acted. Not only did they file suits and attempt to place their bureaucratic strength in the way of the Alaskan coal claims, but Forest Service officials launched a crusade to make the public aware of the injustice. In November 1909, two of Pinchot's men wrote in Collier's Weekly that Ballinger was overseeing the theft of sixty million tons of coal from the Alaskan public lands. In the same month, Pinchot asked the public to help prevent the lands from passing "into private ownership, and be controlled by the monopolistic interests of a few." As Pinchot continued his direct assault on Ballinger and his innuendo against Taft, the nation's newspapers obliged the forester through wide coverage of the conservation fracas. Taft doggedly maintained his support for Ballinger and told Pinchot in no uncertain terms to drop the issue.

Pinchot, of course, had no intention of letting the matter fade away. To a group of New York publishers he declared, "The people of the United States have been the complacent victims of a system of plunder . . . by men who have suffered a curious perversion when it comes to the public trust." Taft seethed in anger at such statements, and, by the beginning of 1910, Pinchot was certain that his days were numbered as chief forester. On January 6, he persuaded his friend John Dolliver of Iowa to read a letter before the Senate condemning Ballinger and the Alaskan coal claims. Taft could no longer endure such insolence. As Pinchot left his house for a dinner engagement on the evening of January 7, a messenger from the White House arrived with an envelope for him. Pinchot opened the envelope to find a letter with a few terse words: "By your own conduct you have destroyed your usefulness as a helpful subordinate of the Government, and it therefore now becomes my duty to direct the Secretary of Agriculture to remove you from your office as the Forester." Pinchot reentered his house, waved the letter at his mother, and announced, "I'm fired." His mother threw her head back, laughed, and said, "Hurrah!" Then they left for dinner, Pinchot glorying in what he regarded as martyrdom to the ideals of Roosevelt and conservation.

After January 7, 1910, Gifford Pinchot found himself without a job and, even worse for a man who harbored political ambitions, without a party. Naturally his thoughts turned to Roosevelt, still on safari, and in April Pinchot traveled to the Italian Riviera to meet with the former president. They talked again, between sets of tennis, when Roosevelt returned to the United States in June. The immediate outcome of the discussions was discouraging for Pinchot. Despite the wave of national sympathy that had followed Pinchot's dismissal (thirty newspaper editors even suggested he should run for the presidency against Taft), Roosevelt was noncommittal about the Ballinger issue. He urged his friend to keep cool and keep the Republican party united. Taft had faults, Roosevelt conceded, but still retained his confidence.

In the next two years Roosevelt's faith in Taft withered into bitter enmity, to the satisfaction of Gifford Pinchot. Throughout the summer of 1910 Ballinger and the Department of the Interior were the subjects of a congressional investigation provoked by Pinchot's charges. The sessions were highlighted by the brilliance of Louis D. Brandeis, the lawyer who carried the case against Ballinger, and the mismanagement of the administration's case. During the course of the investigation it became clear that Taft had withheld documentary evidence, made false statements, and given Ballinger a premature exoneration. While the majority report in the investigation exonerated Ballinger of all misconduct, it removed determination of the Alaskan claims from Ballinger's office. The minority report roundly criticized Ballinger and the president. Public suspicions about Taft were reflected in the congressional elections of 1910, in which the Republicans lost control of the House of Representatives for the first time since 1892. And Ballinger, still under heated criticism, resigned his seat in Taft's cabinet early in 1911.

Thanks in part to Pinchot's influence, the significance of these developments was not lost on Theodore Roosevelt. As early as August 31, 1910, he made an impassioned reaffirmation of his reform philosophy in the course of a speech at Pottawatomie (sometimes Osawatomie), Kansas. Pinchot, who was with Roosevelt on this occasion, had actually ghostwritten the former president's speech. Drawing on the memory of John Brown, whose antislavery fanaticism had put the town on the map in the 1850s, Roosevelt and Pinchot called for the federal government to become sufficiently powerful to ensure equal opportunity and social justice. Following the argument in Herbert Croly's 1909 book *The Promise of American Life*, they asserted that the United States could not retreat to an economy of small, competitive units. Concentration was a fact of twentieth-century life. The task of the reformer was to build a federal government strong enough to counter the strength of big business, big labor, and other concentrations of power in the private sector. On behalf of the people the federal government would become a mighty welfare state, regulating, controlling, and stabilizing American life. Only in this way, Pinchot and Roosevelt believed, could popular sovereignty be preserved and the blessings of an urban-industrial age separated from its liabilities. The New Nationalism, as they called their plan, harked back to Alexander Hamilton and anticipated many aspects of Franklin D. Roosevelt's New Deal.

The Pottawatomie blast provided a reference point for the political maneuverings of the next two years. Taft and the conservative Republican Old Guard regarded Roosevelt and Pinchot as wild-eyed radicals out to destroy the capitalistic system. Democrats distrusted the New Nationalism for quite different reasons. Following the lead of Woodrow Wilson, the scholarly governor of New Jersey who would head the party's ticket in the election of 1912, the Democrats protested Roosevelt's advocacy of big government. "Free men," Wilson explained, "need no guardians." What they did need, in his estimation, was a return to free competition, equal opportunity, and respect for the individual in the tradition of Thomas Jefferson. Concentrations of power, according to Wilson, should be destroyed, not accepted and countered with even more power. The government should be a referee, not a participant, in the economic game. "I don't care how benevolent the master is going to be," Wilson declared, "I will not live under a master." And whereas Roosevelt accepted the label New Nationalism, Wilson referred to his own approach to reform as the New Freedom. The difference, according to Wilson, was between "regulated monopoly" and "regulated competition."

On January 21, 1911, Gifford Pinchot and a small group of Republican progressives or "insurgents" met in Washington at the home of Senator Robert M. La Follette of Wisconsin to organize the National Progressive Republican League. For his part, Pinchot was determined to use the group as a lever to force the Republican party toward the political left. If this move failed, the group would make a fine nucleus for a new third party. At first, most of Pinchot's colleagues were unwilling to go along with the idea of a schism, and gradually La Follette emerged as a challenger to Taft. Pinchot supported his candidacy with time and substantial gifts of money. By early 1912, however, he sensed with mounting excitement that Roosevelt himself might oppose Taft for the Republican nomination. Embarrassed, Pinchot hurriedly changed bandwagons and took to the stump on behalf of his former chief. The campaign trail led to the Republican National Convention in Chicago. Roosevelt arrived in high spirits. Asked by reporters how he felt, he replied, "like a Bull Moose." The term stuck as the emblem of his cause. But in the smoke-filled rooms of the convention, the moose proved no match for the establishment. Taft's control of the national party machinery was so complete that he effectively excluded Roosevelt's delegates and captured the Republican nomination in spite of what was probably a grassroots preference for Roosevelt.

Pinchot, who had been helping to mastermind Roosevelt's candidacy, immediately walked out of the convention and, on June 22, in company with Jane Addams and several thousand other Progressives, gave birth to the new Progressive party. In the weeks that followed, Pinchot helped write a party platform that expressed advanced reform thinking on a variety of topics, from conservation to child labor. Roosevelt promised his followers that they would stand at Armageddon and "battle for the Lord."

As the campaign of 1912 began in earnest, Pinchot was confident Roosevelt could beat Taft, but he was less confident about the Democratic nominee, Woodrow Wilson. Subsequent events proved his fears well founded. The Progressive party had a wealth of enthusiasm, a platform aimed at controlling the powerful and privileged, and the biggest name in American politics. But it lacked a network of organization. Moreover, Wilson's variety of reform proved highly attractive, particularly on the farm, in the small town, and among the urban middle class. Pinchot campaigned furiously for Roosevelt and his running mate, Governor Hiram Johnson of California. In October he expressed the inevitable election-eve optimism, declaring, "The Republican party is done for." But it was the Bull Moose that died. Roosevelt ran well ahead of Taft in both the popular and the electoral vote, but Wilson, taking advantage of the schism in the Republican ranks, swept to victory with 41 percent of the popular vote. Now the Democrats would have their opportunity in reform.

Pinchot's success in persuading Theodore Roosevelt to return to politics had far-reaching implications. Roosevelt's third-party candidacy sealed Taft's fate in 1912, but the schism in the Republican party extended beyond that election. It could be argued that the election of 1912 forever changed both major political parties. Liberal Republicans like Pinchot and Roosevelt never again entered the mainstream of the party because of their dislike of the conservative wing. Many progressive reformers resurfaced as Democrats twenty years later in electing Theodore Roosevelt's cousin, Franklin, to the presidency. At the very least, characterizations of the Democratic party as liberal and the Republican party as conservative became more clearly defined as a result of Pinchot's revenge in 1912.

In the aftermath of the election of 1912, Pinchot conferred with several leading members of the Progressive party, including Jane Addams, in an effort to keep the organization alive. His own preference was to push the party to the political left—to advocate outright government ownership of key businesses and utilities. Extreme individual wealth, he believed, could not be tolerated in a republic. The only exception he admitted was "a man who earned it as Henry Ford has done." In going this far, Pinchot pleased the Socialists and the radical fringe of Progressives, but he parted ways with the great majority of reformers. Undaunted, he set out to finish in Pennsylvania what the Roosevelt administration had started on the national level. His immediate goal was the seat in the U.S. Senate then occupied by the powerful Republican boss of Pennsylvania, Boies Penrose. Pinchot was armed with the nomination of the state's Progressive or Washington party and, for the first time, with a wife. Cornelia Bryce was half the forty-nine-year-old Pinchot's age but was every bit his equal in energy and enthusiasm for politics. The wealthy, attractive, and gracious daughter of a distinguished magazine publisher, Cornelia Bryce Pinchot was outspoken in favor of women's suffrage and rights for working women. She was active in New York politics and often joined striking women on picket lines. Despite their age difference, Cornelia and Gifford were a happy couple and relished their mutual interest in politics. In time, Cornelia would wage two unsuccessful bids for the House of Representatives, and Gifford would actively support her candidacy. But in 1914, it was Cornelia who campaigned hard for her husband.

With his wife's support, Pinchot waged a spirited campaign in 1914. He had the backing of some of the foremost names in the liberal constellation: Jane Addams, Booker T. Washington, Hiram Johnson, and Roosevelt himself. Indeed, the former president mailed over a million postcards to Pennsylvania voters saying that Pinchot was "fighting . . . for the same things for which we fought in 1912." The verdict, however, was the same. Penrose walloped Pinchot, gaining almost twice as many popular votes. Promising not to abandon the fight "for political and economic freedom," the loser and his bride left for Europe.

Although he never was elected to a federal political office, Pinchot's persuasion of Theodore Roosevelt to run as a third-party candidate precipitated the realignment of the Republican party. His ambition and deep belief in the cause of conservation led him to go beyond the bounds of political pragmatism and out of the mainstream of his party. Compromise was not a Pinchot specialty, and his willingness to form and lead a third party may well have cost him the term in the White House that he had coveted for so many years. He did not leave politics, however. Determined to at least bring progressivism to his home state of Pennsylvania, Pinchot accepted an appointment as commissioner of forestry and found his way to the governor's mansion in 1922. In two four-year terms as governor—he was elected again in 1930—Pinchot brought Roosevelt-style progressivism to Pennsylvania in the form of streamlined government and state-controlled power development. In his second term, Pinchot launched what was called the "little New Deal," paving a thousand miles of rural "Pinchot roads," providing broad relief in the Great Depression, and establishing a state-level public works program.

During the 1924 and 1928 Republican campaigns, Pinchot's name came up as a dark-horse candidate, but for too long his views had been too controversial in politics for him to be considered very seriously. Pinchot's support of strong central government found him little favor among the conservative mainstream of the party. After his successful second term as governor of Pennsylvania, the seventy-year-old Pinchot retired from public service to write and travel. He remained deeply interested in conservation and forestry, and in 1936 he and his wife made a long automobile trip to the western national forests. For rangers young and old, it was a great thrill to see the man who was most responsible for both the creation of the Forest Service and the 191 million acres of national forests it managed. To the delight of his listeners, the old forester, still sporting his handlebar mustache, told stories of the early days.

Future generations of environmental intellectuals would take Pinchot to task for his utilitarian views, and scholarship on this enigmatic figure would waver with the political times. During World War II, for example, Pinchot's conservation phi-

THE ELECTION OF 1912

MAINE 6
N.H. 4
VT. 4
MASS. 18
R.I. 5
CONN. 7
N.Y. 45
N.J. 14
DEL. 3
MD. 8
PA. 38
W.VA. 8
VA. 12
N.C. 12
S.C. 9
FLA. 6
GA. 14
OHIO 24
KY. 13
TENN. 12
ALA. 12
MICH. 15
IND. 15
MISS. 10
WIS. 13
ILL. 29
ARK. 9
LA. 10
IOWA 13
MO. 18
MINN. 12
KANS. 10
OKLA. 10
NEBR. 8
TEXAS 20
N.DAK. 5
S.DAK. 5
COLO. 6
N.MEX. 3
WYO. 3
MONT. 4
IDAHO 4
UTAH 4
ARIZ. 3
NEV. 3
WASH. 7
OREG. 5
CALIF. 11

	ELECTORAL	POPULAR (in thousands)
Wilson, Democratic	435	6,297
Taft, Republican	8	3,487
Roosevelt, Progressive	88	4,119

NATIONAL FORESTS 1930

losophy was revered and practiced by a nation determined to ration resources to defeat a powerful enemy. As pollution and the continuing loss of wild land to development accelerated in the postwar era, however, Pinchot and land-use agencies like the Forest Service were criticized for having an anthropocentric (human-centered) ethos, and having ushered in environmental problems through their encouragement of development. By the 1960s and 1970s, biocentric (earth-centered) thinking argued that human beings were just another species of animal and did not have the right to plunder the planet. "Radical ecology" rejected traditional Western development philosophy that celebrated the conquering of nature, and it advocated the peaceful coexistence with nature that existed in preindustrial societies. Pinchot's views were at odds with biocentrism. As a backlash of conservative, prodevelopment thought returned to popularity in the 1980s, Pinchot's utilitarian conservation occupied the broad middle ground of compromise between the two extreme points of view.

Gifford Pinchot himself would not have been surprised by the political and philosophical debate over conservation that went on after his death in 1947. He spent the last ten years of life at Milford, compiling his memoirs, and recalling the give and take during the days of America's conservation awakening. For Pinchot, forestry and conservation were logical, pragmatic, and essential to the future of the human race, and the politics involved was a means to such ends. "I have . . . been a Governor every now and then," Pinchot wrote in those memoirs, "but I am a forester all the time." Through determination and an unwavering belief in "the tonic of conservation," Gifford Pinchot established the framework for the American transition from a pioneer to an ecological perspective.

SELECTED READINGS
The Person

Fausold, Martin L.: *Gifford Pinchot, Bull Moose Progressive* (1961). Pinchot's early political interests as they centered on the election of 1912.

McGeary, M. Nelson: *Gifford Pinchot: Forester-Politician* (1960). The most balanced biography.

Penick, James L.: *Progressive Politics and Conservation: The Ballinger–Pinchot Affair* (1968). The most recent study of the controversy that in 1910 cost Pinchot his job as chief forester.

*Pinchot, Gifford: *Breaking New Ground* (1947): republished in paperback (1987). Pinchot's autobiography covering his career as a forester.

Pinkett, Harold T.: *Gifford Pinchot: Private and Public Forester* (1970). Limited to Pinchot's involvement in forestry.

The Period

*Blum, John: *The Republican Roosevelt* (1954). An excellent short interpretation of Theodore Roosevelt.

Frome, Michael: *The Forest Service* (1984). General history of the creation and evolution of the agency.

*Ginger, Ray: *The Age of Excess: The United States from 1877 to 1914* (1967). A lively interpretation of the years in which the modern United States took shape.

*Hays, Samuel: *Conservation and the Gospel of Efficiency* (1959). Places the progressive conservation movement in a context of science and engineering.

*Hofstadter, Richard: *Social Darwinism in American Thought* (1944). Interpretation of how the rich justified themselves by the application of the evolutionary theses of Charles Darwin.

*Josephson, Matthew: *The Robber Barons* (1934). Criticism of the new breed of industrial leaders who dominated the nation's economic life in the late nineteenth century.

*Nash, Roderick: *Wilderness and the American Mind* (1982). Analysis of the growth of American concern about the environment.

Pringle, Henry F.: *The Life and Times of William Howard Taft* (2 vols., 1939). An exhaustive and laudatory account of Taft's long career in public life.

Richardson, Elmo R.: *The Politics of Conservation: Crusades and Controversies, 1897–1913* (1962). Indepth analysis of the western point of view regarding conservation based on newspapers and manuscript collections.

---

*Available in paperback.

Taylor, Bob Pepperman: *Our Limits Transgressed: Environmental Political Thought in America* (1992). Good historical overview of pastoralism, progressivism, and more recent epochs in environmental history.

FOR CONSIDERATION

1. Individuals like Gifford Pinchot and Theodore Roosevelt did not need to work. Discuss the factors that led to their choices of careers in public service.

2. How did the 1890 U.S. Census Report declaring that there was no more frontier help place Gifford Pinchot's forestry ideas into practice?

3. The first eight years of the 1900s were known as the heyday of conservation and progressivism. Why?

4. Gifford Pinchot was at the center of a major schism in the Republican party beginning in 1909. How did the rift develop? What were some of the short- and long-term impacts of the so-called Ballinger–Pinchot affair?

5. How does Pinchot's conservation philosophy square with recent environmentalism?

FOUR
4

Henry Ford

*T*he rope tightened, strained, and an automobile chassis began to inch along a 250-foot track on the floor of the Ford Motor Company factory. Henry Ford's eyes narrowed in concentration as he watched workmen add part after part. Five hours and fifty minutes later, a finished Model T coughed into life and rolled off the assembly line under its own power. Ford permitted himself a fleeting smile. The previous production record had been cut in half. But for Ford the breakthrough of August 1913 was just a start. Even as he left the experiment, he was thinking about refinements that soon reduced production time to ninety-three minutes. The unbelievable day of a-car-a-minute was not far away. By 1920, every other motor vehicle in the world was a Ford, and Ford himself was a living legend.

The advance guard of the Ford family came to Michigan from Ireland in 1832. Henry's father, William, joined them in 1847, the second year of the great potato famine that persuaded so many Irish to try their luck in the New World. After crossing the Atlantic, the Fords used wagons, canal boats, and finally larger vessels on Lake Erie to reach Detroit.

One day's wagon ride west of Detroit on the road to Chicago lay Dearbornville, or Dearborn, and the River Rouge. At the time William Ford arrived, the region was only a few decades past the frontier stage. Bears and wolves were still part of the everyday scene for the settlers, and dense forests dominated the landscape. But once they were cleared and the swamps drained, southeastern Michigan provided deep, loamy soil, ideal for agriculture. William began as a carpenter for the Michigan Central Railroad, acquired a little cash, forty acres of land, a wife, and a family. Henry, born July 30, 1863, was the first child to live beyond infancy.

The Ford farm in Dearborn typified the variegated pattern of northern agriculture. In sharp contrast to the staple crop system of southern plantations where cotton was king, William kept a variety of livestock, grew several crops, maintained an orchard, tanned hides, cut wood, tapped maple trees for sugar, and supplemented the family income by hunting, fishing, and trapping. Mary Ford churned butter, made candles and soap, fashioned clothes from homespun cloth, kept a vegetable garden, and preserved its harvests. In the absence of slaves or cash for hired hands, Henry got his fill of "chores" at an early age. School was therefore something of a vacation. Henry's formal education began and ended in the one-room Scotch Settlement School a mile-and-a-half walk from the homestead. The curriculum consisted of *McGuffey's Readers* and rulers strong enough for serious spanking. The readers, written by William Holmes McGuffey, were one of the major influences on the American mind in the nineteenth century. McGuffey's six books, published between 1836 and 1857, sold an estimated 122 million copies—more than three times the population of the United States when Ford was a schoolboy. Several generations of Americans grew up on McGuffey's moral-coated language lessons. As in the Puritan sermon, virtue was always rewarded, and delinquency brought instant catastrophe. Benjamin Franklin's prose also graced McGuffey's pages, and young Henry Ford gained from them a clear, if unbending, ethic of hard work and clean living. He never abandoned this system of values. Years after his school days, the billionaire Ford bought and transported to his hometown museum the log cabin birthplace of William Holmes McGuffey.

Another harbinger of the mature Ford was his early fascination with machinery. He was a born mechanic, a natural tinkerer. Clocks and watches were his first love. Before he entered his teens, the neighborhood relied on him to repair its timepieces. He could also build them, as he proved when some friends jokingly gave him a completely empty watch to "repair." In less than an hour Ford returned the watch, running perfectly.

From watches Ford graduated to larger machines. He studied the village sawmill to learn how a sliding steam valve operated. His father's occasional jobs with the Michigan Central provided a chance to learn about locomotives. In Dearborn Henry built waterwheels, wagons, and even a steam turbine that blew up a section of fence and drove a piece of metal through his lip. Sometimes his abilities proved more immediately useful, as when he constructed a device that allowed him to open the farm gate without dismounting from the wagon. As a result, the family accepted his obsession good-naturedly, with only an occasional warning to keep new toys out of Henry's hands for fear he would take them apart.

The history of invention is filled with sudden insights. Ford's first one came on a clear, hot July day in 1876 as he and his father drove the team toward Detroit. The noise came first, a hissing and clanking that shattered the country stillness. Then around a bend lumbered a huge machine: a boiler and engine mounted on wheels with a trailer full of coal in the rear. Of course Ford had seen trains move on tracks, and he knew about stationary engines that used steam to power mills and threshers, but this one moved overland under its own power. The potential rather than the actual appearance of the awkward monster captivated Ford. In an instant the twelve year old was off the wagon, questioning the operator of the vehicle. The answers were disappointing, but Ford could hardly contain his excitement. A whole new challenge—self-propelled overland transportation, a horseless carriage— opened before him. A half century later the automobile king declared, "I remember that engine as though I had seen it only yesterday." He even recalled that it made 200 revolutions per minute.

The year 1876 was the centennial of the United States, and, to mark it, Philadelphia, the "birthplace of liberty," staged a spectacular Centennial Exposition. Machinery was the star of the show. Ford's father made his first long trip since immigrating three decades before in order to attend. He returned to the farm with glowing reports of giant engines. Henry absorbed every detail and in 1879 sought seasonal employment in Detroit's factories, foundries, and jewelry stores. Oblivious of considerations of diet and sleep when absorbed in mechanical problems, he worked a grueling schedule. Everything took second place to engineering. Despite a boyhood of Sunday school, Ford, exactly like Benjamin Franklin, came to a practical conclusion about religion. "I think I saved a lot of valuable time," he noted, "by staying away from church." More to the point, his god was in the machine shop.

Returning to Dearborn to help at harvest time, Ford gained experience operating the kind of self-propelled steam engine he first had seen running on the road when he was twelve. Chancing to meet the agent for the company that had manufactured the engines, Ford became a mechanic and demonstrator for it throughout southern Michigan. He even built a primitive steam-propelled tractor. But steam vehicles were slow, unwieldy, inefficient, and voracious consumers of bulky fuel. So in his little farm workshop Ford began experimenting with alternative sources of power: electricity, illuminating gas, and a little-known liquid called gasoline.

He was in good company. The nineteenth century was the golden age of American invention. The Industrial Revolution, spreading from England, met the challenges of an undeveloped continent and a burgeoning United States. The result was an explosion of revolutionary inventions. Ford's obsession with "building a better mousetrap" sprang from the same ambition that had produced the steamboat (1807), the reaper (1834), the typewriter (1843), the telegraph (1844), and the sewing machine (1846). Cable streetcars had appeared on San Francisco's hills in 1873, and the next year electrically powered cars were operating in New York. But the giants of invention in Ford's youth were Alexander Graham Bell and Thomas A. Edison. The Bell telephone revolutionized communication in 1876, while Edison's phonograph (1877) and incandescent bulb (1879) were only the best known of over a thousand Edison patents.

By 1890, a number of young engineers with prophetic names like Dodge, Buick, Studebaker, and Olds had joined in the pursuit of Ford's dream of a self-propelled carriage. Two breakthroughs inspired their efforts. One was the bicycle. Lightweight, spoke-wheeled, highly maneuverable, and relatively fast, it directed attention to the possibility of independent long-distance travel over ordinary roads. A novelty in the 1880s, bicycles became a national craze in the next decade, and many of the first attempts to build cars took bikes, rather than wagons or carriages, as models. The second significant development was the emergence of an efficient gasoline engine from the shop of Nikolaus Otto in Germany. Otto did not immediately think of his invention as a source of power for vehicles, but several dozen Americans, among them Henry Ford, did. In 1891, Henry excitedly told Clara Bryant Ford, his wife of three years, that he could adapt the Otto engine to move vehicles. A practical young woman for whom transportation meant horses, Clara wondered how. Seizing a convenient piece of sheet music, Henry drew a quick and convincing sketch. He also convinced Clara of the need to settle permanently in Detroit, where he could obtain experience in the field of electrical ignition. The Fords made the move that year, facilitating Henry's work at the Edison Illuminating Company.

Detroit at the start of the 1890s was in the process of rapid growth. The streets were still lined with trees, and Belle Isle in the Detroit River afforded pleasant outdoor recreation, but expansion had brought problems. Horse-drawn vehicles and bicycles jammed unpaved streets that in wet weather turned to quagmires. The city's politics was equally dirty, a condition Mayor Hazen S. Pingree's reform campaign only partially alleviated. Factories, tenements, and saloons tended to replace the fine downtown residences. Their former owners, in turn, took the lead in replacing the surrounding countryside with suburbs. Sprawl was becoming a fact of American city life.

At the Edison plant Ford's abilities as a machinist earned him a modest but respectable fifty dollars per month, but his heart was in his homework: building a gasoline engine. Although Ford attended the Columbian Exposition in 1893 in Chicago, he probably was not aware of the progress that German and French inventors had already made. So it was with the trepidation and the thrill of the pioneer that he began his labors. The finished product was only about eighteen inches long. On Christmas Eve 1893, Henry clamped it to his kitchen sink and called to Clara for help. Busy with seven-week-old Edsel and Christmas preparations, she was not pleased by her assignment of dribbling gas down the intake opening while Henry spun the flywheel. At first nothing happened, and Clara's frown deepened. Then, with a spurt of flame, the tiny motor roared into life. After thirty seconds Henry shut it off.

Now hot on the trail of his car, Ford worked like one obsessed. Every dollar and every hour he could find went into materials and construction. It was a trial-and-error process conducted in a woodshed. In the absence of auto parts shops, everything had to be built from scratch, and the finished product represented not one invention but dozens. By June of 1896, Ford was ready. A warm rain was falling as he applied the finishing touches to the car at 2 A.M. in the presence of a fellow Edison employee and the faithful Clara. The tension mounted as Henry pushed the vehicle to the doorway of the woodshed. Suddenly he stopped, puzzled and embarrassed. The woodshed door was too small to permit the exit of the car. Impulsively Ford grabbed an ax and widened the doorway. He turned on the current from the battery, engaged the choke, and fired the engine. Then he sprang into the driver's seat (taken from a bicycle), pulled the lever transmitting power to the wheels, bumped down the alley onto Bagley Avenue, and disappeared into the rainy night.

Ford's car was not the first gas-powered vehicle to be built in the United States (an honor earned by J. Frank Duryea in the early 1890s), but it was an outstanding achievement. Trim, rugged, reliable, and capable of speeds up to twenty-five miles per hour, the first Ford car still stands in the Ford Museum, ready to run. But in 1896 its future was highly uncertain. Henry Ford was an unknown, unfinanced mechanic who had built a car in a woodshed. He had lots of ambitious competition. Ford, however, caught the wind that drove him to world leadership in less than two decades. His motive? Probably not money (he could, after all, have stopped working and lived far more sumptuously than he actually ever did with his first half million dollars) so much as achievement and self-expression. Putting the nation on cheap yet efficient wheels was for Ford the same kind of challenge as repairing a schoolmate's watch or building his first engine in Clara Ford's kitchen.

The summer of 1896 found Ford in New York at the annual convention of the Edison Illuminating Company, snapping photographs like any gawking tourist from the hinterland. His film records his interest in the Brooklyn Bridge, opened in 1883 and still one of the engineering wonders of the world, and in another engineering wonder: Thomas A. Edison. Like Ford, Edison was a midwesterner and largely self-educated. The men were also similar in their love of machinery and their capacity for sustained application to mechanical problems. Edison, Americans believed, never went to bed, and he encouraged the notion by predicting that in time people would evolve beyond the need for sleep—like machines!

At first, Ford circled warily around the great man, taking an occasional photograph, but his moment came at the end of a banquet when his Detroit superior offhandedly remarked to Edison that this "young fellow here has made a gas car." The statement was made as a joke in the expectation that the assembly would laugh Ford out of his foolish ideas. Instead the humor backfired. The diners, including Edison himself, expressed great interest. Soon Ford was the center of attention. With the aid of sketches on a menu he explained the details of his ignition system. Edison brought his fist down on the table so hard the dishes jumped. "Young man," he roared, "that's the thing! You have it—the self-contained unit carrying its own fuel. Keep at it." Here was the encouragement Ford needed. He later remarked, "I had hoped I was right, sometimes I knew I was, sometimes I only wondered if I was, but here . . . out of a clear sky the greatest inventive genius in the world had given me a complete approval."

Returning to Detroit, Ford began to assemble a team of associates and to search for financial backing. By 1899, he had both, and as chief engineer of the Detroit Automobile Company, he had a golden opportunity to produce cars commercially. The result was total failure. The high point of the company's life was a headline in the Detroit News-Tribune of February 4, 1900, which read, "Swifter Than a Race-Horse It Flew over the Icy Streets." The following article described a journalist's wild ride at speeds up to twenty-five miles per hour in one of Ford's new vehicles. But this was exceptional. Usually the heavy, trucklike machines stood stalled at the curb while horses flew by on the streets.

Discouraged and now considerably behind rival car makers like Ransom Olds, Ford tried another approach. He would build a fast car and go to the races. Not only were there publicity and cash support for the winner but, Ford believed, the best opportunity to test and improve the automobile. In 1901 he had his racer and his first trophy, a cut-glass punch bowl. A year later he developed a car of 100 horsepower. With daredevil Barney Oldfield at the wheel, Ford's car beat the best field of racers in the country by half a mile with a speed of close to a mile a minute. Later Ford himself drove the car ninety miles per hour over the ice of Lake Saint Clair for a new world record.

With the racing program going nicely, Alex Y. Malcomson and Ford organized a group of Detroiters as the Ford Motor Company. Money was hard to raise, but the dozen investors Malcomson talked into contributing were fortunate. They eventually realized the greatest return on their investment in the history of American business. The $100 that a sister of one of the founders contributed ultimately earned her $355,000.

The key to the success of the Ford Motor Company was the vision of Henry Ford. He left something to be desired as a businessman and personnel director, and in truth there were better automobile engineers in the country, but as an associate remarked of Ford, "He had the dream." Its essence was a light, rugged, reliable, and, above all, inexpensive car that the average American could afford. Cars had been the toys of the rich. Constructed individually and by hand, they cost between $3,000 and $5,000. Around Newport, Rhode Island, and other playgrounds of the wealthy, cars were common, but for most turn-of-the-century Americans, they were inconceivable luxuries.

Ford had a different idea. "I will build a motor car for the multitude," he declared. "It will be built of honest materials, by the best workmen that money can hire, after the simplest design that modern engineering can devise. But it shall be so low in price that the man of moderate means may own one." But how? In 1903, it did not seem possible to make something as complicated as a car cheaply. Ford, however, had a plan. "The way to make automobiles," he explained, "is to make one automobile just like another automobile, to make them all alike, to make them come from the factory just alike—just like one pin is like another pin when it comes from a pin factory."

The roots of the mass production system with which Ford revolutionized the manufacture of automobiles were as old as the first American factories. Before 1790 a Delaware farmer's son named Oliver Evans had applied the principle of automation to the milling of flour. Previously, millers had carried bags of wheat to a loft, from which the grain fell between the grindstones. Then the flour was again toted upstairs for drying and sifting. Evans devised a network of vertical and horizontal conveyors that used the power of the waterwheel instead of manual labor. Only two men were needed in Evans's mill. One poured wheat into the system; the other rolled away barrels of flour. A few years later, in Pawtucket, Rhode Island, Samuel Slater constructed a cotton-spinning mill with seventy-two spindles. Falling water provided the power for this pioneering mechanization of textile production in the United States. Subsequent refinements made it possible to transform raw cotton into finished cloth, in a continuous process and under a single roof. The first factory was the Boston Manufacturing Company's plant at Waltham, Massachusetts, established in 1813. The merchant capitalists involved in this undertaking also experimented with a new form of business organization: the corporation. In this arrangement, a group of investors pooled their assets and profited, or lost, only in proportion to their individual involvement. This concept of limited liability made possible the capital accumulation that launched large-scale industry in the middle decades of the nineteenth century.

Along with mass production, corporate financing ended the era of home and small-shop manufacturing. The artisan producing an item from start to finish on a single workbench was replaced by machine operators responsible for only a small portion of the production process. Eli Whitney was the pioneer who turned from his cotton gin to gunmaking in the late 1790s. Before this time, guns had always been fashioned individually by skilled gunsmiths. Whitney thought that unskilled laborers could do the job at less expense and in a shorter time if production was standardized. The key was to make identical parts (Whitney used metal molds) that could be assembled in a series of simple operations. Standardization also facilitated gun repair. From firearms Whitney turned his attention to timepieces, transforming the industry and, incidentally, making it possible for a young Henry Ford to inter-change parts among the watches and clocks in his collection.

In Ford's time the mantle of Oliver Evans and Eli Whitney fell on the shoulders of Frederick W. Taylor. In company with Ford and his contemporaries, Taylor deified efficiency. The concept demanded an obsession with speed, a faith in science and technology, and a pragmatic orientation that put production results above all other considerations. Establishing the nation's first consulting service in a field that came to be known as scientific management, Taylor dissected the manufacturing process. With a stopwatch and a tape measure as his constant companions, he conducted a series of time-and-motion studies. Taylor demonstrated, for example, that, if a worker on an assembly line spent an extra second reaching into a drawer for a screwdriver, time could be saved and production increased by having the tool on a cord as close to the screw in question as possible. In the course of a day, Taylor maintained, the economies would be significant.

Going a step further, Taylor made it a basic principle to replace a worker with a machine whenever possible. Machines, he reasoned, were more precise—and they did not gossip with their neighbors or require sick leaves or strike for higher wages. When people were essential, Taylor advised that they be compensated according to the piecework system, in which production, rather than elapsed time, determined pay. Another Taylor axiom was specialization. Whenever feasible, he broke the manufacturing process into small parts. A worker whose sole function consisted of endlessly tightening the same six screws as they moved past on the assembly line would develop remarkable efficiency. That worker's sanity, however, was another matter. Finally, Taylor stressed the importance of synchronization. All the operations in a plant had to mesh smoothly if maximum speed was to be achieved.

In 1911, when Taylor distilled his ideas into a book entitled *The Principles of Scientific Management*, the automotive industry offered the most fertile ground in the American economy for the application of his ideas. Indeed, Henry Ford had already drawn on them and made some refinements of his own. Efficient production explained why the Ford Motor Company was able to sell a car for $850. This comparatively low price, in turn, was the chief reason for the company's remarkable early record of sales and profits. Ford at first sacrificed efficiency by tinkering with his car and changing the design almost annually, but in 1908 he built the Model T and recognized it as a superior vehicle. Then he made a crucial decision: He would build the Model T and no other for the next twenty years. This policy opened the way to unprecedented efficiency and enormous economies of scale. Consumer choice, to be sure, was a casualty and the subject of endless humorous stories, such as Ford dealers telling purchasers they could have the Model T in any shade of black they desired.

The home of the Model T after 1910 was the Ford Motor Company's new Highland Park plant northwest of Detroit. It was also the showcase of American industry. The factory began by producing about 300 cars a day, but one by one the various manufacturing processes were improved according to the principles of Frederick Taylor and the genius of Henry Ford and his associates. A giant leap forward occurred in the early spring of 1913, when construction of the electrical generator, or magneto, was placed on a continuously moving assembly line. Before, an individual worker had sat down before a pile of materials and put a magneto together in about twenty minutes. The assembly-line technique divided the operation into twenty-nine parts and involved twenty-nine men. It also lowered construction time to five minutes. Now one laborer, working "on the line" as part of a team, could do the work of four.

After this success it was only a matter of months before Ford put the whole car on a moving assembly line. Branch lines, such as the one that produced magnetos, fed into the main track. Again the results were spectacular. From 12 hours and 30 minutes, production time per car dropped to 5 hours and 50 minutes. Further refinement lowered the record in April 1914 to 1 hour and 33 minutes.

By 1916, the Ford Motor Company had outgrown the Highland Park plant. Ford craved still greater automation; he also wanted greater self-sufficiency and envisioned a superplant that would allow almost complete vertical integration of his car building. Ford bought ore-rich land, a 700,000-acre forest, and steel and lumber mills, and then began purchasing land south of Detroit along the River Rouge. Over the next few years a massive complex took shape where everything from windshields to gearshift knobs was made and supplied to the Ford assembly plant at River Rouge, as well as to others around the nation. Henry Ford had for the most part eliminated the middle man—the parts manufacturer who cut into his profit margin—with the completion of River Rouge.

In 1920, with the River Rouge complex pouring out parts, Ford achieved his dream of producing one car for every minute of the working day. Still he was not satisfied. On October 31, 1925, the Ford Motor Company made 9,109 Model T's, one every ten seconds! Sales kept pace, largely because Ford made it a policy to pass on the economies of mass production to the consumer. In 1910, for instance, the basic Model T cost $725, and 34,528 Americans became proud owners. Six years later, the price was down to $345 for the 730,041 purchasers. Eventually it reached an all-time low of $290. Meanwhile, Ford had made millions of dollars and had become the undisputed king of mass production. By 1920 every other car in the world was a Model T, and the Germans, searching for a word to describe revolutionary industrial reorganization, coined *Fordismus*.

As the Ford Motor Company grew, Henry Ford gradually assumed the role of advocate for the business establishment. With the assistance of a stable of ghostwriters, he expounded his philosophy of industry and life to an admiring nation. Predictably, Ford defended the economic and political system under which he had succeeded. His idea of reform was to improve on existing patterns. He had little patience with progressive reformers, especially those critical of the free enterprise system. Such a person, Ford declared, "wants to smash things. He is the sort of man who would tear up a whole shirt because the collar button did not fit the buttonhole. It would never occur to him to enlarge the buttonhole."

Ford singled out for special criticism the reformers who had tried to "start a new world in Russia" with the Revolution of 1917. Their basic error, he opined, was to violate "Nature" by instituting a communistic economy that denied individuals the fruits of their ability and their effort. To Ford, private property was a sacred pillar of civilization and competition the crux of social relations. On the other hand, he did

This is a difficult route to follow and care should be taken, for there is danger in getting off the route.

The roads are good to Carr; small hills and good if dry the balance of the way.

---

357   CHEYENNE TO RAWLINS, WYO.—188.3 m.

Inter- mediate Mileage.	TOWNS.		Inter- mediate Mileage.		TOWNS.
0	0	Cheyenne, Wyo.	18.3	103.4	Rock River
			24.9	128.3	Medicine Bow
20.	20.	Granite Canon	15.3	143.6	Hanna
21.1	41.2	Kask's Ranch	20.7	164.3	Walcott
16.8	58.	Laramie	8.	172.3	Ft. Steele
27.1	85.1	Lookout	16.	188.3	Rawlins, Wyo.

This is the direct route to Rawlins and probably best in dry weather. In wet weather go directly north to Rock Creek 103 m. (June 17th) thence to Medicine Bow. The road gradually rises over the Sherman Divide, through an open grazing country. Good dirt roads with some short steep hills; altitude of 8,000 and 9,000 feet is attained; snow capped peaks in various directions. Route some of the way parallels wire fences; law permits cutting of fences to avoid bad mud holes. From Rock Creek follow old Union Pacific R.R. bed; road good. Just before reaching Medicine Bow cross bridge at a ranch house. Road to Hanna is also over U. P. R.R. and fairly good. Leaving Hanna pass by cemetery on hill and go south of R.R. thru a sage brush country with no water. Road is bad with high centers (and some hills) being nothing but a trail.

At Ft. Steele cross North Platte River on ties of R.R. bridge. Telegraph R.R. office in Omaha for permit if not obtained en-route. Rawlins has the last blacksmith shop before reaching Green River.

Motoring in the early twentieth century often resembled an expedition, as this 1912 description from a guide by the Automobile Association of America suggests. For some years blacksmith shops did double duty for horses and cars.

not defend the status quo. A static "life of ease" or the accumulation of money for its own sake was an invitation to decay in a society as in an individual. With frequent references to his own life, Ford explained that there was always room for

With this assembly line, instituted in 1913, Henry Ford reduced the time needed to construct electrical generators for his Model T from twenty minutes to five.

improvement. And Ford looked forward to the day when machinery, "the new messiah," would usher in a golden age of truth, beauty, and peace.

As the employer of over 32,000 workers in 1916, Ford was acutely conscious of the labor problem in the United States. Since the violence of the 1890s at Homestead, Pullman, and other urban-industrial areas, workers had made little progress toward obtaining a greater share of the profits of business. They still worked long hours at low pay and under trying, often dangerous, conditions. Labor unions like the American Federation of Labor tried to do their best for the skilled laborer, but the unskilled masses had few friends. And even organized workers encountered massive resistance on the part of management.

In May 1902, anthracite coal miners in the United Mine Workers struck for higher wages and shorter hours. The mine owners, who did not even recognize the

Americans exercised considerable imagination in finding ways to use the mobile power plant that Henry Ford perfected. This Model T was converted into a snowmobile.

A great deal of national pride surrounded these six men, whose association included camping trips. From the left are Thomas Edison, Harvey S. Firestone, Jr., Prof. R. J. H. DeLoach, John Burroughs, Henry Ford, and Harvey S. Firestone, Sr. As the attire of the men suggests, some of their camping ventures were not very primitive.

union's existence, much less its right to influence management policy, were incensed. George F. Baer spoke for the owners when he declared that "the rights and interests of the laboring man will be protected and cared for—not by labor agitators, but by the Christian men to whom God in His infinite wisdom has given the control of the property interests of the country."* But the miners, abstaining from violence and asking only for the opportunity to arbitrate, won widespread sympathy. As the strike dragged on into the summer and fall of 1902 with no sign of settlement, President Theodore Roosevelt decided to act. The owners were told that unless they took steps to settle their differences with their employees, the U.S. Army would work the mines in the national interest. At the same time the president secured the assistance of J. P. Morgan in putting financial pressure on the mine owners. Frightened by this unprecedented show of executive power, the owners capitulated and granted a 10 percent wage increase.

Labor's celebration of the anthracite mine settlement was tempered by the knowledge that, with Roosevelt's blessing, the owners were "paying" for their concession by raising the price of coal 10 percent. And there was no union recognition

---

*For a discussion of the premises on which Baer's statement was based, including social Darwinism, see pages 48–49.

in the settlement. Indeed, the completely unionized or "closed" shop had few defenders outside the unions. In the progressive mind, big labor was as much a threat to the public welfare as big business. Several events reflected this point of view. One was the 1905 decision of the U.S. Supreme Court in the case of *Lochner v. New York*, which invalidated a maximum-hour law for bakers on the grounds that it interfered with the free enterprise system. Three years later the Supreme Court unanimously upheld the application of the Sherman Antitrust Act to labor organizations that acted in restraint of trade. This decision in *Loewe v. Lawler* (the Danbury Hatters case) created the possibility of declaring strikes illegal.

Disgusted, many workers began to turn to radical alternatives. Founded in 1905, the Industrial Workers of the World (IWW) grew under the leadership of William "Big Bill" Haywood to have a sizable following in agriculture, mining, and lumbering, particularly in the Pacific Northwest. The IWW advocated the abolition of the wage system, the creation of "one big union" for all laborers, and the creation of a proletarian class consciousness in the Marxist tradition. Also on the political left was the Socialist party in the United States, which had been organized in 1900 by the veteran labor leader Eugene V. Debs. Starting in that year, Debs offered himself as a candidate for the presidency of the United States. At first his candidacy was a joke, but capitalists like Henry Ford gradually became aware that the Socialists struck responsive chords in a significant number of American minds. In the election of 1908, Debs received 420,000 votes; four years later, the figure was 900,000, or almost 6 percent of the national vote. In industrial centers and depressed agricultural regions the percentage was considerably higher. Milwaukee even elected a Socialist to the House of Representatives. Still more frightening to the Establishment was the violence that labor agitation could generate. In 1905, a former governor of Idaho was assassinated, and in 1910 the Los Angeles Times Building was bombed in an act of terrorism attributed to the IWW.

In Detroit Henry Ford faced his own set of problems. The city had a strong open-shop, anti-union tradition. Employers were accustomed to exploiting the concentrations of east European immigrants in the community at virtual slave wages. The Ford Motor Company, for example, adhered to a standard wage of $2.34 a day, or 26 cents an hour. By 1913, the situation in the automotive industry was tense. The Studebaker plant suffered a paralyzing strike that summer, and by fall IWW agents were active at Ford's Highland Park complex. To his credit, Ford recognized the problem. His labor force had long been too large for the kind of personal, inspirational management that was his forte. Lacking it, the existing wage scale and the monotonous assembly-line assignments provided little incentive. The result was a massive turnover among Ford employees. The company had to hire 53,000 men a year in order to keep 14,000 on the job. Constant retraining of this labor force cost Ford millions of dollars annually. Pondering the problem in the winter of 1913–1914, Ford hit on a brilliant solution. On January 5, 1914, he announced a new policy. Henceforth every Ford employee over twenty-two years old would receive "a share in the profits of the house" sufficient to make the minimum wage $5 daily. Moreover, the standard "day" was reduced from nine hours to eight.

Ford grandiosely termed the new plan "the greatest revolution in the matter of rewards for its workers ever known to the industrial world." Previously, by his own admission, Ford had paid "whatever it was necessary to pay." After January 5, 1914, he adopted profit sharing. Labor and capital would pull together; everyone was a partner down to the lowliest sweeper of floors. The workers would rise with the organization they served.

The nation and the world learned about the five-dollar minimum day with amazement. Financiers declared that the Ford Motor Company would be bankrupt within two years. But Henry did not have to worry. Thousands thronged to Detroit seeking jobs at Ford. Those who secured or already possessed them were caught up in a wave of enthusiasm for making automobiles. Production records soared. The IWW organizers quietly left Highland Park, and talk of a union to match the power of management stopped abruptly. So did the costly turnover in the labor force, and despite the higher wages, Ford made more money than ever. At the same time he restored faith in the capitalist system. The five-dollar day was a dramatic, concrete rebuttal to the criticisms of socialists and communists. Instead of resenting the rich men, average Americans resumed their traditional attempts to become rich.

With mass production and the five-dollar day well launched and sales setting new records each year, Henry Ford was free to turn his remarkable energies elsewhere. For the first time in his life he lifted his eyes from the workbench and turned to the larger sphere of world affairs. The result was not always happy. Henry might leave the machine shop, but a machine-shop mentality would not leave Henry. As a master mechanic, he tended to think that all problems were susceptible to mechanical solutions. It was simply a matter of finding the right tools and using them properly according to clearly defined laws. Good planning and careful design, in Ford's opinion, guaranteed a world that would function with the same efficient smoothness as the engine of a Model T. To achieve perfection, human nature and human conduct awaited only the coming of people who, in Ford's words, "can create the working design for all that is right and good and desirable." Such engineers could "mould the political, social, industrial, and moral mass into a sound and shapely whole." Here was a revival of the old idea of American mission complete with its innocence, its confidence, and its faith in reform.

Beginning in 1915, Ford began to offer himself to the world in this messianic capacity. The first dragon against which he threw his energies and his bank accounts was World War I. The war had begun when the assassination of Austro-Hungarian Archduke Franz Ferdinand in 1914 set off a whirlwind of commitments from European countries to uphold alliances in place since the mid-nineteenth century. Austria-Hungary had declared war on the Balkan country of Serbia, which it held responsible for the archduke's assassination. But entangling alliances soon brought Germany and the Ottoman Empire (Turkey) into the war on the side of Austria-Hungary; in turn, Russia, France, Italy, and Great Britain sided with Serbia. When the war began in 1914, President Woodrow Wilson urged impartiality in word and deed. Ford supported the president wholeheartedly. Breaking with his economic peers, the automobile king branded the conflict a capitalists' war. He resurrected the old rural suspicion of New York and Wall Street in attacking the bankers (chiefly J. P. Morgan) and manufacturers who were supplying England and her allies with loans and munitions. This, Ford agreed with Secretary of State William Jennings Bryan, was a clear violation of the spirit, if not the letter, of neutrality. By heavily underwriting the Allied war effort with loans and trade, the United States was, in effect, marrying itself to the Allied cause. Even though most of the loans were secured with collateral, the economic repercussions of Allied defeat would shake the United States. The stakes, moreover, were high. American loans, mainly to England, amounted to $2.3 billion by 1917. The corresponding figure for Germany and the Central Powers was only $27 million.

For his own part, Ford vowed that he would sooner burn his factory to the ground than build a single vehicle for war purposes. Furthermore, he completely rejected preparedness—the idea that the United States should get ready for the possibility of war. But his position was not universally popular in the Ford Motor Company. James Couzens, an original partner and the company treasurer, led the dissent. A Canadian of English parentage, Couzens was vigorously pro-Allies. When a German submarine sank the British liner *Lusitania* on May 7, 1915, Couzens joined many Americans in crying for a declaration of war against Germany. Ford, however, stood firm. Of the *Lusitania*'s passengers he dryly remarked, "Well, they were fools to go on that boat, because they were warned." Furious, Couzens quit the Ford Motor Company in October.

The following month Henry Ford's pacifism took a more active turn. The occasion was a meeting with Rosika Schwimmer, a dashing Hungarian, and Louis Lochner, the young American secretary of the International Federation of Students. Both were militant pacifists and expert persuaders. Ford soon found himself committed to the idea of establishing a commission of neutral nations to devise an acceptable peace for the belligerents. At a meeting in New York on November 21, 1915, Ford jumped at Lochner's half-humorous idea of chartering a ship to take the peace delegates to Europe. Jane Addams, who attended the meeting, protested the flamboyance of the idea, but for Ford that was precisely the point. Before nightfall *Oscar II* had been chartered from an amazed steamship company, and Ford was preparing to meet Woodrow Wilson in Washington. There he received his first reversal. The president was polite, even to the point of sharing his favorite joke about Ford cars with his guests, but he would not endorse the idea of a peace commission. Disgusted, Ford branded Wilson "a small man" who had missed a great opportunity.

With the project hanging in the balance, Ford decided to persevere. Years of engineering experiments had given him a where-there's-a-will-there's-a-way doggedness. On November 24, 1915, he called a news conference in New York. Always an embarrassed public speaker, he managed to tell the assembled reporters that "we're going to get the boys out of the trenches before Christmas. I've chartered a ship, and some of us are going to Europe." The seasoned reporters, who also tended to be pro-British, were first astonished and then convulsed with laughter. Their stories poked fun at the rich rustic who thought he could build a peace the way he built a car. *Oscar II* was termed a "loon ship" and the original "ship of fools." On the floor of the U.S. Senate Ford's delegation was styled "an aggregation of neurotics." Even Ford's wife and closest friends begged him to drop the project. But on December 4, 1915, *Oscar II* left New York harbor after a rousing sendoff. On board was the most distinguished group of Americans Ford's representatives had been able to accumulate with just nine days' notice. But most of the big names, including the now ill Jane Addams, were missing.

During the voyage to Norway, Ford wandered aimlessly among his guests, striking one reporter as "the vaguest of the vague, a comic, charming child." The only exception was when he slipped below deck to study the ship's engines. In Europe the inevitable debacle played itself out quickly. Ford became ill in the bitter Norwegian winter and returned to the United States within a week. Before following him, the delegates toured the nonbelligerent nations and established a Neutral Conference for Continuous Mediation. But the animosities of the belligerents proved too strong to settle at the conference table. When Ford withdrew support early in 1917, the conference collapsed. His flirtation with pacifism had cost him over $450,000. But, in retrospect, Ford's attempt to end the war does not seem as quixotic as it did to some of his compatriots in 1915. The underlying principles of peace that the conference advanced were remarkably similar to Woodrow Wilson's Fourteen Points. And the idea of a permanent organization devoted to world peace subsequently bore fruit in the League of Nations and the United Nations.

Although Ford was a pacifist, he was also a fervent nationalist—a believer in and an exponent of the American way. When the United States declared war on Germany in April 1917, Ford was therefore quick to agree that "we must stand behind the President." Indeed, he had changed his mind about Wilson since the abortive peace ship interview. The president, Ford felt, had sincerely tried to mediate the European war. His "peace without victory" speech of January 22, 1917, seemed to Ford to express some of the ideals behind the *Oscar II.* But Wilson had also failed and come to the reluctant conclusion that militarism could best be fought with militarism, a war to end war. American entry on the Allied side came in April 1917, when Wilson could no longer tolerate German attacks on American shipping. Ford agreed, and after American entrance into World War I, he placed his factory at the disposal of the government and its allies.

Ultimately, the Great War claimed the lives of more than fifteen million people worldwide and introduced the world to tanks, poison gas, submarines, and aerial warfare. Responding to the Allies' technological needs in the eighteen months following America's entry into the war, the Ford Motor Company built aircraft engines, ambulances, tanks, submarine chasers, and even helmets and gas masks. When the armistice came on November 11, 1918, Ford had the satisfaction of knowing he had made a major economic contribution to ending the conflict.

In the 1920s Henry Ford reached the zenith of his career. Few names were better known in the United States. Whether one read his publications (mostly ghostwritten), followed his headline-making public life, or merely drove the Model T, Ford was an inescapable part of the postwar culture. The flivver (as Americans dubbed the Model T), the flask, and the flapper seemed to symbolize the age. Cars, especially, characterized what many thought was a new era. They upset familiar patterns of living, loving, working, recreating, and even thinking. Much of the roar of the twenties came from the internal combustion engine. While providing portable bedrooms in which to enjoy sexual freedom, cars also helped gangsters and bootleggers get away from the authorities. The image of two cars in every garage helped elect a president in 1928. The "lost" generation was a generation on wheels, supposedly spinning to endless parties through the pages of F. Scott Fitzgerald novels. And Henry Ford, preaching the gospel of the machine, seemed to herald the coming of modernity.

Beneath the surface, however, such generalizations ring hollow. Neither Ford nor the 1920s merit the clichés with which each has so frequently been saddled. In the case of the man, both the old and the new mingled in his mind. On the one hand, Ford was a builder and bulwark of the modern, mechanized, urbanized nation; on the other, he devoted a remarkable amount of effort and expense to sustaining traditional America. The nostalgic, backward-looking Ford repeatedly deplored the very conditions that Ford the revolutionary industrialist had done so much to bring about.

This ambivalence did not signify a lack of values so much as a superfluity of them. Hardly "lost," Ford's faith was strong, if bigoted and contradictory. His prescriptions for the United States were clear, if sometimes simpleminded. To the mass of citizens, Ford seemed to demonstrate that there could be change without disruption, and in doing so, he eased the anxieties engendered by a time of rapid and often bewildering change. "The average citizen," editorialized the *New Republic* in 1923, "sees Ford as a sort of enlarged crayon portrait of himself; the man able to fulfill his own suppressed desires, who has achieved enormous riches, fame and power without departing from the pioneer-and-home-spun tradition." In this nervous clinging to old values, even while undermining them, Ford was indeed a "crayon portrait" of the 1920s.

But was Ford typical of Americans in these years? Can he really be said to symbolize the postwar age? He was, after all, in his middle fifties when the decade began. But a great many Americans were also middle-aged in the 1920s, far more, in fact, than the twenty-year-old collegians who have hitherto characterized these years. And at one point even a group of college students ranked Ford as the third greatest figure of all time, behind Napoleon and Jesus. It is also relevant that Ford possessed considerable political appeal after World War I. He narrowly lost a race for the U.S. Senate in 1918, and five years later his candidacy for president of the United States was widely discussed and supported. For many Americans, Ford was the most respected public figure of the time.

Fortunately for the historian, if not always for himself, Ford tended to state his opinions forthrightly on a wide variety of subjects outside his field of competence. He also had the money to publish and otherwise implement his ideas. The resulting portrait is that of a mind steeped in traditional Americanism. For Ford in the 1920s, agrarian simplicity and McGuffey morality were still sacred. So was the United States, with its heritage of freedom, fairness, and hard, honest labor. Ford's confidence in the old-fashioned virtues verged on the fanatical. The "Spirit of '76," equal-opportunity democracy, rugged individualism, the home, and motherhood were his touchstones. "More men are beaten than fail," he declared in 1928. "It is not wisdom they need, or money, or brilliance, or pull, but just plain gristle and bone." In the *Dearborn Independent*, "Mr. Ford's Page" stated that "one of the great things about the American people is that they are pioneers." This thought led easily to a restatement of the concept of American mission. "No one can contemplate the nation to which we belong," Ford continued, "without realizing the distinctive prophetic character of its obvious mission to the world. We are pioneers. We are the pathfinders. We are the road-builders. We are the guides, the vanguards of Humanity." Theodore Roosevelt and Woodrow Wilson had said as much, but Ford was writing *after* the war that had allegedly ended the nation's innocence and mocked its mission.

Ford's intense commitment to the traditional American faith led him to suspect and ultimately to detest whatever was un-American. The same loyalties compelled him to search for explanations for the unpleasant aspects of civilization in the 1920s that exonerated the old-time, "native" citizen. The immigrants were the primary targets of Ford's fire. In editorial after editorial and in several books, Ford argued that aliens who had no conception of "the principles which have made our civilization" were responsible for its "marked deterioration" in the twenties. He enthusiastically supported the Immigration Acts of 1921 and 1924, which used the quota system to reduce sharply the number of immigrants entering the country.

Ford also became a subscriber to the tired myth of an international Jewish conspiracy. When he could not find sufficient evidence for such a plot to take over the country, if not the world, Ford dispatched special agents to probe the affairs of prominent Jews and collect documentation. The search resulted in the "discovery" of the so-called Protocols of the Learned Elders of Zion. Although they were exposed as a forgery in 1921, Ford continued to use the Protocols to prove the existence of a Jewish scheme to overthrow the gentile elite. He also managed to blame everything wrong with the modern United States, from jazz to the "fixing" of the 1919 World Series, on the Jewish presence.

Ford's attack on the Jews was only a part of a general wave of insecurity and intolerance that swept through American society after World War I. First came the Red Scare of 1919, in which suspected communists were hounded and in some cases deported by self-styled patriots. The distorted nativism of nervous minds continued in the 1920s under the white gowns and masks of the second edition of the Ku Klux Klan (KKK). Launched in 1915 by a never-say-die southerner, the KKK had risen to nationwide power and a membership of five million by 1924. Ford was not a Klansman, but his anti-Semitism found a receptive audience in the Klan. In addition, the KKK hated Roman Catholics, blacks, urbanites, "wets" (antiprohibitionists), and liberals of all shades. In the minds of its members, who were not only concentrated in the rural areas and small towns of the South and the Midwest, but also in eastern urban centers, the KKK was a bastion of the national morality. The new Klan was America's front line of defense against evil, degeneracy, and, as it frequently happened, modernism. Nervous about the present and fearful of the future, the Klansmen yearned for a seemingly simpler and purer past.

So did Ford. The tension in his thought between old and new, nostalgia and progress, is dramatically illustrated in his attitude toward farming and farmers. On the one hand, he believed farm life to be a ceaseless round of inefficient drudgery. Indeed, he had abundant personal evidence from his Dearborn boyhood. "I have traveled 10,000 miles behind a plow," he remarked at one point. "I hated the grueling grind of farm work." With the incentive of sparing others this painful experience, Ford addressed himself to the problem of industrializing agriculture. Farmers in Ford's opinion, should become technicians and businesspeople. Tractors (Fords, of course) should replace horses. Mechanization would make it possible to produce in twenty-five working days what formerly required an entire year. Fences would come down, and vast economies of scale would occur. Agriculture, in a word, would be revolutionized by the same techniques of mass production that had transformed American industry. And Ford's modern farmers would not even live on their farms but instead would commute from a city home. To prove his point, Ford bought and operated a 9,000-acre farm near Dearborn.

Yet the Ford who was the so-called father of modern agriculture was only part of the man. He also retained a strong streak of old-fashioned horse-and-buggy agrarianism. Farming, from this perspective, was more than a challenge in production; it was a moral act. So even while his cars made it possible, Ford lashed out at the modern city as a "pestiferous growth." In the manner of Thomas Jefferson, he continually contrasted the "unnatural," "twisted," and "cooped up" lives of city dwellers with the "wholesome" life of "independence" and "sterling honesty" that the rural environment offered. "What children and adults need," he told one reporter, "is a chance to breathe God's fresh air and to stretch their legs and have a little garden in the soil." This ideal led Ford to choose small towns instead of cities as the sites of his branch factories. "Turning back to village industry," Ford declared in 1926, would enable Americans to reestablish a sense of community—with nature and with each other—that urbanization had destroyed.

Ford's enthusiasm for nature did not stop with ruralism. From 1914 to 1924 he sought a more complete escape from civilization on a series of camping trips with Thomas Edison, the naturalist and writer John Burroughs, and the tire king Harvey Firestone. Although the gear these self-styled "vagabonds" took to the woods was far from primitive, they apparently shared a genuine love of the outdoors. In Burroughs's words, Ford and his friends "cheerfully endure wet, cold, smoke, mosquitoes, black flies, and sleepless nights, just to touch naked reality once more."

Ford had a special fondness for birds. Characteristically, he had 500 birdhouses built on his Michigan farm, including one with seventy-six apartments—the "bird hotel." There were also electric heaters and brooders for Ford's fortunate birds. The whole production mixed technology and nature in a way that symbolized his ambivalence.

As for roads and automobiles, Ford saw them not as a threat to natural conditions, but as a way for the average American to come into contact with nature. The machine and the garden were not incompatible. Ford declared he could not agree with those who saw mechanization leading to a "cold, metallic sort of world in which great factories will drive away the trees, the flowers, the birds and the green fields." According to Ford, "Unless we know more about machines and their use . . . we cannot have the time to enjoy" nature. But such statements only partly covered Ford's nervousness about the mechanized, urbanized future. The contradictions persisted. The same man who envisaged fenceless bonanza farms could say, "I love to walk across country and jump fences." The lover of trees could state, in utmost seriousness, "Better wood can be made than is grown."

Ford's attitude toward history has been the subject of considerable misunderstanding. The principal source of confusion is a statement that received wide publicity in 1919 in connection with his libel suit against the *Chicago Tribune*. "History," Ford is supposed to have said, "is more or less the bunk. It is tradition. We don't want tradition. We want to live in the present, and the only history that is worth a tinker's dam is the history we make today." On another occasion Ford admitted that he "wouldn't give a nickel for all the history in the world." Complementing this sentiment is Ford's reputation as a forward-looking inventor and revolutionary industrialist dissatisfied with the old processes. Here, it seems, was a man fully at home in the alleged new era of the 1920s. But in fact Ford idolized the past. His "History is . . . the bunk" remark referred to ancient history as it was taught in the schools. For what had actually happened in America's past, and its tangible evidence, Ford had only praise.

The most obvious evidence of Ford's enthusiasm for history was his collector's instinct. He began with that bastion of his own youth, the *McGuffey Readers*. By sending agents to scour the countryside with no limits on cost, Ford had, by 1925, accumulated one of the few complete collections of the many McGuffey editions. To share their wisdom with his contemporaries, he had thousands of copies of *Old Favorites from the McGuffey Readers* printed in 1926. The book contained such classics as "Try, Try Again" and "The Hare and the Tortoise." It dispensed an ideal of individualism and self-reliance at the same time that Ford's assembly lines were transforming workers into cogs in an impersonal machine.

From books, Ford turned to the collection of things, and during the 1920s, he amassed the most extensive collection of Americana in existence. He bought so widely and so aggressively that he became a major factor in antique market prices. Everything was fair game. Lamps and dolls, bells and grandfather clocks, made their way to his museum, along with machines of all descriptions. Ford delighted in showing visitors around. Playing a few chords on an antique organ, he would remark, "That takes me back to my boyhood days. They were beautiful days." This sentiment undoubtedly figured in Ford's decision to restore his boyhood home. Everything had to be exactly as he remembered it. Furniture, china, and rugs were rehabilitated or reconstructed. He even hired archaeologists to dig the ground around the family homestead to a depth of six feet in the hope of recovering Ford artifacts.

After restoring the homestead, Ford turned to reconstructing an entire pioneer town. Greenfield Village, Michigan, became a monument to Ford's reverence for the past. "I am trying," he explained, "to help America take a step . . . toward the saner and sweeter idea of life that prevailed in pre-war days." Greenfield had gravel roads, gas street lamps, a grassy common, and an old-fashioned country store. The automobile king permitted only horse-drawn vehicles on the premises. The genius of the assembly line engaged individual artisans to practice their crafts in the traditional—and obsolete—manner. In time, the boyhood cottages of Walt Whitman, Patrick Henry, and William Holmes McGuffey were purchased and transported to Greenfield.

Ford's money also saved historic sites in other parts of the country. In 1922, he bought the celebrated Wayside Inn at Sudbury, Massachusetts, and opened it as a museum for the public's edification. But a new highway ran too near; the roar of the automobile disturbed the horse-and-buggy atmosphere. So Ford had the state highway rerouted around the shrine at a cost of $250,000. He also restored the schoolhouse in Sudbury, which was supposed to be the site where Mary had gamboled with her little lamb, and the village blacksmith's shop. History then, was not "bunk" to Henry Ford. The speed of change seemed to increase proportionately his desire to retain contact with a past he believed had been wholesome, happy, and secure. "The Old Ways," as the *Dearborn Independent* declared, "Were Good."

Ford's opinion of the new morality of the Jazz Age was predictably low. He deplored the use of tobacco and even went so far as to publish tracts against smoking. When he had the power, he went beyond exhortation. "No one smokes in the Ford industries," their leader proclaimed in 1929. As for alcohol, Ford was a fanatical prohibitionist. The Eighteenth Amendment and the Volstead Act, which in theory made the United States "dry" after January 16, 1920, were for Ford a great triumph. Any Ford worker suspected of drinking publicly or even keeping liquor at home was immediately dismissed. "There are a million boys growing up in the United States," Ford exulted, "who have never seen a saloon and who will never know the handicap of liquor." When confronted with evidence of bootlegging and the existence of speakeasies, Ford offered his standard explanation of evil: a Jewish conspiracy. The mass of Americans, he believed, "were, like himself, dry by moral conviction as well as by law."

Prohibiting the manufacture and sale of alcohol did reduce American consumption for a time during the 1920s. But despite being an experiment "noble in motive," as Herbert Hoover put it, an edict of total abstinence proved impossible to enforce. Immigrants who had come to the United States from southern and eastern Europe during the past fifty years consumed alcohol daily and were quite reluctant to stop doing so. Meanwhile, wealthy urban whites had stocked up their cellars and clubs with extended liquor supplies before the Volstead Act took effect. As humorist Will Rogers observed during the first full winter of Prohibition, it was a "good thing we have had a nice warm winter this year or people would not have had any room in their Cellars for their coal." Many more Americans resorted to brewing their own beer and distilling their own "bathtub gin." And "bootleggers" (so-called for carrying booze concealed in containers inside their high-topped boots) operated in all parts of the country, selling to whomever could meet their price. Sometimes their liquor was pure enough, but, by the end of the twenties, thousands of Americans had died from drinking lethal concoctions distilled from rubbing alcohol or other toxic substances.

Although many politicians had buckled under the pressure to enact Prohibition, Congress never provided adequate funding to enforce the law. Such lax enforcement gave rise to large-scale organized crime centered in large metropolitan areas. Gangsters like Al Capone and Frank Nitty of Chicago's "Scarface Mob" and Detroit's "Purple Gang" were ready to supply the drinking needs of people willing to break what was becoming an unenforceable law as the Roaring Twenties progressed. Speakeasies sprang up in every town of any size; one simply had to knock, say the password, and enter a swinging nightclub, replete with booze and gambling. Despite the obvious failure of Prohibition, Henry Ford continued to believe in a pure America, dry and sober by choice.

Sex was too delicate a matter to be addressed directly, but Ford conveyed his opinions through a discussion of music and dancing. Few things about the twenties worried him more than jazz. The new music clashed squarely with his ruralism and Bible Belt morality. In 1921, Ford struck out savagely at the "sly suggestion and abandoned sensuousness" of jazz, which sounded like "monkey talk, jungle squeals, grunts and squeaks and gasps suggestive of cave love." To counter the unhealthy influence, Ford promoted traditional folk dances. Backwoods fiddlers were often invited to Dearborn to play "Old Zip Coon" and "The Arkansas Traveler." Ford also undertook the revival of traditional social dancing. In 1926, a guidebook appeared entitled *"Good Morning": After a Sleep of Twenty-five Years Old-fashioned Dancing Is Being Revived by Mr. and Mrs. Henry Ford*. The essential purpose of the book, however, was to revive old-fashioned morality. It began by condemning as promiscuous the newer dances such as the Charleston and the whole flapper syndrome. "A gentleman," the book explained, "should be able to guide his partner through a dance without embracing her as if he were her lover." Proper deportment, according to Ford, minimized physical contact. There were elaborate rules regarding gloves, handkerchiefs, and ways to request a dance. The guidebook, in short, was a monument to nineteenth-century conceptions of morality, decorum, and order. So were the dances Ford and his wife hosted at Dearborn. Precisely at nine, Ford's guests convened in evening dress in a lavish tribute to Victorianism.

Ambivalence is the key to the mind of Henry Ford. He looked both forward and backward. As confidently progressive as he was in some respects, he remained uneasy about the new ways. And the more conditions changed, the more Ford groped nostalgically for the security of traditional values and institutions. He was neither "lost" nor dissipated and "roaring." And in the Jazz Age, he hated jazz. Yet Ford was popular to the point of being a deity in the 1920s. As a plain, honest, old-fashioned billionaire, a technological genius who loved to camp out, he seemed to his contemporaries to resolve the moral dilemmas of the age. Like Charles A. Lindbergh, another god of the era who combined the characteristics of pioneer and technologist, Ford testified to the nation's ability to move into the future without losing sight of the past.

While Ford labored to shape the nation's morality, the continued expansion of his company and his reputation involved him in the mainstream of its politics and economy. Over two decades of effort had left Americans weary of heroics; the ideal of reform now gave way to the pursuit of personal success. The insipid Warren G. Harding was well qualified to preside over the return to what he called "normalcy" in the years immediately following World War I. Ford did not support Harding in the election of 1920. Still a pacifist and a believer in international cooperation such as the League of Nations represented, he voted for and contributed to the unsuccessful Democratic team of James M. Cox and Franklin D. Roosevelt. Warren Harding's administration proved to be one of the most corrupt in American history. The most notorious of the Harding scandals concerned oil. The problem began with the appointment of Albert B. Fall as Harding's secretary of the interior. No sooner was Fall in office than he arranged for the president to transfer federal oil reserves from the jurisdiction of the Department of the Navy to that of his own Department of the Interior operation. It was like putting sheep in the care of a wolf. Fall promptly leased the oil fields at Teapot Dome in Wyoming and Elk Hills in California to two private developers, Edward L. Doheny and Harry F. Sinclair, in return for bribes amounting to almost $500,000. In 1924, a year after Harding had died, a Senate investigating committee convened in Washington, and later in Los Angeles. Although both oilmen were acquitted, Sinclair served prison time for contempt of Congress and tampering with a jury. Fall was convicted in 1929 of bribery, fined $100,000, and jailed for a year—the first cabinet member in American history to achieve this distinction. The oil leases were canceled, and the oil reserves were restored to the jurisdiction of the Department of the Navy.

The Teapot Dome affair was only one of several scandals involving Harding administration officials: Corruption was discovered in the Veterans Bureau; Harding's attorney general was forced to resign amid scandalous revelations; and two of the president's advisers committed suicide. Harding himself may have been honest, but several people in his administration were not. As the dark clouds gathered around his administration, Harding himself died of a heart attack in San Francisco on August 2, 1923.

Almost immediately, Ford found himself seriously considered as a successor to Harding. The "Ford for President" movement had gained momentum rapidly in 1922, and by 1923 Henry seemed ahead of the pack. His stern ethical code and anti-Semitism attracted followers in the South and the Midwest, while his success as a manufacturer had nationwide appeal. At first, Ford was not interested. His narrow loss to Truman H. Newberry in the 1918 Michigan senatorial election had left him disenchanted with politics. But the presidential fever was hard to resist. Running the government, Ford began to think, was no different from running a factory.

The people closest to Henry Ford were amazed by his presidential ambitions. Edison reminded his friend of his chronic shyness in public situations, adding, "You can't speak. You wouldn't say a damned word. You'd be mum." Less friendly critics such as Oswald Garrison Villard of the *Nation* declared they had never encountered a candidate "so absolutely unfit" for the presidency. Even Clara Ford wrote indignantly to her husband's staff, "Since you got him into it, you can just get him out of it. I hate this idea of the name of Ford being dragged down into the gutters of political filth. My name is Ford, and I'm proud of it! If Mr. Ford wants to go to Washington, he can go, but I'll go to England." With this kind of support at home, Ford must have had second thoughts, but the decisive blow came when Harding died. Calvin Coolidge, the taciturn Vermonter who had gained a nationwide reputation by using the power of the governorship of Massachusetts to break a Boston police strike in 1919, proved politically attractive. The professional politicians who had previously shown an interest in Ford now switched to Coolidge. Late in 1923, Ford himself came out for Coolidge.

Behind Ford's decision lay the story of Muscle Shoals, which was a major rapid on the Tennessee River in northern Alabama. During World War I the federal government had made plans to harness its power and develop nitrate plants. Over $100 million went into the Muscle Shoals complex, but funds ran out before it was operative. In 1921, the installations were rusting away, to the disgust of a disciple of efficiency like Henry Ford. So he offered the government $5 million for Muscle Shoals, provided that the United States complete the Wilson Dam at a cost of $50 million. From Ford's point of view, this was surely one of the best buys in the history of business. Furthermore, it opened the possibility of acquiring extensive land holdings in the Tennessee Valley and reaping the monetary rewards of the region's rebirth.

Ford's critics, chiefly Senator George W. Norris of Nebraska, denounced the entire proposition as "the most wonderful real estate speculation since Adam and

Eve lost title to the Garden of Eden." Hostile journalists branded Muscle Shoals "The Biggest GRAB Ever Attempted in America." Still, many fully expected that Ford could do for the Tennessee Valley what he had done for the automobile. Thousands of "pioneers" swarmed into the upper South in 1922. The Ford organization stood ready to swing into action, and the political climate of Harding's Washington was generally favorable. But George Norris, doggedly insisting that the government should develop the area in the public interest, held Ford at bay almost singlehandedly.

This was the context in which Henry Ford and Calvin Coolidge met for private interviews in September and again in December 1923. We will never know precisely what was said, but the topics of discussion were almost certainly the election of 1924 and Muscle Shoals. A few days after the December meeting, Coolidge recommended to Congress the sale of Muscle Shoals to an unnamed private interest. Almost simultaneously, Ford publicly announced the abandonment of his presidential plans, thereby clearing the way for Coolidge in the election of 1924. Ford got the worst of the deal. Coolidge won in 1924, but Ford never got Muscle Shoals. Senator Norris, whose dream eventually materialized into the Tennessee Valley Authority, blocked approval of the sale.

The collapse of Ford's Muscle Shoals bid was one of the few reversals that big business suffered in the United States during the 1920s. Determined to undo the "damage" inflicted on capitalism by the progressive reformers, Harding and his cabinet were unabashedly probusiness. Herbert Hoover, the secretary of commerce, was a self-made millionaire who construed his function as protecting fortunes such as his own. Secretary of the Treasury Andrew Mellon, a multimillionaire from Pittsburgh, declared that "the Government is just a business and can and should be run on business principles." To Mellon, this meant that the taxation of the rich should be sharply reduced. He believed it was better strategy to tax the lower-income groups heavily and thus free the rich to promote economic growth by investment. In time, Mellon argued, the benefits would trickle down to the less fortunate. Ford was a case in point. His enormous, largely tax-free profits had allowed him to institute the five-dollar and later the six-dollar and seven-dollar days for his employees.

Andrew Mellon did not see his soak-the-poor tax structure fully implemented, but the Harding administration was able to help big business with the tariff. The Fordney-McCumber Act of 1922 made possible duties so high as to exclude foreign competition completely. Businesses confined to the United States applauded the protection as a step toward monopoly, but for the Ford Motor Company and other internationally oriented concerns, high tariffs hurt trade. Ford's protest, however, was a minority voice in the business community.

The Harding administration left office on a wave of scandal, but Coolidge continued the postwar Republican tradition of favoritism toward the rich. After prevailing in 1924 over Democrat John Davis and Progressive Robert La Follette, Coolidge declared forthrightly that "the business of America is business." On another occasion, perhaps with Henry Ford in mind, he stated that "the man who builds a factory builds a temple." The federal government, Coolidge believed, should withdraw as much as possible from involvement in the economy. Within the broad framework of the law, business should have an unobstructed opportunity to pursue the main chance. The 1920s witnessed a revival of the socioeconomic philosophy of Andrew Carnegie's Gilded Age.

Herbert Hoover, who defeated Democrat Alfred E. Smith for the presidency in 1928, typified in his career and his thought the ideals of the age. In fact, Hoover was probably the only real competition Henry Ford encountered in the gallery of public heroes of the twenties. Left an orphan in 1884 at the age of ten, Hoover grew up to an international mining career that made him rich. During World War I he became famous as head of the American Relief Commission abroad and the U.S. Food Administration at home. A genius in matters of large-scale efficiency, like Ford, Hoover neatly executed apparent miracles. In 1922, while secretary of commerce under Harding, he set forth his creed in a slender volume entitled *American Individualism*. Its message was one of rugged individualism and free enterprise. Hoover staunchly defended the unregulated profit system. Society and government owed the people only three things: "liberty, justice, and equality of opportunity." Competition took care of the rest, carrying the deserving to their just rewards and the failures to deserved defeat. Any interference, such as philanthropy or favoritism, only dulled "the emery wheel of competition" and retarded progress. Hoover paid lip service to restricting the strong in the interest of society as a whole, but the main thrust of his thought was directed toward awarding the victors their spoils.

When Hoover began his term in the White House early in 1929, there were few surface indications of the economic collapse just around the corner. "I have no fear for the future of our country," the president announced in company with most members of the Establishment. "It is bright with hope." On the surface, there was much to support this prognosis. Riding the momentum of a five-year boom, the stock market pushed to ever higher levels. Business seemed good. In Detroit the Ford Motor Company had just completed a changeover from the Model T to the Model A and, after two lean years, was solidly in the black. Its mighty River Rouge plant was now in full operation in a location accessible to oceangoing vessels using the Saint Lawrence–Great Lakes waterway. Like Carnegie before him, Ford gradually consolidated all phases of production under his ownership. Ford iron ore, Ford logs, and Ford coal came to the Rouge and were converted by Ford smelters and mills into Ford cars by an army of more than 100,000 workers. Prosperity seemed a permanent American possession. When breaks in speculators' confidence in 1928 and early 1929 caused sudden sharp drops in stock prices, most Americans were not overly concerned. The buyers would return. Ford and Hoover agreed with Andrew Mellon, who offered the calm if unfounded assurance that "there is no cause for worry. The high tide of prosperity will continue."

By the late summer of 1929, however, Mellon's "tide" was being sustained largely by statements like his own. The nation's prosperity was one of belief rather than fact, of paper rather than property. Granted that hindsight is always twenty-twenty, still it is surprising that the nation's business and political leaders did not recognize the symptoms. Perhaps they did not want to see, because the signs were there for those who dared to look. One was the limited nature of the prosperity of the 1920s. Substantial segments of society simply had not shared in the allegedly good years of the decade. It was not that they had lost money, but that the gap between their incomes and the cost of living had widened steadily. A dollar bought less and less. The result was a tendency for consumption to lag behind production. America's economy was topheavy and, consequently, unstable.

Agriculture was another area of instability. A host of factors caused the "prosperity decade" to be anything but prosperous for the American farmer. To stimulate commodity production for World War I, the federal government had encouraged farmers to plant more crops. High wartime demand had stimulated prices, but as soon as European farms went back into production, American farm profits began to decline. Heedless of the need to cut back, farmers continued to produce at wartime levels, and prices continued their downward spiral throughout the 1920s. Rural poverty, generated by falling farm prices, no doubt contributed to prosperity in the urban United States. Cheaper food and fabric provided urbanites with more disposable income, but, for farmers, prices fell as costs continued to rise. To combat this situation, farmers lobbied for government support of agricultural prices. Many ideas coalesced in bills sponsored by Senator Charles McNary of Oregon and Representative Gilbert Haugen of Iowa. They proposed that the federal government purchase agricultural surpluses and thereby support prices at "parity" (the pre-World War I level). Advocates of the McNary-Haugen plan argued that they were asking no more than the equivalent of the protective tariff that supported prices on manufactured goods. But in the 1920s the business of the United States was business, and Coolidge vetoed McNary-Haugen bills in 1927 and 1928. His successor, Herbert Hoover, followed suit. Farm incomes and rural purchasing power continued to decline.

The agricultural depression cut a wide swath across the rural United States. Cotton farmers, who had received 35 cents per pound for their crop in 1919, sold "5-cent cotton" in 1932. Wheat farmers had been paid $2.16 per bushel in 1919; by 1931, they could get only 38 cents for the same amount. Between 1929 and 1932, farm commodity prices in the United States dropped 63 percent. Iowa and Nebraska farmers burned ears of corn in their fireplaces to keep warm, while, in 1931, a Colorado rancher brought seven lambs to market for slaughter and received a check for 75 cents! A crisis existed in the rural United States throughout the 1920s.

American laborers also experienced harder and harder times after World War I. In Detroit inflation and the rising cost of living ate into Ford's renowned $5.00 minimum wage. By the end of 1918, the $5.00 was worth $2.80 in prewar currency. To his credit, Ford realized that high wages meant high production, high consumption, and general prosperity. In 1919, he set the minimum in his factories at $6.00 per day. But this gave the worker only $3.36 in 1914 dollars. Labor unions and collective bargaining, which might have alleviated the situation, faced widespread hostility after the war. In 1919, attempts of steelworkers and coalworkers to improve their lot by strikes were put down by the combined might of the federal government and business management. The courts issued injunctions that forced striking workers back to their jobs. They also upheld anti-union "yellow-dog" contracts and allowed the Clayton Act, originally construed as prolabor, to be turned against unions. A decision of the Supreme Court in *Hamer v. Dagenhart* (1918) invalidated all laws aimed at restricting child labor. In 1922, Harding used the threat of federal troops to reopen coal mines with wages slashed 50 percent.

Labor leaders added to their own problems. The craft unions like the American Federation of Labor were still afraid to attempt to organize masses of unskilled workers industrywide. Without organization, laborers in industries such as steel, food packing, chemicals, and automobiles were helpless. Ford, for example, steadfastly refused to permit unions to gain a foothold in his plants; he claimed he knew best how to take care of his workers. Granted that working conditions and wages at Ford in the 1920s were better than the national average, still the refusal of the foremost industrialist of the age to sanction unions had an adverse national effect. Ford had pioneered in wage reforms; he might have set the pace in making negotiation rather than dictation the norm in labor–management relations. As it was, union membership declined steadily in the twenties.

Farmers and laborers were not alone in unsuccessfully trying to gain a larger share of the nation's wealth in the years before the great crash. Small entrepreneurs and professional people such as doctors, lawyers, and teachers also felt the economic pinch. Until late 1929, the luxury and investments of the rich gave the appearance of national prosperity, but a situation in which one-third of all personal income went to one-twentieth of the population was highly vulnerable. When the crash and the subsequent depression curtailed high-income spending, there was insufficient lower- and middle-income consumption to support the economy. Exports might have alleviated the falling demand, but the high-tariff policies of the Republican administrations since Harding discouraged foreign trade just when it was most needed.

Another weakness was the unstable nature of America's corporate and banking structure. Like a row of dominoes, poorly financed organizations were poised to fall. The problem was rampant speculation, which, in the late 1920s, reached the proportions of a national mania. Borrowing far beyond their means, individuals and companies gambled on paper profits. Lending institutions facilitated the overextension. In time, the tangled threads of financial dependency were stretched thinner and thinner. When a break occurred, the whole structure came down with a crash.

With his new Model A outstripping General Motors' Chevrolet and Oldsmobile lines, Henry Ford was in the midst of a very good year when the bottom fell out of the American economy. It happened with sickening suddenness. In early September 1929 the *New York Times* average of selected industrial stocks stood at 452, up an unbelievable 200 points since early the previous year. By mid-November the *Times* stock average was 224. Panic selling, particularly on "Black Thursday" (October 24) and "Black Tuesday" (October 29), caused a paper loss of $26 billion in securities. By the middle of 1932, the *Times* stock average had dropped to 58. In Detroit Henry Ford kept close watch on the collapsing market but derived considerable satisfaction from the thought that "Ford" was not among the big losers on the stock exchange. Indeed, it was not even listed. Many years before, Ford had consolidated ownership of the Ford Motor Company in his immediate family. No stock had been sold to the investing public. As a result, the crash left Ford completely untouched in the short run.

Herbert Hoover, however, was worried. On November 29, 1929, he summoned Ford and other leaders of American business to a conference in Washington, where he pleaded with them not to cut wages or raise prices. Ford was glad to cooperate; in fact, he went the president one better. To the astonishment and dismay of some of the other conferees, he walked out of the meeting and announced that he was *lowering* prices on the Model A coupe by $35 and that his minimum daily wage would be *increased* from $6 to $7.

Ford's spectacular announcements can be understood as a symptom of his instinctive ability to grab the limelight, but they also reflected a basic confidence in the American economy. The crash was certainly disturbing, but along with Herbert Hoover and most fiscal experts of the day, Ford believed almost religiously in the self-regulating nature of the economy. In his opinion, the law of supply and demand would correct temporary economic imbalances provided it was allowed to operate without interference. The nation's only problem was too many people forsaking business for speculation. "A market," he blithely declared in *Moving Forward* (1930), "is never saturated with a good product." If Americans had concentrated on making good products (like the Model A, one presumes), rather than on making dollars, the Great Depression would never have occurred. For the same reason, its cure lay in "quantities of goods pushed out into the world" at low prices and in "building buying power" with high wages. In Ford's mind, "The wages of the workmen are more important to the country than the dividends to stockholders."

As the Depression deepened, Ford was unable to live up to these ideals. The seven-dollar day lasted only a year and three-quarters. And even those who received this rate found that their weekly pay envelopes contained less money because of cutbacks in the number of hours worked. Also, there were fewer laborers. From a high of 174,000 workers in 1929, Ford employment declined to fewer than 50,000 in 1933. River Rouge workers earned a total of $181 million in 1929; four years later the figure had declined to $32.5 million.

In some ways, Henry Ford's intense optimism made the precipitous fall of his company worse. The Ford system of ever-faster production relied on a continually expanding economy. Ford controlled all means of production to such a point that, when the economy slowed down, all elements of his company suffered. His rival carmaker, General Motors (GM), fared better as times got worse, even though GM sales did not reach their 1929 levels again until 1939. The main reasons GM fared better during the 1930s were diversity and the organizational skills of its president, Alfred P. Sloan. Sloan had transformed GM into a far more sophisticated company than Ford during the 1920s. Its products included refrigerators, locomotives, and, of course, an array of automobiles ranging from the inexpensive Chevrolet to the luxurious Cadillac. Sloan introduced long-range planning strategies, and allowed the autonomous divisions of the company to deal with short-term production. With superior marketing and service, interchangeable parts, and a variety of model choices, GM steadily overcame Ford's carmaking supremacy during the Depression. Unlike *Fordismus*, "Sloanism" acknowledged that the American economy would experience good and bad economic times and, through diversification and planning, found ways to make profits even in lean years.

To protect their profits, GM, Ford, and all American manufacturers slashed their work forces after the stock market crash. In Detroit and other urban-industrial areas throughout the nation, the sullen-faced jobless formed bread lines to receive what doles there were. Others trapped gophers for stew or combed garbage dumps in

Ten thousand impoverished New Yorkers were given a free meal on Christmas Day, 1931, at the Municipal Lodging House. Such "bread lines" became a symbol of the Great Depression.

search of edible food. Panhandlers—with their inevitable "Brother, can you spare a dime?"—were legion, but few brothers could. Some women were obliged to turn to prostitution to feed their husbands and children. Home for thousands of Americans was a shack in a makeshift community derisively called a "Hooverville." For bedding they used "Hoover blankets": old newspapers. In the United States, that promised land of abundance and opportunity, a dark age had come.

Aside from a few token contributions to local relief efforts in Dearborn, Ford dismissed the Depression as bad judgment on the part of some and bad luck on the part of others. His belief, like that of Herbert Hoover, was that welfare sapped the strength of American traditions of individualism and self-help. He also agreed with the president that the national budget should not be unbalanced in efforts to revive the economy or even to relieve suffering. This philosophy made Henry Ford appear to be the essence of heartless capitalism. In September 1930, as he boarded a luxurious ocean liner for a European vacation, he casually told the press, "It's a good thing the recovery is prolonged. Otherwise the people won't profit by the illness." In *Moving Forward*, published the same year, Ford echoed William Graham Sumner and Andrew Carnegie in declaring that "the very poor are recruited almost solely

The human pathos of the Great Depression is reflected in this March 1933 photograph of Seattle, Washington. Shantytowns like the one in the foreground were known as Hoovervilles in remembrance of the president whose term coincided with the beginnings of hard times. Looking from this misery to the skyscrapers in the background, many wondered what had gone wrong with the American dream.

from the people who refuse to . . . work diligently." The jobless were urged by farm boy Ford to "cultivate a plot of land" in the "good old pioneer way."

Despite such platitudes, it was clear that by 1932 things were getting worse instead of better. More than 5,000 banks failed between 1929 and 1932, and $15 billion in personal savings was lost with those failures. Fifty percent of all New England textile workers were unemployed by 1932, and months later, fifteen million American heads of household were out of work. The city of Detroit was near the breaking point. In March almost half the city's wage earners were unemployed, with no relief in sight. In this climate of desperation communist organizers succeeded in promoting a "hunger march" to dramatize the plight of the people. The target of the march was Ford's River Rouge plant, and many of the marchers were sometime Ford employees. A mile from the Rouge, Dearborn police intercepted the column, and a running battle involving tear gas, bricks, and bullets ensued. At the end, four marchers lay dead, and the Ford empire, guarded by Harry Bennett's corps of private police, was untouched.

Simultaneously in Washington, DC, thousands of unemployed veterans of World War I marched to reinforce demands for bonuses, which were not actually due until 1945. After House approval of the payment, however, the Senate rejected the measure, and most of the marchers went home. But 2,000 veterans refused to leave; they were driven out on the president's order by the Army under the direction of George Patton, Dwight Eisenhower, and Douglas MacArthur. After banishing the Bonus Army, the troops burned their shantytown near the Capitol. The specter of this incident led many thoughtful Americans to wonder if the political and economic system of their country could withstand the strain of hard times and, even more disturbingly, if it *should*.

Held in an atmosphere of tension verging on desperation, the election of 1932 loomed as the most significant since that of 1860. President Hoover had worked hard with a variety of political and economic tools to halt the Great Depression, but his commitment to free enterprise and the balanced budget hobbled his efforts. Ironically, the hero of American relief efforts in postwar Europe proved ineffective in alleviating the suffering of his own compatriots. Nonetheless, the Republicans renominated him. The Democrats chose the dynamic governor of New York, Franklin Delano Roosevelt.

Henry Ford, however, was not swept off his feet. He had voted Democratic for Wilson and peace in 1916. Four years later he had again supported the Democrats in a losing cause. But in 1924, after the collapse of his own presidential boom, he switched parties and voted for Calvin Coolidge. He was a Hoover man in 1928, and in 1932 he continued to support the man so like himself in origin and philosophy. Signs in Ford plants read: "To prevent times from getting worse and to help them get better, President Hoover must be reelected." In view of the scanty evidence supporting such an assumption, one must seek the real reasons for Ford's decision in 1932 in his incompatibility with Roosevelt.

Although the men had known each other during World War I when Roosevelt, as assistant secretary of the navy, handled Ford war contracts, they had little in common. Roosevelt was a patrician, born to wealth and educated at Harvard. Ford clung to a belief in the open, opportunity-filled world of Horatio Alger, William Holmes McGuffey, and the pioneers, a world in which effort and ability were always rewarded. Let things alone, he insisted, and in time the free enterprise system would find solutions to the country's problems. Roosevelt, on the contrary, believed that with the ending of the frontier the era of relatively equal opportunity had also ended. The government, he reasoned, must do for the country what the frontier had once done: ensure opportunity, security, and prosperity for the individual and for the nation as a whole. In the manner of his cousin Theodore's New Nationalism, Franklin Roosevelt proposed to meet concentrated economic power with the concentrated power of the federal government. The Depression would be legislated away even if it meant stepping on some traditionally sacrosanct toes.

Roosevelt campaigned on the theme of federal action, of "bold, persistent experimentation." He was, to be sure, vague about what this meant, and his economic thinking in 1932 was almost as conservative as Hoover's, but he seemed unafraid to lead in new directions. "Let it be . . . symbolic," he declared after making an unprecedented flight to Chicago to accept the Democratic nomination in person, "that . . . I broke traditions." And he concluded his acceptance speech, "I pledge myself to a new deal for the American people."

Despite Ford's opposition, Roosevelt gained a convincing victory (57 percent of the popular vote) in the election of 1932. It is significant that only one million out of forty million voting Americans opted against repairing the old system by supporting Socialist or Communist candidates. The nation sweated out the last months of the Hoover administration, which, by its own admission, was "at the end of our rope" as far as economic recovery was concerned. With Roosevelt's inauguration on March 4, 1933, the psychological depression, at least, was over. "The only thing we have to fear," the new president shouted into the cold, gray air of his inauguration day, "is fear itself." A whirlwind of action followed. Attacking simultaneously the problems of relief, recovery, and permanent reform, the New Deal at first commanded Henry Ford's respect. On May 8, 1933, he included a personal message in a company advertisement acknowledging Roosevelt as the man who had "turned the Ship of State around" and had set the nation's face toward the future. In particular, Ford approved of the new administration's concern for farmers (the Agricultural Adjustment Act) and its decision to use the neglected resources of Muscle Shoals and other hydropower sites in the Tennessee Valley.

It did not take long for Ford to change his mind, however, after Roosevelt signed the National Industrial Recovery Act (NIRA) in June 1933. This climax of the New Deal's first "hundred days" created the National Recovery Administration (NRA) under Hugh S. Johnson, a hard-boiled veteran of both military and business campaigns. The NRA's purpose was to persuade employers to stop cutting wages and firing employees, thus reducing demand and deepening the Depression. The tools for this task were "codes" of fair competition that established minimum wage and hour standards. Promulgated by the president, the codes had the force of law. They also benefited from favorable public opinion. Johnson exploited this advantage by branding the NRA the nation's best hope to check "the murderous doctrine of savage and wolfish individualism" and calling on everyone to ostracize code violators. Another important part of the NIRA was contained in its Section 7a, a guarantee to labor unions of the right to organize and bargain collectively.

Initially, the NRA was a decided success. Two million employers placed the administration's symbol, a blue eagle, in their places of business and tried to terminate wage and price cutting. Part of the automobile industry cooperated. Chrysler flew blue eagles from every flagstaff, and Chevrolet advertised that it was "proud and glad to do our part." Ford, however, held back. "We know that President Roosevelt wants to do the right and helpful thing," Ford told reporters on the day the NIRA was signed, but "I was always under the impression that to manage a business properly you ought to know something about it." Even the fact that the codes were to be drawn up by the industrialists themselves did not lessen Ford's opposition. He believed, with considerable justification, that his company had already taken steps to maintain high wages, and in his private notes, he grumbled at the New Deal's efforts to "kill competition." Another note read, "I do not think that this country is ready to be treated like Russia for a while. There is a lot of the pioneer spirit here yet." Of course this was unrealistic. It was the New Deal's great achievement that it managed to preserve the essence of capitalism while making it more responsive to national needs. In the desperate atmosphere of 1933, Roosevelt could well have moved toward the extremes of government control that Joseph Stalin and Adolf Hitler were imposing elsewhere at precisely the same time. Instead, the New Deal followed a middle way, reforming the free enterprise system in order to preserve it. In this endeavor Roosevelt had the support of the great majority.

Ford remained firmly in the minority. Despite Hugh Johnson's friendly pleadings and subsequent threats to administer a "sock in the nose" to "chiselers" who did not join the code agreements, the Ford Motor Company, with 24 percent of the nation's automobile production, refused to cooperate. Its leader advised his fellow industrialists to "forget these alphabet schemes [such as NRA] and take hold of their industries and run them with good, sound, American business sense." As a result of his resistance, Ford became a hero to right-wing opponents of the Roosevelt administration who in 1934 organized the Liberty League. Ford's reputation increased as Johnson unwisely overextended his bureau's efforts and invited the 1936 ruling of the Supreme Court (*Schechter Poultry v. U.S.*) that declared the NIRA unconstitutional. There was even talk of the seventy-three-year-old Ford as an opponent to Roosevelt in the election of 1936.

Henry Ford also stood athwart the mainstream of American thinking in his opposition to the organization of labor. As with the NRA codes, he felt the Ford Motor Company knew the interests of the workers and how best to serve them through company welfare programs. The bulk of his workers disagreed. Moreover, they believed they had the support of the majority of their peers. The New Deal had revived unionism after a sleep of a quarter century. Even after the invalidation of Section 7a of the NIRA, the National Labor Relations (Wagner) Act of 1935 maintained the principle of labor's right to organize and management's obligation to bargain in good faith. The American Federation of Labor responded with a successful campaign to organize skilled workers according to the philosophy of craft unionism. But in 1935 a powerful new force, operating on a new philosophy, entered the labor scene. The Committee (later Congress) of Industrial Organizations (CIO), under the leadership of John L. Lewis, operated on the belief that all the workers in a given industry should be organized in one big union. The automobile industry was a prime target of CIO attack. Working through the United Automobile Workers (UAW) under Walter Reuther, the CIO carried the fight to GM in the winter of 1936–1937. Using a new weapon, the "sitdown strike," which prevented the operation of a plant with nonunion workers, the UAW forced GM to the negotiating table in February 1937.

Ford was unmoved and determined to resist the unions, with force if necessary. What his policy meant became clear on May 26, 1937, when Reuther and other union leaders arrived at the gates of the Rouge to distribute circulars. A gang of Ford toughs, including professional wrestlers and boxers, constituted the reception committee. The union men were ordered to leave. As they started to obey, they were slugged from behind; kicked in the groin, head, and abdomen; and finally thrown down a flight of iron steps. The press was on hand to describe and photograph the entire proceedings of the "Battle of the Overpass." These documents later became part of the evidence that the National Labor Relations Board used to accuse the Ford Motor Company of violating federal labor laws and discriminating against unions. Henry Ford personally denounced the charges as gross falsehoods even as similar cases of brutality occurred at Ford plants in Dallas and Kansas City. In lieu of the UAW, he offered workers his own Blue Card Union and seemed to have evaded both unionization and federal authority.

In the winter of 1940–1941 the UAW renewed its attempts to organize the Ford Motor Company. On its side were recent Supreme Court decisions favorable to labor, including the upholding of the Wagner Act. Also influential was the revival of the economy as a consequence of the United States' assumption of a major share of war production for a new set of European belligerents. With workers in increasing demand, Ford could not pick and choose between union and nonunion workers as easily as before. On April 1, 1941, the UAW struck at the Rouge and closed the plant. Growling that he would "never submit to any union," Ford wanted to unleash Harry Bennett's squads of plant police with tear gas and machine guns. But he consented to an election under the auspices of the National Labor Relations Board. The results of the May 21 balloting were definitive: 70 percent of Ford's workers supported the UAW, 27 percent the AFL, and only 2.7 percent Ford's no-union principle.

Deeply hurt, Ford vowed he would quit business rather than accept the verdict of his employees. "Close the plant!" he thundered to his aides. The government, they quickly pointed out, would take it over to service war contracts. Let it be so, Ford snapped back. But he was losing his grip. The judgment that had built an industrial empire had been lost. Ford Motor Company was no longer the world's largest carmaker, that distinction now belonging to the more efficient GM. Already the victim of a stroke, Ford had only two more years of autocratic company management and seven more years of life remaining. His son, Edsel, pleaded with him to alter a business philosophy of rugged individualism that had lost its usefulness decades earlier. Clara Ford threatened divorce if he did not accept unionization. At length, Ford was persuaded to enter or, more exactly, was dragged kicking and screaming into the modern world he had done so much to create.

SELECTED READINGS
The Person

Bennett, Harry H.: *We Never Called Him Henry* (1951). A reminiscence by one of Ford's close business associates.

Bryan, Ford R.: *Beyond the Model T: The Other Ventures of Henry Ford* (1990). Pictorial history of Henry Ford's many enterprises and inventions.

Collier, Peter, and David Horowitz: *The Fords: An American Epic* (1987). Concise, well-presented account of Henry and Henry, Jr.

*Herndon, Booton: *Ford: An Unconventional Biography of the Men and Their Times* (1969). The most recent account of Henry Ford, his son, and their company.

Jardim, Anne: *The First Henry Ford: A Study in Personality and Business Leadership* (1970). Incisive, dispassionate analysis.

Lacey, Robert: *Ford: The Men and the Machine* (1987). Fast-paced history of the Ford Motor Company from its beginnings through the 1970s.

Nevins, Allan, and Frank Ernest Hill: *Ford* (3 vols., 1954–1963). The best source for the man and the company. A fair, thorough treatment.

*Available in paperback.

Nye, David E.: *Henry Ford: Ignorant Idealist.* (1979) An exploration of the contemporary American willingness to overlook Ford's eccentricity and bigotry and retain him as a national hero.

*Rae, John B. (ed.): *Henry Ford* (1969). Ford's own writing and the evaluations of others.

*Sward, Keith: *The Legend of Henry Ford* (1948). A comprehensive account, frequently critical of Ford.

Wik, Reynold M.: *Henry Ford and Grass-Roots America* (1972). Ford's relationship to the ideas and feelings of common people in the United States.

The Period

*Burns, James M.: *Roosevelt: The Lion and the Fox* (1956). The best analysis of Franklin D. Roosevelt as a politician.

*Conkin, Paul: *The New Deal* (1967). A good brief analysis.

*Degler, Carl: *The Age of the Economic Revolution, 1876–1901* (1967). The background to the emergence of the Ford Motor Company and similar enterprises.

Fass, Paul: *The Damned and the Beautiful: American Youth in the 1920s* (1977). A history of college life in the 1920s.

Hawley, Ellis W.: *The Great War and the Search for a Modern Order: A History of the American People and Their Institutions, 1917–1933* (1992). Good general survey of the period.

Hays, Samuel: *The Response to Industrialism, 1885–1914* (1957). A sweeping, often provocative interpretation of one of the forces that transformed American life.

*Higham, John: *Strangers in the Land* (1955). Immigrants and the response of "native" Americans to them in the late nineteenth and early twentieth centuries.

*May, Ernest: *The World War and American Isolation, 1914–1917* (1959). The changing relationship of the United States to the first general European war of the twentieth century.

*May, Henry: *The End of American Innocence* (1959). Intellectual and social history focusing on the impact of World War I.

*Nash, Roderick: *The Nervous Generation: American Thought, 1917–1930* (2d ed., 1989). A revisionist treatment of the social and intellectual history of a much-mythologized era.

Rogers, Daniel T.: *The Work Ethic in Industrial America, 1850–1920* (1975). Studies the ideals of effort and application that drove Henry Ford to achievement.

*Wiebe, Robert: *The Search for Order: 1877–1920* (1967). An imaginative generalization concerning the major forces for change in the life of a maturing nation.

FOR CONSIDERATION

1. Discuss the traits that enabled Henry Ford to become the greatest industrialist of the early twentieth century.

2. What techniques did Henry Ford incorporate to turn his small automobile company into the giant Ford Motor Company?

---

*Available in paperback.

3. In what ways was Henry Ford a "symbol for the age" of the 1920s? How does Ford epitomize the ambivalence of many Americans regarding modernity?

4. Like many other industrialists, Ford opposed government intervention to ease the ravages of the Great Depression. In their view, what were the causes and solutions to the economic downturn?

5. Henry Ford fought against unionization of his automobile plants until the 1940s, believing he had a better idea. What was his better idea, and how did it become increasingly impractical?

FIVE

Eleanor Roosevelt

The door to the hospital tent was so low that the tall woman, dressed in a standard Red Cross uniform, had to duck considerably to enter. It was good to be sheltered from the blazing tropical sun of Christmas Island, in the South Pacific, on that fall day of 1943. But her senses were quickly overcome by the combined odors of antiseptic, bandages, and wounded men. There was little time on this stopover, yet it was important that she spend a few moments with a marine whose torso had been horribly mangled by a mortar shell blast. Extremely worried about the young man's survival, the doctors had asked First Lady Eleanor Roosevelt to sit with him for a while and hopefully brighten his spirits and strengthen his will to live.

Recovering her poise after the initial shock of the hospital scene, she smiled, adjusted her cap, walked to the bedside of the boy shrouded in bandages, and introduced herself as "Mrs. Roosevelt." Heavily drugged and barely conscious, the boy took the hand of the kindly woman, who leaned forward to kiss him on the forehead. In the same unhurried, sincere, and caring manner with which she had spoken to hundreds of Allied soldiers fighting in World War II, Eleanor Roosevelt gently reassured the boy that he would fully recover and come home to the United States. The time was short, and the troop transport plane, on which she had traveled throughout the Pacific, was ready to depart for Honolulu. But she stayed until the very last moment, holding the boy's hand and speaking softly to him. She even promised to visit his mother when she returned to the States. Only when he fell asleep did the first lady leave his bedside.

Some months later, the same young soldier called on Eleanor Roosevelt at the White House to express his deep gratitude for her visit. Her remarkable impact on his recovery—and on the morale of tens of thousands of Allied soldiers fighting in World War II—symbolized the person who has been called the most important public woman of the twentieth century. The wife of President Franklin Roosevelt poured the same kind of boundless energy and tireless concern for the betterment of the world into all of her humanitarian interests. Eleanor Roosevelt was a pacesetter for the expansion of rights for minorities, the disabled, and especially women. Still, she remained an embodiment of the characteristics that defined the traditional Victorian American woman.

"The ability to think for myself did not develop until I was well on in life," wrote Eleanor Roosevelt in her 1958 autobiography, *On My Own.* "Therefore no real personality developed in my early youth." Born in New York City on October 11, 1884, Anna Eleanor Roosevelt was the descendant of several generations of successful merchants and bankers. Even before her Uncle Theodore became a leader of the Republican party as governor of New York (1898–1900) and president of the

United States (1901–1909), the Roosevelt name had been prominent among the eastern elite of the United States. However, women in such social positions as the Republican Roosevelts were not encouraged to develop personalities beyond what was needed to be "charming wives."

Eleanor, the only daughter of Elliot and Anna Hall Roosevelt, was reared to be a charming adornment of wealthy Victorian idleness. Her parents hoped that she would marry well, but even if she remained unmarried, they expected her to take her place alongside the other apolitical Roosevelt women. Most family members believed her fate would be the latter. Her mother, who was disappointed in her daughter's plain physical features, paid far more attention to Eleanor's younger brothers, Elliot, Jr., and Hall. Eleanor's parents were a handsome couple who mingled easily among the young and wealthy of New York society. Anna made it clear that Eleanor, who was always too tall and gangly, was not the daughter she had wanted and was embarrassed to take her out in public. She even nicknamed Eleanor "Granny" because she looked so "old-fashioned."

Eleanor's father compounded the difficulties of her troubled childhood. Elliot, Theodore's younger brother, was a chronic alcoholic who struggled in vain to find his niche in the world. Elliot's drinking placed a heavy burden on all family members. When he was sober, Elliot was kind and loving to Eleanor, but his behavior was more usually irresponsible. On one occasion, Elliot had promised to take Eleanor out on the town. Shortly after the outing began, however, Elliot left her with a hotel doorman while he went on a drinking binge. Heartbroken, Eleanor waited in vain all that day.

Tragedy had rocked Eleanor Roosevelt's world by her tenth birthday. When Eleanor was eight, her mother died suddenly of diphtheria. Shortly thereafter, the same disease took the life of her brother, Elliot, Jr. After Anna's death, Elliot entrusted the children to his mother-in-law. Eleanor longed to be with her father and lived in constant fear that he had abandoned her altogether. Her sense of despair deepened when news came in 1896 that Elliot had died. Eleanor's grandmother, who was preoccupied with her own four children still living at home, had little time for Eleanor and her brother, Hall. She forbade Eleanor to go out on her own, except to attend a small private school at a nearby mansion. Although Eleanor did very well in school, she was rarely allowed to socialize with any of the other girls who attended. Consequently, she was isolated and had little contact with other children. On occasions when the family visited Roosevelt relatives, Eleanor, who was never taken shopping, was invariably dressed in dowdy, out-of-style clothing. Her appearance and apparent lack of social graces led some family members to ridicule the shy young girl privately, while others pitied her. As one of her cousins remembered, "[Eleanor's] was the grimmest childhood I had ever known."

Social position finally paid off for the melancholy child when she was 15. Fulfilling Anna Roosevelt's wish that Eleanor attend school in Europe, her grandmother used a trust fund to send her to Marie Souvestre's finishing school, Allenswood, outside London. In England, Eleanor enjoyed a completely new life. Souvestre, the daughter of a French radical philosopher, provided an atmosphere of warmth and care that Eleanor had never before experienced. The girls were given a well-rounded education in science, literature, language, and history (the last, of course, bearing the interpretation of the daughter of a political radical). The girls were also required to speak French in all classes.

Marie Souvestre was a strong female role model. Except for Eleanor's Aunty Bye (Theodore Roosevelt's sister), whose advice the president often sought, she had grown up among uninspiring and apolitical female socialites. In contrast, Souvestre was deeply interested in world affairs. Her penchant was for underdogs, and she was openly critical of British imperialism. Souvestre took an immediate liking to Eleanor because she was an American at risk of rejection in the British school. Under Souvestre's tutelage, Eleanor learned that women could lead more meaningful lives than merely providing loyal service to a husband.

Eleanor excelled in all phases of her schooling at Allenswood. Consequently, a self-conscious girl ashamed of her six-foot frame was transfigured into a confident and attractive young woman. Eleanor was popular among the students and the favorite of her teacher. When school was out of session, Souvestre took Eleanor on several European tours. Seeing the great cities of Italy, Belgium, France, and Germany with the well-versed Souvestre broadened Eleanor's perspective on the history and culture of the Western world. Eleanor remembered her time at Allenswood as "the happiest years of my life."

Graduation from Allenswood came too soon. With great reluctance, Eleanor boarded the ocean liner to New York to return to life with her grandmother. The year was 1902 and, according to the customs of high society, time for Eleanor's "coming out." Although the seventeen-year-old girl had gained great self-confidence in England, she still regarded herself as an "ugly duckling." The dances and parties of the coming-out season were agonizing to Eleanor. Towering over all the girls, and most of the boys, Eleanor adopted an unbecoming, hunched-over posture. As much as she wished to forgo the parties—many given by the Gettys, the Astors, and other families among the financial aristocracy—New York society demanded her participation. Reluctantly, Eleanor donned her ball gown again and again.

During the course of the coming-out season, Eleanor became reacquainted with her second cousin Franklin. They had known each other since they were small children and had danced once at a family party; later, Franklin wrote his mother a letter expressing how much he enjoyed talking to "Cousin Eleanor." Born in 1882, Franklin was a member of the Democratic side of the Roosevelts of New York. Before the Civil War, the Democratic Roosevelts had been among northerners who helped maintain the sectional balance of compromise. When war broke out, they had aligned themselves with the Lincoln Republicans but returned to the Democratic party after Reconstruction to support such candidates as Grover Cleveland. Democratic support, however, was not written in stone. Franklin's father, James, had bolted from the Democratic party in 1900 to support Theodore Roosevelt's Republican candidacy for vice president. Partisan politics did not prevent close family ties among the two Roosevelt clans: the Oyster Bay Republicans and the Hyde Park Democrats. In fact, Eleanor's father was Franklin's godfather.

To Eleanor's surprise and delight, Franklin found her charming and attractive. Courtship of a distant relative at the turn of the century was not only accepted but still encouraged in high society. Franklin's interest in Eleanor grew during 1902 and 1903. Eleanor was thrilled, especially since her grandmother and aunts had told her she would probably never attract a beau. That she had won the heart of handsome and gregarious Franklin was as much a joy to her as it was a source of envy to many of her relatives. As she and Franklin began to see each other regularly, Eleanor was pleased to discover that Franklin also preferred informal luncheons and country outings to the elegant parties of high society.

Romance in Victorian America moved slowly, and while Franklin was sure he wanted to marry Eleanor by early 1903, her "painfully high ideals" stood in the way of any proposals until the proper length of courtship had been observed. But Eleanor was then nineteen and, in her words, had "a desire to participate in every experience that might be the lot of a woman." So when Franklin Roosevelt asked her to marry him in the fall of 1903, Eleanor hesitated only briefly before accepting his proposal. Although she was uncertain that she was actually in love, her instincts told her that it was the proper thing to do. After all, not only was Franklin charming and good-looking, but his gaiety and ebullient personality reminded her of her father. Franklin was attending Harvard University and looked forward to a promising law career. What more could Eleanor expect from life than to be the wife of a successful and loving husband?

Problems surfaced during the engagement that haunted Eleanor for years to come. Franklin's father had died in 1900 after a long illness, leaving his mother, Sara, to pour all her energy into the affairs of her only son. She wanted Franklin to follow in his father's footsteps as the genteel country squire of the Hyde Park estate. But having grown quite independent while Sara was tending to her husband, Franklin resisted her efforts. Part of that resistance was his proposal to Eleanor. Sara found it intolerable that Franklin should choose a spouse without consulting her. As a result, she did everything in her power to break off the engagement, refusing to accept the fact that she might have to share her son with *any* woman. In the winter of 1904, Sara persuaded Franklin to join her on a cruise of the West Indies, hoping that ocean air, frivolity, and absence from Eleanor would prompt him to change his mind.

To Sara's dismay, Franklin's feelings toward Eleanor did not change. In the fall of 1904, they were officially engaged. The engagement did not keep Sara Roosevelt from resenting Eleanor, even though it stopped her overt attempts to prevent the marriage. Her aloofness toward Eleanor often turned into rudeness and cruelty before the wedding took place. Sara's actions hurt Eleanor deeply, but, as always, they only sharpened her own sensitivity to hurting other people. Franklin and Eleanor prevailed, and a grand wedding was held at a relative's house in New York City on March 17, 1905. The affair was all the more grand because the president of the United States was to give the bride away. But "Uncle Ted's" attendance at the wedding only diminished Eleanor's big day. The commotion of having the popular and recently reelected president in attendance prevented some guests from arriving on time. After the ceremony, the receiving line quickly disintegrated into a crowd around President Roosevelt. Soon, Franklin and Eleanor stood by themselves on their own wedding day. Though neither of them seemed to mind very much, Eleanor was relieved that the "lion of the afternoon" had left by the time they made their own departure. Eleanor's ambivalence about publicity was shaped by this event. Public life, she learned, often meant an almost total loss of privacy.

After a European honeymoon, Franklin and Eleanor began their lives together. Unfortunately for Eleanor, Sara had arranged for them to live in a house that she owned and occupied. By then Franklin was attending law school at Columbia University. Certain that she knew what was best for her son, Sara had bought a house near the university where they would all live together.

At the time of her marriage, Eleanor was working in several settlement houses in the slums of New York City. Like Jane Addams's Hull House in Chicago, the New York houses dealt with the multitude of urban problems. As the main port of entry to the United States, New York City saw hundreds of European immigrants pour in each day. Once naturalized at Ellis Island, they entered a new and perplexing world. Many came with only the clothing on their backs, unable to speak English, and in dire need of housing and work. Eleanor's ability to help the underprivileged filled an emotional void while also giving her tremendous self-satisfaction and the praise of Marie Souvestre. She had also joined the National Consumers League, organized by veteran settlement house worker Florence Kelley. League members strove to improve conditions for workers in the nation's factories and department stores. Through Kelley, Eleanor learned the art of the indepth investigation of a problem, followed by full disclosure—in short, muckraking. Eleanor devoted herself to teaching the new immigrants how to cope in the United States, lobbying for improved workers' conditions, and exposing fraud and abuse in city government. As much as social work meant to Eleanor, Sara Roosevelt insisted it stop. She disapproved of such activism, believing it beneath the dignity of a woman in Eleanor's position. Besides, she told Eleanor, settlement houses bred germs that, undoubtedly, she would bring home.

Childbearing soon became Eleanor Roosevelt's primary occupation. Between 1906 and 1916, she gave birth to six children: one daughter and five sons (one son died in infancy). Although her children gave her great happiness, motherhood was a difficult and painful experience for Eleanor. Never having experienced the frivolity of a happy childhood, she simply did not know how to play with children. She was ill at ease, aloof, and unpredictable as a mother. Moreover, Sara Roosevelt stood in the way of Eleanor's relationship with her children. She domineered to such an extent that Eleanor regarded herself as less of a mother to the children than their grandmother. Constant reminders of her inadequacy as a wife and mother led Eleanor to insecurity and inconsistency in everything she did around the home.

When the Roosevelts moved into a new, larger home in 1908, designed, built, and purchased by Sara, Eleanor's despair nearly overcame her. No sense of her own personality had developed, and none could as long as Sara reigned over her family. But she dared not defy her mother-in-law for fear of losing her husband. A few weeks after moving to the new home, however, Franklin found Eleanor weeping at her dressing table. In a rare display of candor to Franklin concerning his mother, Eleanor sobbed that she was dreadfully unhappy about living in a home that they had not built or bought, "and which did not represent the way [she] wanted to live." Franklin was undoubtedly affected by this emotional outburst; yet he too felt quite powerless concerning his mother. He told Eleanor "gently" to come to her senses and calm down, and Sara's dominance continued.

For some, an unhappy existence leads to a life of lethargy. But a miserable home life inspired Eleanor Roosevelt toward public service. The opportunity un-

folded when Franklin, dissatisfied with working in a New York law firm, sought a
career in politics. The partners in the law firm discouraged Franklin, arguing that he
was jeopardizing a brilliant legal career. Sara Roosevelt objected strongly also, because politics required mingling with the masses. Eleanor, however, supported
Franklin's decision, knowing that her husband aspired to a political career in the
mold of Theodore Roosevelt's. Franklin revered his cousin and visited him often at
the White House. He never really considered Theodore a Republican; rather, he
was a progressive using the party to advance his objectives. Franklin adopted the
same viewpoint toward the Democratic party as he moved back to his birthplace of
Hyde Park, New York, some sixty miles north of the city. In 1910, he successfully
ran for the state assembly, becoming the first Democrat elected from that district in
thirty-two years.

Over the next three years, Franklin established himself as a promising reform
politician in Albany. Meanwhile, Eleanor set about her duty of becoming a politician's wife. A welcome four-year break between pregnancies and life apart from
Sara, who remained in New York City, gave Eleanor a new sense of independence.
Although she had grown up in the Republican Roosevelt clan, Eleanor had little
trouble changing her loyalties. She admired the progressive presidential administration of her Uncle Ted, which had consistently outraged party conservatives. She
also shared her husband's view that political parties were but a means to an end.
And after all, neither Eleanor Roosevelt nor any other woman in the United States
could officially belong to a political party since they could not vote. At first,
Eleanor simply considered it her wifely duty to be involved in her husband's political career, but she quickly learned the dynamics of state politics. She attended state
legislative sessions and began scouring newspapers for further analysis of the issues.
Discussions of politics over the dinner table soon convinced Franklin that his wife
had a clear insight into the affairs of state and was an able adviser.

The New York State Assembly was only a stepping-stone for the charismatic
Franklin Roosevelt. When Democrat Woodrow Wilson was elected president in
1912, he appointed Franklin assistant secretary of the navy. After Wilson's eight
years in office, Franklin was nominated as the running mate of Democratic presidential candidate James B. Cox. These were eventful years for Eleanor as well. Although she never overcame her reservations about large-scale entertaining as a
politician's wife, she adjusted and performed her duties well both in Albany and in
Washington. During World War I, she resumed social work, serving in the Red
Cross in Washington, DC, organizing improvements in military hospitals, and visiting wounded and shell-shocked soldiers. High society approved of this kind of vol-
untarism during wartime as socially acceptable and patriotic, even though Sara argued that Eleanor spent too little time with the children. For Eleanor Roosevelt,
the volunteer work was a revelation. Comforting the sick and wounded amounted
to a rediscovery of the satisfaction she had derived years before through settlement
house work. The human suffering and "the many tragedies" she witnessed during
the war prompted Eleanor Roosevelt to devote herself to making the world a better
place.

As a result of their busy lives she and Franklin were often apart. After American entry into the war, Franklin resigned his post as assistant secretary of the navy

to serve in the armed forces in France. But even before the war, there had been frequent periods during which Franklin and Eleanor were apart. As early as 1916,
Eleanor began to suspect that Franklin might be having an affair with her attractive
social secretary, Lucy Mercer. Her suspicions were confirmed in 1918 when she was
handling Franklin's correspondence. He returned from Europe with double pneu-
monia, and while he lay incapacitated in bed, Eleanor happened onto some love
letters from Lucy. Devastated, she immediately blamed herself for being too dull for
"the gay cavalier." Because her father had been an alcoholic, she felt both fear and
revulsion toward drinking and could never "let herself go." Consequently, Franklin
gravitated toward people who could, including Lucy Mercer. Eleanor confronted
Franklin about his infidelity. With Sara's intervention, Eleanor was persuaded not
to divorce him. The affair would end, but Eleanor made it clear that she was staying
married to Franklin only for the children and for public appearance. The affair was
yet another bitter experience for Eleanor, but it was also a turning point. No longer
would she bend to her mother-in-law's dominance to preserve her husband's love.

One of her first "appearances" was as the happy wife of the Democratic vice
presidential candidate in 1920. The election, however, was a resounding defeat for
the Cox–Roosevelt ticket. Disillusionment with the war and Woodrow Wilson's
internationalist peace stance, as well as a growing conservative mood nationwide,
were factors in the loss. Voters were swayed more by the Republican promises of
isolation and minimal business regulation than by a continuation of Democratic internationalism and progressivism. Exercising their first opportunity to vote in a national election, only about one-third of eligible women voted, underscoring the fact
that most still considered politics a man's affair. This was a great disappointment to
the suffragists, who had devoted their lives to obtaining the vote for women. But
the movement's guiding lights, Susan B. Anthony and Elizabeth Cady Stanton, had
died a decade before the Nineteenth Amendment was ratified, and their leadership
was missed when it came to the first voting opportunity.

Moreover, as recent scholarship has suggested, women reformers became involved in a "social uplift" of the nation during the early 1900s. Immersed in improving the lot of women workers and prohibiting exploitive child labor, many who
supported suffrage had given little thought to a political course of action once they
had secured the vote. What there was of a women's political organization endorsed
the Cox–Roosevelt ticket because of its support of the League of Nations and liberal reform. But more than 60 percent of voters, men and women, preferred Harding and his "return to normalcy" in 1920.

Like many women, Eleanor believed during the same period that "men were superior creatures and knew more about politics than women." As she became active
in politics, however, she grew to doubt this assumption, and saw no reason why
women should not fully participate in the political process. At the 1920 Democratic convention, however, women interested in politics were belittled and unwel-
come. They had little voice in fashioning the party platforms for the 1920 election
and were excluded from all facets of politics except voting. At the 1924 Democratic
convention, Eleanor Roosevelt sat patiently outside a closed-door session that was
determining the platform of candidate John Davis. She had been asked to present
to the platform committee the issues favored by women's organizations, but was re-

The two photographs on this page were taken during Eleanor and Franklin's honeymoon in Europe during 1905. At the right they pose happily for friends with whom they were staying in Strathpeffer, Scotland. Below, Eleanor reads aboard a Venetian gondola. Franklin took the picture.

Eleanor Roosevelt's activities in women's political and world peace organizations were well documented. In 1934, the New York Women's University Club honored the first lady. Carrie Chapman Catt, instrumental in the ratification of the Nineteenth Amendment, a founder of the National Woman's Party, and a long-time proponent of prohibition, stands at the far left (above). Below, Eleanor stands with Elizabeth Christman and Rose Schneiderman as she addresses delegates at the twelfth annual convention of the National Women's Trade Union League.

stricted to passing messages to an envoy. Not surprisingly, few of those issues made their way into the Democratic platform. Although women were attending the conventions, they still had little influence on the policies of the Democratic party.

After the disappointment of 1924, Eleanor Roosevelt and other Democratic women from New York State decided that organization within the system was the only avenue for increased participation. Eleanor Roosevelt became involved in the Democratic party apparatus of New York, the League of Women Voters, and the New York City Women's Club. In the Women's Club, she came to know Molly Dewson. An able administrator who had worked in a women's prison in Massachusetts, had done research for the National Consumers League, and had prepared legal briefs on minimum wage cases, Dewson was a great influence on Roosevelt. They worked together in New York women's political organizations and sought out ways to advance issues they believed were important to women.

In general, however, there was little more political unity among American women than among the men. Although women of all economic and social classes had supported the suffrage movement during the 1910s, a conscious group identity did not materialize after the ratification of the Nineteenth Amendment. Feminism, as defined by historian Nancy F. Cott, was based in the belief "that women perceive themselves not only as a biological sex but (perhaps even more importantly) as a social grouping." Feminism served the suffrage movement by claiming that women deserved rights, not only because women were human beings like men, but also because they were universally altruistic, unlike men. After ratification, however, the ambiguities and divergent motivations of women retarded a movement toward unity.

Feminists of the postratification era rallied around certain issues. But their belief that all women shared their views was a mistake. The unsuccessful attempts of the National Woman's Party to promote women's issues and elect women to office during the 1920s was a case in point. The roots of this party lay in the militant women's suffrage movement in England around the turn of the century. English suffragists had chained themselves to vehicles and street railings and had pounded on the doors of Parliament in their efforts to obtain the vote. Their exhibitions had not been wasted on Alice Paul, an American student at the London School of Economics. Returning to the United States in 1912, the inspired Paul and her friend, Lucy Burns, became members of the Congressional Committee of the National American Woman Suffrage Association (NAWSA). Dissatisfied with the lack of activism in NAWSA, Paul, Burns, and a handful of others on the Congressional Committee organized mass rallies demanding a constitutional amendment granting the vote for women. By 1914 the Congressional Committee had broken off from the NAWSA and become the Congressional Union. Two years later, the same group founded the National Woman's Party. Party leaders attacked the Wilson administration because it had thus far failed to implement national women's suffrage. Through marches, rallies, and blunt editorializing in the party newspaper, the *Suffragist*, the National Woman's Party was instrumental in securing passage of the Nineteenth Amendment. During the 1920s, the National Woman's Party identified with liberal candidates who, more often than not, were defeated at all electoral levels. Alice Paul and other party leaders believed that an independent party of women with liberal leanings could come to dominate American politics. However, many women were voting their husband's wishes in successively electing Harding, Coolidge, and Hoover to the presidency—or perhaps many women were just as conservative as the majority of men.

In light of her experience as a politician's wife, Eleanor Roosevelt believed that women had to work inside the system if they were to become the political equals of men. Although sympathetic to the National Woman's Party, she placed more faith in groups like the League of Women Voters, formed from NAWSA in 1920. With the passage of child labor laws, minimum wage and maximum hour laws for women, and representation in the federal Department of Labor, progressive women like Roosevelt had accomplished many of their goals by the 1920s. New challenges still abounded, such as increased participation in the political process, recruitment of more women into management positions, maternity leave, civil rights, and world peace. "Birth control," however, a term coined by activist Margaret Sanger, remained controversial. Sanger had established a clinic in New York City and had founded the National Birth Control League (later changed to Planned Parenthood). Although Roosevelt probably supported Sanger, who was arrested several times in the 1920s in police raids on the New York clinic, her open support of birth control did not come until the 1930s.

Neither did she actively support the cornerstone of the National Woman's Party: the Equal Rights Amendment (ERA). Proponents of the ERA believed that only a constitutional amendment declaring absolute equality between men and women would guarantee women full economic and political participation in American life. Women like Roosevelt placed their faith in protective legislation addressing abuses case-by-case. The National Woman's Party bristled at this widespread opposition to equal rights. Party leaders argued that protective legislation, often limiting working hours and requiring safer conditions for women, relegated women to certain jobs while eliminating them from consideration for others. With a constitutional amendment mandating equality, women would have equal access to jobs and to union membership. But women and men of all classes denounced the ERA. Women trade unionists saw it as an ill-conceived plan devised by idly rich women that would only cost them jobs; male union members saw the ERA as a threat to their own jobs; and politically active women such as Eleanor Roosevelt believed that the amendment was ambiguous and unenforceable. The National Woman's Party, so successful in achieving women's suffrage, foundered over its support of the ERA during the 1920s.

Three years before the Nineteenth Amendment was ratified, the New York legislature had approved women's suffrage. As a result of implementing early female suffrage in the most populous and wealthy state in the union, New York became the center of national women's politics. The Women's City Club emerged as a powerful force with over 3,000 members by 1920. Dominated by upper-class white women, the club nonetheless promoted all kinds of reform, including social welfare, city planning, standards for living conditions in jails and prisons, and labor reforms. Club leaders, like Eleanor Roosevelt and Gifford Pinchot's wife, Cornelia Bryce Pinchot, developed a working relationship with the Women's Trade Union League (WTUL), thereby establishing a bond between upper-class club members and working-class union women. Many Women's City Club members were involved in settlement house work, and this brought them into contact with the plight of immigrant working women. Together, the settlement house workers and the working women had formed the WTUL in 1903. The league and its president for much of the 1920s, Rose Schneiderman, joined forces with the Women's City Club to bring about reform of women's labor laws through both legislation and picket lines. Schneiderman, a tough-minded first-generation Jewish immigrant from eastern Europe, was an organizer for cap makers. She was also a firebrand speaker for female workers' rights. The lessons of Schneiderman's effective organizing campaigns had a profound impact on her friend Eleanor Roosevelt. In New York, Roosevelt was surrounded by hardworking, concerned women. But her own dedication, combined with the poise and gentility of a patrician upbringing, made her a natural leader and spokesperson.

Eleanor Roosevelt's emergence as a public figure was spurred on by another family tragedy. In August 1921, Franklin Roosevelt was stricken with infantile paralysis, or poliomyelitis. While on vacation at their Campobello retreat in Maine, the family often went sailing. One day in August, they spotted a forest fire and put ashore to fight it. After the exhausting battle was over, Franklin went swimming in a landlocked lake near the family home. Later that day he complained of chills and went to bed. The following day he developed a mild fever that worsened. Soon his arms and legs were paralyzed. When specialists arrived, they diagnosed him as having what was commonly called polio. If Franklin did survive, the family was told, he would probably be an invalid for the rest of his days. After the initial shock, Eleanor gathered her composure and saw to her husband's needs. With strong family support and extraordinary determination, Franklin Roosevelt began to recover, first regaining the use of his upper torso and arms. And though he never walked unaided again, within two years of his illness he was back in politics. Franklin and Eleanor now had a new relationship, probably unique in political history. Although they would never again share the love of their earliest years together, they still needed one another. Franklin would work his way back into the political limelight, and Eleanor would be "his eyes and ears."

Eleanor Roosevelt's contribution to her husband's political ascendancy was crucial. As Franklin recovered, Eleanor became one of the best-known names in New York State politics. She worked within the League of Women Voters, writing digests of election information and learning more about politics from veteran suffragists Esther Lape and Elizabeth Read. She also became involved in the Women's Division of the New York Democratic Party as a spokesperson, policy analyst, and editor of the division bulletin. She benefited from the experience of party activists Nancy Cook and Marion Dickerman. As they became fast friends, the three women oversaw the restructuring of the Women's Division as an effective lobbying apparatus in the Democratic party. Although they failed to get most of their agenda of world peace and progressive reform legislation into the 1924 Democratic national platform, they were less at fault than was Al Smith's failure to wrest the nomination from the more conservative John Davis. Placing their hopes in Smith's nomination, they were shut out when the party chose Davis. Roosevelt, Cook, and Dickerman quickly learned from their mistake. In the future, they worked to make sure that they could guarantee their candidate's nomination.

Even though Eleanor Roosevelt's political activism drew praise from her recovering husband, it earned her great enmity from her mother-in-law. Sara's obstinacy made the winter of 1922 the "most trying" of Eleanor's whole life. Sara could not bear to see her son put through the pain of stretching, massaging, and exercising his crippled legs—even though doctors insisted the regimen be continued. Her son was to be kept "completely quiet," meaning that, until Sara finally relented, Eleanor had to oversee the exercise sessions while her mother-in-law was away. Nurses and therapists were in full-time residence at the Roosevelts' Hyde Park home, and the crowded conditions wore on everyone's nerves. Eleanor's relations with her children were strained—especially those with her teenage daughter, Anna. Eleanor feared that Franklin's affliction would strike her children, but the children viewed her actions as neglect. Eventually, however, Eleanor assumed many of the duties of both mother and father and grew closer to her children.

By late 1922 the crisis was over. Franklin was on a rigorous recovery program. Although the therapy sessions were "torture," Franklin "bore [them] without complaint," according to Eleanor. Her feelings had changed dramatically for the man who had "betrayed" her. Eleanor's compassion was strong, and she now realized that Franklin desperately needed her. At their Hyde Park home, Franklin learned to use crutches and, in time, was able to stand on his own. Swimming was one physical activity that doctors urged, and, in 1924, the Roosevelts made their first trip to Warm Springs, Georgia, a resort in the Appalachians where Franklin could swim for hours at a time in the warm, buoyant mineral waters. Thereafter, he went to Warm Springs every autumn. The purported medicinal powers of the mineral springs did not give Franklin the full recovery he wanted so badly, but swimming in the warm waters revived his spirits and renewed his energy. Warm Springs was Franklin's retreat; he often went there without Eleanor. However, Eleanor also built a retreat, in part to get away from Sara. In 1926, she had a cottage built on Val-Kill, a brook on family property near their Hyde Park estate. While Eleanor lived there periodically, her close friends, Nancy Cook and Marion Dickerman, were permanent residents. Eleanor enjoyed coming to Val-Kill. Her retreat gave her the privacy and sense of belonging that she never felt in any of the homes that her mother-in-law had dominated, and her relations with Cook, Dickerman, and other women gave her the friendship she had never before known.

After his first visit to Warm Springs, Franklin resumed working in New York City in defiance of Sara, who wanted him to retire to her home. His remarkable recovery made him the natural choice for directors' seats by foundations such as the Boy Scouts, the American Legion, and an industrial organization known as the American Construction Council. These positions helped bring him back into the public eye and provided valuable learning experiences in business and nonprofit organization. Eleanor supported his efforts, but the real mastermind throughout Franklin Roosevelt's political career, dating back to the New York Assembly, was his close confidante, Louis Howe. The small bug-eyed man Eleanor called "gnome-like" was an Albany journalist who had very early recognized Franklin's political potential. After running Franklin's successful reelection campaign for the State Assembly in 1912, Howe was never far from the Roosevelt family until his death in 1936. Howe helped with Franklin's recovery and constantly prodded him to get

back into politics. He believed that Franklin could actually use his disability to political advantage. With keen insight and an eye for the rapid political changes developing, Howe was instrumental in Franklin Roosevelt's career.

Louis Howe also recognized Eleanor's political potential. In the wake of
women's suffrage, Howe recognized the impact of the female vote on the electoral
process and also recognized that Eleanor could be an important asset to her husband's career. Howe admired Eleanor's compassion, sincerity, and political acumen.
Because Franklin was not as mobile as other politicians, he saw in Eleanor a vehicle
for effectively representing her husband's name and interests. Eleanor initially disliked Howe because of his shabby appearance and chain smoking, but she eventually came to regard him as a close friend. Howe encouraged her writing efforts and
helped her edit the first editions of the League of Women Voters' bulletin, *City-
State-Nation*. He accompanied an extremely nervous Eleanor Roosevelt when she
gave her first few public speeches. He coached her to avoid annoying habits, such as
laughing nervously when nothing was funny, and he trained her to use her high,
uneven voice effectively. "Have something you want to say," advised Howe, "say it,
and sit down."

By the early 1930s, Eleanor Roosevelt had established herself as a journalist, an
author, a teacher, and a radio personality. Her articles, appearing in periodicals
ranging from *Ladies Home Journal* to *Reader's Digest*, were usually of a highly personal nature. She also wrote on political and social issues in organizational journals
such as the *Women's Democratic News*. Her topics ranged from women's rights in
the workplace to world peace. In 1933, she published her first book, *It's Up to the
Women*, an assessment of changing times and conditions for American women. Although including an analysis of the first decade of female suffrage and the problems
of modern marriage, the book was primarily a guide to helping women economize
during the Great Depression. It offered timely advice, money-saving recipes, and
the philosophy of a woman whom readers regarded as neither radical nor old-fashioned. She was a "modern woman," able to balance family and career. Eleanor Roosevelt exhorted the women of the United States, declaring that they would "tip the
scales and bring us safely out of [the depression]." Occasional radio broadcasts during the 1920s, usually for the Democratic party, gave her a command of the new
mass medium that she and Franklin would both use successfully in years to come. In
addition, she taught American history, literature, and English at a girls' finishing
school in New York City.

One of the most pleasing aspects of Eleanor's work was the additional income
it gave her. Although she had had a trust fund since her father's death, it was small
in relation to the upper-crust style of life that she and Franklin led. Often, Eleanor
and Franklin had to rely on Sara for money and housing. Wives without money
were wives without power in Eleanor's way of thinking. Such powerlessness kept
them isolated in the home. Preventing wives from working outside the home and
earning their own money was only another means of male social control. Her income from publishing, teaching, and broadcasting pleased Eleanor as much as it
irked her mother-in-law. Nor did Sara care for the company Eleanor often kept, especially the working-class women of the trade union movements. But Eleanor was
by then unconcerned about what Sara thought and was pleased that Franklin sup-

ported her activities. As Franklin's income increased, Eleanor began to give large portions of her own annual salary to charity.

As the wife of the governor of New York from 1929 to 1933, Eleanor Roosevelt was often in the public eye. Al Smith's loss to Herbert Hoover in the 1928 presidential election was a blow to Democratic women, but Franklin Roosevelt's gubernatorial victory the same year placed their most effective spokeswoman in the national limelight. Magazine articles by or about Eleanor in national periodicals actually made her better known than Franklin, who was himself establishing a kind of "mini–New Deal" in New York in anticipation of his presidential plan. An overwhelming reelection in 1930 confirmed not only Franklin's popularity, but also large-scale approval of his politically active wife. Whether speaking before New York City Council meetings or visiting mental hospitals in rural New York, Eleanor Roosevelt was changing public perceptions about the way political wives could conduct their lives.

Remembering the experiences of her uncle Theodore Roosevelt and his family during his presidential years, Eleanor viewed her husband's presidential candidacy in 1932 with ambivalence. Public life was hard on the president and on his family. Privacy, so important to Eleanor, would undoubtedly become a thing of the past with Franklin's victory. And she dreaded the time when she could no longer travel without large-scale recognition and the presence of security guards. But as the campaign of 1932 began, the groundswell movement for Franklin to run for president was overwhelming. Dutifully, Eleanor supported her husband, knowing he would make a fine president—and acknowledging that she would further her own political interests by being first lady. Still, she lamented Franklin's presidential aspirations, and after the election, she declared to reporter Lorena Hickok, "If I wanted to be selfish, I could wish Franklin had not been elected."

But elected he was in a landslide over Hoover, and, in March 1933, Franklin and Eleanor Roosevelt prepared themselves for their future. Although she always denied it, Eleanor's frequent discussions with Franklin undoubtedly influenced his decisions. She forcefully advocated the appointment of women to positions in his gubernatorial and presidential administrations. Frances Perkins, for example, who served as New York State's commissioner of industrial relations and later as secretary of labor of the United States, owed her initial appointment to Eleanor Roosevelt's power of persuasion over her husband. Perkins had been a leading suffragist and was active in the National Consumers League and in settlement house work in New York. Eleanor admired her political and administrative abilities, and, with the help of Democratic activist Molly Dewson, she convinced Franklin to appoint Perkins. As FDR's secretary of labor, Perkins held the highest federal appointment of any woman in American history up to that time.

During the first four years of the New Deal, Eleanor rewrote the role of the first lady. She could have been satisfied to keep close to the White House and just be a "tea-and-luncheon" first lady, but this was not her way. Devoting her time and efforts to the plight of others fulfilled both her inner needs and her public philosophical aspirations. The most satisfying part of her political life was her heightened ability to help people. She traveled thousands of miles to assess the extent of human suffering during the Great Depression. She answered thousands of letters from distressed Americans personally and, when possible, even visited the writer. She performed many of the ceremonial functions, such as dedications and commencements, that an ambulatory president would normally have handled. Her pace was so hectic that one Washington newspaper made it headline news when she spent a night *at* the White House!

One morning Eleanor left very early to visit a penitentiary. When Franklin called her secretary to find out where she had gone, the answer was "She's in prison, Mr. President." "I'm not surprised," quipped Franklin dryly, "but what for?" During the bitter coal strikes of 1933, the *New Yorker* published a cartoon in which two surprised coal miners looked up to see "Mrs. Roosevelt" approaching them in the mine shaft. Along with Molly Dewson, now head of the national Women's Division of the Democratic Party, Eleanor lobbied hard for greater female representation in the party and in her husband's administration. When congressional conservatives proposed that married women be banned from working, she decried the inequality of such a notion, and even made the counterproposal that husbands pay their wives wages for running the home. She also carried out the conventional activities of a first lady, which included scheduling and attending dozens of teas and luncheons, banquets and receptions, and hundreds of other engagements each month. Meanwhile, in "overtime," she maintained her writing and broadcasting career.

Eleanor Roosevelt also pioneered press conferences given by first ladies. Women newspaper reporters were constantly looking for ways to advance beyond their limited roles of covering "women's" or "human interest" stories. After years of reporting the activities of the bland first ladies Grace Coolidge and Lou Hoover, the women's press corps leaped at the opportunity to cover the outspoken Roosevelt, "a woman's woman." Lorena Hickok of Associated Press, who became a close friend and personal companion of the new first lady, led a campaign to persuade Eleanor to hold press conferences for women reporters. At first she declined; but Louis Howe and Franklin, aware of the political influence the conferences could have on women voters, urged her on. Although the conferences were nerve-wracking for Eleanor, she adjusted quickly and presented viewpoints not always in accord with the adminstration.

Because of her extensive travels and activities, a great deal of "news" crept into her news conferences as the first New Deal progressed. In 1934, for example, Eleanor defended her activities in a West Virginia project of the Resettlement Administration. One of more than fifty resettlement communities planned for extremely depressed regions of the nation, Arthurdale, West Virginia, was built to house unemployed mining families. After visiting the region and witnessing the squalor of the tent cities surrounding the closed coal mines, Eleanor became involved in the Arthurdale project. Conservative congressmen quickly branded the first lady as having socialist leanings for promoting such big-government projects. Roosevelt responded by challenging her critics to substantiate their claims that Arthurdale, or any other such relief project, was "communistic." More and more, she denounced Republicans and defended the New Deal in her press conferences. While acknowledging the gains American women had made in recent years, she regretted that politics was "still a man's world." She also began to attack racism and sexism openly.

In 1936, the Republicans attempted to cast Eleanor Roosevelt as a domineering woman with total control over a disabled husband whose mind was probably affected by polio. Republican nominee Alf Landon attempted to make an issue out of Eleanor's travels and the politicking of her press conferences. The former Kansas governor promised that his wife would stay close to the White House. Attacking the first lady was a desperate maneuver, but Republican strategists sensed that theirs was an uphill battle. The Democrats' campaign slogan was "Four Years Ago and Now." The first New Deal had been a moderate success. Thousands of farms and homes had been saved through the Farm Credit Administration and the Federal Housing Administration. The Agricultural Adjustment Administration had effectively raised commodity prices, and unemployment had dropped from almost 25 percent in 1933 to under 17 percent in 1936. One lifelong Republican even wrote to the president before the election, "Life is 1000% better since you took charge of the United States."

If the Republicans saw Eleanor Roosevelt as a liability, the Democrats were willing to gamble that she was just the opposite. Rather than curtail her activities, Franklin and Louis Howe continued to encourage her to make public appearances. Although some southern Democrats in the administration, such as Press Secretary Steve Early, wanted her to be less vocal about civil rights, others, such as Interior Secretary Harold Ickes and Works Progress Administration (WPA) head Harry Hopkins, joined her in the crusade against racial discrimination. Her campaign on civil rights for blacks paid rich political rewards in 1936. Blacks had voted almost unanimously with the party of Lincoln since the Civil War, identifying the Democratic party with slavery and oppression. While most impoverished people had been solidly behind Roosevelt in 1932, blacks had largely remained loyal to the Republicans. During the first New Deal, however, many poor blacks, especially in urban areas, could see the tangible differences resulting from relief programs. Black leaders like Walter White, executive secretary of the National Association for the Advancement of Colored People (NAACP), were given frequent audiences with President Roosevelt. Eleanor Roosevelt, who had grown to deplore discrimination of any kind, had been the intermediary between White and her husband. She was among many Americans who were appalled by the fact that twenty to forty blacks were still being murdered each year by white mobs. She corresponded regularly with White and the NAACP while prodding Franklin to support an antilynching bill in Congress.

Black voters in northern and eastern urban centers contributed to Roosevelt's landslide victory in 1936, and Eleanor had no small part in their shift to the Democratic party. Her efforts to help blacks did not end with the electoral victory of 1936. She had long been appalled that disfranchised southern blacks were being prevented from voting through threats and intimidation. In 1939, Eleanor actually joined the NAACP, to the delight of black leaders, and in defiance of those in the administration who believed that her affiliation threatened the national Democratic alliance. Attempting to break down color lines in public places and at public events, Eleanor several times straddled her chair between the white and colored sections at segregated gatherings.

Although Franklin was more cautious in publicly championing civil rights, he did not try to restrain her. This was true even after she outraged many white conservatives by resigning from the Daughters of the American Revolution (DAR) in 1939. Howard University in Washington, DC, had planned to present the celebrated black contralto Marian Anderson in concert at Constitution Hall early that year. The DAR owned the hall, however, and refused to let her perform there. Eleanor Roosevelt, who had entertained Marian Anderson at the White House in 1936, was incensed. In her daily "My Day" newspaper column, which ran from 1936 to 1962, she wrote, "The question is, if you belong to an organization and disapprove of an action . . . should you resign or is it better to work for a changed point of view within the organization?" "To remain as a member implies approval of that action," she wrote further, "and therefore I am resigning." A few months later, Roosevelt awarded Marian Anderson a medal at the NAACP annual meeting, and on Easter Sunday of 1939, the singer performed on the steps of the Lincoln Memorial before an integrated audience of 75,000. Eleanor had arranged the event.

Eleanor Roosevelt's dedication to humanitarian issues led her to become known as the "conscience of the New Deal." To be sure, she regularly bent her husband's ear with matters important to her. Public knowledge of this fact led many people within and outside the administration to approach her first with an idea they hoped eventually to present to the president. One such idea came from Harry Hopkins, the head of the WPA, whose youthful experiences in New York settlement house work had imbued him with the same heightened interest in social reform as Eleanor's. He presented a plan for aiding the vast number of underprivileged American youth, who had "grown up against a shut door." The Great Depression had devastated American young people by disrupting the normal progression of life. With the chief breadwinner out of work, the family savings went fast. Life insurance policies were cashed in. The family car went next, if there was one, along with other luxuries. Children of formerly middle-class families were forced to quit school, to seek out poorly paying jobs, and to help support the household. College plans were, of course, canceled, marriage was forgotten, and, for many young males, the best solution was to leave the household one less mouth to feed and live a life on the road as a "hobo."

To help demoralized youth, Hopkins proposed the establishment of a National Youth Administration (NYA) to create and provide jobs for young people in a fashion similar to that of the WPA and the Civilian Conservation Corps (CCC). But the idea was controversial in 1935, because it bore some similarities to Germany's recent regimentation of its youth into the militaristic Nazi Youth Corps. Hopkins approached Eleanor Roosevelt, hoping she would discuss it with her husband. Eleanor explained the idea fully to Franklin, including the political damage it might cause in light of the cost, as well as its probable comparison to what was happening in Germany. "If it is the right thing to do," said the president, "then it should be done. I guess we can stand the criticism." In a variety of projects over the next few years, the NYA provided part-time work for 2.6 million unemployed youths who had dropped out of school. Eleanor was proud that her husband's administration often did "the right thing" without regard to the political consequences.

Eleanor Roosevelt's support for social welfare organizations sometimes took her far afield of her husband's official position. In 1939, for example, she defended the

American Youth Congress (AYC), an organization formed by the Communist party. When leaders of the group were called before the House Un-American Activities Committee (HUAC), she attended, and reported on the proceedings in her "My Day" column. She knew several members of the AYC (including her friend and later biographer, Joseph Lash) and liked the youthful idealism of their cause as much as she disliked the "Gestapo methods" of the HUAC. When Lash was called to testify, Eleanor put aside the knitting she invariably worked on while listening to hearings or committee meetings, picked up a pencil and pad, went to the front of the room, and began to take notes. This intimidated the HUAC even more than her mere presence. They knew their words would undoubtedly appear in "My Day." While aware of the Communist party influence in the group—and stating that fact in "My Day" to the disapproval of her editors—Roosevelt was a staunch defender of freedom of speech and the necessity of listening to youth. It was important to her that young people be involved in public life instead of riding the rails. She urged her readers in her column of December 13, 1939, "Let's be free to express ourselves." This was what "Democracy and our Bill of Rights" were all about. And, although she strained the support of even her husband by standing up for the AYC, public opinion was squarely behind her in 1939. Sixty-seven percent of those polled approved of her job performance, while Franklin won only 58 percent approval.

In his victory of 1936, FDR had withstood attacks from both the right and the left. On the right were the Alf Landon Republicans, and within their ranks the Liberty League, organized in 1934 by conservative businesspeople to protest the New Deal's modification of the free enterprise system. Those who did not feel Roosevelt had modified it enough constituted the other source of criticism. Their leading representative was the Louisiana "Kingfish," Huey Long, who had risen to national prominence in the year before his assassination (September 1935) with his "Share Our Wealth" plan. Among other things, Long had called for a guaranteed annual income of $2,500. Dr. Francis Townsend of California called for $200 per month for all elderly people in the United States and built a following of five million supporters. Father Charles Coughlin of Michigan, "the Radio Priest," meanwhile formed the National Union for Social Justice and broadcast his message of nationalization of all business institutions and utilities in an overall plan, which—like Long's and Townsend's proposals—took from the rich and gave to the poor. Such ideas had a considerable following during the Depression, not only among the poor but also among many intellectuals. Roosevelt, however, took this "radical fringe" in stride and proceeded to build the most powerful political coalition of the twentieth century.

FDR interpreted his reelection in 1936 as a mandate to carry New Deal measures further. Standing in the way of progress, he believed, was the U.S. Supreme Court. Still dominated by conservatives, the court had dismantled the Agricultural Adjustment Act and the National Recovery Act and had recently overturned a New York minimum wage law. Surprising all but his closest advisers, Roosevelt sent Congress a plan for reorganizing—or "packing," as it came to be called—the entire federal court system. Claiming that the court system was "overburdened," the plan was really an attempt to put enough friendly judges on the bench, including the Supreme Court, to ensure the continuation of New Deal legislation. However, a growing coalition of conservative southern Democrats and midwestern Republicans in Congress viewed the Roosevelt plan as a thinly veiled attempt to increase his power. They also saw an opportunity to rebuke the president for introducing an array of liberal laws that they opposed, and consequently defeated the court reorganization bill.

Roosevelt's popularity plummeted over the court-packing scheme and fell even more as a new economic recession set in. "The Roosevelt Recession of 1937," as Republicans branded it, began to erase the gains made since 1933. Steel production, which had risen to 80 percent of capacity, plunged to 19 percent; the stock market began dropping again after years of steady increase; and by the end of the year, over two million workers were among the ranks of the unemployed. Meanwhile, a series of "sitdown strikes"—such as the one on Memorial Day of 1937 at the Republic Steel plant in Chicago, where ten people were killed—prompted many newspapers to blame unionization for the violence and the Roosevelt administration for its support of organized labor.

The cause of the recession was clear to New Deal economists: Deficit spending had fueled the recovery, and now the federal government was attempting to restore a balanced budget. As soon as the economy had recovered during the first term, Roosevelt had started to reduce federal spending. Most of Roosevelt's economic advisers were adherents of the theories of John Maynard Keynes, the British economist who believed that industrialized societies could recover from recessions by increased government expenditures. Such spending, or "pump priming," would stimulate private sector activity, create jobs, and add disposable income to the economy. Never much of a Keynesian, Roosevelt feared the repercussions of continued deficit spending. But with the recession threatening to become severe, the president authorized $5 billion for new public works programs. In 1938, the second Agricultural Adjustment Act became law, calling for more crop reductions and soil conservation payments, export subsidies, and government purchase and storage of grain and other produce. A guaranteed minimum wage of twenty-five cents per hour was ensured by passage of the Fair Labor Standards Act of 1938. The Supreme Court's negation of New Deal programs became less a threat as archconservative associate justice Willis Van Devanter retired in June 1937. Roosevelt quickly appointed Hugo Black, a justice to his liking, and gained a 5 to 4 majority on the bench.

Deficit spending worked moderately well as the severity of recession declined by 1939. Unemployment, which had risen to 19 percent in 1938, dropped to slightly over 17 percent in 1939. But Franklin Roosevelt's popularity stood on shaky ground. Prosperity itself had mixed blessings, for the better off people became, the less they supported the activist government of the New Deal. Many who had eagerly supported the New Deal earlier were becoming, in Harry Hopkins's words, "bored with the poor, the unemployed and the insecure." Moreover, the perceived liberalism of the New Deal eventually eroded the support of many small-town Democrats even though farmers still supported the agricultural programs. The question of a third term loomed ahead. If Roosevelt did decide to run for a third term, he would be the first president to do so. Republicans, confident because of their success in the 1938 midterm congressional elections, believed their candidate, Wendell Willkie, a former Democrat who had never held public office, was unbeatable. As a utility company executive, Willkie had opposed Roosevelt's regionalized, government-owned electrification enterprise, the Tennessee Valley Authority (TVA). This stance appealed to conservatives. Most of Willkie's views, however, were moderate to liberal. Armed with a powerful speaking ability and good looks, Willkie satisfied both conservative and moderate Republicans.

Franklin and Eleanor Roosevelt pondered the prospects of a third term as the election approached. Eleanor believed that Franklin would not run. He was physically and mentally exhausted and simply "did not want the nomination." Franklin's had been a partnership presidency between him and Eleanor, and both actually looked forward to retiring to their "dream house" currently being built at Hyde Park. Although they still had separate lives and bedrooms, their relationship had slowly improved during the past decades. Retirement seemed wise, considering Franklin's health. But Eleanor was deeply troubled because no preparations were being made for a successor. Every day, people urged Franklin to run again. They argued that his leadership was required for the times that lay ahead. Shortly before the Democratic national convention in Chicago, it became obvious that Roosevelt would be renominated. Reluctantly, the Roosevelts accepted.

Neither Franklin nor Eleanor planned to attend the nominating convention, but controversy soon embroiled the event. John Nance Garner of Texas, Roosevelt's current vice president, had removed himself from consideration because of differences over what he regarded as the too-liberal measures of the second New Deal. Franklin favored his secretary of agriculture, Henry Wallace of Iowa, but many delegates opposed the former Republican for his adherence to a kind of mystical socialism. With several conservatives nominated, party leaders insisted that one of the Roosevelts would have to nominate Wallace personally to break the deadlock. Franklin, who had been enigmatic about the campaign, persuaded Eleanor to make the nomination. Urging Democrats to "sink all personal interests in the interests of the country," her words brought calm and reason to the convention. "You will have to rise above considerations which are narrow and partisan," she declared in her high-pitched, resonating, patrician voice. "This is a time when it is the United States we fight for." Sixteen years earlier, at the 1924 convention, Eleanor Roosevelt had been relegated to sitting outside a committee room and passing messages to the male delegates. In 1940, she stood before the entire convention, bringing about order, unity, leadership, and the nomination of Wallace.

Wendell Willkie ran a vigorous campaign, traveling over 30,000 miles and delivering more than 500 speeches. Willkie opposed Roosevelt's bid for a third term, decried the domination of government by one man, and condemned the recession of 1937. Although Willkie criticized specific measures, he generally agreed with the New Deal's principles and goals. Willkie's early rise in the polls compelled the president to go on well-publicized inspection tours of defense plants that were really campaign junkets. In stirring radio addresses, he called attention to the lines of workers he had seen filing into the Boeing and Douglas factories in Seattle and Los Angeles, and he alluded to the "whirring wheels and beehive of activity" he had seen at New England defense plants. War preparation was taking the issue of the economy away from Willkie as the Roosevelt administration steadily increased defense expenditures after 1939.

Franklin Roosevelt was confident of victory in 1940 for several reasons, but one of the most important was Eleanor. Besides settling the fracas at the convention, the first lady was at the height of her popularity as the election neared. "My Day" was syndicated in over sixty newspapers and reached four million subscribers. While this was only a small fraction of the total number of American newspaper subscribers, Eleanor Roosevelt also made frequent headlines with her travels, press conferences, and commentary. Even those who disagreed with her ideas and causes had to concede begrudgingly that hers was the work of "a genuine do-gooder." Those who called her a "busybody" or a woman who did not know her place only enhanced her reputation among people who celebrated the change in women's roles that she symbolized. Three million more women were in the nation's work force in 1940 than in 1930, many of them working mothers, and the first lady provided inspiration to them.

The election results of November 1940 confirmed the importance of Eleanor's influence. Franklin had won with about 55 percent of the popular vote and a plurality in electoral votes of 449 to 82. Willkie, however, had carried traditionally Republican states, and Roosevelt's appeal in the South had dwindled. He had won the election by carrying metropolitan areas like New York City, Chicago, Cleveland, and Milwaukee, which tipped the balance in New York, Illinois, Ohio, and Wisconsin. New Deal programs had had considerable impact on urban areas, and the first lady's support of civil rights was well publicized. There was a dramatic shift in the urban black vote to the Democratic side in 1940, and the first lady undoubtedly had a role in that transformation as well.

Eleanor's widely publicized associations with blacks overshadowed the reality of her gradualist posture on race. Unwilling to offend certain whites, she commented publicly about her efforts to "understand the southern point of view." As late as the second New Deal, she used the antebellum slave term *darky* until informed by an outraged black reader of its offensive racist overtones. Such comments, however, were probably more a reflection of the amazing level of institutionalized prejudice of the era than of any personal bigotry on Roosevelt's part. She was sincere in her opposition to racism, and actions spoke louder than words. Photographs of the first lady embracing blacks were spread throughout the South in attempts to split the Democratic party. But the same photographs also reached northern urban areas and sent a strong and heartening message to black voters about the Roosevelt administration. By calling attention to the problem of racism in the United States, Eleanor Roosevelt helped win a third term of office for her husband.

One year before the election of 1940, Franklin Roosevelt declared, "I have seen war, and I *hate* war." He was referring to his own experiences in World War I, but at the same time he was also preparing the American people for involvement in another global conflict. World War II began on September 1, 1939, when Nazi Germany launched a "blitzkrieg" invasion against its eastern neighbor, Poland. Two days later, England and France had declared war on Germany. German chancellor Adolf Hitler's fine-tuned war machine smashed through the Polish army—one of the best armed in eastern Europe—in a matter of days, alarming those throughout the world who had believed that another great conflict could be avoided. A brief lull after the Polish conquest led the wishful to call this a "phony war," but few world leaders were willing to curtail military preparations. "This nation will remain neutral," announced Roosevelt after the Polish invasion. But he recognized that American sentiments would not remain so. A few weeks later, Congress repealed the arms embargo clause of the Neutrality Act of 1937 to allow belligerent nations to purchase arms on a "cash-and-carry" basis. Roosevelt succeeded in gaining congressional appropriation of over $4 billion for defense and, in the interests of national unity, appointed Republican Henry Stimson as secretary of war. Americans were becoming resolute that their involvement in the war would be necessary, but they still hoped that providing England and France with arms and supplies would be a sufficient response.

The lull in the war ended abruptly. In the spring of 1940, German troops roared through Denmark, Norway, the Netherlands, Belgium, and France. The English army stood alone, in opposition to the Nazi onslaught, but the outnumbered and inadequately supplied British troops retreated to Dunkirk, France, and then fled ingloriously back across the English Channel in any available craft, including rowboats. By this time, Benito Mussolini's Italian government was allied with Hitler. On June 22, 1940, news of Germany's conquest of France filled the morning papers. Speaking from London, French general Charles de Gaulle vowed to resist the Germans, but with Luftwaffe (German Air Force) bombs pounding England day and night in preparation for a planned land invasion, his chances of liberating France seemed poor.

As the storm clouds of war gathered in the late 1930s, Eleanor Roosevelt still hoped that disarmament and sanity would prevent the "suicide" of another global conflict. "I breathe again this afternoon," she wrote after British concessions to Hitler in 1938, "in the hope that this meeting in Munich may bring about peace instead of war." But the lifelong pacifist who had lobbied with Carrie Chapman Catt and Mary Garret Hay for the Kellogg-Briand treaty of 1929 outlawing war now feared a world where "freedom and democracy would no longer exist." During the 1940 presidential campaign Wendell Willkie made things easier for the Roosevelts by agreeing it was time to move away from neutrality. At a press conference in the fall of 1940, Eleanor announced her support for repealing the Neutrality Act, suggesting that it was time to deal with the fascists. This was an excruciating turnabout for her. For the past two decades, she had stood firmly with women of all nations who had crusaded for peace. With four sons of military age, she also knew that an official movement away from neutrality might lead to active American involvement in the war. However, she had been so appalled by the fascist activities of Francisco Franco in the Spanish Civil War during the late 1930s that she had tried to convince Franklin to send troops to support the loyalists there.

Eleanor Roosevelt was even more outraged by the recent violence in Hitler's Germany. Rabid anti-Semitism throughout Germany and eastern Europe had resulted in a wave of violence against Jews and their systematic concentration into detention camps such as Auschwitz and Dachau. In 1935, the Hitler-devised Nuremberg Laws deprived Jews in Germany of their rights of citizenship and made intermarriage between Jews and gentiles illegal. During a night of ruthless terrorism in November 1938, Nazi vigilantes looted and burned Jewish homes and businesses throughout Germany. In light of such events, Jewish groups in the United States pleaded for a relaxation of the restrictions on German immigration.

As a younger woman Eleanor Roosevelt had made some anti-Semitic remarks in her personal correspondence, for example, in 1918 calling the prominent lawyer Felix Frankfurter "an interesting little man but very jew." But in 1939, Frankfurter was appointed to the U.S. Supreme Court with Eleanor's support. Twenty years of experience had taught Eleanor that prejudice in any form was demeaning to both perpetrator and object. She quickly took up the cause of the Jewish refugees, lobbying and gaining Franklin's endorsement for a congressional act to ease the quotas for refugee children. But Congress, pressured by public opinion against additional immigration and vocal opposition from groups such as the American Legion, defeated the Jewish Refugee Children's bill.

Eleanor Roosevelt now focused her energy on supporting the Allies and women's efforts in the war. As in many New Deal programs, women were being overlooked in the staffing of preparedness organizations, and the first lady actively opposed such discrimination. One agency, the Office of Civilian Defense, headed by New York mayor Fiorello La Guardia, had no women in positions of authority. At a press conference in August 1941, Eleanor praised the excellent work of the women's civil defense organization in England and criticized the lack of female participation at home. La Guardia in turn suggested that the first lady become assistant director of the office. Although she worked briefly in the office for no salary, hostile newspapers expressed outrage over a president's wife's holding an official position. In early 1942, after a few months of controversy, she resigned.

By this time, the United States was officially at war. On December 7, 1941, a date President Roosevelt declared "would live in infamy," Japanese bombs destroyed 19 ships and 150 planes and killed 2,335 Americans in a surprise attack on the American naval base at Pearl Harbor in Hawaii. Aggressive in East Asia since their 1931 invasion of Manchuria and their continuing assault on other Chinese provinces, the Japanese were confirming the suspicions of those who believed that they were intent on building an empire. By September 1940, the Japanese were allied with Hitler and Mussolini, forming the Rome-Berlin-Tokyo Axis.

In an unusual circumstance, both Franklin and Eleanor were at the White House on December 7, 1941. Eleanor remembered that an eerie silence reigned for a few moments after news of the attack arrived. But then a whirlwind of activity began. When the throngs of advisers left late that evening, Eleanor had her first opportunity to talk to her husband. She found him more "serene" than he had been in months; at least the uncertainty was over, he explained, and the difficult business of maintaining neutrality while the rest of the world battled was finished. But Eleanor could only recall 1918, when she had sent her husband and her brother off to one war; now she would have to send four sons off to another.

Congress declared war on Japan the day after Pearl Harbor. Germany and Italy declared war on the United States on December 11. In ringing prose, President Roosevelt characterized the decision to use force as a sacred American mission: "When we resort to force as now we must, we are determined that this force shall be directed toward ultimate good as well as immediate evil. We Americans are not destroyers—we are builders."

Perhaps Eleanor Roosevelt was correct when she argued that the New Deal social agenda had helped prepare Americans to pull together in the war effort. The spirit of cooperation in a nation of rugged individualists had been unprecedented in the 1930s. And at no time in American history was public opinion so unified behind any event as it was at the outset of World War II. Thirty-one million Americans registered for the draft under the Selective Service Act of 1940. Between 1939 and 1945, U.S. Army ranks grew from 174,000 to 8.3 million. An additional 7 million men and women enlisted in other branches of the armed forces. Always outspoken on women's rights, Eleanor Roosevelt favored conscription for young women and witnessed the creation of a women's auxiliary army corps in 1941, which was renamed the Women's Army Corps (WAC) in 1943. Later on in the war years came the women's navy volunteer service known as the WAVES, the Women Marines, the Coast Guard's SPARS, and the Women's Air Force Service Pilots (WASPs). Despite these advances, Eleanor lamented that American auxiliary servicewomen were not being given as many duties as in the British and Australian women's corps. Despite the hardships of military service, she wrote in "My Day," "women can stand up under that type of living as well as men" and therefore should have more "full participation." Because women were declared ineligible for combat duty, their status remained secondary throughout the war, and they were consequently denied many of the veteran's benefits that accrued to men.

As in World War I, the mobilization of the 1940s entailed massive industrial redirection. Whereas in 1939 only 6,000 planes had been produced in the United States, the mass production techniques developed by Henry Ford led to the construction of more than 300,000 aircraft in the next six years. In addition, American factories produced three million machine guns and achieved over sixty million tons of shipping capacity. And while it had taken 105 days to build a ship in 1939, American shipyards were producing a unit every 14 days by 1945. The gross national product (GNP), never greater than $90 billion during the 1930s, soared to over $200 billion in 1945. Not only had the Japanese "awakened a sleeping giant" in their attack on Pearl Harbor, but they had, in effect, ended the Great Depression.

With thirteen million men in military service and wartime industrial production rising, a labor shortage developed, especially in the defense industry. As a result, over six million women entered the national work force in defense jobs. By 1945, women composed 36 percent of the work force and were performing welding, riveting, drilling, and other fabrication jobs that up to that time had been performed only by men. Although government war planners like Secretary of War Henry Stimson and Office of War Mobilization director James Byrnes actively encouraged women to work in industry, shipyards, plants, and factories, women consistently earned much less than men for the same work. Moreover, employers made working mothers' lives even more difficult by granting limited child care and enforcing rigid working hours.

Eleanor Roosevelt celebrated women's entering the work force but was angered by their treatment in comparison to what she witnessed on her tour of England. Winston Churchill, the British prime minister, was a great admirer of Eleanor, and he and Franklin agreed that sending her as a goodwill ambassador would brighten both English spirits and those of American soldiers stationed in Great Britain. She met the royal family and the Churchills, delivered a radio address to British citizens, and visited troops about to be sent overseas. The first lady marveled at the work that women were doing in the British Isles. England had lost nearly one million male soldiers in World War I, and mobilization for World War II left the country desperately short of labor. Women literally ran the country, building cars and trucks, performing maintenance work, managing civil defense, flying Royal Air Force planes away from Nazi target areas, and operating military hospitals. Reporting back to the United States in "My Day," Eleanor wrote, "I hope . . . that the opportunity . . . to see the work which the women are doing in Great Britain may also be of use . . . to our women at home."

The devastating effects of aerial warfare were evident throughout England and Europe in 1942. "It is really appalling what one big bomb can do," Eleanor commented after viewing aerial photographs of Allied bombing raids on Germany, "and certainly a well-organized raid with skilled people in planes can leave a city practically in ruins." The war in Europe raged during her visit. In June 1941, Hitler had broken the Nazi-Soviet Nonaggression Pact, which had allowed for the Nazi invasion of Poland, and had smashed into the Soviet Union in a surprise attack. Armored divisions and infantry totaling fifteen million soldiers moved east from Germany, Hungary, Romania, Czechoslovakia, and Bulgaria. Hitler's objective was to destroy Moscow and the Soviet military capability while capturing the rich oil fields near the Caspian Sea. Because western Europe had fallen so easily, Hitler was able to move the bulk of his fighting forces to the eastern front, where the most intense fighting of the war was taking place. Meanwhile, the Nazi forces invaded northern Africa behind the leadership of Field Marshal Erwin Rommel, the "Desert Fox." By the end of 1941, war had spread from the northwestern corner of the continent, south to Africa, and deep into the Soviet Union.

Since the onset of "Operation Barbarossa" (the Nazi invasion of the Soviet Union), the United States had been supplying the Soviets with arms through the same lend-lease policy that was providing England with American goods. It had been easy for President Roosevelt to work with Churchill; the Americans and the British shared a similar history, language, culture, and worldview. Agreements such as the Atlantic Charter of 1941, which set wartime and postwar goals, were the result of this good working relationship. However, neither leader—especially the conservative Churchill—found it easy to work with his Soviet counterpart, Marshal Joseph Stalin. In addition to the bloody purges that facilitated his rise to power, Stalin was leader of the most powerful communist country in the world. Still adhering to the dogma that workers of the world would eventually overthrow the capitalist bourgeoisie, the Soviets were at least as ideologically threatening to democracies as the fascists. Yet Churchill, Roosevelt, and Stalin all had a common enemy that posed an imminent military threat. Ideological differences and postwar scenarios had to be put aside. Throughout the war, Roosevelt, who in 1933 had supported the official recognition of the Soviet Union by the United States, served as intermediary between the mistrustful Churchill and Stalin.

For every letter received condemning Eleanor Roosevelt's 1942 visit to England, dozens praised it. The condemnations usually followed the same chorus as the hate mail of earlier days by arguing that a woman's place was in the home, but they now added the new complaint of unnecessary travel. Indeed, the War Production

Board (WPB), established in 1942, had restricted travel; it also rationed gasoline, food, fabrics, and metals, and set nationwide thirty-five-mile-per-hour speed limits. Although some branded the English trip as a luxury junket, far more celebrated the morale-boost provided by the engaging first lady's presence. In response to charges of unnecessary travel, Eleanor used her position as "the First Lady of Radio," to urge compliance with the WPB restrictions, and also advocated the purchase of $100 million in war bonds.

The Nazi domination of Europe coincided with Eleanor Roosevelt's return to the United States. On the eastern front, the city of Leningrad (now Saint Petersburg), on the Baltic Sea, was enduring what would become a 900-day siege, while German artillery also hurled shells into Moscow. Advancing Nazi divisions, meanwhile, braced for the Battle of Stalingrad near the Caspian Sea. Stalin had long been upset with other Allied leaders for their delay in establishing a second European front to divert the German onslaught in the east. Whether unable or unwilling, however, Churchill and Roosevelt waited until the end of 1942, when Nazi forces bogged down amid the fierce Russian winter—and an even fiercer Soviet counterattack.

Churchill's "soft underbelly" plan, in which Allied forces would first move through North Africa and the Mediterranean region, began in late 1942. As Allied armies poured into Casablanca, Cairo, and Algiers, it became evident that the Nazi war machine had overexpanded. Field Marshal Rommel's tank corps, although battling brilliantly, literally ran out of gas as supply lines from Europe were cut. By May of 1943, North Africa was in Allied control. Next, Allied forces headed by American general Dwight Eisenhower invaded Italy and brought about the fall of Mussolini's government on July 25; on October 13, Italy joined the Allies. The real turning point of the war in Europe, however, occurred at Stalingrad (now Volgagrad), where 250,000 Nazis and 200,000 Soviets died in blazing tank and infantry battles in 1942 and 1943. The Nazi advance was stopped in September. From Stalingrad, the Red Army began a relentless push toward Berlin.

Meanwhile, the war with Japan took several turns. Pearl Harbor had been a highly successful strategic attack, leaving the Pacific naval forces of the United States devastated. While the Americans regrouped their navy, the Japanese moved quickly to establish a shield of fortified islands across the ocean. By the spring of 1942, however, the American fleets were steaming across the Pacific. Although several American battleships had been damaged or destroyed at Pearl Harbor, none of the navy's aircraft carriers—which, by chance, were out on maneuvers—had been disabled. The strategic value of aerial warfare in naval battles was confirmed in the tactical draw at the Battle of the Coral Sea, north of Australia, in May 1942, and in the American victory in the Midway Islands in June 1942, where American dive bombers sank four Japanese aircraft carriers and with them about 300 planes. Thereafter, two main forces, directed by General Douglas MacArthur and Admiral Chester Nimitz, set out to reverse the Japanese advance through the South Pacific. Retaking islands on which the Japanese military was firmly entrenched required land, sea, and air assaults. The toll on American soldiers was very high in the liberation of such islands as Guadalcanal and the Marshall Islands.

Because of the heavy fighting around Australia and New Zealand, Franklin Roosevelt and his advisers wanted to send their ambassador of morale and goodwill there in 1943. Eleanor Roosevelt had already visited military training bases and hospitals throughout the nation, had entertained Winston Churchill and Madame Chiang (the wife of Chinese leader Chiang Kai-shek), and had visited war plants in Mexico with Franklin. She had also received word that the ship on which her son Franklin, Jr., served had been bombed in the Mediterranean, and that he was slightly injured. At first, she declined to go on the mission to the South Pacific because of the bad press she had received for her trip to England. However, she agreed to make the tour when the Australian government made an official request. Eleanor also persuaded her husband to allow her to visit military combat zones and hospitals in the war-torn South Pacific.

Naval officials were initially reluctant to allow the first lady to come to a war zone. Admiral William Halsey said that he would permit the first lady's visit only "if it did not interfere with the conduct of the war." Eleanor Roosevelt's ability to boost morale among the soldiers, with whom she dined and talked, and her dramatic effect on wounded men were so apparent that even Admiral Halsey had to acknowledge her value. Taking only her typewriter for writing her daily column and a suitcase, and dressed in a Red Cross uniform (which she had paid for), the first lady talked to over 400,000 soldiers during her five-week trip. After visiting Australia and New Zealand, she traveled in military planes along with other soldiers to seventeen Pacific islands. The night before she arrived at Guadalcanal, Japanese planes bombed American beachheads there, inflicting many casualties. Eleanor gathered the names and addresses of hundreds of soldiers, promising to contact the families of each. She told American readers of the hastily dug graves, in which fragments of bodies that never made it to the cemeteries were laid to rest. "Wherever they lie," wrote Roosevelt from Guadalcanal, "is consecrated ground since they gave their lives so others might live in peace and freedom. . . . We must build up the kind of world for which these men died."

If Eleanor Roosevelt's comments hinted at an end to the war and an Allied victory, her opinions were shared by many Americans by 1944. The tide had turned in both theaters of war. In Europe, Churchill, Stalin, and President Roosevelt had met at Tehran, Iran, late in 1943 to discuss new strategies and postwar conduct. While Allied forces led by General George Patton moved northward from Italy, and the Red Army continued to reverse the German advance through eastern Europe, the strategists planned a huge amphibious invasion of northern Europe. The D-Day invasion began on June 6, 1944, and saw three million troops land along the beaches of northern France, initiating a rapid retreat of Nazi forces. In the Pacific, American forces wrenched from the Japanese the occupied islands of Micronesia, while naval victories inflicted heavy damage on the imperial fleet.

Eleanor Roosevelt, meanwhile, made another goodwill trip, this time visiting troops stationed throughout the Caribbean and Latin America. After traveling 13,000 miles and stopping at dozens of military bases, she returned to find only mild disapproval for her trip amid great praise. Complaints did come from New York governor Thomas Dewey, the Republican presidential candidate in 1944, who, like Alf Landon, promised that his wife would stay home as first lady. If Wendell Willkie had received the Republican nomination, it is possible that Franklin Roosevelt might not have run. The president confided his ideas for a postwar world to

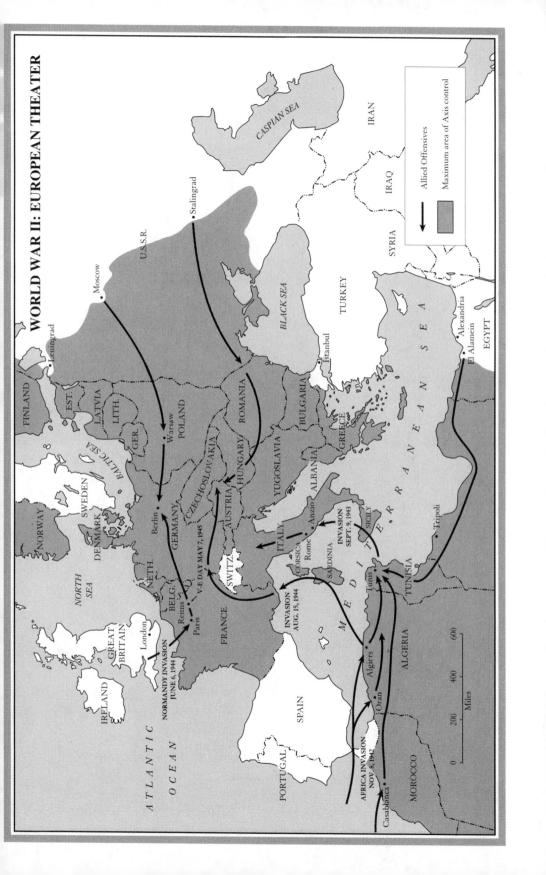

WORLD WAR II: EUROPEAN THEATER

Allied Offensives

Maximum area of Axis control

CASPIAN SEA

IRAN

IRAQ

SYRIA

TURKEY

BLACK SEA

EGYPT

Alexandria
El Alamein

Istanbul

GREECE
Crete

MEDITERRANEAN SEA

Tripoli

TUNISIA
Tunis

SICILY
INVASION
SEPT. 9, 1943

Anzio
Rome
ITALY
Corsica
SARDINIA

ALBANIA

YUGOSLAVIA

BULGARIA

ROMANIA

HUNGARY

AUSTRIA

SWITZ.

Stalingrad

Moscow

U.S.S.R.

Leningrad

FINLAND

EST.
LATVIA
LITH.
GER.

BALTIC SEA

SWEDEN

NORWAY

DENMARK

NETH.
BELG.

Warsaw
POLAND

CZECHOSLOVAKIA

GERMANY
Berlin

V-E DAY MAY 7, 1945

Reims
Paris
FRANCE

INVASION
AUG. 15, 1944

ALGERIA
Algiers
Oran

SPAIN

PORTUGAL

MOROCCO
Casablanca

AFRICA INVASION
NOV. 8, 1942

NORMANDY INVASION
JUNE 6, 1944

London
GREAT
BRITAIN

IRELAND

NORTH
SEA

ATLANTIC OCEAN

Miles
0   200   400   600

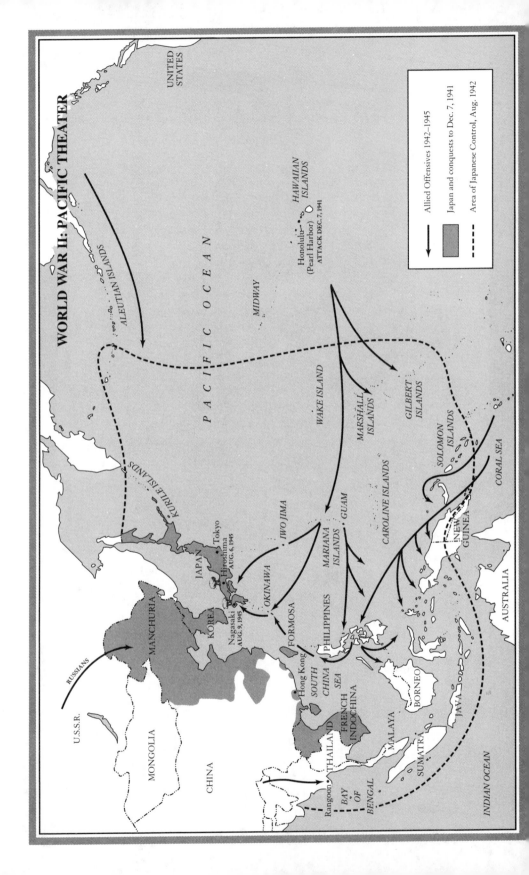

WORLD WAR II: PACIFIC THEATER

UNITED STATES

PACIFIC OCEAN

ALEUTIAN ISLANDS

HAWAIIAN ISLANDS

Honolulu-
(Pearl Harbor)
ATTACK DEC. 7, 1941

MIDWAY

WAKE ISLAND

MARSHALL ISLANDS

GILBERT ISLANDS

SOLOMON ISLANDS

CORAL SEA

KURILE ISLANDS

Tokyo
Hiroshima
AUG. 6, 1945

JAPAN

IWO JIMA

GUAM

CAROLINE ISLANDS

KOREA

OKINAWA

MARIANA ISLANDS

Nagasaki
AUG. 9, 1945

FORMOSA

PHILIPPINES

NEW GUINEA

AUSTRALIA

MANCHURIA

RUSSIANS

Hong Kong

SOUTH CHINA SEA

U.S.S.R.

MONGOLIA

CHINA

THAILAND

FRENCH INDOCHINA

BORNEO

MALAYA

Rangoon

BAY OF BENGAL

SUMATRA

JAVA

INDIAN OCEAN

Allied Offensives 1942–1945

Japan and conquests to Dec. 7, 1941

Area of Japanese Control, Aug. 1942

Willkie. But Willkie died before the 1944 campaign began. Roosevelt disliked Dewey and did not want him to decide the fate of the postwar world. Believing that only he could defeat Dewey, Franklin Roosevelt agreed to run for a fourth term even though the rigors of twelve years as president had seriously eroded his health. When Republicans used the sixty-two-year-old president's age as an issue, Roosevelt launched a vigorous campaign tour while also directing a war. Eleanor campaigned hard for her husband, again ignoring the "stay at home" issue. Attempting to make an issue of the first lady failed this time as well, and the Roosevelt magnetism prevailed in another victory.

After meeting with Stalin and Churchill at Yalta, near the Black Sea, in January 1945, Franklin returned to the United States exhausted. The long flight, the lengthy meetings with the tough Soviet negotiators, and the additional war-progress briefings were extremely taxing on the man who had been president for twelve years. Shrouded in a black cloak, with dark circles under his eyes, and plagued by a nagging cough, Roosevelt appeared in stark contrast to the sagacious Stalin during the sessions. Franklin's health continued to decline after his return to the United States. He began seeing fewer people, and exhaustion forced him to take naps in the afternoon. For the first time ever, he delivered his state of the union address to Congress while sitting down. Eleanor recognized his weakened condition but was afraid to let him slide too far toward invalidism. She continued to occupy him with her agenda for the postwar world and social reform.

Franklin Roosevelt's vacation at Warm Springs in April 1945 was a much needed one. In one respect, Eleanor opposed the respite, fearing that Franklin might never have the strength to work again. However, the first lady knew that rest was imperative as she assumed more and more of his duties. On April 12, 1945, Eleanor, who was attending a benefit in Washington, received an urgent message to return to the White House. On the way there, she feared the worst. Earlier in the day, she had learned that Franklin had fainted while posing for a portrait. Press Secretary Steve Early broke the news to Eleanor when she arrived at the White House: Franklin had died of a cerebral hemorrhage. The tragedy was compounded for Eleanor when she learned that Lucy Mercer Rutherford (Franklin's paramour of the 1910s) had been present at Warm Springs when he died. Against Eleanor's demands, Mercer had visited the White House several times when the first lady was away. Franklin and Eleanor's daughter, Anna, who had arranged the meetings, said their encounters were for dinner and companionship only. But no one dared tell Eleanor. Terribly distressed by both her husband's death and the revelations about Lucy Mercer, Eleanor Roosevelt stared numbly out the window of the Pullman car on the train that carried Franklin's body north from Georgia. Their long and enigmatic relationship, a relationship marked by love and resentment, need and mistrust, was over.

Franklin Roosevelt missed the end of the war in Europe by less than a month, as Allied armies from east and west descended on Berlin. Hitler committed suicide while Allied artillery pounded the capital city of the Nazi empire to rubble. On May 7, 1945, the remnants of Hitler's forces surrendered to the Allies.

The most far-reaching decision of World War II, however, was left to Roosevelt's successor, Harry Truman of Missouri. Truman had replaced the too-liberal

Henry Wallace as Roosevelt's running mate in the 1944 campaign. Truman's decision concerned the war in the Pacific. Recent American victories at Iwo Jima, the Philippines, and Okinawa had pinned the Japanese back to their home islands by mid-1945. After an incendiary bombing raid on Tokyo killed 80,000 people in May, Japan still refused to surrender. President Truman was then given a new and fearsome option in lieu of an invasion of the Japanese mainland: the atomic bomb. In 1939, a group of scientists led by Hungarian refugee physicist Leo Szilard had sent an urgent message to President Roosevelt. They told him of Germany's advanced work in developing atomic weaponry and stated that such weapons could tip the balance of power in any war. Roosevelt responded with the top-secret Manhattan Project, a $2 billion research and development program conducted at Los Alamos, New Mexico; Oak Ridge, Tennessee; Hanford, Washington; and Chicago, Illinois. The government employed top nuclear scientists such as J. Robert Oppenheimer and Edward Teller. Six years later, in July 1945, after the successful detonation of an atomic device at White Sands, New Mexico, the scientists presented the atomic bomb option to Truman. Because of the extreme secrecy of the Manhattan Project, Truman had no prior knowledge of the bomb project.

Truman wrestled with the choice of using the most powerful weapon ever devised or launching an invasion—one that his advisers warned could result in hundreds of thousands of American casualties. At the Potsdam Conference, in July 1945, Truman, Stalin, and Churchill agreed to give one more ultimatum to the Japanese. The ultimatum made no mention of the atomic weapon, and Truman did not tell the leaders at Potsdam about it either. Truman had harsh words for Stalin at Potsdam based on the bomb's potential. If Truman used the bomb on Japan, it would surely send a message to the Soviets to practice restraint in East Asia. On August 6, a lone B-29 bomber, the Enola Gay, dropped the first atomic bomb on Hiroshima. The equivalent of 20,000 tons of TNT devastated the city, killing at least 80,000 people. Three days later, a second B-29 dropped another weapon on Nagasaki, killing 45,000 and maiming many more. On August 14, 1945, Japan surrendered. World War II was over, and the nuclear age had begun.

A week after her husband died, Eleanor Roosevelt wrote in "My Day," "Because I was the wife of the President, certain restrictions were imposed upon me. Now I am on my own." No longer the first lady, Eleanor did not want "to feel old" or to "cease trying to be useful in some way." She had been the first lady for twelve years and had redefined the position. Her human rights crusades had forced the New Deal to respond and Americans to take notice. Millions of troubled Americans had written to her, pouring out their problems to a person they trusted. She had taken up the cause of a generation of American youth displaced by the Great Depression. She had supported black civil rights and had also spoken for all minorities, including American Indians, Asians, and Latinos. Roosevelt had used her position and her example to battle for women's rights and benefits for working mothers. She had expressed herself as an equal in male-dominated politics, and such temerity had earned her the wrath of people who believed that women should stay home and keep silent. Often speaking out without regard to the political consequences, the first lady had set the pace in women's politics and had paved the way for increasing female participation in the system. When the war began, Roosevelt had been campaigning for national health insurance, the expansion of public education, and improved conditions for American workers. But her energy in lobbying for the New Deal had been equaled or exceeded by her support of the Allied war effort. She had served not only as the president's "eyes and ears," but also as his voice to millions of soldiers the world over. At age sixty, Eleanor Roosevelt had every right to retire, but this was not her way.

Having witnessed the violence and suffering of two world wars, the former first lady devoted the rest of her life to world peace. She believed that a peaceful world must emerge from a war in which as many as fifty million lives had been lost. She shared her husband's view of the postwar world, where all nations would work together to avert more wars. She feared the destructive power of the military technology developed in the war, especially the atomic bomb. But Roosevelt believed that, despite the horror of nuclear war, atomic weaponry made world leaders realize that "they must do something about preventing war or there [was] a chance that there might be a morning when we would not wake up." She planned to work for world peace privately, but President Truman gave her no opportunity to retire from public life. In late 1945, he nominated her as a delegate to the first United Nations General Assembly. The postwar world placed great hope in the United Nations (UN). It would be a place, as Roosevelt wrote, "where anything which troubles the world can be brought out and aired." At first, she declined Truman's appointment, fearing that she knew too little about international politics. Truman prevailed, however, and Roosevelt began to view her new position as an opportunity to work for peace. The UN Charter drawn up in San Francisco in April 1945 was signed by fifty nations, but only five—the United States, the Soviet Union, Great Britain, France, and China—had veto power. What emerged as the UN took shape was a bipolar division between Eastern and Western countries (or, in effect, the Soviet Union and the United States).

Harry Truman was a shrewd politician who had served two terms in the Senate before becoming vice president. He recognized Eleanor Roosevelt's widespread popularity, and keeping her in his administration was sound politics. As UN ambassador, Roosevelt brought calm, charm, and patience into a volatile arena. Many male delegates, including the Republican senator Arthur Vandenberg and ambassador John Foster Dulles, opposed her nomination, believing her to be "an emotional, addle-brained woman." They succeeded in placing her on what they viewed as the least important committee (the humanitarian committee). There, they believed, she could not "do much harm."

Roosevelt surprised everyone with her service in the UN. What critics viewed as weaknesses—her declining hearing, her grandmotherly appearance, her politeness, and her idealism—proved to be her strengths. She forced a careful, methodical review of all issues and approached each problem with the calm and patience of a wise elder. Even the Soviet delegates, with whom she often battled, regarded her with respect. Rather than being bullied by the communist delegates, as her opponents had feared, Roosevelt supported Truman's hard line toward Soviet expansion and stood firm when Soviet delegates attempted to abridge clauses of the human rights declaration. Both Dulles and Vandenberg made public statements retracting their doubts about Roosevelt. She was named chairman of the Commission on Human Rights in 1947 and proved to be the driving force behind the Universal Declaration of Human Rights in 1948.

Long outspoken against Nazi atrocities against Europe's Jewish population during the war, Eleanor Roosevelt was instrumental in promoting a postwar state of Israel. Horrified by knowledge of the Holocaust, in which Hitler had begun ordering the systematic slaughter of Jews in concentration camps in 1942, Eleanor had nonetheless been unable to persuade her husband to take action during the war. The fierce "restrictionist" backlash resulting from his support of the Jewish Refugee Children's bill in 1939 had indicated the political volatility of the issue to the president. Even when reports confirmed that Jews were being executed at Auschwitz in late 1942, Franklin Roosevelt rejected rescue plans and strategies to bomb the gas chambers, and he refused to pressure Congress to allow more Jewish immigration. He believed that a quick end to the war was the only way to help the Jews. Only after the war ended, however, did the world learn of the enormity of the Nazi atrocities. To the six million Jews who died in Hitler's death camps, Eleanor Roosevelt felt deep responsibility. Although Americans could not have prevented the Holocaust, they could have saved thousands of the victims. She dedicated her efforts to securing recognition of Israel, which became a formal state in 1948.

As UN ambassador, Eleanor Roosevelt made three trips to Israel, toured the Middle East, visited India and Pakistan, and attended memorial services at Hiroshima in 1953. The former first lady was easily the most respected and well-known person in the UN. However, her popularity and pragmatic competence in the UN did not satisfy FBI director J. Edgar Hoover or Senator Joseph McCarthy. Both men kept her under investigation as a possible "Communist sympathizer." But Roosevelt, with public opinion still strongly behind her, shrugged off their attacks. For her service in the UN, which lasted until Truman left office in 1953, Roosevelt was hailed as "the First Lady of the United Nations."

Refusing to slow down after retiring from UN service, Roosevelt continued to write her column. During the 1950s, she remained the most popular columnist among American women. She also hosted a daily forty-five-minute radio program on NBC, interviewing guests ranging from conservative senator Owen Brister to physicist Albert Einstein. She continued to speak out on civil rights issues, public education, and divorce, and she publicly expressed support for birth control. Traveling to the Soviet Union in 1957, Roosevelt interviewed Premier Nikita Khrushchev, an interview that earned her journalistic acclaim—and the continued surveillance of Hoover's FBI agents. At the age of seventy-five, she accepted a teaching appointment at Brandeis University, continued her writing, fought for disabled citizens' rights, and pursued other social work.

It is appropriate that before she died in 1962 Eleanor Roosevelt served on President John F. Kennedy's Commission on the Status of Women. The commission's 1963 report called national attention to the dramatic changes that had taken place in the postwar United States. The number of working women had increased from 13 million in 1940 to 22.4 million in 1960, and 13.6 million of those women were married. By 1960, over 31 percent of all married women had joined the national work force. The report coincided with Betty Friedan's *Feminine Mystique*, a powerful indictment of the reversion of women back to housewife status during the 1950s.

"Eleanor Was Here" was a common phrase among Allied soldiers during World War II. Here the first lady visits a war zone in the South Pacific.

Less than six months before his death, FDR greets well-wishers on election night, 1944. Eleanor and daughter Anna stand behind.

In 1957, Eleanor Roosevelt interviewed Soviet premier Nikita Khrushchev at Yalta. Although their conversation was "friendly," they differed strongly on the issue of communism.

As a UN delegate, Roosevelt listens alongside Ambassador Adlai Stevenson to a translation of a general assembly address. President Kennedy returned Roosevelt to the UN in 1961 after her eight-year absence during the Eisenhower administration.

Three years later, Friedan was one of the founders of the National Organization for Women (NOW), established to fight sexual discrimination. Its manifesto declared that "NOW is dedicated to the proposition that women . . . are human beings, who, like all other people in society, must have the chance to develop their fullest potential." Eleanor Roosevelt would have approved, but as her own experience had taught, equality was hard won.

Though her health was failing, Eleanor Roosevelt continued work until just a few days before she died of tuberculosis in 1962 at the age of seventy-eight. Without doubt, she would have approved of the gains made in the coming years by the women's movement and all other human rights crusades. Yet her traditionalism might have been offended by the more radical expressions of the women's movement or the militant excesses of the student antiwar movement. She was not a militant feminist; in fact, she opposed the Equal Rights Amendment until a few years before her death. She had chosen to maintain a marriage for the traditional reasons of family and public appearance. Rather than join a political party for women, she had chosen to work within the existing two-party system. She had moved slowly and methodically on civil rights, not wanting to offend segregationists. She had suppressed her heartfelt pacifism to become a leading promoter of the war effort. And she had drawn a firm line for democracy and American interests in the postwar era. Such stances, however, merely demonstrate the human ambivalence and political pragmatism of a person who was a sincere altruist and a firm believer in the merit of the system of government in the United States.

Eleanor Roosevelt did much to change male views toward the proper role of women in society. Never willing to stay at home, she led a life of activism. She helped change the status of women in politics by hard work in political organizations. Redefining the role of a political wife, she gave inspiration to women who recognized new possibilities. She set aside personal comfort and happiness, devoting her life to public service during depression, war, and peace.

After Franklin's death, Eleanor often gathered her children and twenty-four grandchildren together at Val-Kill. The younger grandchildren were often awed and perplexed by their "grandmere," who was always very gentle with them but also obviously revered by all the grown-ups. It always took some time for Eleanor Roosevelt's secretary to explain to the curious grandchildren just who their "grandmere" was.

SELECTED READINGS

The Person

Beasley, Maurine H.: *Eleanor Roosevelt and the Media* (1987). An insightful account of the impact of the mass media on Roosevelt and her use of it.

Black, Allida M.: *Casting Her Own Shadow: Eleanor Roosevelt and the Shaping of Postwar Liberalism* (1996). Traces Roosevelt's causes from the time of her husband's death.

Chadakoff, Rochelle (ed.): *Eleanor Roosevelt's My Day: Her Acclaimed Columns, 1936–1945* (1989). Selected and annotated columns from Roosevelt's days as first lady.

Flemion, Jess, and Colleen M. O'Connor (eds.): *Eleanor Roosevelt: An American Journey* (1987). Illustrated anthology containing scholarly articles and reminiscences.

Goodwin, Doris Kearnes: *No Ordinary Time: Franklin and Eleanor Roosevelt: The Home Front in World War II* (1995). Thorough biography of Franklin and Eleanor during the war years.

Hickok, Lorena: *Reluctant First Lady* (1962). Personal account by one of Eleanor Roosevelt's best friends during the 1930s.

Hoff-Wilson, Joan, and Marjorie Lightman (eds.): *Without Precedent: The Life and Career of Eleanor Roosevelt* (1984). Recent interpretations of Roosevelt's public life.

Lash, Joseph: *Eleanor and Franklin: The Story of Their Relationship Based on Eleanor Roosevelt's Private Papers* (1971). The definitive biography written by one of Eleanor Roosevelt's closest friends.

Roosevelt, Eleanor: *The Autobiography of Eleanor Roosevelt* (1961). An abridged compilation of her three autobiographies: *This Is My Story* (1937), *This I Remember* (1949), and *On My Own* (1958).

Wiesen Cook, Blanche: *Eleanor Roosevelt* (Vol. 1, 1884–1933) (1993). Exhaustive biography of Roosevelt's life before becoming first lady.

Youngs, J. William T.: *Eleanor Roosevelt: A Personal and Public Picture* (1985). A concise, thorough, readable biography.

The Period

Cott, Nancy F.: *The Grounding of Modern Feminism* (1987). An enlightening analysis of the feminist movement in the United States.

Deutrich, Mabel E., and Virginia C. Purdy: *Clio Was a Woman: Studies in the History of American Women* (1980). Papers and discussions from the Berkshire Conference on Women's History in 1976 covering a broad range of issues.

*Evans, Sara M.: *Born for Liberty: A History of Women in America* (1989). A thorough survey history.

*Kraditor, Aileen S. (ed.): *Up from the Pedestal: Selected Writings in the History of American Feminism* (1968). Useful excerpts of American thought on feminism from colonial times to the 1960s.

*Leuchtenberg, William E.: *Franklin D. Roosevelt and the New Deal, 1932–1940* (1963). The best overview of the Roosevelt administration in the years before World War II.

Roosevelt, Eleanor: *It's Up to the Women* (1933). The first lady's "how to" book for American women dealing with the Great Depression.

*Ryan, Mary: *Womanhood in America: From Colonial Times to the Present* (3d ed., 1983). Perhaps the most useful of several general surveys.

*Snell, John L.: *Illusion and Necessity: The Diplomacy of Global War, 1939–1945* (1963). Traces the causes and course of World War II.

*Tugwell, Rexford G.: *The Democratic Roosevelt: A Biography of Franklin D. Roosevelt* (2d ed., 1969). A detailed account of FDR, focusing on the New Deal, and written by the consummate New Dealer.

Ware, Susan: *Holding Their Own: American Women in the 1930s* (1982). An insightful account of women's roles during the Great Depression.

---

*Available in paperback.

Wyman, David S.: *The Abandonment of the Jews: America and the Holocaust, 1941–1945* (1984). Explores the options presented to the Roosevelt administration and the actions not taken.

FOR CONSIDERATION

1. In what ways did Eleanor Roosevelt's childhood propel her into a career of public service?

2. In contrast to those who formed the National Woman's political party in the 1920s, Eleanor Roosevelt remained in the Democratic party. As a feminist and women's rights advocate, why did she stay in the male-dominated party?

3. As a governor's wife and first lady, Roosevelt was known as a "new woman." With regard to her personal life, politics, gender, and race how did she, like Henry Ford, demonstrate ambivalence about being a "new woman."

4. Eleanor Roosevelt's popularity grew steadily as first lady. Discuss the unusual relationship between Eleanor and Franklin with regard to the presidency during depression and war.

5. Eleanor Roosevelt has been called the most important woman of the twentieth century. Do you agree with this statement?

Martin Luther King, Jr.

*P*erspiring *in the sweltering heat of a Washington August afternoon, Martin Luther King, Jr., looked down from the steps of the Lincoln Memorial at the largest assembly ever congregated in the United States. Well over 200,000 people, 70 percent of them blacks, jammed the mile-long mall that swept away to the Washington Monument. Angry yet hopeful, they had come to the nation's capital in 1963, the centennial of the Emancipation Proclamation, to personify black demands for equality in society. But the speakers and singers who preceded King had not been particularly effective, the heat and humidity were oppressive, and the great crowd was starting to thin around the edges. As he mounted the podium King sensed this restlessness and the need for a focus. At first his deep voice was husky, but it soon became resonant with a purpose that quieted and transfixed the multitude and the millions of television viewers. King's eloquence dramatized the anguish of black history. One hundred years after slavery, he pointed out, the black was still "an exile in his own land." It was the future, however, that mattered. "I have a dream," he cried repeatedly, as he sketched his vision of freedom, justice, and harmony. At the end of his speech King prophesied that one day all people would be able to join together in singing the words of an old Negro spiritual: "Free at last! Free at last! Thank God Almighty, we are free at last." There was an awed silence, then an ear-shattering roar; the crowd was applauding wildly. King had galvanized the massive assembly. At that moment he stood at the crest of a mounting wave of African-American protest. Yet, as King must have known, his dream would have an agonizing birth. Just five years after his Washington address, he lay dead on the balcony of a Memphis motel, the victim of the violence he had devoted his life to overcoming.*

On September 2, 1864, the great-grandparents of Martin Luther King, Jr., looked on with astonishment as 100,000 Union soldiers under the command of General William T. Sherman marched triumphantly into their hometown, Atlanta, Georgia. Sherman, on his way from Tennessee to the Atlantic Ocean, was slicing the Confederacy apart. For slaves like the Kings, his presence in Atlanta was reason for both joy and fear. On the one hand, it promised freedom; on the other, it meant changes with which the ex-slaves were ill prepared to cope. Some of the bitter fruits of liberation were already apparent. Sherman's scorched-earth policy had left Atlanta a smoldering ruin. Equally searing were the hatreds and rivalries that swept over the South during Reconstruction. The Kings were caught in the middle of a power struggle in a conquered province. The participants were northern whites determined to maintain federal authority, and old-line Confederates anxious to regain control of their region. In addition, Republican and Democratic politicians fought for control of the votes of a reunified South.

This competition briefly elevated southern blacks to a position of prominence. Between 1868 and 1877, military occupation of the South made "Black Reconstruction" possible. Black votes sent a few blacks to the U.S. Senate and House of Representatives. In South Carolina's lower house, blacks even constituted the majority. But if freed slaves such as the Kings interpreted this as genuine power, they were sadly mistaken. At best, many of the black voters were puppets in the hands of self-seeking white politicians. And when northern zeal for forcing Reconstruction flagged in the late 1870s, the freed slaves found themselves virtually friendless. The restoration of white supremacy in the South followed immediately. For blacks like Frederick Douglass, the promise of the Civil War had turned to ashes. True freedom, it appeared, would not come all at once. The old social relationships would be slow to erode.

Martin Luther King's grandfather, James Albert King, was a case in point. He was born in 1863, the year of the Emancipation Proclamation, and the Union victory two years later seemed to guarantee him equality of opportunity. As James grew up, he, too, had a dream for the future. It consisted of the ownership of a small farm, economic independence, and a measure of self-respect. But even these modest hopes were doomed to frustration. Despite the efforts of the Freedmen's Bureau created by Congress in 1865 to assist ex-slaves, James King's fortunes declined. Within a few years he had sunk to a condition of economic dependence that was tantamount to slavery.

For James King the process began when he moved from Atlanta to Stockbridge, Georgia, in the late 1870s and took work as a sharecropper for a white landlord. Under this arrangement he farmed a white man's land and took a share of the harvest as his wages. He hoped eventually to accumulate the means to purchase his own land, but his economic situation never improved. And even if he had managed to surmount the legal, social, and economic obstacles that southern whites put in the way of would-be black landowners, the crop-lien system waited to strip him of any gains. The local merchant would lend black farmers equipment and provisions against their future crops. At the harvest the merchant often claimed all the crops and more. Keeping black farmers in a state of continual debt worked as a subtle but effective system of social repression. Looking back on his father's life, Martin Luther King, Sr., bitterly commented that James had worked "from sun up to sun down for a whole year and still owed 'the man' $400 for the privilege of working."

In the last two decades of the nineteenth century the southern states took steps to make sure that the James Kings remained on the bottom of the political, economic, and social structure. Segregation laws and customs took firm root after the withdrawal of the last northern troops in 1877. Most southern states eventually revised their constitutions to include discriminatory regulations against blacks. James King found himself in a divided world. Racial ostracism extended to churches, schools, housing, jobs, restaurants, and transportation. Even cemeteries were segregated. Indeed, the separation of the races in the postbellum South was sharper than it had ever been in the slave era.

In 1883, the U.S. Supreme Court found the Civil Rights Act of 1875 guaranteeing African Americans "free and equal enjoyment" of public accommodations unconstitutional. The court's finding symbolized the growing feeling in the North that, once freed, black people had to fend for themselves and succeed on their own. Even former abolitionists and other liberal reformers were reluctant to take up the lance on blacks' behalf. Slavery, it seemed, was one thing; equal opportunity for the former slaves, another. It was quite true that many whites who detested slavery also detested the prospect of having black people as social, economic, and political equals. A backlash of sympathy for the southern whites' "problem" spread rapidly in the North after the Civil War. Few Americans protested when, in 1890, Mississippi led a parade of southern states in instituting a poll tax. These measures, in effect, snuffed out the black male suffrage provided for in the Fifteenth Amendment, which only twenty years earlier had been the pride of Radical Reconstruction.

Although James King and millions like him had received no schooling, education offered one way out of the morass that was black life in the postbellum South. Not only did it promise economic rewards and a genuine role in self-government, but it also offered a road to social respect. John C. Calhoun of South Carolina had inadvertently suggested this before the Civil War, when he remarked, "If a Negro could be found who could parse Greek or explain Euclid, I should be constrained to think he had human possibilities." Calhoun had clearly dismissed the possibility, but his remark was obviously a challenge to those of a different persuasion. After the Civil War many white educators and philanthropists were determined to call Calhoun's bluff. With the help of the Freedmen's Bureau and the tiny corps of educated southern blacks, they launched a system of elementary education for blacks of all ages. A few black colleges appeared, notably Hampton, Fisk, Howard, and Atlanta University. Wealthy northerners such as George Peabody and John D. Rockefeller gave millions for black education. Northern churches contributed additional money as well as numbers of young people who attacked the challenge of educating the ex-slaves with energy and idealism. Southern blacks were glad to have these friends, but frequently the idealism of the educational missionaries did not match the ex-slaves' immediate capacities and needs. Impressive as parsing Greek and explaining Euclid might be in demonstrating innate ability, the usual nineteenth-century college curriculum had little relevance to the blacks' situation. The man who discerned this problem most clearly and, in solving it, became the most significant black American in the generation before Martin Luther King's birth was Booker T. Washington.

Born a slave on a plantation in Franklin County, Virginia, in 1856, Washington determined at an early age to make something of his life, and his autobiography, *Up from Slavery* (1901), reads very much like Benjamin Franklin's. After the Civil War, Washington worked in West Virginia's coal mines and attended school at night. In 1872, he entered the Hampton Institute in Virginia and worked his way through school as a janitor. At Hampton, Washington came under the influence of Samuel Chapman Armstrong, a teacher who emphasized the importance of personal industry and honesty as prerequisites to success. Washington learned, in his words, "thrift, economy and push [in] an atmosphere of business, Christian influences, and the spirit of self help." These values became the hallmark of his approach to the black situation.

After graduating from Hampton in 1875 and teaching for several years, Washington was selected in 1881 to organize a school for blacks at Tuskegee, Alabama.

The resulting Normal and Industrial Institute became Washington's lifework and his key to fame and influence. Martin Luther King, Jr., always referred to Washington's method for uplifting his race as "patient persuasion." Washington believed in a conciliatory approach to the white establishment. He urged blacks to subordinate considerations of political and social equality to those of economic advancement. Respect for the law and cooperation with authority followed.

Washington's formula for black advancement was the one he had learned at Hampton. Through dedication, thrift, and industry, blacks would establish the firm economic base necessary for first-class citizenship. "Let down your buckets where you are," was his advice. "Be content," Martin Luther King interpreted this as meaning, "with doing well what the times permit you to do." The fact that the result was most often humble manual labor for an elite did not disturb Washington in the least. "The opportunity to earn a dollar in a factory just now," he once remarked, "is worth infinitely more than the opportunity to spend a dollar in an opera house." And he illustrated this philosophy by personal example. On one occasion, Washington, by then famous as the president of Tuskegee Institute, was on his way to his office when a wealthy white lady demanded that he stop and chop a pile of wood. Without a word, Washington removed his coat, cut the wood, and carried it to the kitchen. After he left, a maid told the lady that her woodcutter was Professor Booker T. Washington. Mortified, she appeared at his office the next day to make an awkward apology. "It's entirely all right, madam," Washington replied. "I like to work, and I'm delighted to do favors for my friends." From that day on, the lady became one of Tuskegee's most generous benefactors; her gifts and those of her friends amounted to hundreds of thousands of dollars.

Whites everywhere, particularly those in the South, were delighted by Washington's lack of emphasis on civil rights and social equality. Especially after his 1895 address at the Cotton States Exposition in Atlanta, Washington became the national symbol of the "good Negro." The Atlanta Compromise, as his doctrine came to be known, and his emphasis on vocational instead of college education seemed to whites to mark an acceptance by blacks of a servile status. Under Washington's leadership, conservative whites felt confident that blacks would "keep their place."

To Martin Luther King, Jr., Washington's approach to black equality at the turn of the century "had too little freedom in its present and too little promise in its future." King did not call Washington an "Uncle Tom" who compromised rights for the sake of peace; Tuskegee's leader was sincere in desiring full equality for blacks. The problem, King felt, was Washington's optimistic belief that whites would, in time, reward the hardworking, well-behaved black with respect. Looking back on Washington's time and analyzing his own, King believed that this confidence had been misplaced. Washington, according to King, had underestimated the depth of evil that permeated racial discrimination. "As a consequence," King continued, "his philosophy of pressureless persuasion only served as a springboard for racist southerners to dive into deeper and more ruthless oppression of the Negro."

Washington's philosophy also faced criticism in his own time among his own people. William Monroe Trotter and William E. B. Du Bois led the attack on Washington's compromise. The result of it, they feared, would be an American caste system with blacks permanently at the bottom. Du Bois was the leader of the attack on gradualism. A decade younger than Washington, a northerner from Great Barrington, Massachusetts, and the son of a reasonably well-to-do family, Du Bois's perspective was worlds apart from that of the ex-slave. A companion of whites since childhood, he regarded himself as their equal. In intelligence he felt himself to be superior, and he hoped to enter Harvard. Lack of funds thwarted these plans temporarily, and Du Bois accepted a church scholarship at Fisk. Travel and study in Europe followed, and in 1895, Du Bois received a Ph.D. from Harvard University.

In view of their backgrounds, it was to be expected that Du Bois and Washington would differ sharply in their analysis of and prescription for the black problem. Du Bois believed strongly in the value of higher as opposed to vocational education. Proficient himself in science, social science, and literature, Du Bois saw no reason why blacks could not compete as equals with whites and forge to the top. In contrast to Washington's stress on practical, manual training for the masses, Du Bois believed in giving the "exceptional men" of his race intensive higher education. This "talented tenth," to use his phrase, would enter professions like law, medicine, and teaching and win respect for the rest of their race.

Du Bois taught at Wilberforce University in Ohio and at the University of Pennsylvania before moving to Atlanta in 1900 to pursue his pioneering sociological studies of black Americans. Until this time Du Bois had not appreciated the full strength of racism in the Deep South. But his experience in Atlanta, which included witnessing a lynching, removed his illusions. Increasingly militant, he became impatient with Washington and conciliation. Such accommodation, he believed, might work for some blacks, but others should be encouraged to strive for excellence. Refusing an invitation to teach at Tuskegee, Du Bois publicly attacked the "Tuskegee machine" and accused Washington of advocating quasi-slavery. In 1905, Du Bois joined with William Trotter, editor of the Boston *Guardian*, and other black intellectuals in the first organized opposition to postbellum racism. The Niagara Movement proposed to assail America's conscience with loud and unceasing protest, but it lacked funds and white support. As Washington was fond of pointing out, it accomplished little—but a seed had been planted, a seed that people like King would later nourish.

In his impatience with patience, Martin Luther King, Jr. was in tune with William Du Bois. But in regard to the "talented tenth" idea, the men were at odds. According to King, the Du Bois program excluded the masses. "It was," in King's words, "a tactic for an aristocratic elite who would themselves be benefited while leaving behind the 'untalented' 90 percent." King's dream did not leave anyone behind.

For black Americans, the progressive movement offered promise without fulfillment. While writers and politicians filled the air with cries for social justice, blacks' lot continued to be one of broken dreams. The hopes that flared in 1901 when Theodore Roosevelt invited Booker T. Washington to a luncheon in the White House quickly died. None of the three progressive administrations passed significant legislation on behalf of blacks. If anything, discrimination increased in these years. Almost everywhere blacks found themselves stripped of the right to vote, barred from labor unions, denied decent housing, and, as a result of the

Supreme Court decision in *Plessy v. Ferguson* (1896), confined to separate and usually unequal public schools. President Woodrow Wilson even segregated federal employees.

Moreover, the progressive years witnessed a bitter white backlash. Racial violence increased in the North as well as in the South. Over 1,000 blacks were lynched between 1900 and 1914. When black author Ida B. Wells published a book calling for antilynching legislation, her personal property was destroyed and her life threatened. In Brownsville, Texas (1906), and Springfield, Illinois (1908), angry mobs ran roughshod over black communities. One of the worst riots of this period occurred in Atlanta and must have touched the lives of people like the James Kings. At the height of the disturbance in September 1906, whites, enraged by alleged rape charges, attacked every black in sight. When they encountered resistance, tempers flared even higher. White and black eyes could not meet without suspicion, and fear haunted the soft southern nights much as it had in the times of slave insurrections. Like immigrants, blacks were regarded as aliens and resented by a society uneasy over the pangs of rapid growth and change.

The increase in discrimination in the early twentieth century tested the incipient civil rights movement. Booker T. Washington, maintaining his optimism, remarked that no matter how bad his situation was in the United States, he was still far better off than the depressed classes of Europe. But even Washington finally wearied of the continual abuse and called racism a cancer in the nation's heart. William Du Bois continued his militance. In 1909, he joined a number of white liberals, including Jane Addams, to found the National Association for the Advancement of Colored People (NAACP). Although dominated by whites (Du Bois was the only black officer), the NAACP became the most substantial and long-lived organization of its kind. Its Legal Redress Committee attacked all forms of discrimination in an effort to obtain constitutional rights for black people. The NAACP's magazine, *The Crisis*, which Du Bois edited for many years, had 100,000 readers by the end of World War I. After 1911, the NAACP was joined in its crusade by the National Urban League, whose particular concern was the plight of blacks in cities.

These developments did not have much meaning, however, in Stockbridge, Georgia, where James King struggled on under the crushing weight of the crop-lien system. By this time in the Deep South, "the man" was fully in charge, and among illiterate blacks, the spark of resistance had long been extinguished. Fortunately, it was periodically rekindled in the young. James King's son, Martin Luther, Sr., was bright and ambitious. As a teenager he became disgusted with his father's poverty and passivity. Determined not to inherit this condition, Martin left the worn-out fields and crumbling shacks of Stockbridge in 1916. He was seventeen years old, and he was going to try his luck in Atlanta. In the larger city, he reasoned, there would be more job opportunities and, he hoped, more freedom. In time, there might be economic security, perhaps a house he could call his own. Moreover, the bloody race riots of 1906 had left in their aftermath the Atlanta Civic League and a group of white and black citizens determined to ease the city's social tensions. Atlanta was as good a place as any to start the climb toward dignity.

In leaving the rural South, Martin Luther King, Sr., joined a stream of younger, dissatisfied African Americans. By the end of World War I, emigration from the

South had reached flood proportions. Martin chose a southern city, but many of his contemporaries moved to the metropolitan areas of the North and the Middle West, where defense industries were hungry for labor. Hundreds of thousands traveled up the Mississippi River to Saint Louis and on to Chicago, Detroit, and Cleveland. Another path of migration terminated in New York City's Harlem. Those who followed these escape routes from the rural South brought little but hope and frequently found frustration. In fact, the urban ghettos were epitomes of segregation, and the barriers between African Americans and success were just as high as in the southern countryside. Occasionally, however, an individual emerged from the squalor and frustration that was the usual lot of urban blacks. Such was the case with Martin Luther King, Sr. A decade of diligent work in Atlanta left him with a modest bank account and, thanks to evening classes, a high school diploma. He also found time to preside as minister over two small Baptist churches and to marry the daughter of one of Atlanta's foremost black clergymen. The Kings were living with him in Atlanta's best black neighborhood when Martin, Jr., was born on January 15, 1929.

At the time of Martin Luther King, Jr.'s birth the prospects for black Americans were far from promising. Of course the democratic rhetoric and the emphasis on national unity during World War I had raised hopes in much the same way as had the Civil War. Blacks proved eager customers for war bonds and thronged to enlist in the armed forces. Fighting for their nation, they believed, would be a sure way of winning gratitude and respect. But most whites thought otherwise. Military leaders refused to integrate the armed forces or appoint black officers. The most menial and dangerous tasks fell to black soldiers. Discrimination persisted even in the trenches in Europe. Blacks received far more fair treatment at the hands of the French than they did from their own countrymen. There were even reports that the Germans treated captured black soldiers with more consideration than they received from their colleagues in arms.

Nonetheless World War I inspired African Americans, particularly those who fought in Europe, to press forward the crusade for civil rights. William Du Bois expressed the prevalent attitude in *The Crisis* for May 1919 when he wrote, "*We return. We return from fighting. We return fighting.* Make way for Democracy! We saved it in France, and by the Great Jehovah, we will save it in the U.S.A., or know the reason why." But the war to make the world safe for democracy had not secured it in the United States. Equality, it appeared, was still a white possession. The troops had scarcely returned from "over there" when a series of bloody race riots turned the summer of 1919 into a nightmare for blacks. In Chicago alone, thirty-eight persons died in four days of what amounted to civil war. A revived Ku Klux Klan (KKK) spurred the racial strife. Long lines of white-robed whites marched slowly yet menacingly through the black neighborhoods. They were still marching in the 1930s when Martin Luther King, Jr., recalled seeing them from his window. If these tactics did not intimidate minorities, the KKK administered floggings and worse. Hardly a lunatic fringe, the organization's five million members were scattered by the mid-1920s from Mississippi to Maine. Still, much of the bloodshed of the post–World War I years was the consequence of a new spirit among black people. For the first time since the era of slave insurrections, urban blacks fought back from their ghettos in a more or less organized manner. The poet Claude McKay caught the mood of defiance when he wrote that blacks would no longer die "like hogs, hunted and penned in an inglorious spot," but rather "pressed to the wall, dying but fighting back."

The pride implicit in McKay's statement became a factor of increasing importance in African-American history during the decade of Martin Luther King's birth. It also provided the bedrock of confidence on which King subsequently helped construct the freedom movement. Several components figured in the growth of white and black appreciation of black cultural values and traditions. One, of course, was simply the passage of time. The experience of slavery had left a scar on the black mind that healed slowly. Slaves, or the children of slaves, could not easily regard themselves with esteem. But those like Martin Luther King, Jr., who were three generations removed from slavery could begin to look upon themselves and their heritage with new eyes.

The first important herald of race pride was Marcus Moziah Garvey. A Jamaica-born man with piercing eyes and a talent for charismatic leadership, Garvey organized the Universal Negro Improvement Association in New York City in 1916. Its motto was "Back to Africa." Garvey called upon blacks to leave the United States, return to their African homeland, and build a mighty nation. The idea, to be sure, was neither new nor universally accepted among American blacks. King, for example, later termed Garvey's program an admission of defeat, a confession that black people were incapable of winning a just release from discrimination. Moreover, King pointed out, most blacks in the United States could not easily go back to Africa for both practical and psychological reasons. For better or worse, they were Americans. Garvey's grandiose plans, which included orders of nobility such as the Knights of the Nile and a costly Black Star Steamship Line, aroused only jeers on the part of the more sophisticated protest leadership.

Yet, as King recognized, Garvey's message transcended a simplistic back-to-Africanism. "He called," as King put it in 1964, "for a resurgence of race pride." In a manner that anticipated the Black Power advocates of King's own time, Garvey drew attention to a truth long dormant in the black mind: There was no disgrace in being black. Indeed, Garvey went further to suggest that black was beautiful, that black people had a heritage as old and as distinguished as that of whites. Millions of blacks thrilled to Garvey—even after he had been arrested for mail violations and deported to Jamaica—with a degree of emotionalism that testified to the depth of their former sense of inferiority.

Music was one of the first tangible expressions of the African-American pride that Garvey did so much to advance. Since the 1890s, black Americans had played an increasingly important role in influencing popular music in the United States. Ragtime, blues, and jazz were successive outgrowths of black talent and the black experience. Moving north from New Orleans as cultural baggage in the great migration, jazz, especially, took the country by storm. The music of Joe "King" Oliver, Kid Ory, and Louis Armstrong crossed the color line in its appeal. The Harlem area of New York eventually became the nation's jazz capital, and the compelling improvised sounds became closely associated with black identity. Behind the appeal of jazz was the assumption that black culture was freer, wilder, more sensuous, and more joyous than that of whites. Perhaps, more Americans than ever before concluded, these people had a distinctive and distinguished contribution to make to American cultural life. In fact, jazz gained enough prominence to name the age in which Martin Luther King, Jr., was born.

The sense of identity that Marcus Garvey promoted and that jazz portrayed also flowered in the Harlem Renaissance. The term refers to the artistic and intellectual explosion that took place among the residents of New York's black ghetto during the 1920s. The renaissance was the work of the "new Negroes"—militant, proud, wanting to contribute to American culture, yet determined to preserve their racial identity. Writers like Langston Hughes, Claude McKay, Countee Cullen, and Jean Toomer managed to do just that. Also making major contributions to the rise of black art and letters were the respective Harlem-published journals of the NAACP and the National Urban League: *The Crisis* and *Opportunity*. One of the most significant aspects of the Harlem Renaissance was the way it attracted white admirers. Blacks were suddenly more than laborers and servants. The allegedly exotic, primitive, unrepressed quality of black life fascinated young white Americans. Many thronged uptown to Harlem's clubs and cafes to partake of a commodity a later generation would deify as "soul."

Although he was born on the brink of the country's terrifying skid into the Great Depression, Martin Luther King's childhood was more secure and comfortable than that of most southern blacks. Martin's father's determination to break the chains of poverty and illiteracy paid dividends for his son. Sixty-five percent of Atlanta's black population was on relief at one time or another during the Great Depression, but around the Kings' spacious home on Auburn Avenue, sandlot ball games and Christian fellowship continued without interruption. Of course all was not base hits and love for young Martin; inevitably his life crossed the "color line," and he learned the meaning of prejudice. For Martin, the dream was shattered at the age of six. He had been accustomed to playing ball with two white boys in the neighborhood. One day their mother told him in no uncertain terms to leave and not come back because her sons were white and he was black. After tearfully relating the story to his mother, he received an explanation of the extent of race hatred. But he was cautioned never to hate in return. Quite probably Alberta King, the daughter of an NAACP leader, had read in that organization's journal a letter that the Indian pacifist Mahatma Gandhi had written to blacks in the United States. Gandhi counseled them to put their trust in love and nonviolence. He also reminded Americans of color not to be ashamed of their heritage of slavery; there was dishonor only in having been slaveholders. The prejudiced, in other words, were more to be pitied than the objects of their prejudice. Turning the other cheek was a sign of superiority. It was a message that stayed with Martin Luther King as he became one of the greatest proponents of nonviolent protest in American history.

Like many black mothers, Alberta King concluded most of her discussions of race with her son by pointing out, "You are just as good as anyone else, and don't you forget it." But the reality of southern life taught a different lesson. Martin never forgot his father's indignation when an Atlanta shoe store refused him equal service. Taking the bewildered Martin's hand, he stalked out of the store, using the boycott idea Martin would later employ with great effectiveness on a larger scale.

The boy also learned how to organize and influence people by observing his father in action. Martin, Sr., was the local leader of the NAACP, an active member of the Atlanta Voters League, and a director of Morehouse College. Understandably, talk at the King dining table frequently turned to the subject of black rights and the struggle for their realization. Martin, Jr., was never far from the freedom movement he led as an adult.

While Martin Luther King moved through elementary and secondary school at a grade-skipping pace that prepared him for college at the age of fifteen, the nation staggered through the most traumatic decade in its economic history. The Great Depression worked special hardship on American blacks. In times of unemployment they invariably found themselves "the first fired and the last hired." In 1935, the percentage of unemployed blacks was nearly double that of whites. Job discrimination was never more rampant than during hard times.

Because of their traditional allegiance to the "liberating" Republican party, most of the low percentage of African Americans who voted in the election of 1932 cast their ballots for Herbert Hoover. In November 1932, the shape of Franklin D. Roosevelt's New Deal was still unformed and its effectiveness uncertain. But after the 1934 congressional elections, it was apparent that the Democrats were making massive gains among blacks. By 1936, the majority supported Roosevelt. Their vote was in direct response to the effectiveness of New Deal relief and recovery measures in easing their particular plight.

New Deal programs had mixed blessings for blacks. Public works programs like the Works Progress Administration (WPA) provided urban employment, but the Agricultural Adjustment Act (AAA) displaced poor black farmers throughout the South. Still, the New Deal laid the foundations for better days. For the first time since Reconstruction, the federal government was recognizing and endeavoring to ease their conditions of life and work. As president, Roosevelt did more than any of his predecessors. At the behest of First Lady Eleanor Roosevelt, blacks were included in nearly every phase of his administration, some achieving high federal posts. The economist Robert C. Weaver, for example, headed the president's informal "Black Cabinet." Roosevelt's highly publicized refusal to sign an antilynching bill in 1938 for fear of losing the support of southern Democrats should be seen in the broader perspective of his entire record. Summing it up, *The Crisis* reported that "for the first time in their lives government [had] taken on meaning and substance for the Negro masses." The 1930s also witnessed the continued growth in effectiveness of the NAACP. Concentrating on legal rights, the NAACP had the assistance of brilliant black lawyers such as Thurgood Marshall, later a Supreme Court justice, and Hamilton Houston. In 1930, the association put enough pressure on the U.S. Senate to block confirmation of President Hoover's Supreme Court nominee, John H. Parker, an opponent of civil rights. Two years later Nathan R. Margold, head of the NAACP legal defense committee, decided to attack the principle of "separate but equal" education. He did not succeed, but he laid the legal foundation that ultimately led to the desegregation decision of 1954.

While attempting to achieve civil rights reform, the NAACP experienced a sharp internal struggle over ideology. Du Bois headed the faction thoroughly disillusioned by the prospects of reform within the national economic and political system. He proposed that blacks voluntarily segregate themselves from that system and turn instead to Marxism. Immensely impressed by his visit to Russia in 1927, Du Bois believed that if African Americans sided with the communists, their combined force could topple a capitalist order already reeling from the Great Depression. The National Negro Congress, founded in 1935 by Ralph Bunche and E. Franklin Frazier among others, was a step toward the organization of a black proletariat. More conservative leaders of the NAACP, such as Roy Wilkins, Walter White, and Martin Luther King, Sr., disagreed strongly with this approach. Pointing to the success of the Congress of Industrial Organizations (CIO) in advancing the interests of black laborers, they were not prepared to abandon capitalism or white America. Eventually they forced Du Bois out of the NAACP and into the Communist party.

After skipping the ninth grade, Martin Luther King, Jr., entered Atlanta's Booker T. Washington High School as a sophomore in 1942. Already he possessed a flair for oratory and a growing understanding of how to use it on behalf of black people. Part of this insight came from observing the course of the national civil rights movement. The ongoing controversy between his father's position and that of Du Bois and the radicals, for instance, sharpened the young King's faith in the power of love and reason to transcend racial separatism. He also received a lesson in the power of nonviolent protest from African-American labor leader A. Philip Randolph. The background of Randolph's campaign was discrimination in the armed services and defense industries during World War II. Despite the explicit provisions of the Selective Service Act (1940), prejudice permeated the drafting and training of blacks. Defense workers were treated similarly. In early 1941, Randolph, who was president of the Brotherhood of Pullman Porters, threatened President Roosevelt with a massive march on the capital to protest this discrimination.

Roosevelt faced the prospect of international embarrassment. He had publicly referred to the United States as the "great arsenal of democracy" and now feared that Germany would use racial problems in anti-American propaganda. But keen politician that he was, Roosevelt was reluctant to alienate southern Democrats by enforcing civil rights legislation. The president begged Randolph to cancel the march. Randolph held firm, and an estimated 100,000 blacks prepared for the protest. Finally, on June 25, 1941, one week before the scheduled demonstration, Roosevelt issued an executive order banning "discrimination in the employment of workers in defense industries and government because of race, creed, color or national origin." He also established the Fair Employment Practices Committee. Old enough to appreciate what had happened, Martin, Jr., filed the knowledge for future reference. He had occasion to recall it six years later, when Randolph again threatened massive civil disobedience and again secured his goal: desegregation of the armed forces.

World War II was in full swing in 1944 when Martin Luther King, Jr., entered Morehouse College in Atlanta. He responded at once to the "freer atmosphere" and to professors who "were not caught up in the clutches of state funds and could teach what they wanted with academic freedom." Much of Morehouse's concern was with racial problems, and King wanted to help his people, but when his thoughts turned to a career he found himself undecided. His father hoped he would enter the ministry, but Martin, Jr., was suspicious. Too often, he felt, religion had been an anesthetic for blacks, the substitution of a vague heavenly afterlife for happiness and justice in the here and now. Business was another possibility, and King had the ability and the contacts to go to the top. Yet here, too, there were problems. The successful "black bourgeoisie," King observed, frequently cared more for personal success than for the condition of the masses. Law seemed more promising. As a southern black King continued to experience a series of degrading confrontations with prejudice that suggested the importance of legal redress. A particularly bitter experience occurred when King returned from an oratorical contest in Valdosta, Georgia, on a public bus. Ordered by the driver to move from seats reserved for whites, King and his friends at first refused. After the driver became enraged, the students reluctantly moved, but King admitted he would never forget the depth of his anger. There was a need for lawyers to break down, as King put it, "the legal barriers to Negro rights."

Gradually, however, King came back to religion as his lifework. Contact with Morehouse's minister-teachers, such as Benjamin E. Mays and George D. Kelsey, showed him how religion could be made socially relevant and practically useful. Ordained in 1947, a year before graduation, King became assistant pastor in his father's church. He also worked with Atlanta's integrated Intercollegiate Council, an experience that softened his previous resentment of whites. Some of them, he realized, were genuinely sympathetic with the condition of black Americans and were worthy colleagues in the fight to improve it.

Following Morehouse, King embarked on three years of graduate study at Crozer Theological Seminary in Pennsylvania. These were years of intellectual quest, as King sought a philosophy for coping with the race problem. His reading of the German philosopher Hegel helped. King responded positively to Hegel's idea that progress can come only through the painful struggle of one condition against its opposite. He also liked the notion that an individual was capable of advancing, if not causing, great historical changes. Marxism, with its emphasis on breaking the hold of the Establishment on the underprivileged, also seemed relevant to the black situation. "Power," he wrote in agreement with Marx, "concedes nothing without a demand. It never did and never will." But unlike the black Marxists of the 1930s, King could not accept Marx's rejection of God as a moving force in human affairs. More to his taste, as a consequence, was the teaching of Walter Rauschenbusch and other proponents of the Social Gospel. Their advice to take religion out of the churches and into the streets struck responsive chords in King. Any faith that was content with people's souls and oblivious of their social and economic condition, he decided, was "spiritually moribund . . . only waiting for the day to be buried."

The most exciting ideas King encountered at Crozer, however, were those of the Indian pacifist Mahatma Gandhi. Ghandi, deeply influenced by Henry David Thoreau's *On the Duty of Civil Disobedience* (1849), had used nonviolent resistance in the struggle to liberate 350 million Indians from British rule. His success in 1948 made a great impression on the youthful King. Gandhi seemed to prove that love and passive resistance might be a powerful agent of social change. This was not, King realized, to deny the reality of hatred and of evil. King was learning to set aside superficial optimism in constructing a meaningful philosophy of reform. He would face evil—and overcome it—with compassion and love. This was close, of course, to the method of Jesus of Nazareth, whose teachings remained King's principal guide.

At Boston University, where King enrolled in 1951 to seek a doctorate in philosophy, the preparation for leadership continued. An important part of it consisted of meeting and marrying Coretta Scott. She was the daughter of an Alabama family whose color had not prevented them from retaining considerable land holdings ever since Reconstruction. Scott had attended public schools in Alabama and, in 1945, Antioch College in Ohio. Although conscious of her role as a "token of integration," Scott had pursued a program of study in elementary education with high enthusiasm. When it came time to student-teach, however, she was barred from the local school system. Thoroughly disillusioned, Scott told herself that as a black she had to face "the problem" no matter how educated or wealthy she became. "This is the first time it has hit you in the face," she thought, "you might as well accept the fact."

After graduating from Antioch in 1951 without the teaching certificate she had hoped to receive, Coretta Scott turned to music and planned her future around the concert stage. She was studying at the New England Conservatory of Music in Boston when she met Martin. His driving sense of mission "to do something for humanity" in general and blacks in particular was contagious. For his part, Martin was immediately drawn to the attractive and intelligent Coretta Scott.

Married in 1953 during Martin's final year of graduate school, the Kings faced a nation whose climate of opinion was slowly but steadily shifting toward a greater understanding of black conditions and black demands. After his favorable 1947 response to A. Philip Randolph's call for an end to segregation in the military, President Harry S Truman set the tone of the new mood. At his inauguration in 1949, for the first time in American history blacks were invited to the major social events. Truman also ordered (July 1948) complete integration of all units of the military, a process that American involvement in the Korean War hastened considerably. Truman's Fair Deal, in the words of NAACP head Walter White, reflected a nationwide recognition "of the new place of all ordinary Americans." The blacks among them were further heartened by the beginnings of African independence. Beginning in the early 1950s, over two dozen black nations emerged from the wreckage of Europe's colonial system. Another object of pride in these years was Ralph Bunche. A political scientist from the University of California at Los Angeles, Bunche had risen to importance in the Department of State and, after World War II, emerged as a world figure as a result of his role in founding the United Nations. Bunche had also negotiated a settlement of the Arab–Israeli dispute of 1948 and, for his efforts, had received the Nobel Peace Prize.

Unquestionably, however, the most encouraging development in the 1950s, and in many ways since the Emancipation Proclamation, was the Supreme Court's reversal of its stand on school segregation. Since the 1930s the NAACP had picked away steadily at the principle of "separate but equal" as laid down by the Court in *Plessy v. Ferguson* (1896). In 1945, Thurgood Marshall assumed leadership of the legal assault, and for the next decade, a steady stream of cases filed by the NAACP sought to test the law. There were signs of a thaw in 1950. Then on May 17, 1954, the Supreme Court handed down an opinion in the school segregation case of *Brown v. Board of Education of Topeka*. When Chief Justice Earl Warren declared that "separate educational facilities are inherently unequal," the long struggle was over, but in many ways it had just begun.

The gap between principle and practice was apparent immediately after the *Brown* decision. Having cleared its conscience with a declaration, the Supreme Court proved a reluctant reformer. Refraining from setting a timetable for desegregation, the Court in May 1955 merely urged school boards to proceed "with all deliberate speed." In many parts of the country, it was deliberate indeed! Emboldened by hesitant national leadership, reactionary forces, particularly in the South, "declared war" on the *Brown* decision. In a manner reminiscent of Reconstruction and of the 1920s, White Citizens' Councils sprang up across the South, and the Ku Klux Klan was reactivated to obstruct integration. Tom Brady, a judge in Mississippi, epitomized the revived contempt for blacks when he urged white southerners to "blow again and stronger on the dying embers of racial hate." But even responsible southern white leadership was agitated. One hundred United States congressmen issued a manifesto pledging their support of those organized "to resist forced integration by lawful means."

In this atmosphere of tense race relations, Martin Luther King, Jr., arrived in Montgomery, Alabama, in September 1954 to take charge of the Dexter Avenue Baptist Church. For a little more than a year the Kings tried to avoid controversy while quietly building a following for their church. But on December 1, 1955, the main current of the freedom movement swung in their direction. On that day a seamstress named Rosa Parks boarded a Montgomery bus, exhausted by a long day's work. Transit regulations stated that blacks, regardless of gender, must relinquish their seats in the black section to whites when all seats had been taken. When Parks, who had been secretary of the local NAACP, refused to give up her seat to a white man, she was arrested for violating city segregation ordinances. Her arrest sparked a storm of discontent, and prompted the Montgomery African-American community to use the incident as a test case for civil rights. E. D. Nixon, a longtime activist in Montgomery, paid her bail and then conferred with King and Ralph Abernathy about a one-day bus boycott. The idea, as King later suggested, was not simply to protest the arrest of Rosa Parks, but to protest the "series of injustices and indignities that have existed over the years."

When Montgomery's entire black population honored the one-day boycott, it became evident that it would be possible to prolong and coordinate the protest. As president of the newly formed Montgomery Improvement Association, King presided over this expansion. His first step was to set forth his philosophy of protest. Putting together what he had learned from Hegel, Rauschenbusch, and Gandhi with his Christian principles, he convinced his colleagues to operate through "persuasion, not coercion." Quoting Booker T. Washington, he warned Montgomery blacks, "Let no man pull you so low as to make you hate him." Nonviolent resisters, King explained, refuse to hate. They do not seek "to defeat or humiliate the opponent, but to win his friendship and understanding." All life, in King's view, was interrelated, all humans were ultimately members of the same family. It followed that "along the way of life, someone must have the sense enough and the morality enough to cut off the chain of hate." It required courage to take this step. Again and again King explained that *"nonviolent resistance does resist."*

On this note King and the Montgomery Improvement Association launched a boycott that ultimately lasted for 382 days. Before it was over, the city's black population had organized its own transportation system using private cars. Women activists were particularly instrumental in sustaining the boycott, and largely through their influence nonviolent resistance prevailed. There were no riots, no fights. Even when King's house was bombed, he admonished angry blacks to love their enemies and trust in God. Finally, in November 1956, the Supreme Court upheld a lower court decision declaring unconstitutional Alabama's laws requiring segregation on public buses. On December 21, King, Abernathy, E. D. Nixon, and a host of reporters joyfully boarded the first integrated bus in Montgomery.

The *idea* of nonviolent resistance was not unknown in the history of black protest. William Lloyd Garrison had advocated it before the Civil War as a response to slavery, and A. Philip Randolph had urged its adoption during World War II. In fact, in 1942 James Farmer had organized the Congress of Racial Equality (CORE) for purposes of instituting massive, relentless noncooperation. But it was not until Montgomery that the hopes of earlier leaders became reality. King demonstrated the ability and the willingness of blacks to challenge the system without "violence of spirit." Granted, the boycott did not noticeably improve the overall social situation of blacks in Montgomery, but it did signal, in King's words, "a new sense of dignity and destiny" among blacks that would henceforth underlie the freedom movement.

As evidence, bus boycotts soon spread to other southern cities, and thirty-five eventually voluntarily abolished bus segregation. Moreover, Montgomery marked the entrance of the masses into the freedom movement. Organizers like Martin Luther King, Jr., made it possible for thousands of black voices to be added to those of the NAACP's corps of lawyers. The result could only strengthen black demands.

After Montgomery, King, now the recognized leader of nonviolent resistance, gathered black religious leaders together in Atlanta in January 1957 to form the Southern Christian Leadership Conference. King, as expected, became president and immediately put pressure on President Dwight D. Eisenhower to come south and personally support the civil rights laws. When he sidestepped the invitation, King and Roy Wilkins of the NAACP went to Washington in May as part of a Prayer Pilgrimage 35,000 strong. The conviction and eloquence of the twenty-seven-year-old minister dominated the assembly even in competition with figures of the stature of entertainer Sammy Davis, Jr., and baseball star Jackie Robinson. In the major speech of the Prayer Pilgrimage, King demanded that southern blacks be given an opportunity to vote without restriction so that they might "quietly, lawfully implement the Supreme Court desegregation decisions." He followed up his speech with a conference with Vice President Richard M. Nixon and, in June, had the satisfaction of seeing Congress pass a Civil Rights Act, the first since Reconstruction. Texas senator Lyndon B. Johnson led the fight for the measure, which empowered judges to jail anyone who prevented qualified persons from voting. The act also established a Commission on Civil Rights to investigate alleged violations.

As one who put his faith in nonviolence, King's reactions to the Little Rock crisis of September 1957 were mixed. It began when Arkansas governor Orville Faubus defied a court ruling giving black children the right to attend Little Rock's

Central High School. The next move was President Eisenhower's. He was reluctant to enforce integration, but as a military man he knew the necessity of enforcing the principle of federal supremacy. For two months federal troops with fixed bayonets escorted nine black children to and from Central High. A unit of the National Guard remained stationed at the school for the entire 1957–1958 academic year. Feelings ran high throughout the country. Little Rock was unquestionably the most serious challenge to federal authority since the Civil War. In some parts of the South the show of federal force hardened resistance to assertions of civil rights. There was a rash of attacks on the persons and property of blacks. But even the diehards could not mistake the significance of active federal involvement. African Americans had a powerful friend.

Late in 1958, King's nonviolent philosophy received a severe challenge. On Saturday afternoon, September 20, he was seated in a Harlem shoe store autographing copies of his new book, *Stride Toward Freedom*, which described the Montgomery boycott. Looking up, he saw a black woman pushing through the crowd toward him. She asked his name, and on hearing it, she drew a long letter-opener from her dress and plunged it into King's chest. She had not used the loaded pistol police later found in her handbag, but, as doctors discovered after a three-hour operation, the point of the letter-opener rested against King's heart. A sudden movement, or even a cough, would have killed him instantly. After he recovered, King told a crowded press conference that he felt "no ill will" toward his assailant; he hoped she would receive the help she obviously needed. Then he added that the real tragedy of the incident was not the injury to himself, but the demonstration "that a climate of hatred and bitterness so permeates areas of our nation that inevitably deeds of extreme violence must erupt." It was King's mission to abolish such violence and still secure freedom for his race.

In February 1959, Martin and Coretta King made a pilgrimage of their own to India. Their host was Prime Minister Nehru, a close observer of the racial problems in the United States and an admirer of King. After visiting the places where Gandhi had worked and taught, the Kings were even more deeply convinced that his technique of massive nonviolent resistance was applicable to black social protest. But on his return to the United States King found a challenge to his philosophy in the growing impatience of black youth and in the ideas of Elijah Muhammad and the Black Muslims. Indeed, in Malcolm X the Muslims had an emerging leader as compelling as King himself. And Malcolm gave no quarter in his criticism of King's methods. Passive resistance, the Muslim contended, made the black defenseless in the face of white hatred. He called for race pride, black nationalism, and the end of integration. The Black Muslims wanted no part of what they considered an inferior white civilization. A campaign for civil rights within that civilization was meaningless. The twenty million blacks in the United States, Malcolm declared, should think in terms of their own superior culture.

Martin Luther King did not agree. There was no salvation for blacks or anyone else, he believed, through separatism and isolation. The only real solution to the problem was the establishment of true harmony among all people. In the eyes of many frustrated black Americans, however, the Muslim solution glittered. King realized that his leadership of the freedom movement hung in the balance, as did

When a federal court order failed to open Little Rock's Central High School to black students, President Dwight D. Eisenhower had no alternative but to send in troops. With their assistance, people like fifteen-year-old Elizabeth Echford were able to attend classes, but at the price of the kind of hostility she is receiving here.

When Martin Luther King, Jr., decided to take the freedom movement to Birmingham, Alabama, in the spring of 1963, he deliberately challenged one of the bastions of race prejudice in the United States. Widely publicized photographs of the protest, like this one of May 3, 1963, aroused the conscience of the nation and the world.

nonviolence. He resigned as pastor of the Dexter Avenue Church in Montgomery and, on January 24, 1960, moved to Atlanta and prepared to devote his life to "a bold, broad advance of the Southern campaign for equality." In particular, he sought "new methods of struggle involving the masses of people"—methods, moreover, that were not violent or unlawful.

The sit-in was one answer. It started as an idea in the minds of several students at North Carolina Agricultural and Technical College in Greensboro. Like most southern blacks, they knew and revered Martin Luther King as the man who had taken on the power structure in Montgomery and won. The students also owned *Martin Luther King and the Montgomery Story*, a booklet which had sold over 200,000 copies since the bus boycott. King's example and an insult suffered by one of the boys the day before inspired a group of four to sit down at a Woolworth's lunch counter in Greensboro and order coffee. The date was February 1, 1960. The students expected to be refused service by the white waitress, and they were not disappointed. What was unusual was that they remained sitting, in silent protest, until the counter closed. And they returned for many days thereafter, suffering verbal and even physical abuse, but supported by the conviction that this was the kind of nonviolent protest King would endorse. On February 4, the blacks were joined at Woolworth's by sympathetic white students from a local women's college. A news story about the sit-in followed, and a new chapter in the freedom movement began.

From Greensboro, sit-ins spread across the South to more than fifty cities, and there were marches and other expressions of support throughout the nation. King and the Southern Christian Leadership Conference presided over the growing movement. It pleased him to hear reports such as one in May 1960 from Nashville, Tennessee, which described the behavior of participants in a sit-in: "When called names, they keep quiet. When hit, they do not strike back. Even when hostile white youth pull hair and snuff out burning cigarettes on the backs of Negro girls, the girls do not retaliate. They pray and take what comes, in dignity." This was the essence of nonviolence, and the stature of King, its chief exponent, increased daily. The demonstrators in many parts of the South carried with them a printed card: "Remember the teachings of Jesus Christ, Mahatma Gandhi and Martin Luther King. Remember love and nonviolence." When harassed, they asked one another what King's response would be. When arrested and jailed, as many were, they sang and prayed as King had taught. But sometimes there was victory. Not only did nonviolence put the onus of brutality on the white segregationists, it also exerted considerable economic leverage. After several weeks of sit-ins, store owners in twenty-seven southern cities agreed to desegregate their operations.

To expand and coordinate the sit-in form of protest, King and his associates in the Southern Christian Leadership Conference helped students organize the Student Nonviolent Coordinating Committee (SNCC) in April and May 1960. Along with a revived Congress of Racial Equality (CORE), it sponsored a series of Freedom Rides across the South. Using interstate buses for transportation and determined to test civil rights laws everywhere they went, riders of both colors put the sit-ins on the road. In May 1961, in Anniston, Birmingham, and Montgomery, Alabama, local police stood aside as white mobs beat the Freedom Riders savagely. Unfortunately for the cause of segregation, they also beat several representatives of the national news services. The resulting pictures were front-page news everywhere. Southern white resistance had also backfired the previous autumn when the story of Martin Luther King's being placed in leg irons and sentenced to four months at hard labor for failing to renew his Georgia driver's license made the headlines. The commotion not only brought the intervention of Senator John F. Kennedy, then running for the presidency, on King's behalf, but it discredited and ridiculed the white supremacists. Nonviolent resistance seemed to be working.

Still, there were moments during the acceleration of the freedom movement in the early 1960s when King had doubts about its future. He knew that the line between passive and violent resistance was very thin. The black protest he had done so much to arouse would be increasingly hard to control and discipline. Young blacks, especially, were chafing at the bit on nonviolence. They demanded action, now, and they were not oblivious of the example of Africa, where dynamic native leaders were violently asserting the independence of their countries. The members of SNCC and CORE, in particular, had serious reservations about King's Southern Christian Leadership Conference and the still more conservative NAACP and Urban League.

Seeking ways to reassert his philosophy and his leadership, King lashed out with criticism of the Kennedy administration. There was too little civil rights legislation and too little enforcement of what laws existed. Responding to Kennedy's promise to put a man on the moon within a decade, King pointed out the absence of a plan "to put a Negro in the state legislature of Alabama" in the same amount of time. The latter, he implied, would be more difficult. It was not just a matter of justice long overdue. King warned Kennedy that he would have to act quickly and decisively if he wished to prevent black discontent from reaching "an explosion point." He also warned him about tokenism. In the fall of 1962, federal authorities literally forced a black named James Meredith into the University of Mississippi. The Kennedy administration and the nation as a whole made much of the "breakthrough," but King pointed out that Meredith's admission was merely a crumb thrown black Americans in lieu of real equality for all. King contended further that tokenism was worse than useless: "It is a palliative which relieves emotional distress, but leaves the disease and its ravages unaffected. It tends to demobilize and relax the militant spirit which alone drives us forward to real change." On another occasion, he put it more bluntly: "It does no good to apply Vaseline to a cancer."

What did do good, in King's opinion, was a massive nonviolent protest campaign like the one he had conducted in Montgomery, which had left in its wake a real and permanent change in institutions and attitudes. With this in mind, in 1962 he led a prolonged effort to "liberate" Albany, Georgia. The local power structure retaliated calmly and efficiently, arresting marchers and closing facilities threatened with integration. As a result, the blacks accomplished little. Even King's supporters had to recognize the ineffectiveness of nonviolent protest against the well-organized hard-core prejudice it had encountered in Albany.

The disappointment of Albany and the rising criticism by impatient black militants left King keenly aware of the need to make passive resistance work. Early in 1963, he set his strategy. He would take the freedom movement to Birmingham, Alabama. He would lead a nonviolent attack on the power structure of what he called "the most segregated city in America." And he would avoid the spontaneity of Albany in favor of meticulous planning and coordination. The results justified his hopes. Birmingham became another great stride toward freedom. The explanation lay partly in King's talent for leadership, but even more in the conduct of his opponents. Birmingham officials, led by the racist commissioner of public safety, Eugene "Bull" Connor, responded in a manner calculated to advance King's cause. Connor and his police met every move of peaceful protest King staged with brutal repression. Men, women, and children were swept down streets and sidewalks by powerful streams of water from fire hoses. Snarling police dogs were unleashed on crowds. Clubbings and beatings of demonstrators were commonplace. And thanks to comprehensive newspaper and television coverage, all of it occurred in full view of the country and the world. The shock was general. Many Americans agreed with one senator, who declared Birmingham a "national debacle." White supremacists had not appeared in so unfavorable a light since before the Civil War.

The demonstrators, on the other hand, won widespread respect for their ability to withstand provocation. King and the other black leaders succeeded in controlling the protest. The urge to riot and attack Bull Connor's men was sublimated, for the most part, into prayer and into singing the battle hymn of Birmingham: folksinger Pete Seeger's adaptation of the old hymn "We Shall Overcome." Still, thousands were arrested in April of 1963, including King himself, who was placed in solitary confinement and denied communication. Many feared for his life, but a telephone call from Coretta, who had just given birth to their fourth child, to President John F. Kennedy brought an immediate improvement in the conditions of King's detention. While he waited to be released, he received news that Birmingham's white religious leaders had publicly denounced both the demonstrations and King's right to be called a man of God. In response, King wrote his widely publicized "Letter from Birmingham Jail," dated April 16, 1963. A ringing defense of nonviolent protest and civil disobedience, it linked his cause to that of Lincoln, Jefferson, and Jesus. Accepting the label of "extremist," King defended the role of "creative extremists" as agents for righting wrongs. Finally, he expressed his deep disappointment that clergymen of any color could align themselves against the black struggle for equality.

After serving eight days, King accepted bond money raised by entertainer Harry Belafonte and left the Birmingham jail. He plunged at once into the task of keeping the pressure on the city's leadership. Demonstrations and an effective boycott of segregated businesses continued. At the same time, he struggled desperately to keep the movement nonviolent in the face of bombings and beatings. By May 1963, there were signs of success. A large number of Birmingham businesspeople were prepared to come to terms with the blacks. A program of desegregation was arranged for stores and restaurants. Bull Connor was ousted. Plans were made to integrate schools the following autumn. Hearts, to be sure, did not change as fast as rules, but for the blacks of Birmingham, Alabama, there was a new sense of dignity. And on the national level the events in Birmingham spurred the campaign for more effective federal civil rights legislation. On June 11, over national television, John F. Kennedy became the first president to declare racial discrimination a moral as well as a legal issue. It was time, he said, for government at every level to act on behalf of equality for every American. "Those who do nothing," Kennedy added, "are inviting shame as well as violence." A week later he submitted to Congress a program calling for the complete desegregation of all public accommodations.

Looking back on Birmingham, Martin Luther King believed that the freedom movement had turned an important corner in Alabama in 1963. Nonviolence had produced meaningful change, and there was hope for black Americans. "I have this hope," King wrote in *Why We Can't Wait*, "because, once on a summer day, a dream came true. The city of Birmingham discovered a conscience."

Despite the satisfactions of Birmingham and the great March on Washington, 1963 was a bitter year for Martin Luther King. On June 12, Medgar Evers, NAACP field secretary and King's counterpart in the Jackson, Mississippi, demonstrations, was shot and killed by a white terrorist. For King and his family, it must have been clear that sooner or later he would become prey to this kind of violence. But pausing only to grieve for Evers, he launched a nationwide speaking tour that was interrupted by tragedy on September 14. A bomb had been thrown through a window of the Sixteenth Street Baptist Church in Birmingham. When the smoke cleared, four little girls who had been attending a Sunday school class lay dead. The event threatened to undo the settlements of May and precipitate a full-scale racial war. King rushed back to Birmingham and, with the help of local clergy, barely managed to avert violence. On November 22 of this tense, emotion-charged year, the nation lost its president to an assassin's bullet. For King, who thought John F. Kennedy had undergone a "transformation from hesitant leader to a strong figure with deeply appealing objectives," the sense of loss was great.

The new president, Lyndon B. Johnson, immediately dedicated his considerable talents in political infighting to securing the passage of Kennedy's still-pending Civil Rights Bill. Finally passed in June 1964, it prohibited racial discrimination in accommodations and employment. The bill's teeth came from a section withdrawing federal funds from states found to be practicing discrimination. Many Americans celebrated the measure as an important milestone on the road to equality. King regarded it as the outcome of Montgomery, Birmingham, and the Washington March. But a few dissented. Diehard segregationist Strom Thurmond, for example, the senator from South Carolina, greeted the Civil Rights Act with the opinion, "This is a sad day for America."

The accelerating freedom movement also produced an acceleration in militancy. There were 758 separate civil rights demonstrations in the ten weeks following King's Birmingham campaign. King had long anticipated and dreaded such a development. Speaking shortly after Birmingham, he warned that the urban ghettos in particular contained "certain elements [which] will respond with violence if the people of the nation do not recognize the desperate plight of the Negro. . . . The brutality they are experiencing as a result of their quest for equality may call for retaliation." King, of course, did not advocate such a development; he never wavered from a nonviolent stand. But he realized that nonviolent protest was no substitute for freedom. Unless the Civil Rights Bill and other legislation brought tangible gains for African Americans, he foresaw "a season of terror and violence."

In October 1964, Martin Luther King learned from a radio bulletin that he had been awarded the Nobel Peace Prize for his efforts in furthering "brotherhood among men." The award stirred controversy. In many eyes King's role had been anything but that of peacemaker. On the other hand, if the roots of true brother-hood lay in social equality, as others believed, then King's honor was richly de-served. But for King personally, the award was an added burden. After it, he felt even more responsible for the course of American race relations. And, by 1964, he was increasingly uneasy. What disturbed him most was the prospect of losing con-trol of the black protest movement he had done so much to bring about. More radi-cal aspirants to black leadership, preaching a doctrine of black nationalism and re-taliatory violence, were waiting for King to falter. They were evident at the Washington rally in the person of John Lewis, who asserted that a revolutionary change in American institutions was a necessary prelude to freedom. His speech broke the otherwise solid front of the civil rights movement and portended a deeper split in the future. The rioting that engulfed Harlem in the summer of 1964, despite King's plea for peace, was evidence that the schism in the freedom movement would not be restricted to philosophical grounds.

The new year began with several indications that the movement was nearing the boiling point. In February, Malcolm X was murdered by a rival Black Muslim faction. Fearing a black civil war, King volunteered to mediate the dispute but was rejected by both sides. The militants wanted no part of a man they regarded as pa-tient and docile to a fault—an "Uncle Tom." A month later, in Selma, Alabama, King again encountered the stinging charge of "chickening out." The occasion was a series of marches protesting the denial of suffrage, and the critics were the young blacks whom King himself had rallied to the movement just a few years before. Even when President Johnson submitted a strong Voting Rights Bill to Congress, these young blacks questioned its credibility. Finally, in August 1965, the most shocking of a series of riots by urban blacks erupted in the Watts district of Los An-geles after white police officers beat two black men they had arrested. King left a re-ligious convention in Puerto Rico to rush to the West Coast. In King's opinion, ri-oting was "absolutely wrong" as a form of protest, "socially detestable and self-defeating." But the blacks of Watts proved indifferent or openly hostile to King's efforts at mediation. Their anger transcended passive resistance; their feeling of powerlessness was not alleviated by King's philosophy of nonviolent dignity.

Moved by both the dejection of urban blacks and the pressure of the radicals, King went to Chicago in January 1966 to launch a massive campaign against social and economic deprivation. For nine months he directed the Chicago Movement from a slum tenement. It was not a success. Even though one-third of Chicago's population was black, the scarcity of local black leadership and a boss-dominated city government combined to limit King's effectiveness. Moreover, the movement got away from King on several occasions. A vicious three-day riot, for instance, was touched off when police denied the use of a fire hydrant to children trying to get some relief from the sweltering heat. And, to his dismay, King found that many Chicago blacks, like those in Watts the year before, were proud of the riot, proud to have "shaken whitey up." The Chicago Movement failed to produce tangible re-sults, and black militants seized on it as an example of the ineffectiveness of nonvi-olence and publicly jeered King.

King understood the radical position put forth in 1966 by Stokely Carmichael, the new leader of SNCC, Floyd McKissick of CORE, and black power advocate H.

Martin Luther King, Jr., helped lead 200,000 people in an August 1963 March on Washington. Shortly after this photograph was taken, King delivered his "I have a dream" speech from the steps of the Lincoln Memorial.

Rap Brown. He knew the reason for the organization that year in Oakland, California, of the Black Panther Party for Self-Defense under the leadership of Huey Newton and Bobby Seale. Nor was he surprised to see the Black Muslims recover from the defection of Malcolm X and go on to gain the support of many young people, including heavyweight boxing champion Cassius Clay (Muhammad Ali). "I had urged them," King wrote, "to have faith in America and in white society. Their hopes had soared. . . . They were now hostile because they were watching the dream that they had so readily accepted turn into a frustrating nightmare." The rising appeal of black radicalism in the 1960s was a function of changes in black demography. In 1910, only 9 percent of American blacks had lived outside the South, and only 27 percent were in urban areas. Sixty years later, the figures had risen to 47 percent living outside the South and an astonishing 70 percent living in urban areas. Whereas support for King's position had traditionally come from southern, rural, religiously oriented blacks, the new breed had too little patience for and faith in nonviolent methods of protest. Heeding the lesson of Vietnam and white countercultural dissent, increasing numbers of blacks distrusted the American Establishment. Still, King clung to his original postulates: nonviolent protest, reform

In the riots in the Watts area of Los Angeles in 1965, looting and arson were commonplace. The usual targets were white-owned businesses, but A. Z. Smith, who owned this barbershop, was an exception. Martin Luther King, Jr., found that the Watts rioters had little patience with his philosophy of nonviolence.

through the existing system, and acceptance by and integration into white America. With an ecologist's insight, King constantly maintained that "all life is interrelated—tied into a single garment of destiny."

When James Meredith, who had integrated the University of Mississippi, was shot on June 6, 1966 near Memphis, King rushed to the scene pleading for peace. He preserved it, too, although at one point he had to physically restrain Stokely Carmichael from lunging at a state trooper. It was more difficult, in a way, to restrain the growth of black hatred, black separatism, and reverse racism. In King's view these would only call forth a backlash of white racism that would inevitably crush the black minority (only 15 percent of the American people). Black violence, moreover, would undo King's painstaking efforts to encourage respect for a people brave enough to turn the other cheek. He cringed, therefore, when young militants altered his theme song to "We Shall Overrun." He was similarly disturbed by their growing reluctance to accept the aid of white liberals. Carmichael and his colleagues, King came to realize, were of a different generation. Lacking the Christian element that figured so strongly in King's life and thought, they were children of violence. Carmichael had been arrested twenty-seven times between the ages of nineteen and twenty-four. He had seen nonviolent blacks abused too often. Like H. Rap Brown, he was prepared to admit that "violence was as American as apple pie." In the summers of 1966 and 1967, poor urban areas were awash in violence, as major riots broke out in Newark, Detroit, Milwaukee, and several other cities.

During the summer of 1966, King and Carmichael engaged in a running debate. Carmichael was anxious to have the freedom movement accept his "Black

Power" slogan. King preferred "Black Equality" or "Power for Poor People" or "Freedom Now." For hours on end he attempted to bring the militants around to his view, but to no avail. "Black Power" prevailed in Jackson and, a year later, in Cambridge, Maryland, when H. Rap Brown told a rally to "burn this town to the ground if [it] don't grant the demands of Negroes." King could only shudder and watch the white backlash gather force. It took various forms, from the defeat of a civil rights bill in 1966 to segregationist George Wallace's relatively strong showing (13 percent of the national vote) as a third-party candidate in the election of 1968.

But, in the vicious circle King dreaded, blacks responded to the growing white backlash with behavior calculated to accelerate it still more. The summer of 1967 brought the most serious race riots yet to American cities: forty-one incidents in thirty-nine communities. With every new headline, white resistance to civil rights stiffened. King remained convinced that only a reemphasis on nonviolence and civil disobedience could regain white support and bring real improvement. The riots were killing the freedom movement, King explained in a 1967 book, *Where Do We Go from Here: Chaos or Community?*

With this problem in mind, King, Ralph Abernathy, and the Southern Christian Leadership Conference began preparations in the winter of 1967–1968 for a Poor People's March on Washington. In keeping with King's beliefs, it would be a fully integrated, nonviolent appeal to the nation's conscience. The marchers planned to request federal support in the amount of $12 billion to fund the proposals in an "economic bill of rights." There was reason to think President Johnson would respond to such a request, even though King had broken sharply with him over the issue of the Vietnam War. As a proponent of peace and nonviolence, King could not accept the rationales advanced in support of that conflict. In 1967, he condemned the United States as "the greatest purveyor of violence in the world." He maintained his position even in the face of pointed criticism by the NAACP and the Urban League, whose leaders preferred to keep the issues of war and civil rights separate in the hope of gaining support from the administration.

The Poor People's March was set for June 1968, but the whirlwind pace King had kept since the beginning of the decade allowed him only occasional participation in the planning. One of the detours took him to Memphis, where a garbage strike threatened to evolve into a racial encounter of crisis proportions. Local black leaders wanted King to organize a peaceful demonstration, but once again he had difficulty working with Black Power militants. Uncontrollable black looters, arsonists, and street fighters were another source of difficulty. On March 28, they had transformed a nonviolent march into an orgy of destruction that had provoked an even greater measure of police brutality. As a self-styled "riot preventer," King was sick at heart. If Memphis exploded, he feared, the approaching summer of 1968 would be chaos. Already, black leaders like Harlem congressman Adam Clayton Powell were arousing the urban masses and, as part of their campaign, making references to "Martin Loser King" and his Uncle Tom tactics. Nonviolence, King felt, was on trial in Memphis.

On April 3, 1968, on the eve of the crucial Memphis march, King addressed a capacity crowd at the Masonic Temple located in that city. His mood was strangely somber and introspective. "Like anybody," he mused, "I would like to live a long life." But longevity, he added, was not his chief concern; he would rather do God's will. Some of his aides were reminded of the great Washington rally of 1963, where King had expressed his belief that "if a man hasn't discovered something that he will die for, he isn't fit to live!" The following evening, on the way to yet another mass meeting, King walked onto the balcony of his motel room and leaned over the railing to talk with a colleague. A moment later he crumpled to the ground. An assassin's bullet, fired from a hotel room across the street, had pierced his skull. The killer, arrested two months later and identified as James Earl Ray, was a white drifter with a long criminal record.

Following Ray's confession, investigations of King's murder continued until 1977. Exhaustive reviews of the evidence seemed to prove conclusively that Ray had acted alone in the assassination, and there was no conspiracy. The research did reveal that the Federal Bureau of Investigation, under orders of its director, J. Edgar Hoover, had complicated the last six years of King's life with a program of systematic harassment on the spurious grounds that he was under the influence of the Communist party. The conspiracy theory surrounding King's death re-emerged in the 1990s when James Earl Ray, in prison and in dire health, recanted his confession. Talk of Ray being brought to trial—there had been none due to his confession—ended abruptly when Ray died in early 1998.

The murder of Martin Luther King, Jr., moved the American people as had few events in recent years. The immediate response in all but the most prejudiced white minds was shame. Millions of whites felt compelled to apologize to black people as a whole and went to their churches for services honoring King. But even among the mourners, white and black eyes did not meet easily. Everyone seemed to recognize that, with King's death, a powerful influence for interracial compassion and understanding had been eliminated—the basis of ordered change and reform. The evidence came almost at once in the rioting that broke out in over 130 cities. There were 20,000 arrests, with fifty people dead (forty-five of them blacks). Stokely Carmichael summed up the prevalent feeling when he declared that white America "declared war on us" in killing King. Floyd McKissick added that "nonviolence is a dead philosophy, and it was not the black people that killed it." Black Panther spokesman Eldridge Cleaver made it clear that he saw in King's death the "final repudiation by white America of any hope of reconciliation, of any hope of change by peaceful and nonviolent means." Added to this bitterness was the discouraging report, in March 1968, of President Johnson's National Advisory Commission on Civil Disorders, which found white racism at the root of a process of polarization that threatened democratic values and the nation itself.

The assassination on June 5 of presidential aspirant Robert F. Kennedy deepened the pessimism of 1968. True, the Civil Rights Act of that year was encouraging in its attempt to end racial discrimination in the rental and sale of property. But the 1968 elections brought to the presidency a man, Richard Nixon, and a party, the Republicans, who generally favored withdrawing federal involvement from the struggle for black rights. Freedom, Nixon believed, could not be forced. Self-help and individual effort were the keys. In building Republican ties with the white South and the followers of Alabama governor George Wallace, the Nixon administration appeared to be willing to leave blacks to the then-powerless Democrats.

"Benign neglect" characterized Nixon's policy toward civil rights. The hopes, based on federal support, that had flared briefly under Kennedy and Johnson dimmed throughout black America. With Martin Luther King dead and Richard Nixon in the White House, there seemed to be little to stem the bitter and violent spiral of rising black expectations and countervailing white resistance. American society, many feared, would deteriorate into clusters of armed camps. King's cause had been lost.

In fact, the tide of race relations swung the other way. If King's influence faded in the final years of his life, it revived markedly after his death. King's martyrdom aided his message. Black protests, for the most part, remained nonviolent. The Poor People's March that came to Washington in June 1968 might have resulted in a bloodbath. Instead, the Reverend Ralph Abernathy, King's colleague since Montgomery and the first to bend over his fallen body in Memphis, guided the demonstration according to King's principles. In memory of King, Abernathy gave the marchers' encampment around the Lincoln Memorial the name Resurrection City. To many it did indeed seem that King was a black Jesus. Coretta King wrote a month after her husband's death that he was a man "who refused to lose faith in the ultimate redemption of mankind." Symbolism, not violence, dominated the black protest later that summer. At the Olympic games in Mexico City, the black American medalists in the 200-meter dash stood on the victory stand with upraised, clenched fists while the national anthem was being played and the American flag raised. It was a gesture King would have approved of, and the worldwide publicity that the photograph capturing that moment received was likewise in the tradition of King's flare for the dramatic.

One reason that black militancy had lost momentum by the late 1960s was the arrest, self-exile, or death of many of the radical leaders. By 1971, Huey Newton, Bobby Seale, and Angela Davis were all involved in complex court trials. Eldridge Cleaver had fled to Algeria. Stokely Carmichael had also gone to Africa. George Jackson, who had written *Soledad Brother* in his jail cell, and Fred Hampton, a member of the Black Panthers, had been shot to death. Moreover, the message of the remaining radical leaders was blunted by a recognition in the black community that rioting had not accomplished very much beyond the destruction of black neighborhoods. Appealing as it was on the soapbox, militancy did not put food in the pantry or money in the bank. Like most disgruntled minorities in the nation's past, the African Americans of the 1970s came to the realization that the best chances of improvement lay inside, not outside, the system.

The eclipse of radicalism that King regrettably did not live to see produced remarkable philosophical turnabouts. Eldridge Cleaver is a case in point. In 1968 Cleaver's *Soul on Ice* had drawn a parallel between the status of the Vietnamese and black Americans. Both were victims of colonialism, of systematic exploitation by the American majority. "In their rage against . . . police brutality," Cleaver wrote, "blacks lose sight of the fundamental reality: that the police are only an instrument for the implementation of the policies of those who make the decisions. Police brutality is only one facet of the crystal of terror and oppression." In 1968, Cleaver felt that the only way open to blacks was violent resistance. But six years later Cleaver announced his intention to give up his self-imposed exile and return to the United

States to face criminal charges. "In the end," he told *Rolling Stone* magazine on September 11, 1975, "the system rejected President Nixon and rearmed its own basic principles. A fabulous new era of progress is opening up. . . . With all its faults, the American political system is the freest and most democratic in the world."

The concept of using the system rather than overturning it meant a renewed emphasis by blacks on politics and economics. Abandoning the marches and prayers that had been King's means, blacks of the 1970s used civil rights legislation, particularly the Voting Rights Act of 1965, to attain King's ends. Blacks saw that they could gain power—and not necessarily "black power" in the old radical sense. The new approach found blacks using the ballot box as the cutting edge of the reconceived black revolution. The achievements were undeniable. In 1965, the ex-Confederate states had a total of seventy-two black elected officials. A decade later there were over 1,500. Eighteen blacks served in the Congress of the United States; Edward Brooke, the senator from Massachusetts, was the first black senator to hold office since the forced elections of Reconstruction. Thurgood Marshall sat on the Supreme Court, Barbara Jordan (breaking two kinds of social barriers) delivered the keynote address at the 1976 Democratic National Convention, and Andrew Young represented the United States in the United Nations. Black mayors were elected by the people of Los Angeles, Newark, Gary, and Washington, DC, and other cities. In many parts of the nation large voting blocs put blacks in crucial balance-of-power situations. As Gerald R. Ford learned to his dismay in the 1976 presidential election, concentrated black voting could swing elections. The black mayor of Atlanta drew the obvious conclusion: "Anyone looking for the civil rights movement in the streets is fooling himself. Politics is the civil rights movement of the seventies."

Even more significant, because it came from a one-time radical, was the 1972 revelation of Huey Newton that the Black Panthers had decided to put away their guns and work within the system. The challenge of the future, Newton explained, was not to *fight* the white Establishment but "to organize the black communities politically."

Economics was the other principal avenue to meaningful power that black Americans began to explore in the decade following King's death. Jesse Jackson, a protégé of King who saw his hero fall at Memphis, is typical of aggressive, business-oriented blacks. Jackson, to be sure, remained sharply critical of King's religious approach to protest, personified by Ralph Abernathy, but Jackson's idea of working peacefully within the system was true to the views of his teacher. In Chicago and other cities Jackson organized Operation Breadbasket. Designed to consolidate and apply black economic power, Operation Breadbasket campaigns stressed cooperative buying, the end of job discrimination, and, more significantly, the development of black-operated business alternatives. Early in 1972 Jackson reorganized Operation Breadbasket as People United to Save Humanity (PUSH). Its membership, he made clear, would be a "rainbow coalition" of poor people of all races. Jackson's weapons were, again, legal economic leverage. On higher business levels it was possible, by the bicentennial year, to say that a black alternative existed in the worlds of construction, banking, and insurance. Black incomes remained low and unemployment rates were high in relation to those of whites, but the expectation of gradual improvement in these areas sustained black optimism.

The recent political career of Jesse Jackson in many ways reflects the black experience in the American political system. Disillusioned by the Democratic administration of Jimmy Carter (1977–1981), Jackson and other blacks gave the Georgian lukewarm support in his reelection bid in 1980. Charging that Carter had not done enough to help African Americans, some even switched party loyalties to support conservative Republican Ronald Reagan. They believed that his laissez-faire fiscal policies would create a stronger economy and consequently improve the plight of struggling blacks. Jesse Jackson unveiled his own presidential aspirations as the Reagan administration began a systematic effort to roll back civil rights and affirmative action legislation. In 1984, Jackson declared his candidacy for the Democratic party nomination, denouncing Reagan for his indifference to minority problems, and attempting to establish a broad liberal coalition. Jackson vied for the nomination again in 1988. Although he fared well in primaries in both elections, the party turned its back on Jackson, nominating Walter Mondale in 1984 and Michael Dukakis in 1988. In 1992 and 1996, Jackson's name was mentioned again as a presidential candidate, and his presence at both Democratic conventions underscored his importance as an African-American leader.

Martin Luther King, Jr., might have been surprised that the bitterest racial clashes of the 1970s and 1980s involved northern communities. Busing was the immediate cause: Schoolchildren were transported in buses from neighborhood to neighborhood in order to obtain a desegregated education. The 1954 Supreme Court decision in *Brown v. Board of Education* (see page 195) laid the legal foundation for attaining racial balance in public schools. A 1971 Supreme Court decision upheld busing as a means to achieve this end, and the policy worked reasonably well in the South. By 1975, southern schools were the most integrated in the nation. But northern communities with highly segregated residential patterns exploded in protest over busing. There was extensive violence in South Boston, Massachusetts, which pundits quickly dubbed the "New South." Presidents Nixon and Ford were not inclined to enforce the court orders on busing, and many blacks had little interest in the success of the policy. After two decades of trying to change hearts and minds with laws, increasing numbers of thoughtful Americans, both white and black, were beginning to recognize that the vitality of their nation's culture stemmed not from its homogeneity so much as from its respectful tolerance of diversity.

With the passage of time and the healing of factional cleavages that had torn apart the freedom movement during his lifetime, Martin Luther King's reputation has acquired legendary proportions, including making his birthday a national holiday. The eclipse of militancy in the 1970s and 1980s brought King's idea of making the American system work in the interest of black rights back into the prominence it had enjoyed in the late 1950s and early 1960s. The way King's memory is used is instructive. In the rural South, the revived Southern Christian Leadership Conference (SCLC) still has a difficult time getting many blacks to vote on election day. The long history of intimidation has added to the difficulty, as has a sense of hopelessness and resignation. But one SCLC technique has succeeded. It consists of a simple poster at the top of which is the date of the election in which African-American voters are urged to participate, and at the bottom of which is the statement: "Martin Luther King died for this day."

SELECTED READINGS
The Person

*Bennett, Lerone: *What Manner of Man: A Biography of Martin Luther King, Jr.* (3d ed., 1968). A readable and informative biography.

Bishop, Jim: *The Days of Martin Luther King, Jr.* (1971). The full story behind King's assassination, with details of his earlier life.

Colaiaco, James A.: *Martin Luther King, Jr.: Apostle of Militant Nonviolence* (1983). A good, brief biography of King's influence during his adult life from the perspective of the 1980s.

Garrow, David J.: *Bearing the Cross: Martin Luther King, Jr., and the Southern Christian Leadership Conference* (1986). Detailed history of King and his role in the SCLC.

Hanes, Walton, Jr.: *The Political Philosophy of Martin Luther King, Jr.* (1971). A political scientist's critical examination of King's method in influencing the political system of the United States.

*Harding, Vincent: *Martin Luther King: The Inconvenient Hero* (1996). Good, brief biography reflecting recent scholarship.

*King, Coretta Scott: *My Life with Martin Luther King, Jr.* (1969). King's widow's reminiscences.

*King, Martin Luther, Jr.: *Stride Toward Freedom: The Montgomery Story* (1958). King's own account of his struggle to end segregation in public transportation in Montgomery, Alabama.

*King, Martin Luther, Jr.: *Why We Can't Wait* (1964). In the opinion of some, the classic expression of King's philosophy of protest and reform.

*King, Martin Luther, Jr.: *Where Do We Go from Here: Chaos or Community?* (1967). A review of black history and the civil rights movement since 1964 plus speculation about the future.

*King, Martin Luther, Jr.: *Documentary . . . Montgomery to Memphis* (1976). The most comprehensive collection of King's writings.

*Lewis, David L.: *King: A Critical Biography* (1970). Another perspective on a controversial figure.

*Lincoln, Eric (ed.): *Martin Luther King, Jr.* (1970). A collection of profiles of King by his contemporaries.

*Miller, William Robert: *Martin Luther King, Jr.: His Life, Martyrdom, and Meaning for the World* (1968). A full, factual account.

*Oates, Stephen B.: *Let the Trumpet Sound: The Life of Martin Luther King, Jr.* (1982). A well-written, comprehensive one-volume biography.

*Patterson, Lillie: *Martin Luther King, Jr.* (1972). A brief biography written long enough after King's murder to ensure a greater degree of objectivity than was possible in earlier efforts.

Schulke, Flip, and Penelope Ortner McPhee: *King Remembered* (1986). Graphically illustrated account of King's struggle based on empirical sources and many interviews.

---

*Available in paperback.

The Period

Archer, Jules: *They Had a Dream: The Civil Rights Struggle from Frederick Douglass to Marcus Garvey to Martin Luther King and Malcolm X* (1993). Brief overview of the civil rights movement.

Chafe, William H., and Harvard Sitkoff (eds.): *A History of Our Times: Readings on Postwar America* (1995). Social and political history essays.

Draper, Theodore: *The Rediscovery of Black Nationalism* (1970). An examination of radical black thought in the 1960s.

*Franklin, John Hope: *From Slavery to Freedom: A History of American Negroes* (3d ed., 1967). General treatment of black history by a distinguished black scholar.

Golden, Harry: *Mr. Kennedy and the Negroes* (1964). John F. Kennedy's involvement in civil rights.

*Hampton, Henry, and Steve Facer: *Voices of Freedom: An Oral History of the Civil Rights Movement from the 1950s through the 1980s* (1990). Companion volume to the acclaimed television series, "Eyes on the Prize: America's Civil Rights Years, 1954–1965."

*Harrington, Michael: *The Other America* (1962). The history of poor people of all colors.

*Lincoln, Eric: *The Black Muslims in America* (1961). An examination of the more radical wing of the black revolution.

Lomax, Louis: *The Negro Revolt* (1963). An analysis of the freedom movement since 1955.

*Meier, August, and Elliott M. Rudwick: *From Plantation to Ghetto* (rev. ed., 1970). An interpretive history of blacks in the United States, especially valuable for its use of scholarly findings.

*Muse, Benjamin: *The American Negro Revolution: From Nonviolence to Black Power, 1963–1967* (1968). The best general account of the developing freedom movement.

*Peeks, Edward: *The Long Struggle for Black Power* (1971). Interpretation of black history in the United States.

Raines, Howell (ed.): *My Soul Is Rested: Movement Days in the Deep South Remembered* (1977). A vivid, moving account of the civil rights movement told by some of its participants.

FOR CONSIDERATION

1. Two schools of thought on achieving advancement for black people dominated late-nineteenth and early-twentieth-century America. Compare and contrast the philosophies and practices of Booker T. Washington and William E. B. Du Bois.

2. By the time of Martin Luther King, Jr.'s birth in 1929, black culture was making an increasing mark on the national culture. Identify the factors that made this so.

3. What influences were most important in the development of King's philosophy of nonviolent resistance regarding civil rights?

---

*Available in paperback.

4. Legal decisions and nonviolent resistance proved successful during the 1950s in promoting black civil rights. Identify and discuss some of the watershed events of that decade.

5. By the 1960s, King's nonviolent resistance was challenged by younger African Americans who believed his methods outmoded. Why did these militant individuals reject King? Does King's philosophy still have merit in the late twentieth century?

6. Upon King's assassination in April 1968, many people feared nationwide, violent militance. What actually transpired in subsequent years?

SEVEN

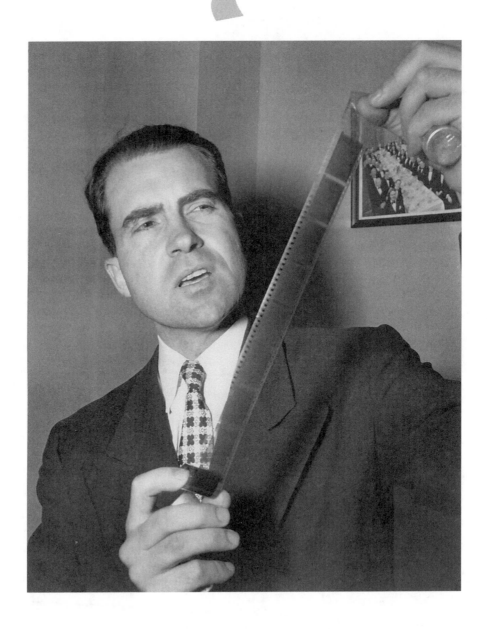

Richard Nixon

The bright lights behind the television cameras were more blinding than ever to a man who had just sobbed uncontrollably in front of the people who had stood by him the longest. But now, on the night of August 8, 1974, he was alone with only his memories of the thousands of other speeches that underlay one of the nation's most spectacular political success stories. This was his last speech. "I have never been a quitter," he told the nation. "To leave office before my term is completed is abhorrent to every instinct in my body." He had considered turning back on his decision right to the end, but there was no reversing it. He had lied to the people. He had lied to Congress and the courts. He had lied to family and lawyers. In a sense he had even lied to himself about a series of events called Watergate. Now the price must be paid. He had heard the cries of the people who were clustered outside the White House when he appeared that morning: "Jail to the Chief!" Yet Nixon still could not bring himself to admit guilt. "I would say only," he continued, "that if some of my judgments were wrong, and some were wrong, they were made in what I believed at the time to be the best interest of the Nation." The voice broke slightly. Nixon admitted he had no support left in the Congress. He would not consume the time and energy of the nation in a lengthy impeachment trial. The end came quickly. "Therefore, I shall resign the Presidency effective at noon tomorrow."

Noon of August 9 found Richard Nixon on his way home to California, flying somewhere over Illinois or Iowa. Beneath him, at the moment power passed to his successor, was that Middle America on which his political strength had always depended. Yet it was the innate morality of the average American that Nixon had betrayed and that, in the end, saw justice done. If the Watergate scandal represented tragedy for a man, it marked an hour of triumph for the nation and its constituted system of government. Certainly Watergate disgraced the United States, but around the world people paused to consider the way their nations would have handled a comparable situation. Firing squads for the critics, not the resignation of the criticized, were standard procedure in many countries. Paradoxically, one of the darkest hours for the United States was also one of its brightest.

The roots of Richard Milhous Nixon's family tree run deep in American history. An ancestor on his mother's side left Wales for Delaware in 1690. The warm reception that the Quakers received in William Penn's colony attracted other Milhouses in the eighteenth century. On the paternal side the Nixon lineage dates from 1753, when James Nixon arrived at Brandywine Hundred, Delaware. From these beginnings, the Milhouses and Nixons went on to help build the American experience. One of Richard Nixon's forefathers crossed the Delaware River with George Washington in 1776 and saw action in a dozen other engagements of the Revolutionary War. Another Nixon fell on the Civil War battlefield at Gettysburg. Mostly farming people, the Nixons and the Milhouses followed the rainbow to new land out west—to western Pennsylvania, Ohio, Indiana, and finally to the end of the trail in southern California.

Frank Nixon, the future president's father, had been educated through the fourth grade. He was a trolley-car motorman when he met Hannah Milhous in February 1908. They were married four months later and set up a household in Yorba Linda, a rural village about thirty miles east of Los Angeles. Richard, the second son, was born January 9, 1913, on a near-freezing night. The only heat in the modest house came from a battery of wood-burning stoves that Frank Nixon had assembled for the occasion. It was just a small step away from a log-cabin existence, but the Nixon family lacked the cohesiveness of pioneers. By all reports Frank was a surly, loud-mouthed man with a vicious temper. In order to escape some of his father's wrath, Richard learned at an early age how to lie expertly. As he put it later, being a child of Frank Nixon taught him "to be pretty convincing to avoid punishment." But he also learned how to punish when he held the reins of power.

In sharp contrast to the families of many recent American presidents—one thinks especially of the two Roosevelts and John F. Kennedy—Richard Nixon was never a member of, nor comfortable among, the nation's higher economic and social echelons. From the time he was old enough to work, at about age eleven, Dick was expected to help pay the family bills. He picked beans, pumped gasoline, sold groceries at the family store, swept a meat-packing plant, cleaned a public swimming pool, and hustled customers for a gaming concession at the Slippery Gulch Rodeo. When his father gave him the proceeds from the vegetable counter, Dick, emulating Benjamin Franklin, rose before dawn to shop at the Los Angeles wholesale markets and arrange his display before school. Nixon's stern Methodist and Quaker background did not permit much in the way of recreation. Neither did the Great Depression. The Nixon boys became well acquainted with sixteen-hour working days. Understandably, they learned to detest people who did not work as hard. Even during the Depression, when many of the well-meaning simply could not find work, Frank Nixon called unemployed people "bums." When they came to his back door asking for leftover food, he made sure they paid for the handout with several hours' work in the yard. Richard grew up in an atmosphere hostile to the welfare and social security programs of the Democrats' New Deal.

Money and the power it bought remained just beyond the Nixons' grasp. When Dick was nine, his father had to choose between two locations for a gasoline station. The location he finally chose, in Whittier, California, yielded a modest income. A year later drillers discovered oil beneath the property Frank Nixon had turned down. The family tried hard to pretend it did not care, but Richard Nixon was developing anxieties and ambitions that shaped the course of his future life.

Athletics was another disappointment. Although Nixon dreamed of Harvard, it was beyond his economic reach. He entered Whittier College, the hometown Quaker institution, in 1930 and tried out for the football team four years in a row. He made it only during his freshman year, when exactly eleven men came to the first practice. But Nixon doggedly warmed the bench throughout his college years, cheering men whose grace and coordination he never possessed. Nixon started and presided over his own fraternity, the Orthagonians, at Whittier. It offered an alternative to the elite fraternity, the Franklins, which Richard Nixon was never asked to join.

Nothing came easily to the young Nixon. His achievements in college and high school were the result of extraordinary effort. He won school elections by exhaustive electioneering. His good grades resulted from months of all-night study. His outstanding record as a college debater was the result of diligent research into every aspect of the assigned topic. The Nixon his youthful companions remembered was no prodigy, no brilliant intellect, no charismatic leader. His forte was an ability to drive himself in relentless pursuit of specific ends.

Upon graduating from Whittier College in 1934, Nixon was determined to enter the legal profession. As a boy of twelve, he had listened to his father berate the "crooked politicians" and "crooked lawyers" whose mismanagement of public oil reserves, notably those at Teapot Dome, Wyoming, caused the Warren G. Harding administration to end in shame and chaos, with one cabinet member in jail. Hannah Nixon recalled the long family discussions of the Harding scandals and her son's vow to "be an old-fashioned kind of lawyer, a lawyer who can't be bought."

The year 1934 was an inauspicious one in which to graduate from college. Franklin D. Roosevelt's New Deal had lifted some of the nation's psychological clouds, but the Great Depression persisted like a bad dream. Ten million Americans were still unemployed; the gross national product was down $30 billion from 1929, the last "good" year. The congressional elections of 1934 reaffirmed public confidence in Roosevelt and the Democrats, but recovery was not coming nearly as fast, nor as completely, as many expected. Roosevelt's federal spending programs had "primed the pump" of economic recovery, but the policies were slow to take effect. Middle-class families like the Nixons were not in soup lines, but they did not have the necessary money to send their sons to graduate school. If Dick was going to become a lawyer, he would have to do it on his own.

Fortunately for his professional plans, Nixon's persistence began to pay off. He had graduated second in his class at Whittier. On the basis of his college grades, Duke University Law School in Durham, North Carolina, offered Nixon a full-tuition scholarship. To supplement this grant, he obtained a part-time job funded by the National Youth Administration—another Roosevelt idea for reducing unemployment and injecting money into the economy. Between classes at Duke, Nixon cranked the handle of a mimeograph machine. He received thirty-five cents an hour. His rented room in Durham had no water or electricity. Only a dedicated man could have survived the ordeal. Nixon, however, rose to the challenge. He was used to supporting himself. Fear impelled him, the fear of failing and falling behind his fellow students. Ambition also figured in his motivation. Nixon yearned to become a member of a "great" law firm, as he put it, with "thick, luxurious carpets and fine oak paneling." This affluence, and the power that accompanied it, seemed an appropriate end of the American dream, from the perspective of the produce counter and gas pumps of Nixon's Whittier boyhood.

Although he graduated third in his law school class, Nixon had no connections with the eastern Establishment, and he failed to land a job in one of the prestigious

New York law firms he admired. His alternative was to return to California, cram for the bar exams, and begin practice in the Whittier firm of Wingert and Bewley. Local people who remembered Dick Nixon, the diligent grocer's son, were not surprised by the young lawyer. He rose early and worked late, frequently right through his lunch hour. There may have been more talented members of the California bar, but few outranked Nixon in dogged determination. His colleagues said he won cases by means of exhaustive research.

If Nixon had married into the eastern gentility, some of the pressures that complicated his life might have been alleviated. But on June 21, 1940, he married not a debutante but a woman who paralleled his own circumstances and complemented his attitudes. Thelma Catherine "Pat" Ryan came from a dismal blue-collar background. Her father mined for a living. Pat Ryan had been born in 1912 in the drab copper town of Ely, Nevada. Both her parents had died before she was eighteen, leaving her to face the Great Depression alone. When she met Nixon in Whittier in 1938, she had already worked at odd jobs for a decade and had managed to obtain a teacher's certificate. She also knew what it meant to persevere. Later, reflecting on her own background and that of her husband, Pat Nixon remarked, "We come from typical, everyday American families that have had to work for what they got out of life but always knew there was unlimited opportunity."

War was perhaps the only thing that could have disengaged a man of Richard Nixon's ambition from total absorption in his quest for success. In the hectic days following Pearl Harbor, Nixon offered his services to the government. On January 9, 1942, he walked unannounced into the Office of Price Administration (OPA) in Washington, DC, and said he wanted to help with the war effort. The director, Thomas I. Emerson, recalled that "Dick Nixon . . . was a nice-looking boy, seemed intelligent and had an excellent record. . . . I gave him a job right then and there." It paid sixty-one dollars a week. Nixon asked for the lowest possible salary because, as he put it, "the boys who . . . hit the beaches were paid a lot less." His assignment was the coordination of rubber rationing, rubber being one of the vital war materials held off the free domestic market during the years of emergency.

A few months after joining the OPA, Nixon applied for a commission in the navy and sea duty. The desk job he was first given was not very satisfying; he wanted to fight. Nixon's first application for active duty was turned down, and he remained mired in the bureaucratic anonymity of the OPA for nine months. The experience left him with a distaste for incompetency and inefficiency in government. "I saw government overlapping and government empire-building at first hand," he recalled. In September 1942, Nixon's commission finally came through. The unfinished naval air base at Ottumuta, Iowa, was a long way from the fighting front, but Nixon, as always, knuckled down to the job at hand. The following May brought exciting news for Lieutenant (Junior Grade) Richard Nixon. His new orders assigned him to the post of operations officer with the South Pacific Air Transport Command. For the next sixteen months, Nixon concerned himself with the movement of airborne cargo to the combat zones. He built airstrips and supply stockpiles on the chain of islands across which American forces moved toward the Japanese homeland. Only on rare occasions during World War II did Nixon see military action.

V-J (Victory in Japan) Day, celebrated on August 14, 1945, allowed Americans to concentrate on domestic affairs for the first time in four years. In California's Twelfth Congressional District, the local kingmakers of the Republican party again considered an embarrassing situation. Although this was staunch Republican territory, a Democrat named Jerry Voorhis had been elected to Congress in the 1936 Democratic landslide; he still represented the district. Voorhis was a liberal. He had been voted the best congressman west of the Mississippi by Washington press correspondents. But the bankers and businesspeople of his district saw him as the epitome of what was wrong with the hated New Deal. The Twelfth District Republicans hoped to unseat Voorhis in the 1946 elections. To that end they placed an advertisement in twenty-six southern California newspapers:

> WANTED: Congressman candidate with no previous experience to defeat a man who has represented the district in the House for ten years. Any young man, resident of the district, preferably a veteran, fair education, no political strings or obligations, and possessed of a few ideas for betterment of [the] country at large, may apply for the job.

The first respondents were unimpressive. Then Herman L. Perry, head of the Bank of America in Whittier, proposed the name of Richard Milhous Nixon, who was still in Washington working as a navy lawyer. Yes, Nixon told Perry over the telephone, he was available and was interested, and he thought he was a Republican because he had voted for Willkie (1940) and Thomas E. Dewey (1944) in the national elections. Moreover, he did not believe in the New Deal philosophy of "government control in regulating our lives."

The California Republicans found Nixon an almost ideal candidate. He projected the image of a clean-cut, hardworking, young (he was then thirty-three years old) go-getter. Moreover, he was politically naive and malleable. This fact pleased Murray Chotiner, a Los Angeles lawyer who had considerable skill in marketing candidates with a bagful of public relations tricks learned from Hollywood and the mass media. The Chotiner method featured the "smear," a way of associating an opponent with an unpopular position by insinuation. Truth was always subordinate to the practical consideration of winning—in this case, the election. Richard Nixon understood this philosophy. It was part of his background and character to pursue his ends with bulldog determination. He might not be the best man, but he simply refused to lose. This was especially true in regard to Jerry Voorhis, who in midsummer of 1946 appeared to hold a comfortable lead over the upstart Republican. Voorhis was everything Nixon wanted to be: wealthy, important, and famous. To beat Voorhis would help banish the devil of inferiority that had clung to Nixon's back like a burr throughout his life.

So it was that Nixon readily accepted the change in campaign strategy suggested by his advisers: to link Voorhis to organized labor and organized communism. The association had no basis in fact, but Nixon and his supporters were not hampered by such considerations. Ads placed in newspapers in the Twelfth District implied that Voorhis had communist sympathies. He denied it, but public confidence eroded. It was guilt by implication. A telephone campaign began, in which anonymous callers simply said, "This is a friend of yours. I just want you to know that Jerry Voorhis is a communist," and the phone clicked dead. Nixon later denied that such calls had been made, but the damage had been done. A public debate in South Pasadena sealed Voorhis's fate. The congressman tried to be polite, to reply to Nixon's wild accusations with rambling explanations. Nixon, the skilled college debater, attacked relentlessly. The audience left believing that Voorhis was at best a bumbler and at worst what Nixon pictured him as being: a communist sympathizer. In the November election Nixon won handily.

On January 3, 1947, Richard Nixon took the oath of office as a U.S. congressman. He received an assignment to the Education and Labor Committee, which soon began consideration of the power of giant labor unions like the Congress of Industrial Organizations (CIO). Nixon played a minor role in shaping and securing approval of the Taft-Hartley Act. Passed by a Republican-dominated Congress in June 1947, over the veto of Democratic president Harry S. Truman, the measure outlawed the closed shop, in which only union members could work, and revived the injunction as a means of delaying strikes in vital industries for an eight-day "cooling-off" period. As part of his Taft-Hartley efforts, Nixon met and debated a freshman Democratic congressman from Massachusetts. His name was John Fitzgerald Kennedy.

Nixon's other committee assignment was to prove much more significant in his developing political career. The House Un-American Activities Committee (HUAC) was concerned with investigating the activities of the Communist party and other allegedly subversive organizations and individuals in the United States. Nixon knew from the Voorhis campaign what political dividends could be reaped from the skillful exploitation of this issue. But it was not all politics. Nixon also felt a genuine commitment to defending his nation against those who would bore at its strength from within. Enthusiastically, he took the chairmanship of the legislation subcommittee of HUAC and introduced a bill designed to crack down on communism. Thomas E. Dewey, the Republican nominee for presidency in 1948, called the Mundt-Nixon bill "thought control" and a "surrender of everything we believe in," and it did not pass the House.

But on August 3, 1948, Nixon's fortunes experienced a sudden upward surge. On that eventful day, HUAC called before it for testimony an admitted former communist of the 1930s named Whittaker Chambers. In an emotional statement, Chambers named communists who had worked for the government of the United States. The most notable of them was Alger Hiss, an elegant product of the Harvard law school who had served in the State Department in the 1930s before becoming president of the prestigious Carnegie Endowment for International Peace. Hiss demanded the opportunity to deny Chambers's allegation, and after his testimony on August 5, most of the members of HUAC felt it pointless to pursue the case. President Truman dismissed the whole thing as a Republican attempt to smear Hiss.

Nixon, however, was not convinced of Hiss's innocence. The man, he said, "was just too slick"; he might be lying, although skillfully, to the committee. Nixon's attitude toward Hiss had deeper, almost subconscious, levels as well. Hiss was the embodiment of everything the younger Nixon coveted but could not have: a place in the eastern Establishment, a Harvard education, wealth, social grace, and importance. Being in a position to embarrass Hiss and his similarly aristocratic supporters, such as Truman's secretary of state, Dean Acheson, must have been enormously satisfying for the small-town grocer's son.

The matter might have ended there had not Alger Hiss filed a libel suit, in September 1948, against Whittaker Chambers. In response, Chambers produced top-secret documents that he claimed Hiss, as a government employee, had stolen and given to him for transmission to the Soviets. Nixon, as the first person to raise doubts about Hiss, remained close to the case and in touch with Chambers. On December 1, Nixon revealed that Chambers had even more incriminating evidence and issued a subpoena on the former communist. The following night a HUAC staff member went with Chambers to his Maryland farm and, in a hollowed pumpkin, found five rolls of microfilm containing more confidential State Department documents supposedly supplied by Hiss. The case was now headline news throughout the country, and Richard Nixon, testifying at grand jury hearings in New York, received nationwide publicity as well as unopposed reelection to Congress in 1948. On December 15, 1949, the grand jury indicted Hiss for perjury. After a series of trials, he went to prison early in 1950.

The advancement of Richard Nixon and the escalation of the entire Hiss controversy must be understood in the context of what people in the late 1940s came to call the Cold War. Its roots ran back to the middle years of World War II. The Atlantic Charter of August 14, 1941, with its disavowal of any territorial ambitions on the part of the Allies, laid a groundwork of principles for postwar reconstruction. But how these idealistic sentiments would survive the test of the real world was largely up to the three new superpowers: Great Britain, the United States, and the Soviet Union.

When their heads of state met for the first time late in November 1943 at Tehran, Iran, differences in policy and procedure were already apparent. Great Britain and the United States were willing to abide by the Atlantic Charter, but the Soviets, who had also signed this document, found it at odds with their avowed intention of advancing communism internationally. Joseph Stalin, in fact, left no doubt at Tehran that he intended to retain the Baltic republics and eastern Poland, which he had recently annexed. Moreover, he was prepared to support the newborn communist movements in the unannexed part of Poland, in Yugoslavia, and in Greece. Franklin D. Roosevelt and Winston Churchill were well aware that the Soviet Union's "support" would prove decisive in eastern Europe, but at Tehran they were prepared to play down their misgivings in the interest of winning the war.

The next meeting of the Big Three took place at Yalta in the Crimea in February 1945. An aging and weary Roosevelt had been elected to an unprecedented fourth term the previous November over the young Republican governor of New York, Thomas E. Dewey. With the victory, Roosevelt had received a mandate from the majority of Americans to construct the peace. The aftermath of World War I was relatively fresh in their minds, and the people hoped this one would be a just and lasting settlement. Yalta was a crucial milestone, and it provided few reasons for encouragement. Great Britain and the United States, still anxious about winning the war and feeling the need of Soviet support, gave in to the Soviet Union's demands for territory in eastern Europe and in the Far East. Churchill and Stalin also accepted without close scrutiny the concept of "free popular elections" in the European countries liberated from Axis control.

Although victory over the Axis powers was sweet, it was tempered by the realization that the result might be only the replacement of the Nazi juggernaut with a new version under the red flag of communism. By the summer of 1945, Churchill was already speaking of an "iron curtain" between the Soviet Union and the West. What went on behind it, he implied, was unknown and, presumably, unfree. Stalin confirmed this impression before a shocked and angry Churchill and Roosevelt's successor, Harry Truman, at the last Big Three conference at Potsdam, Germany, late in July. The pledges of Yalta, it appeared, were only so much paper in the face of the Soviet Union's postwar ambitions for communism. Once again it seemed that the United States had won the war but lost the peace.

By the time Richard Nixon entered the House in 1947, it was clear that conflict with the Soviet Union was the dominant theme of American foreign relations. The expectations of the 1930s and the early war years that democracy and communism shared a common denominator of respect for popular self-determination gave way to the realization that these systems, as defined by the current leadership, were implacably opposed.

The United States had several strategies available for meeting the postwar communist challenge. One was liberation. It called for positive American action aimed at freeing peoples trapped behind the iron curtain. The rationale here was to force Russia to keep its Yalta pledges concerning free elections. Apathy was immoral. "What we need to do," declared the belligerent secretary of state of the 1950s, John Foster Dulles, "is recapture the kind of crusading spirit of the early days of the Republic." The United States had a mission to liberate the world.

The second strategy also took a hard line. *Massive retaliation*, as it was called, entailed an immediate and all-out (that is, nuclear) response to Russian expansion whenever and wherever it appeared. The hope was that the threat of such a severe reprisal would stop Soviet aggression before it began. The result was an arms race between the world's two major powers and a dark cloud of fear over all humankind.

The third strategy, *disengagement*, involved reducing Soviet–American tension by withdrawing the American presence from hot spots such as central Europe and Southeast Asia. Its proponents were willing to allow the peoples of these regions to choose the political system they desired. If the choice went against democracy, it had to be accepted. In its extreme form, disengagement was comparable to the isolationism that had been the major theme in American foreign policy after World War I.

A fourth strategy was the United Nations (UN). A successor to the League of Nations, the UN began as a wartime coalition of Allied countries. Its function in times of peace was defined at the Dumbarton Oaks Conference, held near Washington, DC, in 1944, and at the Yalta meeting early the following year. The final charter was adopted April 29, 1945, in San Francisco; it provided for a General Assembly and a Security Council. The latter body consisted of five permanent members (the United States, Great Britain, the Soviet Union, France, and China) and six elected members. It had the power to invoke military sanctions against actions threatening world peace, but any one of the permanent members could veto such a decision. Still, the UN was a possible deterrent to Soviet aggression. In marked contrast to its policy toward the League of Nations, the United States gave the new world organization its full support.

The fifth strategy in relation to the Soviet presence in the postwar world was *containment*. The term originated with foreign service officer George Kennan and meant "the adroit and vigilant application of counterforce" at every point where the Soviet Union attempted to expand its circle of influence. Full-scale war was not contemplated. Indeed, the proponents of containment hoped never to engage the Soviets face to face and never to involve nuclear weapons. Rather, a series of limited wars and wars of nerves were envisaged, many of them to be fought "second-hand" for the superpowers by other peoples or by the UN. Containment, in essence, meant a patient snuffing out of sparks before they ignited a third world war. The strategy rested on the belief that if communism did not grow, it would eventually mellow or even wither and die.

A vital aspect of containment was the creation and maintenance of sufficient strength, both material and ideological, in the noncommunist world to resist Soviet pressures. President Harry Truman took the first step in this direction on March 12, 1947, when he announced that the United States would not stand by and watch Greece and Turkey fall to the communists. "I believe," Truman told the Congress, "that it must be the policy of the United States to support free peoples who are resisting attempted subjugation by armed minorities or outside pressures." The president further suggested that totalitarianism was "nurtured by misery and want." It followed that the United States could support freedom by economic and financial aid to hard-pressed peoples. The Truman Doctrine resulted in the immediate appropriation of $400 million in foreign aid for Greece and Turkey, and eventually it ended the communist revolutions in those countries. America's security, it seemed certain, could not be divorced from that of the free world as a whole.

On June 5, 1947, three months after Truman had set forth his doctrine, Secretary of State George C. Marshall proposed a broader plan for helping Europe recover from the ravages of war. Directed at the causes rather than the symptoms, the Marshall Plan called for the commitment of billions of dollars to fight poverty, increase production and trade, and promote economic cooperation in Europe. The long-range objective was to create a social and economic setting conducive to free institutions. Surprisingly, the Soviet Union was initially included in America's program for European economic recovery. "Our policy," Marshall declared, "is directed not against any country or doctrine but against hunger, poverty, desperation, and chaos." Yet after just one preliminary meeting of the nations involved, the Soviets abandoned the attempt to cooperate with the West.

A few months later, in the fall of 1947, they announced their own plan for helping the world: The Cominform, a new agency dedicated to the extension of communism, would assist any nation in launching a communist revolution. A demonstration of what the Russians had in mind occurred on February 25, 1948, when a coup d'état and several key assassinations and convenient suicides gave communists control of Czechoslovakia. The next month, the U.S. Congress answered with the first of what, in time, amounted to $12 billion in appropriations under the Marshall Plan. Congressman Nixon strongly supported this form of internationalism and made fifty speeches in his district justifying his stand.

The next move in the Cold-War chess game was the Soviet Union's. On June 24, 1948, it blockaded Berlin, which lay deep in the Soviet-occupied part of Germany. At the end of World War II, the city had been divided into four Allied zones. With the blockade the American, French, and British zones of Berlin, and the two million people who lived there, were isolated behind the iron curtain. The Western nations faced a crisis. They could not afford to yield to this show of Soviet strength if communism was to be contained; neither could they risk a major war by invading Soviet-held Germany. The solution to the dilemma was an airlift that supplied West Berlin for 321 days, until the Soviet Union lifted the blockade. It was a dramatic demonstration of the value of patience and determination and of the vitality of the noncommunist world. The Berlin airlift helped inspire the founding of the North Atlantic Treaty Organization (NATO), which established mutual defense arrangements among twelve nations on April 4, 1949. But Americans still preferred to fight with dollars rather than bullets, and President Truman's Point Four Program early the same year extended the Marshall Plan's concept to the entire underdeveloped world.

In September 1949, Nixon and his compatriots were astonished to learn that the Soviet Union had detonated its first atomic bomb. The superiority that the United States had held in that area since 1945 was now gone; the prospect of a nuclear holocaust that would leave few survivors on any side was very real. Added to the American agony was the revelation in February 1950 that a British scientist named Klaus Fuchs had collaborated with staff members Julius and Ethel Rosenberg of the Los Alamos, New Mexico, nuclear laboratory to channel details about the production of atomic bombs to the Soviets. The Rosenbergs were executed as traitors in 1953, although there was doubt about Ethel's involvement. Liberal intellectuals and many Democrats might deplore such actions, as they had deplored the investigation and imprisonment of Alger Hiss, but the charge that the communists had a foothold in the government of the United States could not be shaken off.

More and more Americans remembered that it was Richard Nixon who, almost alone, had dared to get tough with Hiss in the summer of 1948. "The conviction of Alger Hiss," former President Hoover wrote to Nixon early in 1950, "was due to your patience and persistence alone. At last the stream of treason that existed in our government has been exposed in a fashion that all may believe." Encouraged by this kind of support, Nixon decided to offer himself to the voters of California in the election of 1950 as a candidate for the U.S. Senate. As a young Republican who had made aggressive opposition to internal and international communism his major political stock in trade, Nixon timed his decision astutely.

In 1950, many Americans were worried about the global balance of power between their country and the Soviet Union. The Soviets had the atomic bomb and expansionist ideas, and, in 1949, communists under Mao Tse-tung prevailed in a civil war in China and drove pro-Western Chiang Kai-shek's Nationalist government to the island of Formosa. The way was now clear for the Soviet Union to challenge the status quo in Korea. Japan had held the Korean peninsula during World War II. At its conclusion, the Soviet Union and the United States had taken joint occupation of the peninsula, with the thirty-eighth parallel of latitude as the dividing line. Americans hoped the Koreans would eventually establish a free and unified nation, but on June 25, 1950, Soviet-backed North Korean troops stormed across the thirty-eighth parallel. Their fast-paced invasion, reminiscent of

Hitler's blitzkrieg, almost succeeded. The troops of the UN, whose Security Council voted to resist the North Korean aggression on a day when the Soviet delegation was absent, retreated to the very edge of the peninsula before beginning a counter-attack.

To Richard Nixon, the series of international reversals suffered by his country since World War II seemed too consistent to be explained fully by the ability of the Soviets. He suspected that communist sympathizers in his own country had aided and abetted the process. "Traitors in the high councils of our government," Nixon declared, "have made sure that the deck is stacked on the Soviet side of the diplomatic tables." Many Americans were prepared by the anxieties of the Cold War to believe such a statement and to support those who promised a remedy.

The communist-conspiracy idea to which Nixon subscribed received its most extreme domestic expression from Senator Joseph R. McCarthy of Wisconsin. A veteran, like Nixon, of the Pacific theater, McCarthy won election to the Senate in 1946 with the same crude campaign tactics that the Californian had used so successfully against Jerry Voorhis. On February 9, 1950, Senator McCarthy, hungry for an issue, stood up in Wheeling, West Virginia, and stated, "I have here in my hand a list of 205 names known to the Secretary of State as being members of the communist party and who nevertheless are still working and shaping the policy of the State Department!" That McCarthy produced no proof of his charge did not prevent its becoming headline news. In the following months, the senator pointed at communism in every corner of the nation's political house and reveled in his role as dragon-slayer.

Responsible people denounced McCarthy as a demagogue but found it hard to deny his vague and undocumented allegations. Anyone who challenged him ran the risk of being branded a communist sympathizer. Senator Millard Tydings of Maryland, for example, chaired hearings that examined McCarthy's charges and found them a "fraud and a hoax." But in the 1950 elections, McCarthy "smeared" Tydings himself with communist sympathies and brought about his defeat. Thereafter few dared to challenge the senator from Wisconsin. The truth, they realized, had very little to do with the public response to his charges. Americans were searching for a scapegoat that would relieve their frustrations in the Cold War. McCarthy provided one in the form of an internal communist conspiracy.

Nixon had known McCarthy since 1947, and their attitudes about communism were similar. Indeed, after the 1950 Wheeling speech, McCarthy asked Nixon to help prove his charges of communism in the State Department. Nixon was immediately uneasy—for practical political considerations, it appears, rather than ideological ones. He told McCarthy that in such matters understatement was much more effective than overstatement. Most important, Nixon added, the charges had to be based on proof. That Alger Hiss had known Whittaker Chambers in the 1930s was an example of a provable charge. To accuse the State Department of being communists, as McCarthy did, was fruitless in Nixon's opinion. While it might generate headlines, it could never win cases.

McCarthy, however, scarcely paused to listen to such advice, and Nixon courteously dissociated himself from McCarthyism. But while McCarthy's brand of anti-communism was too rabid for Nixon, he warmly supported the McCarran Internal

Security Act, which Congress passed in September 1950. Actually a reformation of the old Mundt-Nixon bill of two years before, the McCarran Act created a board to follow communist activities in the United States and barred anyone who had ever been a member of a totalitarian organization from admission to the United States. President Truman angrily vetoed the bill, stating, "We need not fear the expression of ideas—we do need to fear their suppression. . . . Let us not, in cowering and foolish fear, throw away the ideas which are the fundamental basis of our free society." Congress, however, overrode the veto.

Richard Nixon approached the 1950 senatorial campaign in California with a clear and simple philosophy. The issue, he declared, is "the choice between freedom and state socialism." The United States could either maintain its traditions of individual freedom or follow the planners and social welfare theorists of the New Deal and the Fair Deal toward "the slave state in its ultimate development," which was, as Nixon saw it, the Soviet Union. The only problem with campaigning on such an issue was finding an opponent who disagreed with Nixon's philosophy and could therefore be labeled an exponent of communism. The Democratic nominee for the senate seat Nixon desired was Congresswoman Helen Gahagan Douglas. As a protégé of the outspoken Eleanor Roosevelt, Douglas fit nicely into Nixon's smear methodology. Roosevelt had encouraged Douglas to get into politics in the 1930s. After being elected to Congress in 1944, Douglas was appointed as an alternate delegate to the UN two years later. Although a liberal and a critic of hard-liners in the Cold War, Douglas stood firm against Soviet expansionism. However, Douglas's friendship with Roosevelt and her dismissal from the UN in 1948 for criticism of Harry Truman were all that Nixon and his campaign manager, Murray Chotiner, needed. Irresponsibly disregarding the facts, the Nixon campaign simply branded Helen Gahagan Douglas a communist: "the Pink Lady."

Pamphlets printed on pink paper linked her voting record to that of Vito Marcantonio, the New York congressman with avowed communist principles. With a tangle of half-truths and distorted statistics, the "Pink Sheet" purported to prove a "Douglas–Marcantonio Axis." From the standpoint of winning elections, Nixon's strategy was effective. Tricks of language planted suspicions. Douglas could not ignore Nixon's taunts in such a sensitive area. So instead of developing her own platform for the voters, she was obliged to spend the great majority of her time correcting Nixon. Even when she did manage to present an alternative interpretation of her record, the seeds of doubt sown in the minds of less discerning or uninterested voters were hard to remove. It was in the 1950 campaign that Nixon picked up the label he never shook: "Tricky Dick."

In the concluding weeks, the Nixon campaign against Douglas turned into nothing less than character assassination. Even the fact that Douglas's husband was part Jewish was shamelessly dragged into the fray, although not by Nixon personally. Convinced by Republican propaganda, the *Los Angeles Times* called Douglas the "glamorous actress who, though not a communist, voted the communist party line in Congress innumerable times" and "the darling of the Hollywood parlor pinks and Reds." For his part, Nixon waged his characteristically comprehensive campaign. In sixteen weeks he gave a thousand speeches, most of them over a loudspeaker mounted on the station wagon in which he traveled from town to town.

The payoff came on election day. Nixon received 2,183,454 votes to 1,502,507 for Douglas.

As the returns came in, Nixon was ecstatic. That night he went from party to party banging out "Happy Days Are Here Again" on every piano he saw. But there was a price to pay for winning Nixon's way. Seven years later, as vice president, he granted an interview to an English publisher. Perhaps because the man was laudatory in his discussion of Nixon's command of international problems, Nixon was inclined to be more open than usual. At the conclusion of the interview the question of the 1950 campaign came up. How, the English visitor wondered, could Nixon explain what he had done to Helen Gahagan Douglas seven years before? With as much dignity as he could muster, Nixon sadly replied, "I'm sorry about the episode. I was a very young man."

The election of Richard Nixon as vice president of the United States climaxed one of the most outstanding rags-to-riches stories in the history of American politics. After just two terms in the House and twenty months in the Senate, the thirty-nine-year-old grocer's son became the second highest elected official in the country. Nixon's reputation as the determined, patriotic congressman who "got Alger Hiss" was his main springboard to success in the public's mind. But Republican professionals tended to emphasize Nixon's 1950 senatorial victory in a state in which Democrats outregistered Republicans by a million voters. Indeed, Nixon's victory was hailed as one of the signs that the Republican party was emerging from the long dry spell of Democratic control of the federal government. Nixon on the presidential ticket might ensure that California, second only to New York in population and electoral votes, would go Republican in 1952. Also important to the Republicans was Nixon's success in maintaining independence from the growing McCarthy bandwagon. Although the Helen Gahagan Douglas campaign seemed to prove the opposite, Nixon urged that, in cleaning communists out of American government, the Republicans avoid "indiscriminate name-calling and professional Red-baiting."

A far better star than McCarthy's to hitch his political wagon to was that of Dwight D. Eisenhower. Although completely inexperienced in politics, the general was the essence of patriotism and fatherly strength. At a time of increasing anxiety about the Cold War, and its hot front in Korea, there could be few better choices to offer the American people as a leader than "Ike." In May of 1951 Richard Nixon called briefly on Eisenhower at NATO headquarters in Paris. He returned with news that the general might be available for the presidential nomination the next year.

At the Republican convention in July 1952, Eisenhower defeated Senator Robert A. Taft of Ohio. A conservative who favored toughness with communism abroad and at home, Taft had the support of a sizable segment of right-wing Republicans. To appease them in the face of a presidential nominee associated with both the Roosevelt and the Truman administrations, the convention turned to Nixon as a forthright exponent of orthodox republicanism. Senator William Knowland of California nominated him as a man whose "bulldog determination" had enabled the "government to hunt out and unravel the Alger Hiss case." Eisenhower introduced him as a man with "a special talent . . . to ferret out any kind of subversive influence wherever it may be found, and the strength and persistence to get rid of it."

Nixon is all smiles as he checks the election scoreboard in the 1950 senatorial race in California, in which he defeated Democrat Helen Gahagan Douglas. With two terms as a congressman behind him, the thirty-seven-year-old Nixon's political future seemed bright at this point.

Because Eisenhower had never previously campaigned for political office and because the Republicans wanted him to be considered "above" politics, Nixon led the assault on the Democrats. The urbane liberal governor of Illinois, Adlai E. Stevenson, headed their ticket. His running mate, Senator John J. Sparkman of Alabama, was also liberal. Nixon went right for their throats with his familiar hatchet. The issues in 1952, he said, were "Korea, communism, and corruption." The last referred to recent exposures of influence-peddling in the Truman administration as well as the links between local politics and organized crime that Estes Kefauver's Senate Crime Investigation committee was exposing in nationally televised hearings. The Korean War was, by the summer of 1952, dragging into its third year and on its way to costing the United States 25,000 lives and $22 billion. Nixon charged that Democratic bungling had led to the assumption by the United States of an unfair amount of the United Nations' resistance. Plans to end the war quickly, notably the nuclear bombing suggested by General Douglas MacArthur before his dismissal by President Truman on April 5, 1951, had been ignored.

It was the issue of communist sympathy, however, that Nixon especially relished. Here was a chance to do on a national scale what he had done twice in California. In his campaign speeches, Stevenson became "Adlai the appeaser . . . who got a Ph.D. from Dean Acheson's College of Cowardly Communist Containment."

Nixon added that the Truman government had "covered up" the communist conspiracy for political reasons and that communists still lurked in the executive branch. Nixon constantly reminded the electorate that Stevenson had defended Alger Hiss, and he could always get a chuckle from an audience by a reference to "Alger, I mean Adlai, Stevenson." On other occasions Nixon fell back on what for him was a very characteristic anti-intellectualism. The balding Stevenson and his intellectual supporters were labeled "eggheads." Eisenhower chimed in with a definition of an intellectual as someone "who takes more words than are necessary to tell more than he knows." Sometimes the mood turned uglier, as when Nixon came close to calling Harry Truman and other Democrats traitors.

The Republican campaign was progressing nicely into September. Nixon had just completed a major speech on corruption and Truman's "scandal-a-day administration" with its "bribes" and "fixes" and "favors." Then, on September 18, 1952, the *New York Post* published a rare full-page headline: "Secret Nixon Fund." The story followed. After the 1950 campaign, Nixon and his advisers had recognized the need for this young "comer" to maintain visibility between elections. He needed to travel, give speeches, and distribute mailings. But Nixon was not independently wealthy, and his salary as senator was then a modest $12,500. The idea of the fund was a response to this situation. Donations were solicited from wealthy southern California businesspeople to enable Nixon to publicize his political and economic philosophy, which was, decidedly, in the American free enterprise tradition. At the time the story about the Nixon fund broke, about $18,000 had been collected and disbursed for airplane tickets, printing costs, Christmas cards, and the like.

News of the Nixon "slush fund" spread quickly throughout the country. At first, Nixon lashed back at the story, calling it an attempt by "the communists and crooks in this administration" to "smear" him. Then, as Eisenhower and his staff seriously considered dropping Nixon from the ticket, the young senator realized his desperate predicament. In fairness to Nixon, it should be noted that he had used the contributions for precisely the kinds of publicity purposes for which they had been solicited. But whatever justification he used for the fund, the fact remained that Nixon could be considered, as the *Sacramento Bee* said, "the pet and protégé of a special-interest group of rich southern Californians." Real estate, manufacturing, and oil interests had given over three-quarters of the fund, and Nixon had invariably voted in ways they applauded.

It was Thomas E. Dewey, former governor of New York and 1948 Republican presidential nominee, who first advised Nixon that his only hope was a national television appearance in which he explained his situation fully and frankly. Eisenhower agreed. Nixon, he said, had to prove himself "to be clean as a hound's tooth." Quick financial arrangements by the Republican National Committee opened a prime-time hour for Nixon on September 23, 1952. A combined radio and television audience of fifty-eight million watched and listened. It was make-or-break time for Richard Milhous Nixon—up to that time, his gravest personal and political crisis.

Minutes before air time, Nixon took a call from Dewey. Most of the Republican campaign leaders and, Dewey implied, Eisenhower himself felt that Nixon should resign. "Dick looked like someone had smashed him," an associate who was present recalled. For thirty minutes he sat alone pondering his future. Then it was airtime. The telecast opened with a shot of Nixon seated behind a desk. "My fellow Americans," he began, "I come before you tonight as a candidate for the vice-presidency . . . and as a man whose honesty and integrity has been questioned." What followed was a remarkable performance in American political history. Nixon freely acknowledged the existence of the fund. He said that not a cent of the money had gone to him for his personal use, and a careful unbiased audit later substantiated this claim. He added that no contributor had ever received any special consideration, but, with an instinct for drama, he pointed out that he had used the fund to buy stamps for mailing Christmas cards to his constituents. Then he launched into a personal financial history. It featured the blue-collar boy clawing his way up to success. His wife, he said, had never had a mink coat, just a "respectable Republican cloth coat." But he had accepted one personal gift. The gift, Nixon continued, was "a little cocker spaniel dog" that his daughters had named Checkers. The girls loved that dog, Nixon added, "and I just want to say this right now, that regardless of what they say about it, we're going to keep it."

The "Checkers speech," as it came to be called, was anticlimactic from then on. Nixon said he wasn't a quitter. He lauded Eisenhower. And he concluded with an invitation for Americans to contact the Republican National Committee and tell them if he should be retained on the ticket or dropped. Moments after the cameras clicked off, Nixon dissolved in tears. Then the telephones began to ring. Sophisticates later ridiculed the speech, but the nation had been overwhelmed. Eisenhower wired, "Your presentation was magnificent." The next day he met Nixon in Wheeling, West Virginia, and told him, "You're my boy." Again there were tears. But the reunited Republicans laughed last. On election day in November 1952, Eisenhower and Nixon crushed the Democrats by six million popular votes and a 442 to 89 margin in the electoral college. The slush fund episode revealed Nixon succeeding in a game he would ultimately lose in the Watergate scandals. There was the extreme self-righteousness, the talent for obscuring or circling the truth, and the instinct for political survival. And there was the paranoia and self-pity. People were "out to get" Richard Nixon, but he would "get" them. The 1952 campaign taught him, in his own words, that "in politics most people are your friends only as long as you can do something for them or something to them."

The continuing Korean War was a major issue of the 1952 presidential campaign. Americans were increasingly disgusted by bearing some 90 percent of the costs (both human and material) of this UN police action. Eisenhower attracted much attention with his campaign promise that, if elected, he would go to Korea to begin building an honorable peace. As good as his word, the general went to the front lines even before his inauguration. He made it clear to the communists that although the United States was sick of the war, it would insist on a territorial settlement at approximately the prewar line of the thirty-eighth parallel. The United States, Eisenhower added, also intended to honor the wishes of 100,000 North Korean war prisoners who did not wish to be returned to a communist society. Eisenhower and his secretary of state, John Foster Dulles, made it clear that if progress toward a satisfactory peace was not begun at once, the North Koreans and their allies could expect nuclear attack and a greatly expanded theater of military operations.

With his political life on the line as a result of the exposure of a secret campaign fund, vice presidential candidate Nixon (top) appeared on national television to defend himself. His successful performance in 1952 featured a reference to his beloved family dog, Checkers (bottom). The animal had been a gift from a political admirer, and Nixon tearfully vowed he would not return him.

Dulles explained the theory behind the tough talk: "The necessary art" in dealing with the communists was "the ability to get to the verge without getting into the war. If you are scared to go to the brink, you are lost." While Dulles's skill in so-called brinksmanship helped, so did the death of Soviet dictator Joseph Stalin on March 5, 1953. An armistice on American terms was concluded on July 27, and the North and South Korean people settled back into a condition of uneasy coexistence. In Nixon's interpretation, firm Republican action had extricated the nation from the mess in Asia resulting from inept Democratic leadership.

Less partisan observers explained the Cold War in terms of Soviet ambition rather than by using differences between American political parties. By the time Nixon assumed the vice presidency, it was apparent that the Soviet strategy was aimed at winning over the uncommitted and mostly underdeveloped world to communism. Revolutionary movements against the old colonial powers were applauded in Moscow. Soviet economic and technical assistance stood ready to support challenges to the status quo. Ideas also figured in the fight. The Soviets were anxious to show the world that they, rather than the Americans, carried the key to the future.

To that end, Moscow delighted in pointing out that the growth rate of the Soviet economy in the 1950s averaged three times that of the United States. The construction of a hydrogen bomb in 1953 symbolized the new Soviet competence. But the greatest Soviet triumph of Nixon's vice presidential years was the successful launching on October 4, 1957, of the world's first orbiting space craft, *Sputnik I*. Eisenhower and Nixon tried to make light of the achievement. "One small ball in the air," the president remarked, "does not raise my apprehensions, not one iota." But especially after the ludicrous failure, on December 6, of America's initial attempt to duplicate *Sputnik* (the U.S. rocket rose only a few inches from the ground before collapsing), there was no denying the country's anxiety.

At the conclusion of the Korean War, the action in the broader Cold War shifted south to Indochina. The French colonial empire was collapsing under a wave of rising indigenous expectations. Despite massive transfusions of American supplies and dollars, nationalist revolutionaries under Ho Chi Minh threatened to end French control. Russia and mainland China welcomed that prospect and lavished economic and military assistance on Ho's troops. In March 1954, France informed Eisenhower and Nixon that it could not hold its main fortress, Dienbienphu, without direct American aid. The request posed a dilemma for the Eisenhower administration, which had sharply criticized American involvement in Korea.

Eisenhower reasoned that the integrity of free nations could be likened to a "row of dominoes." If Indochina fell to the communists, it could trigger a chain reaction that would bring down other governments and ultimately threaten the security of the United States. As Dienbienphu tottered, Secretary of State Dulles advocated using nuclear bombs to relieve the French. On April 16, 1954, Nixon told reporters that "the United States is the leader of the free world and the free world cannot afford in Asia a further retreat to the communists." Nixon added, in a statement that received wide publicity around the world, that if the French withdrew from Indochina "we must take the risk now by putting American boys in."

In the aftermath of Korea, this was too much. Congressional leaders, notably Senator John F. Kennedy, were strongly opposed to Nixon's idea. Even Dulles and Eisenhower did not support the use of American troops, and on April 28, Nixon reversed his position. On May 7, 1954, communists overran Dienbienphu, ending French colonialism. The ensuing settlement created the independent nations of Laos, Cambodia, and Vietnam, but, to the disappointment of the United States, there were no provisions for free elections. In the manner of Korea, Vietnam was divided at the seventeenth parallel, with a communist government in North Vietnam and an American-supported republican government in South Vietnam. On September 8, 1954, Dulles completed the details of a mutual-defense plan known as the Southeast Asia Treaty Organization (SEATO)—an Asian counterpart of NATO. Thereafter the United States was committed to maintaining the balance of power on the very doorstep of the communist world. That fact would become one of the most significant in Richard Nixon's future.

Of more direct concern to Nixon at this time was a domestic aspect of the cold war: "McCarthyism." The Wisconsin senator reached the zenith of his power in the first year of the Eisenhower–Nixon administration. Despite his failure to prove his wild charges of communist influence in American government, polls showed that McCarthy had the confidence of a majority of the American people. Big names continued to be smeared, notably that of the brilliant nuclear physicist J. Robert Oppenheimer. President Eisenhower refused to have anything to do with McCarthy, saying, "I will not get in the gutter with *that* guy." This put the problem in Nixon's lap. His foremost concern was with the unity of the Republican party. Beginning in late 1953, he tried to restrain (some would say "appease") McCarthy, but the senator forged ahead in his accusations that the U.S. Army had been infiltrated by communists at the uppermost levels.

On March 13, 1954, Nixon spoke for the administration in a nationwide broadcast on the McCarthy problem. It was not an easy assignment for a man who, if honest with himself, could see in the senator only an exaggeration of his own attitudes and methods. Nixon compromised effectively: "Men who have in the past done effective work exposing communists in this country have, by reckless talk and questionable methods, made themselves the issue rather than the cause they believe in so deeply." Nixon also commented on McCarthy's philosophy of anticommunism, expressed as "why worry about being fair when you are shooting rats." The vice president said he agreed about the "rat" characterization but stood firmly for fairness in the hunt "because when you shoot wildly it . . . means that the rats may get away more easily [and] you might hit someone else who is trying to shoot rats too." At the conclusion of his broadcast, just to show he had not gone "soft" on communism, Nixon used his favorite trick of indirect accusation, saying, "Incidentally, in mentioning Secretary Dulles, isn't it wonderful, finally, to have a secretary of state who isn't taken in by the communists, who stands up to them?"

Despite Nixon's reprimand, McCarthy remained undaunted. On April 22, 1954, the Senate committee he chaired began hearings on communism in the armed forces. McCarthy floundered in a morass of partial truths and untruths that he himself had created. National television exposed the whole ugly spectacle. Even Nixon was disgusted by the posturing and false melodrama. "I prefer professionals to amateur actors," he remarked. On December 2, 1954, in a rare move, the U.S. Senate censured McCarthy by a sixty-seven to twenty-two vote. Within three years he drank himself to death.

The embarrassment of McCarthyism could not dispel the elation the Republicans felt in coming to national power after two long decades. With great enthusiasm the Eisenhower–Nixon administration tried to live up to its conservative image. Eisenhower appointed a General Motors executive, Charles Wilson, to the position of secretary of defense. Wilson's biases were so ingrained he could not even understand the uproar that greeted a casual statement of what he had always believed: "What was good for our country was good for General Motors, and vice versa." Another millionaire headed the Department of the Treasury, and Eisenhower's secretary of the interior, former Chevrolet dealer Douglas McKay, frankly stated that Republicans were "in the saddle as an administration representing business and industry." In Eisenhower's view, Roosevelt and Truman had dangerously increased the power of the executive branch of the federal government at the expense of Congress, the courts, and the states. He deplored the presidential steamrolling of the early New Deal and Roosevelt's later efforts to pack the Supreme Court. Deliberately refusing to cast the shadow of his office over Capitol Hill, Ike hid his preferences behind the orderly veneer of an efficient military-style staff.

The other hallmark of Eisenhower's domestic policy was a preference for economic stability with as little federal management as possible. For him, as for Herbert Hoover and Calvin Coolidge, free enterprise was the taproot of America's strength. Eisenhower distrusted the government's entrance into the nation's socioeconomic life with projects like the Tennessee Valley Authority (TVA). Such developments represented "creeping socialism," and in 1954, the Eisenhower administration unsuccessfully attempted to provide a private alternative to TVA hydropower with the Dixon-Yates contract for a steam-generating facility. The Republicans did manage, however, to reduce the federal budget by 10 percent, and they allowed some New Deal agencies and economic controls imposed during the Korean War to expire. But overall, Eisenhower accepted far more of the New Deal than he rejected. Just like Roosevelt, Eisenhower loosened credit, increased subsidies, reduced taxes, and raised federal spending in an effort to pump vigor into the economy. Even the archconservative secretary of agriculture, Ezra Taft Benson, was obliged to relent and pay out billions of dollars in an effort to support farm prices. This compensatory fiscal policy ended recessions, but the Eisenhower Republicans regretted every departure from the balanced budget and the ideal of federal nonintervention.

On behalf of the Republican party, Nixon campaigned with his characteristic aggressiveness in the congressional elections of 1954. In terms of issues, he had a formula: K_1C_3. It meant one part reference to the Korean War, caused by Democrats and ended by Republicans, and three parts each of communism, corruption, and controls by the government over the economic system. The strategy did not succeed. Nixon traveled 28,000 miles and made 200 speeches, but the Democrats reversed their minority status in both the House and the Senate.

At 3:30 P.M. on September 24, 1955, Eisenhower's press secretary telephoned Nixon with the news that the president had suffered a heart attack in Colorado. The announcement began eleven months of anguish for Nixon. For a time he ran the federal government, and he could not avoid contemplating the possibility of Eisenhower's death or at least an opening at the top of the 1956 Republican ticket.

But Nixon's political sixth sense, which had once saved him from too close an alignment with Joseph McCarthy, warned him not to appear too ambitious. Outwardly calm and self-effacing, Nixon churned inwardly. People close to him said he aged ten years in appearance.

Finally, on February 27, 1956, the president announced he had been given medical clearance to consider another nomination by the Republican party. Nothing was said about a running mate. In fact, Eisenhower conferred with Nixon about the possibility of accepting a cabinet appointment instead of the vice presidency. Insulted by the offer, Nixon considered quitting politics. His wife, still distraught over the secret fund revelation and the tearful "Checkers speech," urged him to do so, and for different reasons, so did several high-ranking Republicans. Nixon, they said, was too controversial and was losing popularity. The "dump Nixon" effort flared up irregularly in the summer of 1956 as the vice president, according to friends, "ate his heart out." Eisenhower, it seems certain, was not enthusiastic about running with Nixon again. But at the Republican convention, no stronger candidate appeared. It was "Ike and Dick" one more time.

In 1956, Nixon campaigned with his eyes on the presidency. Everyone commented on the "new Nixon." He was mellower, more subdued, more statesmanlike. He did not resort to the no-holds-barred slugging of his previous campaigns. Some felt he was less effective in his new role, but the ticket won easily over Democrats Adlai Stevenson and Estes Kefauver by more than nine million popular votes. Yet for any Republican considering himself a presidential contender of the future, the course of events over the next four years was not encouraging. Economic recession gripped the nation in 1957 and 1958, forcing the Republicans away from their traditional opposition to compensatory fiscal policy and federal intervention in the private sector.

On top of this, the party that had made the "corruption" of the Democrats a campaign slogan had its own taste of scandal. Bribe taking and influence peddling brought about the resignation of numerous highly placed officials, including the chairman of the Republican National Committee and, in September 1958, Sherman Adams, the influential assistant to the president. The congressional elections two months later reflected the public disappointment in a party that could offer little more than the president's health as an issue, particularly since Eisenhower had suffered another heart attack late in 1957. The Democrats gained the largest majorities in Congress since 1936, the heyday of Franklin Roosevelt's New Deal.

The Republican record in foreign affairs offered little consolation for these reversals at home. There was hope that the 1955 "summit" meeting between Eisenhower and the Soviet leaders in Geneva, Switzerland, would lead to a lessening of Cold-War tensions. In fact, they escalated. In Asia, Chiang Kai-shek continued to voice his determination to return to the Chinese mainland. Any such move threatened to involve his supporters, chiefly the United States, in a major Asian war. Half a world away, Germany remained divided and a source of continuing tension, as thousands of refugees from Soviet-dominated East Germany fled to the west. There was even an abortive attempt at revolution in East Germany. In Hungary, an uprising in October 1956 proved successful in overthrowing the local communist party. Although the Hungarians immediately appealed to the UN for support, the Soviets moved in quickly with troops and tanks. For once, John Foster Dulles was not willing to risk a confrontation, and the noncommunist world stood by as the Hungarians were brutally forced back into the Soviet camp.

Then the focus of the Cold War shifted to the Suez Canal, where the Soviet Union's support of Egypt and the military strongman Gamal Abdel Nasser threatened the freedom of access to this vital waterway. In the ensuing war between Israel, France, and Great Britain, on the one hand, and a Soviet-backed Egypt, on the other, the United States managed to alienate both sides. Finally, in the late 1950s, the Cold War reached the New World in a series of communist uprisings in Latin America. For the United States, the most serious of these occurred in 1959 only ninety miles away on the island of Cuba, placing the charismatic young Fidel Castro in power. Almost immediately, he turned to the Soviet Union for guidance and support.

Eisenhower, in failing health, desperately wanted to end his last term in office on a wave of renewed hope for world peace. Richard Nixon became a goodwill ambassador, but the results of his trips were not always goodwill. In Venezuela in May 1958, the Nixons were almost killed by a spitting, rock-throwing crowd of pro-communists. The vice president did better in his July 1959 meeting with Soviet premier Nikita Khrushchev. Hopes were high for the scheduled summit meeting of May 1960 between Khrushchev and Eisenhower. Just before it began, however, the United States was embarrassed by the Soviet Union's announcement that an American high-altitude reconnaissance plane, a U-2, had been shot down 1,200 miles inside the Soviet border. For a few days, the Eisenhower administration denied any knowledge of the flight. But on May 7, 1960, Khrushchev said the pilot of the U-2 had parachuted from the plane, had been captured, and had confessed to espionage. Eisenhower quickly accepted full responsibility for the mission but saw his plans for the summit and for peace scuttled over the incident.

With eight years as vice president in which to build support among the insiders, Richard Nixon did not have significant opposition in his bid for the 1960 Republican presidential nomination. When he accepted at the Chicago convention, Nixon said: "I believe in the American dream because I have seen it come true in my own life." Henry Cabot Lodge of Massachusetts was the Republican choice for the vice presidential nomination. The Democrats nominated Senator John F. Kennedy from Massachusetts, who had scored well in the primaries. Lyndon Baines Johnson, a senator from Texas, completed the slate. Being so near what must have been a long-standing goal, Nixon pushed himself through a punishing campaign schedule. His standard speech emphasized his experience. Kennedy attacked the eight-year Republican record and promised to "get this country moving again." Neither candidate dared to make much of an issue of Kennedy's Roman Catholicism.

In retrospect, what seemed to be the determining phase of the campaign began on September 26, 1960, when Nixon and Kennedy held the first of four nationally televised debates. In theory, Nixon had little to gain by debating Kennedy. He was the better known of the two and the front-runner. Traditionally, an incumbent such as Nixon would have remained aloof from man-to-man confrontations. But it was not Nixon's style to dodge a political fight. He had been a successful college debater, and his first political victory over Jerry Voorhis had been the result of a 1946 debate. Nixon was confident that he could outtalk Kennedy. He did not, however, accurately assess the importance of two realities: First, the anticommunist mud-slinging that had characterized his earlier campaign successes was now less than effective against fellow anticommunist, John F. Kennedy. Second, the outcome of the crucial first debate was being shaped by Kennedy. The Massachusetts senator benefited from many advantages and experiences denied to Nixon. Kennedy had been born rich. He had attended Harvard. He was handsome. He had won a Pulitzer Prize for biography. While Nixon had warmed the bench at Whittier, Kennedy had been a varsity athlete. While Nixon was stacking boxes of supplies in the wartime Pacific, Kennedy had commanded a PT boat, had seen heavy fighting, and had been injured. Kennedy's wife, Jacqueline, was an international beauty; the most anyone said for Pat Nixon was that she wore a respectable cloth coat. If the Nixons were blue-collar in their background, the Kennedys were white-collar. John Kennedy, in sum, had the elegance and grace that had led easily to the goals that Nixon had always had to sweat to achieve.

The difference was clearly evident to seventy-five million viewers on September 26. Nixon, looking haggard, sweaty, and nervous, spoke as if addressing a panel of debate judges. Kennedy, exuding vigor and confidence, addressed the nation as a leader. Nixon probably won the verbal battle on technicalities of subject matter, but he lost in the area of public relations. Given the closeness of the election (Kennedy had a popular vote margin of about 119,000 votes out of 68.3 million), the debates proved decisive. The spread in the electoral college was greater (303 for Kennedy, 219 for Nixon), but a change of a few hundred votes in several key states could have altered that result as well. To his credit, Nixon did not call for a recount even in the face of reports of ballot-box tampering, particularly in Illinois and Texas, both of which he had lost by narrow margins. "Our country," he declared, "can't afford the agony of a constitutional crisis—and I damn well will not be a party to creating one just to become president."

At noon on January 20, 1961, Richard M. Nixon became a private citizen for the first time in fourteen years. He held no public office and had no job. With Pat he tried vacationing in the Bahamas, but beach sitting was decidedly not his style. In less than two weeks, Nixon was back and ready to work. He accepted a position with a Los Angeles law firm and resumed his old career. In late April 1961, Tricia, the Nixons' twelve-year-old daughter, left a note on her father's desk: "Dear Daddy, I knew it would happen! JFK called and wants you to come down to see him. I knew he would have to come begging for your help." Tricia was correct in guessing that Kennedy needed help. Despite all the bravado about "new frontiers," his administration had not enjoyed an encouraging start in foreign affairs.

On April 12, 1961, the Soviets had succeeded in orbiting the first man in space, an achievement that enhanced the Soviet image in the Third World. Frustrated and annoyed, Kennedy had reacted impulsively and ineffectively. He had authorized the invasion on April 17 of Fidel Castro's communist-aligned Cuba by Cuban refugees trained and equipped by the United States Central Intelligence Agency (CIA). Landing at the Bay of Pigs on the southern coast of Cuba, the invaders quickly became disordered and collapsed. The fiasco, for which Kennedy had accepted full blame, made the United States a laughingstock around the world. Kennedy's call to Nixon had followed. At their meeting, Nixon stated in regard to

Cuba, "I would find a proper legal cover and I would go in." This would mean a full-scale invasion by American armed forces under the guise of protecting the American military bases and the Americans still living on the island. Nixon later criticized Kennedy for undertaking the Bay of Pigs invasion with so blunt an instrument. "When a decision is made to commit American prestige," Nixon explained, "we must be prepared to commit an adequate amount of American power."

Relishing his role as chief Republican critic of the Kennedy administration, Nixon fell back into his accustomed brass-knuckle style of politics. In dealing with communism abroad, he said, Kennedy displayed "a Hamlet-like psychosis which seems to paralyze." What bothered Nixon the most were American setbacks in the continuing Cold War, particularly in Southeast Asia. When Kennedy entered the White House in January 1961, a bitter civil war was in progress in the swamps and jungles of Laos. And despite American aid that amounted to $150 for every Laotian, the pro-Western government in that country remained in jeopardy. The same was true in neighboring South Vietnam, where an indigenous guerrilla group, the Viet Cong, was challenging the republican regime. The government of Ho Chi Minh in North Vietnam supported the Viet Cong. The United States, in turn, rushed supplies to support the incumbent administration of Ngo Dinh Diem and, after 1961, provided military advisers and special "Green Beret" troops. But in November 1963, Diem was overthrown and murdered by his own people. By this time it was becoming evident that Vietnam had the potential for entangling the United States to a far greater extent than any previous Cold-War commitment.

In Europe, the inability of the superpowers to deal with the problems of a conquered Germany continued to undermine peace. For fifteen years, an ideological wall had separated East Germany from West Germany and the Soviet-controlled from the Western-controlled sectors of Berlin. In August 1961, after a summit-level showdown between Kennedy and Khrushchev in Vienna, the Soviets transformed the ideological wall into concrete and barbed wire. They also vowed to drive the Western powers out of Berlin by the end of the year. They were concerned because, since World War II, over three million East Germans had fled from communist control and had sought refuge in Berlin's western sector. In the battle for world prestige, this unequivocal demonstration of communism's lack of appeal had had the same effect on the Soviet ego as *Sputnik* had had on that of the United States. The Berlin Wall stopped the flow of defectors, and, to Nixon's great joy, Kennedy's firmness in dealing with Khrushchev caused a postponement of the Soviet's end-of-the-year deadline for driving the Western powers out of Berlin.

As the 1961 Berlin crisis showed, neither the Soviet Union nor the United States was willing, in the last analysis, to press to the point of direct war. Both sides realized that, given their possession of nuclear bombs that were now thousands of times more powerful than those that had devastated Hiroshima and Nagasaki, there would be no victors and few survivors of an unlimited war.

This bipartisan realization also figured in the settlement of the Cuban missile crisis of 1962. This frightening confrontation arose as a result of the Soviet delivery to Cuba of long-range missiles capable of reaching most of the United States. When U-2 reconnaissance flights in October confirmed the presence of the missile stations, Kennedy faced the most serious possibility of world war since 1945. His re-

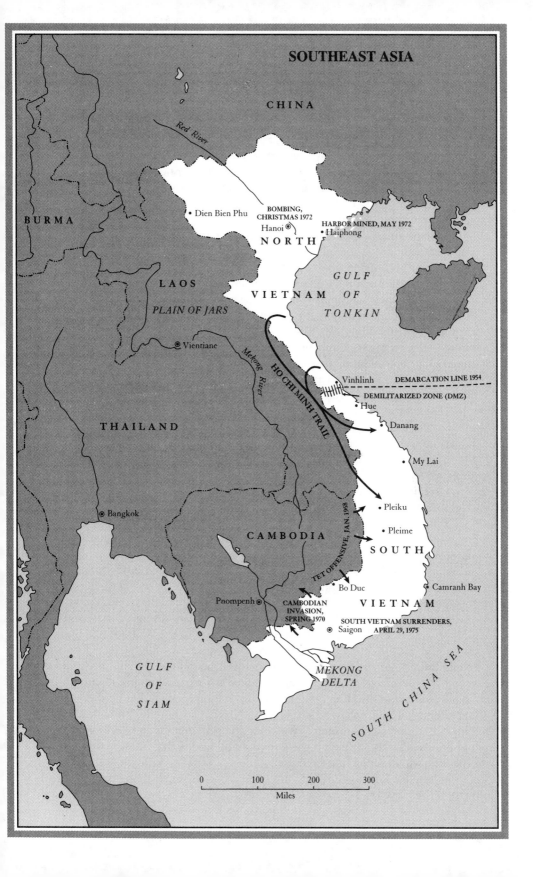

SOUTHEAST ASIA

CHINA

Red River

BURMA

Dien Bien Phu

BOMBING,
CHRISTMAS 1972

HARBOR MINED, MAY 1972

Hanoi

Haiphong

NORTH

LAOS

VIETNAM

GULF

PLAIN OF JARS

OF

Vientiane

TONKIN

Mekong River

HO CHI MINH TRAIL

Vinhlinh

DEMARCATION LINE 1954

DEMILITARIZED ZONE (DMZ)

Hue

THAILAND

Danang

My Lai

Bangkok

Pleiku

TET OFFENSIVE, JAN. 1968

Pleime

CAMBODIA

SOUTH

Bo Duc

Camranh Bay

Pnompenh

VIETNAM

CAMBODIAN
INVASION,
SPRING 1970

SOUTH VIETNAM SURRENDERS,
APRIL 29, 1975

Saigon

GULF

MEKONG
DELTA

OF

SOUTH CHINA SEA

SIAM

0   100   200   300

Miles

sponse was to establish a naval blockade of Cuba, to demand the removal of the existing missiles, and to inform Krushchev in no uncertain terms that a Cuban missile attack on the United States would result in instant, direct retaliation on the Soviet Union. Nixon strongly supported these actions. They were in the tradition of the "brinksmanship" he had learned from Secretary of State Dulles in the Eisenhower administration. For several days a war of nerves prevailed. Then the Soviets and the Cubans removed the missiles. It was a great day for Kennedy's foreign policy, but the real credit belonged to the universal fear of a nuclear holocaust. Fear also inspired the 1963 treaty that banned atmospheric nuclear tests, ending the panic regarding radioactive fallout.

If Nixon thought Kennedy was becoming a hard-liner on the issue of international communism as a result of Berlin and the Cuban missile crisis, he was mistaken. After his unimpressive beginning at the Bay of Pigs, Kennedy was developing a more mature and realistic view of the problems and possibilities of America's role in world affairs. He came to see the danger and arrogance inherent in assuming American infallibility. In direct contrast to Nixon, Kennedy did not believe that the Cold War was a holy war. "We must face the fact," Kennedy declared, "that the United States is neither omnipotent nor omniscient; that we are only 6 percent of the world's population; that we cannot impose our will upon the other 94 percent of mankind; that we cannot right every wrong or reverse each adversity; and that therefore there cannot be an American solution to every world problem."

The corollary of this belief was the acceptance of the ideas and institutions of others. "If we cannot end now all our differences," Kennedy told an audience at American University on June 10, 1963, "at least we can help make the world safe for diversity." Here was a direct repudiation of the idealism that Richard Nixon had inherited from Woodrow Wilson and other champions of the liberation philosophy. Here, too, was a rejection of the Nixon philosophy that communists were devils always bent on undermining republican institutions.

The ambition that drove Richard Nixon did not allow him to rest content for long with writing newspaper articles about foreign policy and delivering after-dinner speeches. He dreamed of the presidency, and he needed to maintain his political visibility for the eight Kennedy years that were anticipated in 1961. Such considerations prompted Nixon to declare his candidacy for the governorship of California in the 1962 elections. His opponent, Democrat Edmund G. Brown, was the incumbent. The belief of a great number of California voters that Nixon was only seeking to be their governor as a stepping-stone to the White House hurt his cause. On the eve of the election, Nixon uncharacteristically predicted that he would lose. He proved an accurate prophet. But he did not take his defeat gracefully. On November 6, Nixon verbally attacked a group of a hundred reporters who, he alleged, had wanted him defeated and had misinterpreted what he said at every opportunity. Toward the end of the talk, Nixon said bitterly, "You won't have Nixon to kick around anymore." Watching the performance on television, Governor Brown observed, "Nixon is going to regret all his life that he made that speech. The press will never let him forget it."

In June 1963, Nixon fulfilled a dream held since his graduation from law school in 1937; he moved to New York City, entered a prestigious law firm, and joined the monied eastern Establishment. Shortly after the move Nixon disavowed all political ambitions. He told an interviewer, "Anybody who thinks I could be a candidate for anything in any year is off his rocker." And then Kennedy died. Coincidentally, Nixon was in Dallas, Texas, on a business trip on November 22, 1963, but he did not learn of Kennedy's assassination until returning to New York that evening. He made a graceful statement about "a man of history struck down in the tragic panorama of history" and almost immediately began considering the effect of Kennedy's death on national politics.

Lyndon Johnson, he realized, was totally lacking in the style that had generated a renaissance of hope during the brief Kennedy presidency. But Johnson was a master politician, and his Great Society program had enough diversity and enough federal expenditures to please almost everyone. It would be hard for any Republican to beat Johnson in 1964. Nonetheless, Nixon campaigned hard in thirty-six states for Arizona senator Barry Goldwater. He was not surprised, however, to see Johnson carry forty-four states in the biggest landslide since Franklin Roosevelt's in 1936.

Johnson's smashing victory in 1964 changed the political horizon substantially. Instead of a vacant White House after two Kennedy terms, Nixon could now contemplate Johnson in office until 1972. By that time Richard Nixon would be forgotten. Vietnam changed all of that. At first it did not seem much of an issue. Johnson failed to mention the situation in Southeast Asia at all in his January 1964 state of the union address. Yet the civil war in that divided country was rapidly becoming a quagmire from which the United States could not easily escape. Johnson, as Kennedy's vice president, had phrased what had come to be the dominant point of view as early as 1961: "We must decide whether to help these countries to the best of our ability or throw in the towel in the area and pull back our defenses to San Francisco."

Kennedy had not been so sure. He had sent "military advisers" to South Vietnam but had realized that this policy was "like taking a drink; the effect wears off, and you have to take another." Fewer than a hundred Americans had been killed in combat in Vietnam during Kennedy's presidency. In August 1964, however, Congress responded to alleged attacks on American destroyers by North Vietnamese gunboats by passing almost unanimously the Gulf of Tonkin Resolution. It authorized the president to "take all necessary steps" to help South Vietnam. By early 1965, this resolution had been translated by the newly elected Johnson into a mandate to send thousands of American troops to the front, and to begin a systematic and increasing program of bombing North Vietnam.

Although always sympathetic with resisting communist aggression, Richard Nixon became increasingly uncomfortable with the growth of American involvement in Vietnam. He did not believe that the United States should fight in Southeast Asia without allies. Regionally organized collective security was Nixon's formula, together with American economic and technical assistance, not troops. Yet Nixon watched the numbers of Americans fighting without allies in Vietnam grow to more than half a million. He saw his nation's total monetary commitment approach $150 billion. Like other Americans, he read with shock and grief the weekly death tolls; at the peak of the fighting in 1967 and 1968, they reached 300 per week.

Most disturbing of all was the lack of a clear case for American involvement. Johnson talked about deterring "a wider pattern of aggressive purpose," but unlike the situation in World War II and the Korean War, there was no totalitarian aggression. The Viet Cong guerrillas appeared to have widespread support in South Vietnam. No one seemed to want American involvement except war profiteers. The "democratic" government upheld by the American presence in South Vietnam did not seem to be desired by the people. Vietnam was, by every measure, the most unpopular war the United States had ever fought.

As the protests mounted, Nixon commented on the "terrible American disillusionment" regarding the war. He knew it was tearing the nation apart. He knew President Johnson was ineptly trying to keep the full truth about Vietnam from the people. When his daughter Julie became engaged to David Eisenhower in 1967, Nixon had occasion to reflect on the warning that David's grandfather had issued as part of his farewell address in 1961. "We must guard," Ike had declared, "against the acquisition of unwarranted influence . . . by the military-industrial complex." There were few better explanations for the escalation of the Vietnam War.

In March 1968, Lyndon Johnson did what had seemed impossible four years before. After a poor showing in the early primaries, he declared he would *not* run for a second term as president. Vietnam had taken its toll. So had the quieter criticism Johnson had received from the eastern Establishment for his "country" manners and Texas accent. Johnson had always suffered from disparaging references to his being a graduate of Southwest Texas State Teachers College. If he had only been a Harvard man, Johnson bitterly said, he would have been treated more respectfully. Nixon, who had delighted in bringing Harvard men like Alger Hiss to their knees, knew exactly what Johnson meant.

With Johnson unexpectedly out of the presidential picture for 1968, Nixon's political star rose dramatically. Republicans discovered that he had never lost his nationwide basis of support, particularly among middle-class Americans who empathized with his poor-boy beginnings and narrow defeat in 1960. They admired his tenacity and respected his considerable experience in foreign affairs. Voters remembered that he had been part of the team that had extricated the nation from Korea in 1953. Perhaps he could repeat the performance for Vietnam. Nixon was, after all, Mr. Republican, the best-known man that that party could nominate. When liberal Republicans realized that Nixon supported peace, not escalation or total victory in Vietnam, his nomination on August 8, 1968, in Miami was assured. The little-known governor of Maryland, Spiro T. Agnew, was Nixon's choice as running mate.

The 1968 election was complicated by the presence on the ballot of George Wallace, former governor of Alabama, as the candidate of the right-wing American Independent party. Wallace's avowed racism and his hawkish stand on Vietnam put Nixon in the unusual role of filling the center of the political spectrum. Senator Hubert Humphrey of Minnesota, the Democratic nominee, was on his left. At the polls in November, Wallace received a surprising 13.5 percent of the popular vote. Most of this support would have otherwise gone to Nixon. As it was, Nixon won by only a few tenths of a percent over Humphrey in the popular vote. But narrowly or not, the miracle of twentieth-century American politics occurred. Twice pronounced politically dead, after his 1960 and 1962 defeats, Nixon rose from the ashes to become president of the United States. The early despair made the ultimate satisfaction all the sweeter. Fifty-six years old at his inauguration in January 1969, Richard Nixon had at last realized his dream.

In choosing the men who would govern the country with him and, as it turned out, *for* him, Nixon turned to the inner circle of political loyalists who had engineered his successful campaign. None of those who were closest to Nixon had had any experience in government. John Mitchell, the attorney general, had been a bond lawyer from Nixon's New York firm. H. R. Haldeman—who, as chief of the White House staff, would become the instrument through which the new president exercised his authority—had been an advertising executive from southern California and the advance man in the Nixon presidential campaign. Self-righteous and arrogant, Haldeman was fanatically loyal to Richard Nixon and his view of what was good for the United States. He neither drank nor smoked, he was deeply religious, and like Nixon, he was capable of prodigious quantities of work. If there was an incarnation of sociologist William Whyte's "organization man," it was crew-cut management expert Haldeman. John Ehrlichman was chosen by Haldeman and was cut from the same cloth. A Seattle lawyer, Ehrlichman had been schooled in government only by virtue of assisting in the Nixon campaign. He became the president's personal counsel. William Rogers became secretary of state. Completing the Nixon inner circle was Harvard political scientist Henry Kissinger serving as foreign policy adviser.

The Nixon family beams after Richard Nixon's defeat of Hubert Humphrey in the 1968 presidential election. David Eisenhower (far left) stands beside his fiancée, Julie Nixon. Daughter Tricia and Mrs. Pat Nixon complete the family grouping. Nixon holds a needlework of the presidential seal that an optimistic Julie had done in the final weeks of the campaign.

National Security Adviser Henry Kissinger (far left), Domestic Counsel John Ehrlichman (left), Budget Director Robert Mayor (center), and President Nixon.

The Vietnam morass was the most difficult problem that the Nixon administration inherited. The conflict, Nixon was convinced, could not be won by eliminating communism in Indochina. He also knew that the great majority of the American people were sick of Vietnam. But too precipitous a withdrawal would weaken the nation's reputation as a leader of the free world. It would, Nixon thought, encourage communists everywhere. The answer seemed to be "Vietnamization," the gradual reduction of American ground troops and the assumption of more and more military responsibility by the South Vietnamese under President Nguyen Van Thieu. So in the summer of 1969 Nixon began substantial and always well-publicized withdrawals of ground combat troops.

But in the final analysis, Nixon hated to lose, especially to the communists. In one form or another, he had made a political career of fighting them. The answer to this problem seemed to be secrecy. Nixon and his military advisers found ways to falsify reports so that neither Congress nor the people nor the press were aware of an incredible 3,500 air strikes against North Vietnamese strongholds in the nation of Cambodia. On April 30, 1970, Nixon accepted the advice of his military leaders and ordered an invasion of Cambodia, complete with ground action.

Although Nixon attempted to keep the actions in Cambodia secret, the evidence of escalation did not escape the media. By this time, polls showed that 65 percent of the American people felt that the Vietnam War was "morally wrong," and television brought the war direct from the front every evening to the nation's living rooms. Morale in the armed forces in Indochina had sunk to a low never before seen in American military history.

Although discontent over the war grew, the Nixon administration, kept at a distance from criticism by Haldeman and Ehrlichman's carefully designed hierarchy, did not get the message. Nixon referred to the student demonstrators as "bums," but let his vice president, Spiro Agnew, become the primary critic of the antiwar movement. Attributing the escalating protest to "an effete corps of impudent snobs who characterize themselves as intellectuals," Agnew went on to state that he would trade "the whole damn zoo" for one good American boy. Agnew's zoo remark was in reference to militant organizations such as the Youth Independent party (Yippies), the Black Panthers, Weathermen, Students for a Democratic Society (SDS), and more generally hippies which had been protesting the Vietnam war since the mid-1960s. After harassing Lyndon Johnson to the point of declining to run for reelection, these groups disrupted the 1968 Democratic National Convention in Chicago.

Agnew's reference to intellectuals was quite accurate in characterizing the antiwar movement. American radicalism of the 1960s took place under the label *New Left*, which definitely had its origins in the university. The term referred more to a point of view than an organized political movement. It stressed the presence of oppression in the United States and the world and, as a remedial measure, proposed a largely ideological fight against the established power structure. Even before the Vietnam escalation, SDS, inspired by Thomas Hayden, organized at the University of Michigan to oppose racism. In company with most New Left pioneers, Hayden believed that racial prejudice was only a part of a broader and deeper malaise in society. Ultimately, he argued, the Establishment's fixation on power and profit explained America's involvement in wars of aggression abroad. This linkage of antidemocratic practices at home and imperialism abroad was one base of SDS ideology. The other was that the mainstay of the New Left would not be the laboring classes, but the campus communities. In the words of the 1962 Port Huron Statement, largely the work of Hayden, "social relevance, the accessibility of knowledge, and internal openness—these together make the university a potential base and agency in a movement of social change."

Tom Hayden had seemed a prophet of extraordinary ability in the fall of 1964, when students at the Berkeley campus of the University of California escalated the civil rights movement into a full-blown assault against the Establishment. The immediate issue was university opposition to campus-based political activism. For several months a virtual state of war existed between university and local law enforcement authorities, on the one hand, and social activists, informally organized as the Free Speech Movement, on the other. At the height of the confrontation in December, a student leader named Mario Savio applied protest techniques he had learned while working for black civil rights the previous summer in Mississippi. Students took over several university buildings and, when the police arrived, went limp in the nonviolent manner advocated by Martin Luther King, Jr. When Joan Baez appeared on the disrupted campus and sang "We Shall Overcome," the connection between the causes of students and blacks was clearly drawn. Both social groups contended they were second-class citizens and the victims of a repressive, powerful elite. The remedy, Savio declared, was to "put our bodies against the gears, against the wheels . . . and make the machine stop until we're free." The success of the Berkeley militants in actually stopping academic processes and the subsequent resignation of University of California president Clark Kerr lent credibility to Savio's formula. But the Establishment showed its own muscle when conservative Republican Ronald Reagan won the governorship of California in 1966 on a "get-tough" platform aimed particularly at the university community. Older people, in general, supported Reagan, a fact that prompted the student slogan, "You can't trust anyone over thirty." In such a sentiment was the flowering of the generation gap implicit from the beginning of the counterculture protest.

By mid-decade, the Vietnam War had become the primary target of American radicalism, and when Nixon, the president who promised to wind down the war, appeared to be escalating it, protest turned more violent. The largest public demonstrations in the nation's history (some 500,000 held a "March Against Death" in Washington late in 1969) showed Nixon that it was not just student radicals who opposed the war. Following additional disclosures about Cambodia in April 1970, the nation exploded. On May 4, inexperienced national guardsmen fired into a group of antiwar demonstrators at Kent State University in Ohio and took the lives of four students. Ten days later, police killed two black demonstrators at Jackson State College in Mississippi. Angry demonstrations occurred on college campuses from coast to coast, with draft card burning and denunciations of Nixon regular events.

Had the escalations of 1970 accomplished their goals, Nixon might have emerged victorious again. But as Nixon's ineffectiveness in Vietnam became more evident, the Democrat-controlled Congress grew impatient, then angry. The president, it seemed to many, had usurped the constitutional authority of the Congress to declare war. This was especially apparent after Congress repealed the 1964 Gulf of Tonkin Resolution and made Vietnam a completely undeclared war. In June 1971, the rage of Nixon's critics increased when former Pentagon official Daniel Ellsberg unlawfully released to several newspapers documents pertaining to the Vietnam War. The so-called Pentagon Papers revealed a complex series of concealments and outright lies through which the military and the Johnson and Nixon administrations had kept the truth about Vietnam from the nation. From the president's point of view, Daniel Ellsberg was disloyal to the United States, another Alger Hiss.

Nixon continued the bombing, dropping more tons of explosives in three years than Johnson had in five. He mined harbors, talked about "decisive military action to end the war," and used the domino theory to justify the need to stop communism in Vietnam. Only the approaching election of 1972 and the obvious disgust of a large majority of Americans with the war changed Nixon's line. In August, he completed the withdrawal of American ground troops and softened American conditions for a peace settlement. A week before the November elections, which Nixon won in a landslide over Senator George McGovern of South Dakota, came the timely announcement from Henry Kissinger: "Peace is at hand." That was, however, not the case. Both North Vietnam and President Thieu balked at the draft agreement of the peace settlement. In brutal bombing raids over the 1972 Christmas season, Nixon devastated North Vietnam cities. On January 23, 1973, Thieu was virtually forced to sign the peace agreement that left him with little long-term protection from the communists in his country.

The aftermath in Vietnam confirmed the fears of Johnson's and Nixon's critics. Thieu's allegedly democratic government could not last without American military support. The Vietnamese people, even in the south, did not want Thieu. At best, the United States had intervened in a civil war. At worst, it had tried to impose its conception of political order on a nation with other ideas. No one expected Thieu's regime to last very long alone. The best Nixon could hope for was a "decent interval" between the American withdrawal and Thieu's collapse. That, at least, occurred. North Vietnam did not launch a major offensive until March 1975. In the United States there was no will left to resist. Thieu fell in April 1975.

While the Vietnam War conclusion could hardly be regarded as a triumph for the United States, Richard Nixon did better in other aspects of foreign policy. One of his major contributions to recent American history was a start toward the implementation of a new relationship with the communist world, based not on conquest or intimidation, but on the refurbished concept of balance of power. For a legendary cold warrior such as Nixon, détente, as the new policy came to be known, was a major about-face. Nixon saw the peril of an uncontrolled nuclear arms race. He also realized that, on the constantly changing international scene, the United States could not impose its will. Better to be flexible and swing the power of the United States this way and that in an effort to maintain a dynamic equilibrium.

Illustrative of the "Nixon Doctrine" was the remarkable and unexpected initiation of friendly relations with communist China. The president's national security adviser (and beginning September 22, 1973, his secretary of state), Henry Kissinger, paved the way for Nixon's dramatic week-long visit to Beijing in February 1972. A genuine triumph of his presidency, the trip demonstrated Nixon's new perspective on communism as a political system that the United States had to accept as a part of the world order. After the China initiative, Nixon turned Kissinger's attention to the explosive Middle East. Playing the Arabs and the Israelis like chessmen, Kissinger's "shuttle diplomacy" succeeded in 1973 and 1974 in lessening the prospects of war. But effective as Kissinger and Nixon were in foreign policy, by 1974 no one in the United States cared. The domestic situation occupied center stage.

Watergate began so simply. On the night of June 17, 1972, five burglars were arrested in a Washington, DC, office, a routine police matter in a city where crime, unfortunately, was common. But this break-in was different. The target was the Democratic National Committee headquarters, where there was little of value to steal, and the burglars were armed with tape recorders and cameras. One of them turned out to be James McCord, a member of the Committee to Reelect the President. The building's name, the Watergate (it was adjacent to the Potomac River), soon became a generic term for perhaps the most serious political crisis—apart from the Civil War—in American history.

The roots of Watergate lay in the way Richard Nixon governed, as well as in the way he thought. On winning the election of 1968, Nixon had begun a concentration of power unprecedented in the history of the American presidency. Congress learned that this "imperial" presidency would not spend the funds Congress had voted—amounting to some $15 billion—a practice called "impoundment," which the federal judiciary pronounced unconstitutional. The Nixon administration also exercised discretion in enforcing the laws Congress had passed. Spurred by the need to obscure the bad news from Vietnam, Nixon upheld and greatly expanded the president's privilege to withhold information from Congress and the people. Even cabinet members found their access to the president firmly controlled by a corps of "special assistants," particularly H. R. Haldeman and John D. Ehrlichman. Nixon claimed these exceptional powers on behalf of the "great silent majority," middle-class people like himself whose hard work and law-abiding lives were allegedly being undermined by communists. More recently, hippies, "welfare chiselers," college antiwar demonstrators, and black-rights advocates had assumed the role of the enemy, but the rationale was the same one that Richard Nixon had used all his political life.

Vice President Spiro Agnew, continuing to play the traditional role of presidential mouthpiece, lashed out in defense of law and order, and against a press corps that was critical of the administration. If such attacks polarized the American people, Nixon and Agnew welcomed such polarization. It was entirely consistent with Nixon's political style to divide and label. He invariably saw his opponents as sinister threats, not merely the representatives of alternative viewpoints. Campaigns, for Nixon, were crusades. Throughout his first term the president's paranoia mounted as he found himself frustrated in Vietnam and the object of increasingly bitter attacks at home.

His fears intensified after Daniel Ellsberg's "leak" of the Pentagon Papers to the press in June 1971. Somebody must be out to "get" Nixon, but he would "get" them instead. This was the way Richard Nixon talked and thought. On one occasion, for example, Nixon told a White House staffer, "One day we'll get them—we'll get them on the ground where we want them. And we'll stick our heels in, step on them hard and twist, right, Chuck?" So after Daniel Ellsberg had "played dirty" by releasing the embarrassing truth about the Vietnam War, Nixon felt no compunction about creating the White House special investigation unit. Under Ehrlichman's direction, the group was known as "the plumbers" ("I fix leaks," one of them explained). They "tapped" telephones and "bugged" the offices of government officials and newspeople. Less subtle activities included a break-in at the Los Angeles office of Ellsberg's psychiatrist.

An atmosphere of suspicion and self-righteousness, emanating from Nixon, generated the frightening "enemies list." For counsel John Dean and other eager young assistants who put loyalty to Nixon ahead of the law, the list was the first step in using "the available federal machinery to screw our political enemies." Anything illegal about such activities was justified under the blanket rationalization of "national security."

The election of 1972 saw the White House extend police-state methods from the foreign to the domestic sphere. Nixon, quite simply, did not want to lose in 1972, and early polls showed that the front-runner for the Democratic nomination, Senator Edmund G. Muskie of Maine, had a substantial lead. That fact alone, from Nixon's perspective, justified campaign sabotage, just as it had in his first race against Jerry Voorhis back in 1946. But in 1972, Nixon had a huge staff and a $55-million campaign fund with which to work. The Committee to Reelect the President, which the press soon dubbed CREEP, moved ahead with a series of "dirty tricks" against the Democrats. The Watergate break-ins (the building had been entered illegally several times before June 17) were part of a broader plan to win in

1972 at all costs. It was not just a lust for power. Richard Nixon sincerely believed that his election was absolutely essential to the national security of the United States. This end, he felt, justified any means.

Whether Nixon knew in advance about the Watergate break-in is immaterial, because he certainly sanctioned this type of activity. Moreover, as tape recordings subsequently showed, Nixon had made plans with Haldeman to cover up the Watergate affair within a week after it had occurred. The first step was directing the CIA to halt an FBI investigation of the break-in. Initially, Nixon succeeded. Watergate did not influence the election of 1972, which was a landslide for the Republicans. Nixon and Agnew received 520 electoral votes compared to 17 for Democrat George McGovern. It was characteristic of Nixon's "zeal for overreach," in the words of political analyst Theodore White, that Nixon felt it necessary to stoop so low in order to win so big.

Although reelected in 1972 by an overwhelming majority, Nixon stood in the center of a closing circle. Two young reporters on the *Washington Post*, Robert Woodward and Carl Bernstein, were discovering more and more about the Watergate cover-up. The trial of the Watergate burglars left unanswered so many questions about their motivation that the Senate established a special committee, under Senator Sam Ervin of North Carolina, to investigate the 1972 Republican campaign. Following a course parallel to that of the Ervin Committee was Archibald Cox, the Harvard law professor appointed by Nixon himself to be an independent special prosecutor in the Watergate affair.

Nixon might, of course, have made a full and frank confession. As in the case of John F. Kennedy's assumption of the blame for the Bay of Pigs fiasco or Nixon's own Checkers speech, immediate confession might have proved to be his salvation. But Nixon chose to "tough it out," as he put it. He was president, after all, and he persisted in believing that he was right in putting his conception of national security ahead of the law. "When the president does it," he told David Frost on national television in 1977, "that means it's not illegal." But in early 1973, it was clear that some White House scapegoat had to be sacrificed. John Dean and the deputy director of CREEP, Jeb Stuart Magruder, finally abandoned their loyalty to Nixon and began unraveling the thread. On April 30, 1973, the identity of two scapegoats became known: H. R. Haldeman and John D. Ehrlichman submitted their resignations.

But the wolves did not stop howling. Disclosure that Nixon's White House conversations were routinely recorded on tape led to a sensitive new area of evidence. Even with key post-Watergate sections "accidentally" erased by loyal members of the Nixon staff, the tapes revealed the private personality of the man as unscrupulous, insecure, bigoted, and foul-mouthed. Nixon's judgment was further impugned when federal prosecutors charged Spiro Agnew with taking bribes both as governor of Maryland and as vice president. Plea bargaining resulted in minor charges against Agnew in return for his resignation from the government on October 10, 1973. Nixon appointed Gerald R. Ford of Michigan, the minority leader of the House of Representatives, in his place.

Besieged on all sides, Nixon lashed out desperately. Special Prosecutor Cox was doing too good a job, so Nixon ordered Attorney General Elliot Richardson to fire him. Instead, Richardson and his deputy resigned on October 23, 1973. The nation exploded in anger. The White House received a half million communications protesting the Cox–Richardson action, and Nixon reluctantly appointed Leon Jaworski, a Texas lawyer, to succeed Cox. "I am not a crook," he told Americans in November, but fewer and fewer believed him. In December the House Judiciary Committee began inquiry into whether grounds existed for impeachment of the president. As the hearings progressed into early 1974, Nixon began to lose control of his office and of himself. "I can pick up my phone," he told a group of astonished congressmen, "and seventy million Russians can be killed in twenty minutes." It was the old fighting Nixon now armed with frightening powers. Hastily, Nixon's own aides arranged to block the president's ability to push the button of nuclear war.

Late in July 1974 the House committee, including many of its Republican members, voted three articles of impeachment against Richard Nixon. But there were still many Nixon supporters in Congress, and the president himself said he had no intention of resigning. Then, under order from the Supreme Court, the White House released the actual tapes of Nixon's conversations. As his horrified aides quickly discovered, the president was caught in a web of lies. Despite his explicit denials, he *had* used the CIA in an effort to cover up Watergate. A taped conversation of June 23, 1972, between Nixon and Haldeman left no doubt on the matter. As one shocked staff member put it, "Those bastards . . . who've been saying all the things about the president all year—those bastards I hated, they were right."

Fearful and mentally exhausted, Nixon was in the White House only a few days of his final weeks. Hoping to draw strength from Middle America, he agreed to speak at the Oklahoma State University commencement in May 1974. But here too, support was tempered by hundreds who lined the streets, chanting, "Jail to the Chief!" In June 1974, desperate to salvage what popularity he could from his reputation in foreign affairs, he traveled to the Middle East and to the Soviet Union. A painful attack of phlebitis that he experienced overseas somewhat offset the growing mood of national hatred. July found Nixon back at his home in San Clemente, California. He remained in seclusion, accessible only to the last few defenders, notably his daughters and their husbands. On July 28, 1974, Nixon returned to Washington, DC, where General Alexander Haig, his chief of staff since Haldeman's departure, attempted to show him that resignation was his best course of action.

Nixon could, of course, fight. It was his nature to do so. In that event, Haig knew, impeachment proceedings in the House and the trial in the Senate could drag on for a year, paralyzing the government. Knowing he was dealing with an unstable and haunted man who could explode at any moment, Haig carefully showed Nixon that, after the incriminating evidence (i.e., the famous "smoking pistol") in the June 23, 1972, tape had been disclosed, Nixon's remaining support had vanished. Henry Kissinger suggested that he resign. So did Republican leaders in Congress. Dazed, Nixon shook his head when he heard of the deserters. "I helped some of these people," he said. He could not understand that political favors did not extend to sanctioning the breaking of the law.

On August 7, after learning from Senator Barry Goldwater that he could count on only a dozen votes of support in the event of a Senate conviction trial, Nixon decided to resign. He told his family that evening but forbade them to discuss it at the table. After dinner he sat alone, periodically telephoning the speech writer who was preparing his statement of resignation for delivery the next day. The old ghosts he had fought so long were with him that evening. He was the outsider, the unloved, the grocer's boy from Whittier who had never made it to Harvard and had always had to work so hard for what he achieved. The very fears that had made him run so furiously and so ruthlessly most of his life were now impossible to deny. For a paranoiac like Nixon, there was comfort in seeing one's anxieties assume substance. "They" had got him. It was an explanation, however mythical, with which Nixon could at least live.

The next day, just before his television broadcast, the president met with a group of congressmen who had supported him to the bitter end. He told them that he would prefer to fight this one out just as he had fought previous adversities. For a moment it seemed as if the resignation message would not be delivered. Then Nixon reflected on the agony for the country of his impeachment trial. Ignoring the question of whether he would win or lose, Nixon put the national interest ahead of his own. "I just hope," he concluded, "I haven't let you down." Then he collapsed in tears.

At noon the following day, August 9, 1974, Gerald R. Ford became president of a traumatized nation. Using his impeccable long-term congressional credentials, Ford began the process of restoring public confidence in the federal government. Disdaining the grandiose gestures of the Nixon years, Ford moved slowly and carefully to deal with the foreign and domestic problems that had accumulated during nearly two years of national preoccupation with Watergate. The nation breathed a sigh of relief and began to return to business as usual after two years of tumult that even the most apolitical American could not ignore.

Disgraced and downhearted, Richard Nixon returned to private life. A pardon from President Ford on September 8, 1974, eliminated the possibility that the former president would serve any jail time, but Nixon chafed at the thought of retirement and inactivity. He watched as Gerald Ford barely survived a nomination bid by conservative California governor Ronald Reagan in the 1976 Republican primary campaign, only to lose to a relatively unknown Democratic governor from Georgia, Jimmy Carter. He then watched as the Carter administration self-destructed over both foreign and domestic crises, and as Carter himself was trounced in 1980 by a Reagan campaign that exploited a hard line on communism similar to the one Nixon had espoused years before.

In September 1977, Richard Nixon taped a series of interviews for television with the talk-show host David Frost. By prearrangement, sensitive issues were skirted, but Nixon did have the opportunity to say that Watergate had changed the nation and for that he was sorry. As for his personal conduct in the scandal, he offered neither explanation nor apology. This stance was consistent with his earlier declaration that he was not a "crook," and in one sense he was correct. Like everyone, he was the product of his historical context. Nixon's political ascendance had occurred in an era when his nation had tended toward paranoia about communism. He had developed a tendency to view the world in terms of the forces of light and the forces of darkness, good and evil, we and they. Politics, for Nixon, was never just a profession. It was a crusade, a holy war. On that basis he had waged his early

On August 9, 1974, after taking a tearful leave of the White House staff, Nixon walked to the helicopter waiting to take him to Air Force One for his final official flight back home to California. Here he waves from the helicopter steps.

ruthless campaigns, had attacked Alger Hiss, and had fought the Cold War. It was a perspective that made Nixon an excellent partisan but a poor national leader. When he finally possessed the power of the presidency, the crusading mentality that had carried him so far became a fatal liability.

Richard Nixon never eased into a life of leisure. Instead, he became an author, pouring the same boundless energy into writing that he had earlier given to politics. After his resignation, Nixon published six books, including his memoirs in 1978.

Each book reflected a Richard Nixon well attuned to events. In *The Real War* (1980), Nixon expressed his enduring conviction that the United States and the Soviet Union were locked in a global struggle for survival. While the aged hard-line Soviet leadership and President Ronald Reagan continued their sword rattling through the mid-1980s, Nixon continued to espouse his own concepts of good and evil with *Leaders* (1982), *Real Peace* (1984), and *No More Vietnams* (1985).

In 1985, however, Mikhail Gorbachev, a young, charismatic populist, rose to power in the Soviet Union. Initiating sweeping new policies of *glasnost* (openness) and *perestroika* (restructuring), Gorbachev inspired democratic movements throughout the communist world. Gorbachev's mere presence—as evidenced by the summer 1989 student democracy demonstration in Beijing, China, the tearing down of the Berlin Wall, the proliferation of independence movements in Eastern Europe, and accelerating efforts toward German reunification—sparked massive populist movements for change wherever repressive governments existed. Gorbachev's reforms resulted in his own demise, however, as the Soviet Union and its republics broke apart in the early 1990s. In 1991, Gorbachev was himself replaced, and, on December 31, the Soviet Union astonishingly disbanded.

In *1999: Victory without War* (1988), Nixon recognized the dramatic changes in the world and credited Gorbachev with being a catalyst for many of them. He predicted with hope that World War III would never occur and viewed the conflicts of the future as being political and economic, rather than military. However, Nixon, the veteran cold warrior, political bulldog, tough negotiator, and power politician, also believed until his death in May 1994 that conflict would always be with the human race. This, perhaps, because conflict was never a stranger to Richard Nixon.

SELECTED READINGS
The Person

Brodie, Fawn M.: *Richard Nixon: The Shaping of His Character* (1981). The start of a definitive biography, this volume traces Nixon's life and thought up to the assassination of John F. Kennedy, with occasional comments on subsequent events.

Costello, William: *The Facts about Nixon: An Unauthorized Biography* (1960). An unfriendly but thorough examination of Nixon through his vice presidential years.

Evans, Rowland, Jr., and R. D. Novak: *Nixon in the White House: A Critical Portrait* (1971). A description of the workings of Nixon's presidency before the scandals.

Hoff, Joan: *Nixon Reconsidered* (1994). One of the first biographical looks at Nixon after his death.

Klein, Herbert G.: *Making It Perfectly Clear* (1980). Nixon's former press secretary discusses the president's relationship with the news media.

*Mankiewicz, Frank: *Perfectly Clear: Nixon from Whittier to Watergate* (1972). Written before the revelations of 1974 and the resignation, this extremely unfriendly book makes the case against Nixon in strong terms.

*Available in paperback.

*Mankiewicz, Frank: *U.S. vs. Richard M. Nixon: The Final Crisis* (1975). A continuation of the above book with events through the resignation. The volume focuses on the White House, the Judiciary Committee of the House of Representatives, the press, and the work of the special prosecutors, Cox and Jaworski.

*Mazlish, Bruce: *In Search of Nixon: A Psychohistorical Inquiry* (1972). The best of the psychological studies of the mind and motives of Richard Nixon.

Mazo, Earl, and Stephen Hess: *Nixon: A Political Portrait* (1968). A campaign biography strong on the early years. The book updates Earl Mazo's *Richard Nixon: A Political and Personal Portrait* (1959).

Nixon, Richard: *Six Crises* (1962). Beginning with the Alger Hiss episode, Nixon discusses his own life and work as well as his view of national developments.

Nixon, Richard: *The Memoirs of Richard Nixon* (1978). A thousand-page book in which Nixon tells his life story and tries to explain his presidency.

Nixon, Richard: *The Real War* (1980). A summary of Nixon's paranoia regarding the Soviet Union.

Nixon, Richard: *1999: Victory without War* (1988). The world according to Nixon in the late 1980s, as well as prospects for the future.

Parmet, Herbert S.: *Richard Nixon and His America* (1990). A thorough and thoughtful biography of both the thirty-seventh president and the society in which he came to power.

*White, Theodore H.: *Breach of Faith: The Fall of Richard Nixon* (1975). An exceptionally readable and detailed account of the last years of the Nixon presidency. White also wrote *The Making of the President—1968* and *The Making of the President—1972*.

*Wills, Gary: *Nixon Agonistes* (1970). A critical biographical analysis. A second edition, subtitled *The Crisis of the Self-Made Man*, appeared in 1979.

Witcover, Jules: *The Resurrection of Richard Nixon* (1970). A description of the years between Nixon's defeat in the California gubernatorial election and his election to the presidency.

Woods, John R.: *Watergate Revisited: A Pictorial History* (1985). A graphically illustrated tour of the entire Watergate affair.

The Period

Ambrose, Stephen E.: *Rise to Globalism: American Foreign Policy, 1938–1980* (1980). The third edition of a comprehensive survey of the events that shaped Nixon's life and thought.

*Bernstein, Carl, and Robert Woodward: *All the President's Men* (1974). The story of how the press helped expose the truth about the Nixon administration, written by the reporters most responsible. The same team published *The Final Days* (1976).

Congressional Quarterly: "Watergate: Chronology of a Crisis" (1973, 1974). A useful compilation, in two volumes, of the entire Watergate affair as it unfolded week by week.

Dean, John: *Blind Ambition: The White House Years* (1976). Understandably biased, the unique account of an insider in the Nixon administration.

*Drew, Elizabeth: *Washington Journal: A Diary of the Events of 1973–1974* (1975). A journalist's recollections and analyses of two years on the national political scene.

---

*Available in paperback.

Gorbachev, Mikhail: *Perestroika: New Thinking for Our Country and the World* (1987). A broad explanation of Gorbachev's vision for the Soviet Union and the world.

*Halberstam, David: *The Best and the Brightest* (1972). An evaluation of the strengths and weaknesses of the men inspired by the presidency of John F. Kennedy, with particular attention to the beginnings of American involvement in Vietnam.

Herring, George: *America's Longest War: The United States and Vietnam, 1950–1975* (1979). An excellent volume on U.S. involvement in Southeast Asia.

Jaworski, Leon: *The Right and the Power: The Prosecution of Watergate* (1976). The special prosecutor's account of the events surrounding Watergate.

Johnson, Haynes: *In the Absence of Power: Governing America* (1980). A critical look at the Carter administration.

Kearns, Doris: *Lyndon Johnson and the American Dream* (1976). An excellent life-and-times biography.

Kissinger, Henry: *White House Years* (1979). In 1,500 pages, Nixon's secretary of state recalls his years in office.

Matthews, Christopher: *Kennedy and Nixon: The Rivalry That Shaped Postwar America* (1996). Reflections on key encounters between the two eventual presidents.

Pach, Chester J., and Elmo Richardson: *The Presidency of Dwight David Eisenhower* (1992). A thorough analysis of Ike's presidential style.

Poole, Peter A.: *The United States and Indochina from FDR to Nixon* (1973). A useful overview and review.

Schell, Jonathan: *The Time of Illusion* (1976). An evaluation and description of the Watergate affair.

*Schlesinger, Arthur M., Jr.: *A Thousand Days: John F. Kennedy in the White House* (1965). A detailed account of the Kennedy administration by a participant.

*Schlesinger, Arthur M., Jr.: *The Bitter Heritage: Vietnam and American Democracy, 1941–1966* (1967). Reviews the reasons for and the consequences of American involvement in Southeast Asia.

Schlesinger, Arthur M., Jr.: *The Imperial President* (1973). Insights into the changes in American political history that made possible Richard Nixon's abuse of power.

Shawcross, William: *Sideshow: Kissinger, Nixon, and the Destruction of Cambodia* (1979). A detailed, if sensational, account of the secret bombing of Cambodia.

FOR CONSIDERATION

1. It could be said that Richard Nixon grew up with a chip on his shoulder that he never really shed. If this is accurate, why did Nixon feel this way? What political views did Nixon's father instill in his son?

2. Discuss Nixon's electioneering tactics in his first bid for Congress and in his 1950 senatorial campaign. Why was Nixon compelled to deliver the "Checkers speech"?

Available in paperback.

3. Why did Nixon take special satisfaction in successfully prosecuting Alger Hiss? How did Nixon respond to the activities of Senator Joseph McCarthy?

4. Why was Richard Nixon's election to the presidency in 1968 considered a political miracle?

5. Discuss Nixon's strategy for ending the war in Vietnam. How successful was it?

6. Aside from the fact of the Watergate break-in, how could it be argued that Nixon mishandled the controversy? What elements in Nixon's personality worked against him during the crisis?

E I G H T

Elvis Presley

O n Sunday September 9, 1956, more than 80 percent of the nation's television viewers tuned into Toast of the Town hosted by Ed Sullivan. The live audience in CBS's New York studios buzzed with excitement as the curtain opened to reveal a trio of musicians. Standing front and center, a tall, thin young man with long dark hair slicked back in a ducktail nodded at the host. Dressed in a shiny gray sport coat, black shirt, white tie, black pants with pink stripes down the sides, and two-tone loafers, Elvis Presley all but sneered at the audience. Next, he nodded to his band members and began strumming his guitar. Crooning out the lyrics to Don't Be Cruel, the singer began gyrating his hips and wiggling his knees to the delight of the largely teenage studio audience. Applause turned to screams as the band played and Elvis Presley sang and danced across the stage. After a frenzied four songs the act was over, but superstardom for the King of Rock and Roll had only just begun.

On a bitter-cold morning January 8, 1935, in a tiny house in East Tupelo, Mississippi, Elvis Aron Presley was born. Thirty-five minutes earlier Gladys Presley had given birth to a twin brother, Jesse Garon, who died in delivery. Elvis was born strong and healthy, and Gladys regularly reminded him of her feeling that he gained part of that strength from his brother Jesse. Elvis was his father Vernon's middle name, and Jesse was named after his paternal grandfather. Their middle names, Aron and Garon, both were pronounced with a long "a" so they would rhyme.

To classify the Presleys as "dirt poor" would not be an overstatement. In fact, most people who lived on the wrong side of the tracks separating Tupelo from East Tupelo lived in poverty. Elvis was born in a "shotgun-style house," meaning that one could fire a gun at the front door and shoot out the back door. Only ten paces separated the front door from the back in the two-room dwelling that Vernon, and his father and brother built next to his parents' four-room house in anticipation of the twins. The day after the birth, Jesse Garon was buried at a nearby cemetery. Since the family could not afford a headstone, Jesse was laid to rest in an unmarked grave. Gladys's difficult pregnancy and delivery forced her hospitalization, and there she learned she could have no more children. Upon her release, welfare paid the bills for the impoverished Presleys.

Elvis's parents knew little of their heritage, but believed their ancestors had been cotton sharecroppers in northeastern Mississippi for generations. One thing they did know for certain was that their families had been poor and uneducated for generations. Vernon, who referred to himself as a "common laborer," worked occasionally at a nearby dairy farm, while Gladys (née Smith) worked at the Tupelo Garment Plant, earning two dollars for a twelve-hour workday. Both had dropped out of school at early ages. They met in 1933 during services at the First Assembly of God Church in Tupelo and quickly fell in love; after a few dates they eloped to a nearby town. Using a borrowed three dollars for a marriage license, both lied about their ages. Vernon, still a minor at sixteen, filed as a twenty-one-year-old, while Gladys, who was twenty-one, declared she was nineteen.

The Presleys' poverty was typical of rural, white Mississippians of the 1930s. Always severe, rural poverty was only exacerbated by the Great Depression. Farm income dropped to record lows by the 1930s. Nationally, more than 1.7 million farm families had annual incomes under $500 in 1935, and tenant farmers occupied 42 percent of all farms. Although Franklin Roosevelt's Tennessee Valley Authority had brought electricity to Tupelo by the mid-1930s, kerosene lanterns lit the Presley home when Elvis was born. Dirt floors and an outhouse in the backyard further attested to the lack of amenities, but the Presleys were hardly alone in such living conditions. Running water and electricity were the exception, not the norm, on the American farm in the 1930s, with only 10 percent electrified by 1936.

Despite their financial struggle, Gladys and Vernon Presley provided a warm, loving household for their only child. Elvis was extraordinarily close to his mother, and Gladys adored her son to the point of overprotection. Elvis later remembered: "My mama never let me out of her sight. I couldn't [even] go down to the creek with the other kids." Indeed Gladys lavished Elvis with love and her undivided attention, in stark contrast to Vernon, a taciturn, brooding, emotionless man. Despite such shortcomings, he was a devoted husband and father.

Vernon had continual difficulty holding jobs, which meant continual hardships for his family. He also had his share of bad luck. In 1937, Vernon and two other men, one of them Gladys's brother, cashed a forged check for four dollars and were caught. In May 1938, they were each sentenced to three years in prison. In Vernon's absence the Presleys lost their house to creditors, and Gladys and Elvis were forced to move in with relatives. To make ends meet, Gladys went to work as a seamstress, but the hard times continued. Although Vernon spent only eight months behind bars, he left prison in February 1939 a changed man. Never regarding his abilities highly, he now felt even more inept. Never very motivated, he now had absolutely no direction. The family drifted, first to East Tupelo, then to Pascagoula on the Gulf Coast, and then back to East Tupelo where the family spent the war years. With plenty of work available, even Vernon succeeded for awhile. First, he worked on a prisoner-of-war camp forty miles from East Tupelo, and later moved to Memphis, Tennessee, to work in a munitions plant. Unable to find housing for his family, Vernon lived apart from them, only coming home on weekends. By late 1942, however, Vernon's poor work ethic surfaced again, and he came back to East Tupelo, unemployed.

In 1943, Elvis entered the first grade at East Tupelo's Lawhon Elementary School. Despite regular moves to new housing, there was a degree of normalcy to Elvis's elementary school years. His teachers regarded him as a polite, well-mannered, and bright boy. There was little money, but the family never went hungry.

Gladys, Elvis, and Vernon Presley pose for a photograph around Elvis's third birthday. This photograph is a testament to Presley's humble beginnings.

On Sundays the Presleys attended the Assembly of God services. The Assemblies of God churches, founded in 1914, were part of an evangelical movement that swept the South and Midwest in the 1910s and 1920s. Partly a response to the modernity of the Jazz Age, the new fundamentalism of the 1920s also reflected a major rift in Protestantism. Modernists, usually educated urban churchgoers, were adapting their religious practices to the sweeping societal changes of the day. Fundamentalists, usually undereducated, rural, and white, fought to preserve traditional faith and Christian values they feared were disappearing from society. Specifically, they believed in a literal interpretation of the Bible and bitterly opposed the Darwinian theory of evolution.

The Assemblies of God combined such fundamentalist values with a strong element of mysticism. While the faith took a conservative view of Biblical scripture, and adhered to the "old time religion" of eternal damnation and suffering for the wicked, Assemblies of God ministers often spoke in tongues, uttering an unintelligible language that was said to be a direct communication with God. Assembly of God faithful frequently and loudly praised the Lord during the pastor's "fire and brimstone" sermons. Services also included lots of hymn-singing and individual musical performances.

Elvis Presley's first exposure to music came at these church services, and at the family home where the three Presleys often sang gospel songs. Even as a small child, Elvis was strongly moved by music. His voice filled with emotion as he sang the old Christian hymns. Elvis simply loved to sing: with his parents, in the congregation, at school, or by himself. One of his elementary school teachers was impressed enough by his musical abilities that she arranged for his entry into a talent contest sponsored by a local radio station in 1945. There Elvis sang in front of hundreds of people at the annual Mississippi-Alabama Fair and Dairy Show in Tupelo. Although he did not win the contest with his rendition of Red Foley's tear-jerking ballad, *Old Shep*, Elvis remembered the event vividly as his first public singing experience.

As Elvis's eleventh birthday approached, he asked for a bicycle. But Gladys and Vernon knew they could not afford the $60 for a new one. Instead they bought him a small, six-string guitar. Vernon's brother, Vester, taught him the rudiments of guitar, and later a pastor at the church taught him more chords. Before long the pastor was calling on Elvis regularly to sing and play during Sunday services. Parishioners recalled a lanky, blond-haired boy with large, dark eyes facing the congregation. They also recalled him singing and playing with a kind of mystical passion that would characterize his entire musical career.

By the time Elvis received his guitar, the Presley home had electricity and a radio. Elvis listened intently to the local radio programs which featured the music of the region: country. Because of his ability to pick up tunes on his guitar and learn lyrics with an incredibly quick recollection, Elvis could do renditions of the best-known country performers of the day: Ernest Tubb, Roy Acuff, Bob Wills, and the acknowledged father of country music, Jimmy Rodgers of Meridian, Mississippi. Elvis also tuned into music that white kids throughout the region were listening to—the blues performed by black musicians. On the black stations artists such as B.B. King, John Lee Hooker, and McKinley (Muddy Waters) Morganfield belted out raw, sensual, rhythmic lyrics based on experiences in the Mississippi Delta country. In time Elvis had a repertoire of songs that included country, blues, and gospel. In East Tupelo, he willingly played for friends, schoolmates, and relatives. They all agreed on one thing: Elvis had talent.

Continuing hard times for Vernon led the Presleys to seek greener pastures in 1948. Loading all the family possessions into a few boxes that fit easily into the trunk of their 1939 Plymouth, they departed for Memphis, Tennessee. The "big city" along the banks of the Mississippi River at least promised more opportunity for Vernon. Memphis had grown to more than 300,000 people, and abounded with industry, manufacturing, and service jobs. But for Vernon, a man with a prison record, it remained difficult to find or hold a job. The Presleys struggled mightily during their first year in Memphis, but in May 1949 their prospects brightened. Having successfully applied for assistance, the Presleys moved into a two-bedroom apartment in the federally funded Lauderdale Courts housing complex. Their rent was $35 per month. The idea behind the 433-unit complex was to provide low-income families with a clean, modern place to live at below-market rental that would get them out of slums and tenements. The Presleys, for example, had been living in a rat-infested room in a run-down boarding house their first year in Memphis. Lauderdale Court, like other federal housing projects nationwide, was developed to bring order to the lives of poor families, and subsidize their rental expenses so they could advance to home ownership. The two-bedroom unit with a separate kitchen and bathroom was a definite step up for the Presleys. Presumably, Elvis enjoyed the first real bath of his life at the Courts.

When the family moved to Lauderdale Courts, Elvis was completing his first year at L.C. Humes High School. Initially overwhelmed by a school that had 1,600 students, Elvis also feared that his classmates would make fun of his "country hick" ways. And although he was more reserved and shy than he had been in East Tupelo, Elvis soon adapted and discovered that the bigger school offered new opportunities. He grew interested in football, actually playing on the team during his eleventh-grade year. Though smallish for football—about six feet tall and 150 pounds—Elvis played end and was considered quite good.

Elvis's football career ended, however, over a dispute about his appearance. When the coach demanded Elvis cut his hair before his senior season began, he quit the team rather than comply. Long, slicked back in a ducktail, with long sideburns, Elvis's hairdo was of immense personal importance. It was part of his style; part of his answer to being a country boy in the big city. The vast majority of his schoolmates wore crew cuts, and almost no one had sideburns in the early 1950s. Explaining his hair to a friend, Elvis said he wanted to look like the long-distance truck drivers who passed through Memphis in their diesel big-rigs. Brightly colored, or "loud," shirts and pants also began to set him apart from the crowd. When he had the money, he bought clothing from a store that catered to flashy country and western performers. His favorite colors were pink and black.

Despite the new look, Elvis remained shy, especially when it came to singing and guitar playing. For the first couple of years in Memphis he never brought his guitar to school or even played outside at the Courts. Few of his classmates even knew that he could sing or play so many songs. But Elvis's repertoire continued to grow in high school, as he privately immersed himself in the ever-expanding world of Memphis radio. During the early 1950s, white Memphis "disk jockeys" or "deejays" such as Dewey "Daddy-O-Dewey" Phillips were becoming late-night celebrities, playing records of both the big companies and local musicians. Phillips played both black and white artists, challenging a tradition of radio segregation that had existed since its invention in the 1920s. In the daytime several country stations played the latest hillbilly music. A midday gospel program featured quartets such as the Blackwoods and the Statesmen, both favorites among the Presleys. Another station in Memphis, WDIA, touted itself as the "mother station of the Negroes." All-black programming included the blues, spirituals live from local churches, comedy, and deejays whose lively talk electrified the airwaves.

The phenomenon of white deejays playing black music for white teenagers on AM radio began early in the decade. Alan Freed, a deejay in Cleveland, Ohio, noticed in 1951 that white teenagers were buying black rhythm and blues (R&B) records in increasing numbers at a local record store. Recognizing the potential, Freed talked his station manager into starting a late-night program called the

Moondog Show that played mostly R&B. Freed promoted performers, played their records, and hosted live shows for consistent sell-out audiences of teens. Freed's immense success propelled him to New York City, and radio station WABC, where his *Moondog Show* became nationally syndicated. The roots of rock and roll had been planted.

Elvis was not alone in tuning into the black stations and white stations that were beginning to cross over to playing black artists; millions of teenagers did the same nationwide. Late-night shows became the standard of powerful AM radio, which at night could send signals hundreds of miles. Long-distance radio brought the larger, constantly changing world of popular music to cities and small towns alike throughout the nation as eager teenagers sought out a new sound in the early 1950s. Postwar teens sought something different than the prevailing popular, or "pop," music of the 1940s. Early postwar pop included love ballads, soft beats, and precision harmonies. Songs such as *How Much Is That Doggie in the Window?* and *Mockingbird Hill,* sung by Patti Page, or *Young at Heart* by Frank Sinatra dominated the popular music sales charts as the 1950s unfolded. Such music reflected the musical tastes of the soldiers who were now home from war. For them, stability, security, predictability, and familiarity were paramount.

But war babies, those born during or shortly before World War II, viewed not only the music but also the cultural values of their older siblings and parents as passé; or, in the parlance of the day, "square." In general, this characterization could also serve to describe the status quo in the United States in the decade and a half following World War II. It was a time of prudent, crew-cut complacency. Daniel Bell explored this mood in a book entitled *The End of Ideology: On the Exhaustion of Political Ideas in the Fifties.* Risks were to be minimized at all costs. The ideal was to keep one's cool, to refrain from rocking the boat or veering it off course. With the Great Depression of the 1930s and the austerity of World War II still facts of enormous significance in their lives, aspirations centered on security. The accepted credo emphasized a college degree, a steady job, a house in the suburbs, a family, and a station wagon. Girls were obsessed with making a "good" marriage, boys with advantageous retirement plans.

Success through competition remained a paramount virtue in the United States, but now the competitive unit was the organization rather than the individual. The person who succeeded in this setting was what *Fortune* editor William Whyte termed in 1956 the "organization man." His chief traits were loyalty to the company and a thoroughgoing conservatism. Dressed in a gray flannel suit and a white shirt with a button-down collar, legions of junior executives practiced the art of getting ahead by getting along. Values and goals were absorbed from one's peers rather than evolved from personal preferences, a characteristic that sociologist David Riesman labeled "other-direction." The perfection and omnipresence of advertising that Vance Packard described in *The Hidden Persuaders* (1957) also contributed to this standardization of attitudes and lifestyles.

The growing popularity of music that appealed primarily to young people represented a sweeping transition from the Great Depression–World War II era to the postwar period. And while Elvis Presley was not middle class, he shared the feelings of America's youthful desire to find something new. As he listened to black performers belt out the blues and the lyrics of hard times or love gone bad, Elvis, who grew up in poverty, understood their plight well. In the South, such music was undermining the traditions of segregation in place since the end of the Civil War. Like Elvis, many southern white youths laid down their traditional bigotry to embrace the blues and the black experience.

By listening to black musicians and all-black stations young southern whites like Elvis exposed themselves to a culture their elders ignored or rejected. At the Lauderdale Courts Elvis made three good friends, and the boys regularly roamed their rough neighborhood and downtown. Frequently, they ventured to the nearby black section of town, and its main drag Beale Street, to see the sights and observe the people. Memphis was a hearth of the blues, and a magnet city for the Mississippi Delta region of the South. Black musicians from the cotton belt of the lower Mississippi Valley either made their way downstream to New Orleans or upstream to Memphis. In addition to hearing blues on the streets of Memphis, Elvis and friends sometimes sneaked out of the white Assembly of God services to drop in on services in black churches. There they reveled in their songs, testimonials, and congregational participation. The gyrations that would define Elvis's early singing career were learned from watching the singers in black church services. The barriers of Jim Crowism were slowly but surely being broken down, and music was playing a major role in the process. As *Billboard* editor Paul Ackerman observed in 1958 in reference to the influence of black music on white youth: "Integration has already taken place." Indeed music had a pivotal role in the civil rights movement simultaneously occurring in the South.

Momentous events marked Elvis Presley's senior year of high school. Vernon continued to move from job to job until he hurt his back and could not work. In response, Elvis and Gladys both found jobs, Gladys as a nurses' aide, and Elvis finding a night job at Marl Metal Products. Almost immediately his studies and grades suffered; he fell asleep in class, and then began missing classes altogether. After two months Gladys made him quit the job, but by that time the increased family income disqualified them from public assistance housing. In January 1951 they left the Courts and rented two rooms in a house. In April, after two more moves, the Presleys settled into an apartment on Alabama Street.

That same month Elvis made his first public performance in Memphis. The Humes High Band Annual Minstrel Show featured Elvis as the sixteenth act. His rendition of *Till I Waltz Again with You* by Teresa Brewer left the audience demanding an encore. Most of his classmates were stunned by Elvis's electrifying performance, and rightly so. "Nobody knew I sang," Elvis remembered. "I wasn't popular in school, I wasn't dating anybody . . . I failed music—only thing I ever failed." No wonder students were surprised when the shy and quiet boy came alive on stage.

In June 1953, Elvis became the first Presley to graduate from high school, majoring in shop, history, and English. His grade point was slightly above average, but he did not ever think of going to college. First of all, there was no money. Secondly, music was his greatest interest; but music did not pay bills. The day after graduation Elvis took a job at Parker Machinists Shop. The end of the summer found him driving a delivery truck for Crown Electric Company, with the modest aspirations of becoming an electrician.

During that summer, however, Elvis did something that eventually took his life in a dramatically different direction. On a hot, sticky Saturday afternoon in July 1963, he walked in the doorway of Sam Phillips's Memphis Recording Service. Phillips was an entrepreneur who recognized that white kids were looking for a new sound. Born in rural Alabama, Phillips grew up believing in the power of music and radio to break down the stultifying traditions of the South. The other part of his recording service was Sun Records, which made master disks of local musicians and leased them to bigger companies for larger distribution. Phillips's studio, which began operating in 1950, was the only one in the South that allowed blacks to record. By the time Elvis came in to cut a record, Phillips had recorded blues musicians such as Bobby "Blue" Bland, B.B. King, and Big Walter Horton, and had sold their songs to large recording studios in Los Angeles. The Memphis Recording Service advertised regularly on local radio, offering musicians a chance to make their own record at a price of two songs for four dollars. Phillips ran the recording operations with Marion Keisker, a woman in her thirties who had been a Memphis radio personality since she was a child.

When finances and confidence grew sufficiently, Elvis Presley came to the service. On this particular July afternoon, Sam Phillips was away and Marion Keisker handled the front-desk operations herself. It was a busy day, and Keisker told Elvis he would have to wait his turn. Politely acknowledging, Elvis sat quietly, clutching his guitar. As the reception room emptied with each musician's recording, Keisker observed the boy with the sideburns thoughtfully. "What kind of singer are you?," she eventually asked. "I sing all kinds," replied Elvis. "Who do you sound like?" "I don't sound like nobody." "What do you sing, hillbilly?" "I sing hillbilly." "Well, who do you sound like in hillbilly?" "I don't sound like nobody."

It was a conversation Keisker would never forget. Hundreds of musicians passed through the door of the recording service, but this young man with the soulful eyes, long dark hair, and hesitant politeness impressed her. (Recently, Elvis had begun dyeing his hair black after seeing country star Roy Orbison perform.) As he sang *My Happiness*, a song made famous by the black group the Ink Spots, Keisker decided to make a tape recording to play back for Phillips. His second number was *That's When Your Heartaches Begin*, a tearful, country ballad that had talking, or recitation, as part of the lyrics. Keisker taped all of the second song, remembering what Phillips had recently said to her: "If I could find a white man who had the Negro sound and the Negro feel, I could make a billion dollars." When Phillips heard the recording of Elvis he agreed that the young performer had possibilities, but was very "rough."

Elvis hoped the recording would help him locate a band that needed a singer, but nothing happened for a long time. Elvis called periodically on Keisker to find if she had heard of any singing work, but to no avail. He continued working at Crown Electric, studying to be an electrician, and began dating Dixie Locke, a high school junior he had met at the Memphis Assembly of God church. Their relationship blossomed in 1954, and there was talk of marriage.

On the way to the altar, however, Elvis Presley was sidetracked. In January 1954 Memphis Recording Company gained the recording rights to two songs that Marion Keisker believed would be right for the kid with the sideburns. Elvis returned to the studio at Phillips's request to record *Casual Love Affair* and *I'll Never*

Stand in Your Way. The session was a disappointment for all. Elvis was nervous and ill at ease. After several attempts to record the numbers, Phillips resolutely asked Presley to play what he liked. Elvis sang snippets of gospel, western, country, and even Dean Martin love songs. There was something special about Presley, but Phillips knew he had not yet connected him to the right music. To be sure, Elvis was a lot of practice away from professionalism.

After some soul-searching, Phillips decided that Elvis needed solid instrumentation to back up his voice and marginal guitar expertise. To that end, he brought guitarist Scotty Moore and stand-up bass player Bill Black together with Elvis. Both Moore and Black were in their early twenties, and had been playing with other bands around Memphis for the past few years. Phillips and Keisker hoped that the three musicians could coalesce as a group, and eventually develop their own style. Style did not come easily, however. After several home sessions in June 1954, the trio's music satisfied no one. Not only could they not agree what to play; neither could they agree *how* to play the numbers they agreed upon.

On July 5, unprepared and with enthusiasm wavering, Presley, Moore, and Black met at 7:00 P.M. at Sun Studios to record. First they tried a Bing Crosby number, followed by a country ballad called *I Love You Because*. Neither worked, and Elvis seemed more ill at ease than ever. After a few hours Sam Phillips resolutely called for a break. Everyone was tired and frustrated, and tomorrow was another work day. Perhaps they should call it a night.

Suddenly, in a gesture of complete frustration, Elvis stood up, grabbed his guitar, and started singing an old blues song by Arthur "Big Boy" Crudup called *That's All Right [Mama]*. Scotty and Bill immediately perked up and smiled as Elvis went into wild gyrations and jumps in rhythm to the song. Bill picked up his bass and joined in; Scotty followed. Phillips, almost asleep, suddenly brightened. He was surprised Elvis even knew the tune, written and performed by Crudup in the mid-1940s. But quickly he discerned that this was the sound. It was new; a young, white man singing black blues with innocence and passion.

The session continued for hours as they worked out the details of the number. Elvis, whose nervousness had stifled the earlier numbers, gained confidence with each outtake. By the end of the session, the trio listened to what Sam believed was a sure hit. Raw, ragged, and soulful, *That's All Right [Mama]* featured Elvis's high-tenor vocals and rhythm guitar, Scotty's smooth lead guitar chords and riffs played on a Gibson hollow-body electric, and Bill's thumping, slapping bass. The number had hints of country, bluegrass, and rhythm and blues.

Sam Phillips was so convinced he had a hit with *That's All Right [Mama]* that he persuaded local deejay Dewey Phillips to play it on his *Red, Hot and Blue* radio program. After fourteen playings and almost 500 phone calls of inquiry, Dewey Phillips agreed. Hopeful hit songs of the 1950s were recorded on 45-rpm vinyl disks. One side could accommodate a song of not more than five minutes, but then there was the flip side. For marketing there had to be second song; and so far the trio had only one recording. Five days after recording *That's All Right [Mama]*, the trio settled on a bluesy version of a hillbilly waltz recorded by Bill Monroe in 1946, entitled *Blue Moon of Kentucky*. Far more "country sounding" than *That's All Right [Mama]*, the number nonetheless had the same energy as Elvis bellowed out one of the anthems of country music in a powerful baritone voice. Now the trio now had a 45 to market. When Sun Records released the single in July, it eventually sold 20,000 copies, mostly in the Memphis area where people had heard it on Dewey Phillips's show. Elsewhere, sales were scant. Pop disk jockeys listened to side one and decided Elvis was too black—or thought he *was* black. When they listened to side two, they determined he was too country.

The remainder of 1954 saw Elvis and his band—Elvis quickly became the headliner—performing almost nightly. Playing in Memphis-area clubs first, they soon branched out to Louisiana and Texas by the end of the year. If Elvis responded well to the studio setting, he truly came alive on stage. Scotty Moore said it was as if someone turned on a switch, and the mild-mannered southern boy turned into a gyrating, passionate performer mesmerized by his music. Elvis shrugged when asked about his movements, and said it was just how the music made him feel. He had an uncanny ability to size up an audience and draw them in with words and body language. Often setting his guitar aside, Elvis swung his arms forward, turned his heels out, and shook his torso around and around, forward and back. His soulful voice, alternating from an almost childlike tenor to a booming baritone, electrified his audiences. Quickly Presley became the top draw in any show. Girls screamed with delight and boys cheered as Elvis sang, played, and moved. Although a late-year *Grand Ole Opry* performance, the pinnacle for country singers, was less than successful since Elvis's gyrations and the band's upbeat renditions disagreed with country purists, four more single recordings rounded out a remarkable year for the Crown Electric truck driver.

Success meant many things. There was money; his first royalty checks from Sun Records began to roll in during late 1954. For Elvis the money meant he could now afford to give his parents more. Elvis seemed to know even before his musical success that he would need to support his parents. Dutifully, as he had done since obtaining his first job, Elvis presented his mother with his paychecks. By mid-1955 the Presleys were living in a new home in a nice Memphis neighborhood financed entirely by Elvis.

There was also fame. Elvis and his fiancé Dixie could go nowhere in the Memphis area without being noticed. Crowds waited anxiously for the band's car to arrive in front of music halls, clubs, and show grounds. Screaming teenage girls literally threw themselves at Elvis. Despite such fame, Elvis remained remarkably unchanged privately in the early days of his music career. He called his mother after every performance, and went home as quickly as possible after being on the road. Dixie, who had become good friends with Gladys, would come over and together they would revel in Elvis's new-found stardom. Elvis neither drank nor smoked, and Dixie was still the love of his life. But this was not to last. As it became increasingly difficult for Elvis to go anywhere in Memphis without creating a stir, Dixie began to sense she was losing him to the world of fame and fortune.

With live bookings soaring, regular recording sessions at Sun, and frequent interviews, Presley's schedule became too full for the band and Sam Phillips to manage. In early 1955, Elvis signed a contract with Memphis deejay Bob Neal to manage his career for a 15 percent commission of all live performances. Soon Neal added a drummer, D.J. Fontana, and the band became known as The Blue Moon

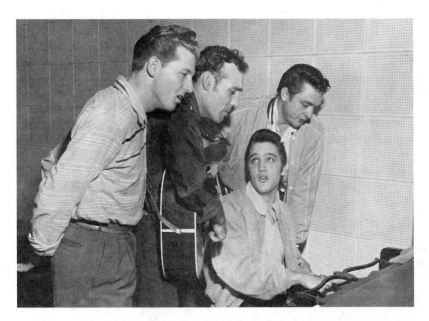

At Sun Records in Memphis, Elvis Presley leads an informal gospel session. The 1956 gathering also includes (from left to right) Jerry Lee Lewis, Carl Perkins, and Johnny Cash. This members of this ad hoc "million-dollar quartet" would go on produce dozens of gold records as solo artists.

Boys. They recorded eight singles in 1955, and the 45, *Mystery Train* and *I Forgot to Remember to Forget*, reached #7 on the country charts. Throughout the year the band played almost constantly, traveling to radio program bookings like *Louisiana Hayride* in Shreveport, as well as to dozens of county fairs, schoolhouse shows, and one-night-stands at clubs and honky-tonks. The power Elvis had over live audiences became clearly evident at a May show at the Gator Bowl in Jacksonville, Florida. As the show ended Elvis joked that he would see all the girls backstage. Frenetically, many took him up on the offer, storming the backstage and ripping most of Elvis's clothing off. Frightened police had to use crowd control measures to restore order. It was after a few incidents such as these that Scotty Moore, for one, began to wonder, "What is going on?"

Touring throughout the South, Elvis caught the attention of Colonel Tom Parker. A native of the Netherlands, Parker had emigrated to the United States in 1929. Although he spent two years in the Army, the title "Colonel" was self-proclaimed and not earned. Even the name Tom Parker was an alias. As a young man, Parker became a carnival promoter with acts like The Great Parker Pony Circus. Later he managed the career of country star Eddy Arnold. Boisterous and brimming over with confidence, Parker resembled, in the words of Presley biographer Jerry Hopkins, "a cross between P.T. Barnum and W.C. Fields." The 300-pound promoter, looking for his next big product, saw in the kinetic moves of Elvis Presley an underused commodity. It was not so much the music, Parker believed, it was

Presley's wild gyrations on stage earned him the nickname "Elvis the Pelvis," and the adoration of fans as his singing career skyrocketed in the mid-1950s.

Elvis's charisma and ability to enchant an audience that would make him a star—and the Colonel wealthy. In 1955, Parker began following Elvis and the band from stop to stop.

Twenty months after signing with Bob Neal, Elvis found himself under the management of the aggressive Tom Parker. Parker wasted no time in promoting his client. By September 1955 Parker had arranged the sale of Elvis's recording contract with Sun Records to media giant RCA. For $40,000 Sam Phillips released Elvis. Phillips intended to use the money to promote other performers, including Carl Perkins, Jerry Lee Lewis, and Johnny Cash. From the day of the buyout on, Elvis Presley was the property of RCA and Colonel Parker. RCA quickly compiled most of the Sun recordings into Elvis' first long playing album (LP), released in December 1955.

The events of 1954 and 1955 had been dizzying, but paled in comparison to those of 1956. Traveling to the RCA Nashville studio in January, Elvis and the band recorded five songs accompanied by two of country music's biggest stars: guitarist Chet Atkins and pianist Floyd Cramer. Included in those was *Heartbreak Hotel*, a soulful, blues number written by Tommy Durden and Mae Axton. Also in January the band made its national television debut on *Stage Show*, hosted by big band leaders Tommy and Jimmy Dorsey and produced by Jackie Gleason. The Colonel had worked hard to get a national booking for Elvis because he recognized that television was the key to superstardom. Now Elvis would be seen by millions via the invention that was revolutionizing the world. Two years after the end of World War II, there were approximately 10,000 TV sets in American homes; at the end of 1956, there were forty *million*. By the end of the decade televisions glowed in 90 percent of American homes, only to approach 100 percent a few years later. As with national radio programs, network television enabled advertisers to reach half the population simultaneously. Expenditures for television advertising increased accordingly, from $170 million in 1950 to $1.6 billion in 1960. Big money enticed the three networks, CBS, NBC, and ABC, to expand programming dramatically. While situation comedies, westerns, drama, and game shows dominated the early days of television, news and sports began to occupy an increasing share of air time as the 1950s progressed.

Colonel Parker demonstrated his business acumen in arranging Elvis's national television debut. Playing the networks off against one another, he obtained the most money and viewers for the debut of the "hillbilly cat." Jackie Gleason, star of the highly successful *Honeymooners*, was one of television's biggest celebrities. However, the variety show he produced that followed *The Honeymooners* suffered from poor ratings. Hoping to upstage NBC's *Perry Como Show*, CBS outbid the rival network to place Elvis on the thirty-minute *Stage Show*. Desperate for a ratings boost, Gleason and his associates saw a photograph of Elvis and believed this "guitar-playing Marlon Brando" might help save the show.

The CBS studio in New York City was about half full on that cold, rainy night of January 28, 1956. Bill Randle, a New York deejay who had been promoting the relatively unknown Elvis, was introduced by the band-leader host of the program, Tommy Dorsey. Randle announced, "We'd like at this time to introduce you to a young fellow . . . we think tonight [is] going to make television history for you. We'd like you to meet him now—Elvis Presley."

Black and white televisions across the nation went dark for a moment, and then there was Elvis, dressed in a black shirt, white tie, dark pants with a stripe, and a tweed jacket, which combined to mimic the image of a test pattern. Giving a nod to Scotty and Bill, Elvis sneered back at the audience and began to gyrate, sing, and play the band's rendition of Big Joe Turner's *Shake, Rattle, and Roll*. They followed with *Flip, Flop, and Fly*, *I Got a Woman*, and *Heartbreak Hotel*. The mail that flooded into the studio following the performance made it clear that Elvis was both popular and controversial. Some wrote of their outrage at his overly sexual movements, but those letters were far outnumbered by fans who wanted to see and hear more of Elvis Presley.

In the wake of his television debut, Elvis Presley's stock rose dramatically. *Heartbreak Hotel* quickly rose to #1 on both the pop and country charts with more than a million copies sold. *I Forgot to Remember to Forget* reached #1 on the country charts by the end of February. Recording sessions in New York produced nine more singles by mid-year, and Presley and his band played twice more on the *Stage Show*, twice on NBC's *Milton Berle Show*, and once on NBC's *Steve Allen Show*. Elvis's date on the Allen show resulted in that show rating higher than the normally best rated program in the Sunday night prime-time slot: CBS's *Ed Sullivan Show*. Sullivan, television's best-known variety host, called Colonel Parker the following day to book Elvis. Parker took particular satisfaction in the call, because Sullivan had shortly before said the controversial and overly sexual Presley would never perform on his show. On September 9, 1956, Sullivan announced Elvis to an estimated audience of fifty-four million. Singing *Hound Dog, Don't Be Cruel, Ready Teddy,* and *Love Me Tender,* Elvis gyrated and wiggled. The television audience, however, did not know this—cameras only filmed him from the waist up. CBS had caved in to sponsors who feared repercussions of a full-image Elvis. Hiding his lower torso did little to dissuade fans who gave him the enduring moniker: "Elvis the Pelvis." From this point on all of America knew about Elvis Presley.

It was precisely at the moment Elvis Presley became a national celebrity that he also became a national threat. He outraged the status quo of America on several fronts. The first was music. Elvis borrowed from all the sources of his childhood to produce a unique sound. *Billboard,* the weekly journal of pop music, declared in 1955 that his music appealed to fans of country, rhythm and blues, and pop, and therefore Elvis was in his own category: rockabilly, or rock and roll. The only other white rock and roll performers of note in those categories at that time were Bill Haley and Comets whose *Rock Around the Clock* had been an anthem of disillusioned youth in 1955. The rock and roll of the 1950s, like the jazz of the 1920s, was the music of youth. With Elvis Presley as its leader, rock and roll moved teenagers as surely as it scandalized adults.

After his network television performances, Elvis's appearance provoked controversy nationwide. Elvis said the look emulated truck drivers, but he also fashioned himself after the teenage heartthrob of the early 1950s, James Dean. The son of a Quaker dentist from Indiana, Dean had dropped out of college to pursue an acting career. In movies of the early 1950s, he played resentful adolescents looking for ways to express their frustration in a world that had failed to fulfill their expectations. Although rebellious, these people had no creed except their discontent with the middle-class United States. Dean's best-known film, pointedly titled *Rebel without a Cause,* showed three types of high school rebellion: juvenile delinquency, violence, and fast cars.

What made James Dean so charismatic for Presley and his contemporaries was that he lived the life he portrayed on the screen. The dress was the same—black leather jacket, blue jeans, boots—and so were the hard, scornful expression, the suspicious eyes, the dangling cigarette. In the jargon of the time, Dean was a "hood." Then, in 1955, Dean paid the supreme price for his way of life when his white Porsche Spyder, moving at well over a hundred miles per hour, slammed into another vehicle near Paso Robles, California. The steering column of the Porsche passed completely through Dean's body. He was dead at the age of twenty-four.

The reaction to Dean's death was a product of the anxieties and ambitions of his youthful admirers. Dean provided an alternative to conventional ways of living and dying. Some of his fans hysterically insisted that he had not died but was recuperating in secret and, like a messiah, would return. Thousands of teenagers wrote to him every month; a year after his death, the mail still poured in. Fan clubs flourished. Magazines, books, and even plastic casts of his head enjoyed a brisk sale. James Dean was a legend, but contemporaries copied his rebellious demeanor, including Elvis. In a 1956 interview, Presley said of Dean, Marlon Brando, and himself: "We're sullen, we're broodin', we're something of a menace. I don't understand it exactly, but that's what girls like in men. I don't know anything about Hollywood, but I know you can't be sexy if you smile. You can't be a rebel if you grin."

Rebellion was part and parcel for those of James Dean's generation. Some of the intellectual dynamite behind that rebellion appeared in the literature of the day, and the quiet desperation of Holden Caulfield was a prime example. Caulfield appeared in 1951 as the protagonist of J. D. Salinger's novel *The Catcher in the Rye*. He was a high school adolescent with all the alleged advantages of wealth and education, but his life was a series of dissatisfactions that ended in expulsion from a private school. Nothing had meaning: school, society, the standard definitions of success. Caulfield's struggle was for what the fifties generation came to call *identity*, and Salinger's novel became a kind of bible for those searching for their own.

The "beatniks" or "beats" of the 1950s also gave direction to the music and culture of rebellion. They were heirs of a bohemian tradition dating back to the art colonies of the 1920s and the itinerant existence of depression vagabonds. Only a handful actually lived the life Jack Kerouac described in *On the Road* (1955), but beatniks were important as symbols of nonconformity. Expressing contempt for the social norms that governed relations between the sexes for most Americans, they followed a sexual style their defenders called liberated and their critics called irresponsible. The beatniks also began experimenting with drugs and Far Eastern philosophies and talking about forms of perception that transcended rational intelligence. Their emphasis was on personal freedom rather than public issues. Like James Dean, their rebellion had no clear cause. "We gotta go and never stop going till we get there," a Kerouac character declared. "Where we going, man?" his friend inquired. "I don't know, but we gotta go."

The rebellious look and sensual sounds of Elvis Presley earned him both adoration and enmity. Conservative critics wrote scathing reviews of his Ed Sullivan performance, and condemned Sullivan for televising, as one wrote, a "gross national disservice." To another Elvis's music was "emotional TNT," and Elvis himself "a new monster, a sort of nightmare of rhythm." In the wake of the Sullivan performances, Elvis was burned in effigy in Saint Louis and hanged in Nashville. Some country deejays called for people to bring Elvis records to their stations where they would be smashed or burned. Religious leaders joined in the lambaste of Elvis. A Catholic newspaper called for a boycott of the *Ed Sullivan Show*, while an Episcopalian priest branded Elvis as "the whirling dervish of sex."

For all the controversy, Elvis never considered himself a threat to national morality or a leader of rebellion. In interviews (one of them recorded on a 45-rpm record) he simply said music made him move and get "real gone." In his polite southern drawl laced with sirs and ma'ams, he said he did not intend to offend adults, pointing out that many of them had danced to the controversial Charleston and the jitterbug to the dismay of their parents. Elvis told an interviewer in 1956 that just hearing rock and roll on the radio did not "get him on fire." On stage, however, he felt compelled to give the audience a show—something that radio or records could not convey.

In the wake of Elvis Presley came a multitude of rock and roll musicians. Many had been singing and playing before Elvis, but until the "King of Rock and Roll" made his national debut in 1956 venues for their talents were limited. After the first of three Sullivan performances by Elvis, radio stations, record companies, and television shows scrambled to adjust their products to meet the tastes of the burgeoning postwar youth culture. The Top Forty pop charts changed dramatically, with rock and roll soon dominant over traditional pop. Single performers, duos, trios, and small bands were cutting records as never before. In addition to Elvis and Bill Haley, the Everly Brothers, Buddy Holly and the Crickets, Jerry Lee Lewis, Ritchie Valens, Gene Vincent, and young Ricky Nelson (who patterned his look after Elvis) captured the imagination of teenagers. Other "teen idols" like Frankie Avalon, Paul Anka, Dion, and Bobby Darin straddled the line between rock and traditional pop with ballads and "fun at the beach songs." Female performers like the Shirelles, Martha and the Vandellas, Gladys Knight and the Pips, Brenda Lee, and Leslie Gore belted out pop, soul, and rock and roll. Black R&B musicians, including Little Richard Penniman, Chuck Berry, Ray Charles, Fats Domino, James Brown, the Platters, and the Temptations found they no longer had to let white "cover" performers sing their songs in order to reach white audiences. A revolution had come to popular music, and Elvis Presley was its leader.

Across the Atlantic the Elvis phenomenon had its impact as well. Juvenile delinquents, or hoods, in England had thrived on James Dean, the controversial 1955 film *Blackboard Jungle*, and Bill Haley just as they had in the United States. Motorcycle riders dressed in leather with long hair and sideburns were known as Teddy Boys in England, and they "dug" Dean, Presley, and rock and roll with a passion. Their descendants, the Rockers of the 1960s, looked to early Marlon Brando, who starred in a motorcycle gang drama *The Wild One* (1953), for their look, and to Gene Vincent, Chuck Berry, and Elvis Presley for their sound.

In early 1956, Elvis Presley said he knew nothing about Hollywood. That was about to change. While Elvis performed live and recorded, Colonel Parker, who in March had engineered a 25 percent cut of all public performances, worked out the details for a Hollywood screen test. After two favorable tests in April 1956, producers scrambled to sign Elvis. Although he had hoped his acting career would mean real acting, and intended to pattern himself after James Dean or Marlon Brando, Colonel Parker and the Hollywood movie moguls had other ideas. Quick to maintain control of his client and maximize profits, the Colonel stipulated that Elvis had to sing in every film. The clause generally limited his roles to light comedy and romance films and made serious acting impossible.

Before this limitation was imposed, Elvis was well into making his first film, a Civil War drama. In *Love Me Tender*, produced by 20th Century-Fox, Elvis sang the title song and drew third billing behind Richard Egan and Debra Paget. For this largely dramatic role he received $100,000. In the original release Elvis was killed in the end, but negative fan reaction in pre-screenings led to a reshoot of the conclusion. In the final release, Elvis lives. Opening in November to mixed reviews—but to box office success—*Love Me Tender* made Presley an instant movie star.

The shy, polite country boy who walked into Sam Phillips studio in 1953 was the best-known performer in the world by the beginning of 1957. Two more films were in the making that starred Elvis. He already had the most songs listed in the history of Billboard's Top 100, and Elvis sheet music, clothing, and souvenirs were impossible to keep in stock at the nation's stores. Throngs of screaming fans attended his every public appearance; Elvis fan clubs were in every city in the nation; and Elvis was commonly known as America's most eligible bachelor.

Such fame and fortune eventually had its inevitable impact on Elvis Presley. Dixie Locke was long gone, and a series of girlfriends followed—some local beauty queens and others Hollywood starlets. He lost some good friends, too. In September, Scotty Moore and Bill Black resigned from the band for monetary reasons. The two were angry that Elvis and the Colonel were getting the lion's share of the take for their music. For Parker, who had never thought highly of either Black or Moore, it was just business. Elvis, however, took the split personally and brooded about it for weeks.

Aside from the financial differences, Elvis was moving in circles in which Bill and Scotty were uncomfortable. Elvis's new best friends included the young and famous of Hollywood, particularly Nick Adams, Vince Edwards, Russ Tamblyn, and Natalie Wood. Elvis attended parties frequently in California but abstained from alcohol and the increasingly popular marijuana. Although he enjoyed jet-setting in the glamour capital of the world, Elvis still liked to spend time with his parents. In mid-1956, he paid cash for a spacious ranch-style home, but less than a year later Vernon and Gladys found an estate outside Memphis that they believed could serve as a home and refuge for their son. The eighteen-room mansion with eighteen beautifully landscaped acres was called Graceland. In April 1957, the Presleys moved in.

A year of hectic touring, recording, and filmmaking was preceded by Presley's induction into the U.S. Army in March 1958. While it seems astonishing by contemporary standards that the world's biggest star could not have avoided the draft, it is important to note that Elvis wanted to do his patriotic duty with no special favors. Moreover, the nation was gripped by some of the most tense days of the Cold War and even hints of disloyalty could result in a House Un-American Activities Committee inquiry. Believing his career could be ruined by evading military service, Elvis made no challenges to being drafted. When he received his notice in late 1957 filming of *King Creole* was taking place. At first Elvis shrugged and said it was time to go, but his father and the Colonel wrote the draft board to ask for an extension until filming was completed. Because the nation was not at war, draft board officials granted the extension.

The induction of Elvis Presley, which took place in Memphis, was an item of intense media attention. After receiving perhaps the most famous haircut in history, Private Elvis Presley reported for boot camp at Fort Chaffee, Arkansas. For the next two years, Presley served honorably, stationed mostly in West Germany. He served as a jeep driver and tank corps member, and was promoted several times. During his service Elvis did not perform publicly. Although it is impossible to calculate his lost income during his military service, conservative estimates run into the tens of millions of dollars. Meanwhile, Presley received his GI salary of less than $200 per month.

Shortly after his induction, Elvis received the news that his mother Gladys was gravely ill. Suffering from acute hepatitis, she was hospitalized in early August 1958. She passed away on August 13 at age 46, with her husband and Elvis, who had flown in from basic training in Texas the day before, at her side. Her body lay in state at Graceland until the funeral on August 16. Elvis's grief was uncontrollable, even in public. He refused to leave her side at Graceland, and had to be consoled constantly by friends and relatives. Yet consolation was futile as he lamented the loss of everything dear to him. At the funeral he had to be helped in and out of cars, to his seat in the church, and to the burial site at the cemetery. The death of his mother left Elvis Presley a changed man.

On March 5, 1960, amid much hoopla, Sergeant Elvis Presley received his honorable discharge from the Army. As he stepped off the train in Memphis in full dress uniform, thousands of fans cheered and screamed wildly despite a bitter cold ice storm. After a brief rest at Graceland, Elvis was back in full swing under the relentless scheduling of Tom Parker. On the 26th, he taped a segment on a Frank Sinatra television special from Miami, being paid $125,000 for a six-minute performance. Sinatra, who in 1957 had branded rock and roll as "brutal, ugly, [and] vicious," now welcomed its king with open arms. The two sang *Witchcraft* and *Love Me Tender*. Exhausting recording sessions followed, in which Elvis, with new band members selected by the Colonel, recorded more than sixty songs by year's end.

Elvis's main occupation for the remainder of 1960—and for the rest of the decade—was acting. Returning triumphantly to Hollywood, Elvis launched into an exhausting number of motion pictures whose plots had been carefully engineered for him. Elvis was the property of no studio, and therefore made pictures with all the majors, including Fox, MGM, Paramount, and United Artists. But his main producer was Hal B. Wallis, who produced ten of the thirty-three Elvis films released between 1956 and 1969. Given his incredible popularity, Presley's films were almost guaranteed to be box office successes. Invariably, the films also featured some of Hollywood's most beautiful actresses and a bevy of handsome young bodies of both sexes.

Settling into a Hollywood career designed for him, Elvis ceased to be a threat to the status quo. In fact, with each new film he increasingly *became* the status quo. Certainly he had been changed by military service and his mother's death, but wealth and stardom had also begun to smooth the rough edges of the once dangerous performer. Elvis was now a multimillionaire, and slowly but surely more and more an icon of what historians call "consensus America." Consensus America can be explained in theoretical terms as an unorganized coalition of entertainment marketers and the government itself. Together these entities present entertainment designed to promote proper American behavior and the mass consumption of particular products. Threatening entertainment forms, the theory continues, were suppressed. The Elvis Presley of the mid-1950s, for example, had been a raw, sensual talent, with openly sexual overtones in his performances. As such, critics alleged, he was a threat to moral American society. Early attempts to package him for mass audiences included filming him from the waist up, but eventually immense success took care of any threat he presented to American morals.

By the early 1960s, Elvis the movie superstar displaced Elvis the King of Rock and Roll. In a steady progression of films, Presley toed the party line of the consensus America he had once challenged. The films of 1962 are typical of his Hollywood period. The year opened with the filming of United Artists' *Follow That Dream*, in which Elvis plays the son of a poor family on welfare living in Florida. A light comedy, *Follow That Dream* showcases Presley's knack for humor, but continues to portray him as an uneducated hillbilly. The film's love interest, Anne Helm, and Elvis get together in the end. United Artists' *Kid Galahad*, a remake of a 1937 film, stars Elvis as ex-serviceman turned boxer. In the end, Elvis overcomes all odds to win a big bout, and marries his manager's sister, Rose Grogan, played by Joan Blackman. The film highlights Presley's handsome physique, and the karate skills he had learned in the Army. (Recently, he had earned a black belt.) The third film of the year was Paramount's *Girls, Girls, Girls*. Filmed in Hawaii, *Girls, Girls, Girls* casts Elvis as a young man who is trying to recover the sailboat he and his father built but lost through financial hardship. Lots of music and a roller-coaster romance with starlet Stella Stevens propel a thin plot across the beautiful setting of the island of Oahu. *Girls, Girls, Girls* placed sixth on the year's top grossing films, while *Kid Galahad* was ninth.

Following military service, Elvis returned for movie stardom. Above, Elvis poses with Nancy Sinatra, his co-star in the 1968 film, *Speedway*. In all, Presley made thirty-three films, many with Hollywood's leading young actresses.

By and large the Elvis films were pure formula in various settings. Handsome boy meets wholesome girl; like all other girls in the film, wholesome girl falls in love with handsome boy; handsome boy's head is turned by other girls, but he really loves only wholesome girl; conflict and controversy arise, but wholesome (and lucky) girl finally prevails and wins the heart of handsome boy. This may not have been what Elvis wanted, but it was what the film business and Colonel Parker wanted of him. (Parker served as technical adviser on nearly every film.) Elvis found it difficult, if not impossible, as many other actors have, to maintain independence and integrity. From the beginning of motion pictures in the early 1900s, filmmakers have eyed the bottom line. Whatever sells is produced; whatever does not is shelved. It was hard to argue with success when it came to the Elvis films. Easily produced, usually at low cost, his films had a guaranteed audience of Elvis faithful. Moreover, nineteen of the thirty-three Elvis films included LP soundtracks. The soundtrack to *Girls, Girls, Girls*, for example, included thirteen songs from the film, and became a million-selling gold record. Midway though the 1960s, Presley had become consensus America. The tenor of his films, moreover, fitted traditional gender roles perfectly. Superstardom was the "velvet hammer" that smoothed out the erstwhile rough and dangerous performer. And honoring a tradition that characterizes Hollywood productions, Elvis films almost always had happy endings.

Since the early days of his music career Elvis Presley had driven large crowds into hysteria. He had had his clothes torn off more than once by female fans, and had received several death threats by the early 1960s. By the time he entered military service, Presley could go nowhere without drawing crowds. Fan intrusion into his life increased even more after his discharge. For protection, security, and companionship, Elvis began employing a group of mostly old friends from Memphis to be his bodyguards. The first member of what became known as the "Memphis Mafia" was childhood friend Lamar Fike, who joined Presley in 1957. After leaving military service, Elvis hired two Army friends and as many as six others from Memphis to serve as his protectors. The world's most popular man was for all intents and purposes becoming an extremely isolated man.

If round-the-clock bodyguards were not enough to change one's life, Elvis Presley's personal life took other major turns during his movie period. There were many women in his life; mostly they were actresses, some of whom were in films with him. Yet during the 1960s he remained serious about only one. During his tour of duty in West Germany, Elvis met fourteen-year-old Priscilla Beaulieu, the step-daughter of an Air Force captain. Immediately captivated, Elvis made long-term plans. In 1961, he invited her for Christmas at Graceland. In 1962, her parents permitted her to move to Memphis and attend high school and finishing school. While Elvis maintained his most eligible bachelor in Hollywood status in word and deed, he privately wooed Priscilla with gifts, cars, and jewelry. In May 1967 they were married in a private ceremony in Las Vegas. The King of Rock and Roll was thirty-two, and his bride was twenty-two. Nine months later Priscilla gave birth to their daughter, Lisa Marie.

Although Elvis was now a father, he remained the King of Rock and Roll to his millions of loyal fans. Despite such popularity, Elvis was not getting any younger, and popular music serves youth. Presley and other performers of the 1950s opened the floodgates for the new music of the coming decade, but it is informative to note that Elvis's last number-one hit for several years was the 1961, *Good Luck Charm*. Throughout the 1960s, rock and roll underwent sweeping transitions. The popular music charts of the early part of the decade revealed an eclectic mix of traditional pop; instrumental and vocal surf music; African-American soul, which would collectively be known as Motown after its hearth, Detroit, Michigan, the Motor City; folk music; teen tragedy songs where young lovers are separated by class or death; and female and male individual vocalists (many of the males still emulating the Presley sound).

Then, in February 1964, came the second revolution in rock and rock (Elvis being the first). On Sunday the ninth, sixty million television sets simultaneously glowed with the image of Ed Sullivan, who now, as he had done eight years earlier with Elvis, introduced four young men from Liverpool, England, with longish hair and bangs and wearing mod suits. Barely audible over the deafening screams of teenagers in the studio audience, The Beatles played their first hit songs, *She Loves You*, and *I Wanna Hold Your Hand*. The sobbing, frantic, ecstatic faces in the audience were clearly reminiscent of the Elvis Presley spots on Sullivan. It also became clear that the King now faced his first real challenge to the throne of rock and roll.

Who were these four lads from Liverpool, and what was their tremendous appeal? During the late 1950s, John Lennon, Paul McCartney, George Harrison, and Ringo Starr formed a band in their hometown of Liverpool, an industrial city on the Mersy River in northern England. Born in the early 1940s, they and their urban counterparts in the United Kingdom were caught up in the hysteria about Elvis Presley. Lennon and McCartney, the band's charter members, early on acknowledged their debts to Elvis, Buddy Holly, and various black rhythm and blues artists. Trained musicians, Lennon and McCartney found one another in their early teens and began playing the popular music of the day on their guitars. Eventually, Paul switched to bass guitar, and lead guitarist George Harrison and drummer Richard Starkey (Ringo Starr) joined the band. Performing the music of others—and a growing number of Lennon and McCartney compositions—the Beatles played the English and western European club circuit in the early 1960s. When shrewd businessman George Martin took over management of the group in the early 1960s, he transformed the Fab Four into a huge success in England and western Europe.

The Beatles' performance on the Sullivan show heralded the "British invasion" of the United States. The Beatles combined rhythm and blues, blues, and even show tunes to produce their own brand of rock and roll. Their tight harmonies and lively lyrics were fresh and immediately appealing to young people. Both of the songs they played on Ed Sullivan's show subsequently soared to number one on the American pop charts, with many more to come. Within a year of the show, the Beatles came to dominate rock music.

To be sure, the Beatles were not the only members of the invasion. In their wake came bands such as the Dave Clark Five, Chad and Jeremy, Peter and Gordon, Herman's Hermits, the Searchers, and the Zombies. These bands reflected the mod culture of urban England. Tailored suits, pointed boots, tab collar shirts, and longish hair with bangs (not oiled) were the look for boys. Girls wore short skirts, white boots, and brightly colored blouses. The look for mods was called Carnaby Street after the row of shops in London where the apparel was sold.

The Beatles and the other clean-cut bands that began the British invasion were followed by a second, more radical, wave. The raunchy and sensual Rolling Stones looked disheveled and menacing, while their songs spoke openly of sexual desire and frustration, and explored social themes that made parents uncomfortable. Rhythm and blues bands, the ancestors of recent heavy metal, also became popular. The Who, Led Zepplin, Traffic, Cream, Pink Floyd, and Jethro Tull all brought their "maximum R&B" to the states. Sometimes sensual, sometimes socially poignant, sometimes outright sexual, but always loud, English R&B bands took rock music in ever new directions. From such bands emerged rock legends such as Peter Townshend, Roger Daltrey, Jimmy Page, Robert Plant, Eric Clapton, Steve Winwood, Roger Waters, and Ian Anderson.

Coinciding with the metamorphosis in British rock came dramatic changes in American popular music. Changes were inspired by England but also by powerful social forces in the United States. The civil rights movement of the 1950s carried on strongly into the 1960s, and folk music in particular took up its cause. Perhaps the best folk musician and composer of the era, Hibbing, Minnesota–born Bob Dylan, shared many of the same early inspirations as Elvis Presley, but with a folk music tradition that also idolized 1930s "dust-bowl balladeer" Woody Guthrie. Dylan's early music had strong social meaning. His 1962 *Ballad of Emmett Till*, for example, told the story of a young black from Chicago who was beaten and killed in Mississippi for whistling at a white woman. Another contemporary concern, the nuclear fallout scare, lay behind Dylan's *I Will Not Go Under the Ground. Blowin' in the Wind*, also written in 1962, dazzled those who first heard it and went on to become the spiritual anthem of the civil rights and antiwar movements. Like most of Dylan's best work, it was understated—simply a series of questions about when justice and peace would come. But there was poetry in the lyrics, and the music conveyed the growing tension of the 1960s.

When James Meredith's attempted to break the color line on the Oxford campus of the University of Mississippi in 1962, Dylan responded with one of his "finger-pointin' songs," as he termed them: *Oxford Town. A Hard Rain's A-Gonna Fall* and other songs used rich but veiled imagery to drive home Dylan's point that lies, hatred, and inhumanity were on the verge of undoing civilization. Fear and anger underlay the song, and Dylan found himself expressing the emotions of many of his contemporaries. Their world, their lives were on the thin line of survival. Continuing to explore this theme, Dylan composed *Only a Pawn in Their Game*. Ostensibly about the shooting of black civil rights leader Medgar Evers, the song implied that evil was largely the result of the Establishment's game of power politics.

Dylan's fear and lack of respect for authority was increasingly echoed by American youth as the Sixties proceeded. Added to the Cold War, the threat of nuclear annihilation, poverty, and bigotry was the escalating American involvement in Vietnam. While folk music took up the banner of opposition to the war, American rock performers began devoting whole albums to protest themes. Bands like the Jefferson Airplane, Buffalo Springfield, the Doors, Country Joe and the Fish, the Grateful Dead, and the Steve Miller Band openly protested the war and the draft in song and performance. Their "look" included very long hair, beads, bell-bottoms, and chukka boots or sandals. Their music was often laced with acknowledgments and endorsement of drug use, especially the hallucinogenic narcotics which spawned the term "acid rock." Their fans included "hippies," the counterculture icons of the decade who drew back from mainstream society to partake in alternative lifestyles that included drug use and communal living. The rock bands of the late 1960s pushed the envelope of decency and respect for institutions to proportions unimaginable a few years earlier.

As Elvis Presley viewed the Beatles' performances in 1964, he immediately believed they were a personal threat. No one had come close to matching the sensation of the King of Rock and Roll until then. Now, while Elvis cranked out a succession of mundane film and musical soundtracks, the Beatles-led British invasion was making music history. Thirty years old as of January 1965, Presley was, in the admonition of the youth of the sixties, not to be trusted. As rock music underwent its gyrations during the remainder of the decade, Presley became increasingly hostile toward its icons. He laid blame particularly on the Beatles, and especially John Lennon, for starting the invasion and then leading the world of rock and roll into its excesses.

Indeed the Beatles had undergone a significant transformation from the wholesome band of 1964. And John Lennon led the way to writing music of social protest and alternative lifestyles. However, each band member contributed to the metamorphosis. Each Beatles album after 1965 was increasingly thematic and philosophical, exploring social issues, politics, everyday life, and fantasies. The Beatles also experimented with new recording techniques, full orchestration, and instruments like the sitar. The sound they created was unique, but compared to many other rock bands of the day the Beatles remained fairly mainstream. Lennon and McCartney's *Revolution*, on the 1968 *White Album*, for example, advocates changing the world through peaceful, rather than destructive revolutionary, actions.

Despite having a host of other targets, Elvis continued to jealously view the Beatles as foreign invaders, drug advocates, and revolutionaries. So strongly did he oppose the connection of rock music and illegal drugs that he visited President Nixon in the White House in 1970. After launching into a tirade against the "anti-American" Beatles that confused even Nixon, Elvis offered his and the Memphis Mafia's services as narcotics agents. He promised to work in Beverly Hills, Memphis, and Palm Springs (where he had homes) to root out drug users and dealers. Nixon, equally concerned about illegal drugs and anxious to do anything to quell the antiwar movement, seized the opportunity and made Elvis a federal narcotics officer. In a well-publicized ceremony, the president presented Elvis with a special assistant's badge.

The Nixon meeting truly captured the mindset of the King of Rock and Roll by the early 1970s. Never interested in politics at any level, Presley's basic underpinnings were those of a conservative, high-school-educated, southern country boy. He loved his country, served in the military, and now was willing to serve again in a different capacity. His concern was for young people whom he believed were being led down a path of destruction by people like outspoken critic of Vietnam, Jane Fonda, radicals such as Abbey Hoffman and Jerry Rubin, and musicians like John Lennon. Presley also viewed the ground swell of youth protest against Vietnam as a threat to the nation's basic institutions.

Presley, sporting his new "Las Vegas" look, and President Nixon shake hands after their 1970 meeting on combating illegal drug use. Nixon later made Elvis a special federal narcotics agent.

The supreme irony of the narcotics agent incident was that Elvis Presley used drugs extensively by the time of his meeting with Richard Nixon. Adamantly opposed to illegal drugs, Elvis was a regular user of prescription drugs. While it is impossible to determine when his drug use began, a good friend later disclosed her belief that actor Nick Adams had introduced Elvis to amphetamines in 1957. (Adams died of a drug overdose in 1968.) Given Presley's grueling film, recording, and performing schedule, the use of speed early in his career seems plausible. Amphetamines were in wide use in Hollywood, as were barbiturates and marijuana. For Elvis, drugs were a way to get his job done. Hollywood physicians willingly prescribed amphetamines to perk an actor up, and barbiturates to help him or her sleep. Throughout the 1960s, Elvis made three films a year. He starred with Hollywood's best young actresses, including Shelley Fabares, Nancy Sinatra, Ann-Margaret, and Mary Tyler Moore. He recorded at least three albums a year and made numerous public appearances. He married and had a child, and traveled hundreds of thousands of miles each year. Uppers and downers undoubtedly helped him maintain this breakneck pace.

After making thirty films, few of which satisfied him, Elvis Presley decided to retire from Hollywood after fulfilling commitments made through 1968. After making three more movies, including *Charro*, his only non-singing film, Elvis persuaded Colonel Parker to let him go back to live performing. By then Parker had renegotiated his contract, and now received an incredible 50 percent of Presley's revenues. Parker was swayed to allow Elvis to leave Hollywood only by the prospect of his client being able to make even more money in live performances.

And make money Elvis Presley did. His exhausting performance period began in 1968 with a highly rated comeback television special on NBC, and the *Elvis* LP that reached #8 in national sales. After making his last feature film in 1969, Elvis stepped up his recording and performing. The single *Suspicious Minds* reached #1, and *In the Ghetto*, a poignant tune about urban poverty and crime, reached #8. He took particular pride in reaching #1 on the national pop charts amid the acid rock and British invasion music. One evening he told his young step-brother David Stanley, "I been wrong for so long, but I'm right tonight."* In July, Elvis opened for the first of many concerts in Las Vegas. More than 100,000 people attended the series of shows, and Elvis thereafter did a series each year in Vegas. Ironically, Elvis, Scotty, Bill, and D.J. had flopped playing Las Vegas night clubs in 1956 because they were too wild. Now Elvis dominated the Vegas entertainment scene.

The pace of the Elvis Presley entertainment machine quickened as the decade of the 1970s unfolded. In February 1970 he did four shows at Houston's Astrodome to more than 210,000 wildly enthusiastic fans. Traveling the nation, Elvis played gigs from Oklahoma City to Boston to Seattle. Each national tour was punctuated by a long concert series in Las Vegas. This became his normal lifestyle beginning in 1970, and increasingly Elvis acknowledged that he was only happy while performing. The pace was dizzying, and he had little time for his family or his health. His family dissolved first when Priscilla, feeling abandoned and unloved, requested and gained a divorce in August 1972.

With the hectic touring pace, Presley's weight began to fluctuate; he weighed as much as 300 pounds on some brief breaks from performing. By performance time, however, the weight had dropped—at least visibly. Elvis had begun wearing white, and sometimes black, beaded, sequined jumpsuits which, he believed, hid his waistline. He also began to suffer vision problems, and was diagnosed with secondary glaucoma in 1971. Recurrent laryngitis forced cancellation of several shows in 1973 and 1975.

Despite these problems, Elvis Presley was never more popular. He had aged, but so had the fans who had adored him since 1956. Elvis played to packed houses each night, and gave electrifying performances that included old and new hits. The King had his fans among rock's new elite as well. When George Harrison attended a concert, Elvis talked to him backstage before the show. After telling Harrison he and Paul were the best talents of the recently broken-up Beatles, Elvis patted him on the back and said "I know you'll do well." At another performance, the members of Led Zepplin came to Elvis's hotel to meet him. According to David Stanley, the British superstars were like awestruck children after seeing and then meeting the King. In 1975, Elvis was introduced to Eric Clapton. "What do you do?" asked Presley, who reportedly never listened to radio after the early 1960s. Clapton replied politely that he played guitar. When Presley offered lessons from his lead guitarist,

---

*In 1960, Vernon Presley re-married. His new wife was Dee Stanley, who had three sons.

James Burton, Eric Clapton said he would love to sit in on a session and play guitar with Burton.

As appealing as the potential jam session with Clapton, Presley, and Burton might have been, it was never to be. The grueling performing pace was taking its toll. Elvis Presley, long isolated in superstardom, now lived an entirely cloistered life. In 1975, he purchased a four-engine Convair jet aircraft. Converting the plane, which he named the Lisa Marie after his daughter, Elvis made private quarters for himself and also quarters for his bodyguards. Now Elvis could literally remain unseen by the public except in performance. The rest of his time was spent on the aircraft, in limousines, or in hotel rooms.

By the mid-1970s Presley had become extremely eccentric, if not psychopathic. His country boy obsession with firearms had never left him, and he carried loaded guns with him at all times. Several times he shot out television sets in anger, especially when challengers to his crown were on. He had a series of girlfriends after his divorce who generally saw to his needs between concerts. A typical tour day, according to David Stanley who was a member of the Memphis Mafia during the 1970s, included waking at four in the afternoon for breakfast: multiple cheese omelets, a pound of burnt bacon, coffee, and cantaloupe. By nine, he began performing, and afterward jumped into a limousine and then the Lisa Marie. By 11:30 Elvis was sedated with Quaaludes, percodan, and/or dilaudid, administered by his personal physician to bring him down from the show. After changing out of his costume, he sat down to eat—chicken fried steak, fried chicken, five cheeseburgers and fries, and burnt beefsteak were among his favorite after-concert meals. By the time he had finished eating, the plane had landed in the next city. Limousines escorted Presley and his entourage to their hotel, where Elvis met his girlfriend in his suite, ate again, and had a second administration of drugs. Sometime in the wee hours of the morning Presley would fall into a deep, drug-induced sleep, where he would remain until four in the afternoon to begin the whole process again.

Ominous portents surrounded Elvis Presley's 1977 tour. Worst of all was the drug use, which, according to those close to him, grew massively. Elvis consulted a large pharmaceutical guide daily and willingly experimented with drug combinations designed to bring him up or make him unconscious. While his confidants tried to get him to stop and seek help, Elvis remained in denial and with a pointed gun threatened anyone who attempted to intervene. Elvis increasingly relied on the Bible and spiritual guidances such as *The Prophet* for solace between shows. The breakneck touring continued, with eight shows in February, seven in March (one was canceled due to Elvis being hospitalized for two weeks for exhaustion), nine in April, eight in May, and six in June.

July found Elvis in seclusion at Graceland, but weighing in at 260 pounds by the end of the month. With three days to go before the next tour, Elvis launched another crash weight-loss campaign. However, his self-prescribed measures proved too extreme. At two in the afternoon of August 16, 1977, Elvis's girlfriend, Ginger Alden, discovered him lying in a fetal position on the floor of his bathroom at Graceland. She called the bodyguards, who called the fire department. It was too late, however. Elvis Presley was dead. While the coroner's report identified the cause as a heart attack, a drug overdose was most likely the cause of his heart failure.

Photographs of Presley in the concerts shortly before his death reveal a man in poor health. Face flaccid, eyes red and irritated, once-perfect hair now not so, and once-taut body flabby, the Elvis of 1977 was a shadow of his former self. Still the performer would not quit, and with the exception of a few shows toward the end, Elvis continued to electrify sold-out arenas around the nation. Performing live was what he had done since he was eighteen—the only consistency in his life, and in the end, his only joy. The King would not quit, but his body did. News of Presley's death catapulted around the world. Grieving fans refused to believe the stories about his death, but the thousands who dropped everything to see Elvis's body lying in state at Graceland knew the news was true. The King of Rock and Roll was dead at forty-two.

In the more than two decades that have passed since his death, Elvis Presley's legend continues to grow. He is probably the only performer who is talked about more in death than during his life. Elvis impersonators, musicians, and cartoon characters make it impossible to observe popular culture anywhere on the globe and not see references to Presley. Controversy arose in 1998 when the U.S. Postal Service announced its commemorative stamp for the King. Elvis fans could not agree whether the stamp should depict the young Elvis of the 1950s or the jumpsuit-clad Las Vegas Presley of the 1970s. More than 700,000 people took the Graceland tour in 1997 alone, and every August, thousands place flowers on his grave in Memphis. Elvis sightings remain regular fodder for national tabloids, and stories that aver that Presley still lives make their way into mainstream periodicals. Academicians devote serious scholarship to analyzing the Presley phenomenon as an exponent of modern American popular culture. The afterlife of Elvis Presley is what one researcher calls "the story that never ends."

The world of rock and roll music that Elvis Presley did so much to create continues to evolve after his death. Rhythm and blues became heavy metal; pop became bubble gum and then punk rock; new wave became grunge; then came reggae and rap. Hundreds and even thousands of bands sought and seek out the new sound that will separate them from the pack. Few succeed, however, and most rock and roll bands are quickly forgotten. A recent phenomenon in broadcast media are the "oldies" radio stations. Some feature the hits of the 1950s, some the 1960s, and others the 1970s and even the 1980s. Some feature pop, some country, and others classic rock. Most of these stations, however, have a full complement of Presley tunes on their playlists. When they play songs like *Heartbreak Hotel*, *Hound Dog*, *Good Luck Charm*, *Suspicious Minds*, or *In the Ghetto*, deejays need only give one quick statement of identification: "That was the King."

SELECTED READINGS
The Person

Guralnick, Peter: *Last Train to Memphis: The Rise of Elvis Presley* (1994). Thorough biography of Presley's childhood and rise to fame up to 1958.

Hammontree, Patsy Guy: *Elvis Presley: A Bio-Bibliography* (1985). Good analysis, including chronology, discography, and extensive interviews.

Hopkins, Jerry: *Elvis: A Biography* (1971). The first full-length and detailed biography.

Plasketes, George: *Images of Elvis Presley in American Culture, 1977–1997: The Mystery Terrain* (1997). An examination of the Presley-after-death phenomenon.

Stanley, David, with Frank Coffey: *The Elvis Encyclopedia: The Complete and Definitive Reference Book on the King of Rock and Roll* (1994). Just as the title suggests, with excellent photographs.

Whitmer, Peter: *The Inner Elvis: A Psychological Biography of Elvis Aron Presley* (1996). Examines Elvis Presley's mind through events and statements.

The Period

Berger, Peter L., and John Neuhaus: *Movement and Revolution* (1970). An analysis of the youth movement in the years since 1955.

*Berman, Ronald: *America in the Sixties: An Intellectual History* (1968). Especially good on the emergence and various manifestations of the New Left.

Gittlin, Todd: *The Sixties: Years of Hope, Days of Rage* (1987). Intellectual history of the counterculture.

*Giuliano, Geoffrey: *Behind Blue Eyes: The Life of Pete Townshend* (1996). Explores the British invasion through the life of one of rhythm and blues' best.

*Goldman, Eric F.: *The Crucial Decade: America, 1945–1955.* (1965). Political and social history.

Leuchtenburg, William E.: *A Troubled Feast: American Society since 1945* (1983). Concise, well-presented outline of popular cultural history as well as mainstream national events.

*Lora, Ronald (ed.): *America in the 60's: Cultural Authorities in Transition* (1974). Representative anthology of the significant sources of cultural history.

O'Neill, William L.: *Coming Apart: An Informal History of America in the 1960s* (1971). The best account of American thought and society in Presley's early adulthood.

Pichaske, David: *A Generation in Motion: Popular Music and Culture in the Sixties* (1979). Uses music to interpret social and intellectual changes that influenced Presley and to which he contributed.

*Roszak, Theodore: *The Making of a Counter Culture* (1969). Reviews the history of American social and cultural criticism in the 1960s.

FOR CONSIDERATION

1. As evidence suggests in the Martin Luther King, Jr. chapter, racism was widespread and deep-seated in the South during the 1940s and 1950s. What factors contributed to Elvis Presley's apparent lack of bigotry toward African Americans?
2. What influences combined to create the Elvis Presley sound?
3. What influences combined to create the Elvis Presley look, and the general rebelliousness of American youth in the 1950s?
4. What void did Elvis Presley's music fill in post–World War II America?
5. How does one account for the posthumous sensation over Elvis Presley?

*Available in paperback.

NINE

9

Gloria Steinem

The tall, stylishly dressed woman with long, straight brown hair and tortoise-shell glasses sat calmly, even though she was under attack by some members of the studio audience of the syndicated television "talk show" during early 1993. The host passed the microphone to a woman who confronted Gloria Steinem about "selling out the women's movement" in her recently published book, Revolution from Within: A Book of Self-Esteem. *Hoots, boos, jeers, and applause rang out from the audience. The book was, at the very least, controversial. It was also a bestseller. For that notoriety, however, Steinem had endured biting personal condemnation, ranging from accusations that she had retreated as an activist to rebukes from conservatives about the failure of the women's movement. Her personal reflections and romances, revealed in the book, were cannon fodder for critics and gossip columnists. Steinem had also included men in her analysis of self-esteem, and critics attacked this action as a capitulation merely to gain readers.*

But many people in the audience rose to support her, and Gloria Steinem made no apologies for writing what the Los Angeles Times *called "the ultimate self-help book." Answering her critics on that day as she also had in the book's afterword, Steinem explained that* Revolution from Within *strived "for inclusiveness across lines of sex and race, class, sexuality, and ability." Everyone, she argued, could benefit from introspection, from asking themselves why they did things, and "unlearning" habits that damaged their self-esteem. She told tales of empowerment, individual improvement, and hope. Her stories reflected three decades as a professional writer, and nearly as long as an icon of the women's movement in the United States. But Gloria Steinem had never been comfortable as an icon of feminism. Her childhood and career were testaments to her individuality and her commitment to the inclusion of all people in the women's rights movement—and the view that "women's liberation would mean the liberation of both sexes."*

In 1904, thirty years before Gloria Steinem's birth, her feminist grandmother wrote: "Men must acquire more of the qualities of women, and women must acquire more of the qualities of men." Pauline Perlmutter Steinem and her husband Joseph had migrated from Poland to Toledo, Ohio, in the 1880s, where Pauline became a suffragist, author, and activist in the local Jewish community. In a 1912 article entitled "Why I Am a Suffragist," Pauline argued that equality between the sexes was based on "Divine Wisdom." Gloria's father, Leo Steinem, was the fourth son of Pauline and Joseph, who had established himself as a successful businessman in

Toledo. Gloria's mother, Ruth Nuneviller, was the daughter of a railroad engineer and a teacher, both Protestants by faith. That Gloria Steinem was the child of an interfaith marriage explains in part the humanitarian causes she championed as an adult.

The Nunevillers had had high hopes for their daughter in the wake of women's suffrage and the giddy economic prospects of the 1920s. They sent Ruth to Oberlin College in Ohio—the first college to admit minorities and women along with white males. Before she could finish, however, the family had to bring her home because of financial troubles. Ruth graduated with a journalism degree from Toledo State University. While working on her degree, Ruth came to work for the school newspaper and there met its editor, Leo Steinem. Steinem was immediately drawn to the attractive and intelligent woman, and Nuneviller found Leo charming and gregarious. Their resulting romance and engagement brought hostility from both families. The Steinems condemned Leo for his desire to marry out of the faith, while members of the Nuneviller family believed Ruth would be marrying beneath her class. Such feelings did not cool their relationship, however, and in 1923 they were secretly married. When, a year later, they had a formal ceremony, some members of both families refused to attend. Two years after their secret marriage, Gloria's sister, Susanne, was born.

Leo Steinem was a fun-loving, impetuous man who had grand designs on fame and fortune in the entertainment business. He had none of his father's business sense, but even his father had lost everything in the stock market crash of 1929. This made the plight of Ruth and the irresponsible Leo even worse, for there was no family money to help them out as the Depression worsened. Ruth had worked as an editor for two Toledo newspapers before 1929, but those jobs disappeared after the crash. Leo had drifted from job to job through the 1920s; by the 1930s he was just another of the jobless millions who were pounding the pavement for work. As unemployment in the industrial town of Toledo soared past 50 percent, Leo Steinem's employment prospects dimmed further. While Leo took the hard times in stride, the insecurity proved debilitating to Ruth. In 1930, she slipped into a severe depression and was eventually hospitalized with a nervous breakdown. As Gloria remembered, Ruth's illness "followed years of trying to take care of a baby, be the wife of a kind but financially irresponsible man with show-business dreams, and still keep her much-loved job as reporter and newspaper editor."

On March 25, 1934, Gloria was born. Ruth had composed herself through pregnancy and provided adequate care for her infant daughter. But the spirit of the former career women was broken; she was unstable, and caring for Gloria and Susanne overwhelmed her. In addition, the family's financial woes continued. Leo remained an incurably optimistic dream-chaser, and was always planning new ways to strike it rich. In 1938, he converted an old lodge in Michigan, which he had bought in better times, into a summer resort. By bringing big bands there to perform for the resort guests, Leo Steinem would make his fortune. Until Gloria was ten, each summer was spent at Leo's Clark Lake Resort. The Steinems were on the road the rest of the year, living in a trailer from which Leo bought and sold antiques. Leo's get-rich-quick attitude reflected his aversion to the work-a-day world and a humdrum existence. As Gloria remembered, "He loved travel and change and uncertainty.

He never put a real bathroom or real heating in our summer place because he was afraid we'd insist on staying home during the winter."

Leo's enterprises bore little fruit. Clark Lake was never more than a moderate success, and the antique dealing produced, at best, an inconsistent income. But the Steinems were better off than millions of other Americans during the hard times of the Depression. They owned no home and therefore faced no foreclosure. Being on the road was exciting, and the resort was a pleasant place to spend summers. Still, there were disadvantages. Gloria never attended school in one place for more than a few weeks, and she was largely educated by Ruth. She had no yard to play in or friends to play with. Gloria made up for isolation by helping her mother with housework and her father with his antique business, learning to tap-dance during summers at Clark Lake, and reading everything she could get her hands on.

The Steinems' precarious lifestyle took a turn for the worse with the beginning of World War II. The frivolity of idylls at resorts became a low priority for Americans after Pearl Harbor. With fifteen million people in the armed services by the following year, much of the clientele for Clark Lake was in uniform, on domestic military bases, or in action overseas. Gas rationing was imposed by the War Production Board, and omnipresent inquiries asking, "Is this trip really necessary?" had transformed Leo Steinem's summer resort into a ghost town by 1943. To make up for the lost income at Clark Lake, Leo decided to go on the road full time, dealing antiques and leaving his family in Toledo. Susanne had gone away to college two years earlier, and only Gloria and her mother remained in Toledo. Nearly a decade on the road had been extremely hard on Ruth. Housekeeping and cooking were really beyond her capacity and, as a result, those tasks fell to ten-year-old Gloria.

World War II ended with Leo Steinem on the road, and Gloria caring for her mother. It was impossible for Gloria not to lament the stark contrast of her life in comparison to her middle-class schoolmates. With stability the paramount consideration of postwar Americans, many of the gender barriers that had been breached during the war were restored. Women, who had served in the armed forces and worked in defense plants and other industries, were now expected to return to their traditional roles in the home. With the disruptions of depression and war over, members of both sexes looked to return to traditional ways, and government and society encouraged the transformation. Congress passed the GI Bill and other federal assistance programs to pay for education and enable families to buy or build homes. Postwar advertisers promoted products that made women better housekeepers and nurturers of children. Not surprisingly, the birthrate in the United States soared to proportions not seen since the nineteenth century. Middle-class children grew up with material goods unknown to previous generations.

Middle-class comforts were well beyond Gloria Steinem's reach. For a brief time she and her mother lived in an apartment in a nice section of town, but they were later forced to move to Ruth's parents' rat-infested farmhouse in a declining neighborhood in East Toledo. They lived upstairs and rented out the downstairs as two apartments. However, when the health department condemned their furnace, the renters disappeared, and Gloria and Ruth lived alone, without heat, through the cold winters of northeastern Ohio. Although doctors treated Ruth's depression with powerful tranquilizers, she nonetheless suffered spells of severe depression and delusions. The drugs often made her drowsy and sometimes incoherent. Gloria therefore had to care for her increasingly dependent mother, maintain a household on a shoestring budget, and attend school. To earn extra money, she tap-danced at a men's fraternal organization called the Eagles Club in Toledo on Saturday nights, earning ten dollars for two shows. She also worked part time after school selling clothes at a local department store.

To cope with her troubles, Gloria fantasized that she had been adopted, and that her real parents would some day come to rescue her. She also dreamed that her dancing skills would eventually bring her out of poverty; she would become a New York City Rockette, find the right man, and marry well. Such thoughts helped sustain her through junior high and most of high school. Before her senior year in high school, however, family members came to Gloria's rescue. Her sister, Susanne, now working in Washington, DC, persuaded Leo Steinem to take Ruth to California to live with him for a year even though they had earlier divorced. Leo acquiesced, grudgingly agreeing that Gloria deserved "at least one year of normal high school experience."

As a result of the agreement, Gloria spent her senior year living with her sister and two friends in a rented house in Washington, DC, where she attended a local high school. The hardships and fear of the last seven years were now a memory; she lived in a stable, clean home, attended a good school, enjoyed free time, and had some spending money. Her high school was highly intellectual in comparison to the one in Toledo, and Gloria marveled at the boys and the girls who read and spoke their minds. Although her overall school record was less than stellar considering her educational background, Gloria had been an avid reader throughout those years. She scored in the highest percentiles on her college placement exams and was able to qualify for a number of colleges. Her choice was one of the best women's institutions in the nation, Smith College in Northampton, Massachusetts. When her mother learned of Gloria's choice, she agreed to sell the farmhouse in Toledo to help with Gloria's college expenses.

In the fall of 1952, Gloria Steinem traveled to Massachusetts to begin her studies at Smith. It was a dream come true. Regular meals, warm clothes, schoolwork, and a social life seemed all a person could or should ever want. A part-time job as a waitress and full-time work in the summers seemed a small price to pay for attending college. Steinem reveled in her good fortune, and her warm personality and good looks made her popular among her fellow students and young men from neighboring colleges. Majoring in government, Steinem excelled in writing and foreign policy studies. Skilled female professors convinced her that she could use her mind for success. And success would enable her to escape the terror that still haunted her: being forced back into poverty and caring for her sick mother in East Toledo. She did not waste the opportunity at Smith College, graduating *magna cum laude* and being elected to the Phi Beta Kappa scholastic honor society.

As a female college graduate in 1956, Gloria Steinem had limited horizons. She had gone against the trend of the day by majoring in government when most of her wealthy peers had studied art or English. Like most female students of the 1950s, Smith graduates generally majored in fields that would make them better wives—not competitors for jobs. The traditionalism of the postwar years had effectively taken women out of the workplace and put them back into the home. As in the Victorian era, most women of the 1950s went to college to become school-teachers or charming, talented, and educated wives. In many ways, the 1950s saw a revival of the "cult of domesticity" celebrating the importance of homemaking. But pressures for conformity to tradition were even stronger than before. Images of perfect housewives such as June Cleaver and Harriet Nelson appeared nightly on the omnipresent television.

The career world Gloria Steinem entered on graduation seemed confusing, stultifying, and unfair. She questioned why barriers, both legal and cultural, were put up against women in their careers. Her sentiments were shared by an increasing number of women during the 1950s. One was Simone de Beauvoir, who published *The Second Sex* in France in 1953. According to de Beauvoir, contemporary society viewed women as the inferior gender, a "second sex": "Man never thinks of himself without thinking of the Other. . . . But being different from man, who sets himself up as the Same, it is naturally to the category of the Other that woman is consigned." De Beauvoir advocated liberation for women throughout the world from this "yoke of oppression."

Ten years after the publication of *The Second Sex*, a Smith College graduate shocked the nation with her book, *The Feminine Mystique*. Selling over one million copies following its publication in 1963, Betty Friedan's book reviewed the status of women in American society during the twentieth century. Friedan was among the first to postulate that women's rights had peaked in 1920 with the ratification of the Nineteenth Amendment to the Constitution guaranteeing women the vote. Friedan believed that the women's movement had exhausted itself in gaining the vote and then had declined. She pointed out, for example, that the proportion of women attending colleges had dropped from 47 percent of the total student population in 1920 to 35 percent by the mid-1950s. The number of women earning graduate degrees and entering the professions had also declined. There seemed to have been a marked shift in female aspirations, particularly after World War II. By then, Friedan argued, increasing numbers of American women had subscribed to a "mystique of feminine fulfillment" centered on husbands, homes, and families. By the end of the 1950s the average age at which American women married was barely twenty and dropping. Fourteen million girls were engaged by age seventeen. Understandably, the birthrate rose. College women of Steinem's generation were looking for the "right man," and the lucky ones wore engagement rings by their junior year in college.

In 1957, Gloria Steinem faced the housewife trap that Friedan later publicized. She had dated frequently in college and had met a newspaper reporter from New York to whom she became engaged. Shortly after graduation, she discovered she was pregnant. Her fiancé wanted to marry her right away to "legitimize" the union and the baby, but Steinem resisted. She did not want to fall into the "feminine mystique" of domesticity and motherhood yet, and was not really sure she loved her fiancé. Her decision, one that would later bring her into the women's liberation movement, was to travel to England and have a legal abortion rather than risk having an illegal "back-alley" abortion in the United States.

During her senior year at Smith, Steinem won a two-year fellowship to study in India. After breaking off her engagement and having an abortion which was, at that time, considered a shameful act, traveling to a different part of the world to live for two years was a welcome event. The experience in India broadened her understanding of the world and its problems. She saw unbelievable poverty, walked and talked with Indian people, and experienced how women were treated in other societies. After living in India, the United States appeared to her to be "an enormous frosted cupcake in the middle of millions of starving poor."

During her two years in India, Steinem kept a diary and, on her return to the United States, tried to find a market for her recollections. She was certain she wanted to become a professional writer—a political writer who would tell the American public about what was happening in Asia. Steinem moved to New York City and began pounding the pavement to find publishers for her work. But the year was 1958, and Steinem was doubly disadvantaged. Magazines were simply not interested in depressing articles about world poverty; neither were they receptive to buying the work of a "girl writer." Frustrated, she left New York to work for the Independent Research Service in Cambridge, Massachusetts, only to return in 1961 to pursue her writing career again. In the wake of the election of John F. Kennedy, Steinem, like so many other young and idealistic Americans, believed that better times were ahead. After campaigning for Kennedy, she moved into a one-room Manhattan apartment with a friend and struggled to find anything resembling journalistic work. Her first job came late in 1961, when she took on most of the editorial duties of the humor magazine *Help*, an offshoot of the satirical *Mad* magazine. At *Help*, Steinem learned the basics of producing a magazine, and at the same time developed a humorous writing style. In the meantime she continued to seek freelance work and, in 1962, published her first signed article, "The Moral Disarmament of Betty Coed," in the men's magazine *Esquire*. The article explored recent advances in birth control, including oral contraceptives, and their effect on American society. While she applauded the new freedom that birth control gave women, she also cautioned that such sexual freedom might have a negative impact on many women. "The real danger of the contraceptive revolution," she concluded, "may be the acceleration of woman's role-change without any corresponding change of man's attitude toward her role." As the women's rights movement advanced, Steinem's predictions rang true in more ways than she could then imagine.

Despite this well-received article, Steinem still struggled to obtain work as a writer in the man's world of New York journalism. Assignments were scarce, as men doubted any woman's ability to cover hard news stories. As a result, Steinem had to take what was offered. In 1963, for example, she agreed to take on an assignment proposed by the editor of *Show* magazine. Steinem agreed to use a fake identity in the New York City Playboy Club and attempt to secure a job as a Playboy Bunny. The *Show* editor hoped that the attractive Steinem could "get inside" the Playboy Club and work there long enough to learn about the real life of a Bunny. In the 1960s, Hugh Hefner's Playboy empire was riding a crest of immense success. Since the first issue of the "men's magazine" *Playboy* in 1953, the Playboy enterprises had grown dramatically. The monthly magazine featured articles for men ranging from style guides on clothing and cars to enhancement of sexual performance. Sexual jokes and explicit photographs of young, attractive women highlighted the issues. The Playboy phenomenon had given Hefner a legitimacy unknown among other "girly magazine" publishers.

By the 1960s, the Hefner enterprise was so successful it had begun establishing Playboy Clubs in major cities throughout the nation. The clubs offered food, drink, and entertainment—the entertainment primarily being the Playboy Bunnies, young women clad in tight-fitting costumes with cottontails, three-inch high heels, copious amounts of makeup and false eyelashes, and rabbit ears. Gloria Steinem walked into the New York City Playboy Club on January 26, 1963, posing as Marie Catherine Ochs, and answering an advertisement that stated, "Attractive young girls can now earn $200–$300 a week at the fabulous New York Playboy Club, enjoy the exciting aura of show business, and have the opportunity to travel to other Playboy Clubs throughout the world."

Steinem carefully chronicled her experiences as she was interviewed, persevered in her false identity, and acquired the job as a Bunny. For the next three weeks, she served in various roles at the Playboy Club, including as a hatcheck girl and a cocktail waitress. The two-part article that resulted in *Show* was entitled "A Bunny's Tale." The immensely clever piece revealed Steinem's skill with words, as well as her sense of humor and objectivity in dealing with matters with which she disagreed. Recalling a costume interview for which she had donned a tight-fitting blue satin swimsuitlike outfit, she wrote, "A blue satin band with matching Bunny ears attached was fitted around my head like an enlarged bicycle clip, and a grapefruit-sized hemisphere of white fluff was attached at the costume's rear-most point. . . . I looked in the mirror. The Bunny image looked back." Steinem wrote of the job in unglamorous terms: of standing at the front door of the club in her Bunny costume in the cold February night; of being on her feet for eight hours without a break, lugging heavy platters of food in three-inch high heels; of enduring the nightly "If you're my Bunny, can I take you home?" comments; and of never coming close to making the wages that had been promised in the ad.

When the article appeared, Steinem became known throughout New York. Yet it was the kind of recognition she quickly came to regret. Editors refused to take her seriously, even though the article was a veiled statement for women workers' rights, as well as a condemnation of the Playboy façade of gentility. Instead, "A Bunny's Tale" became known as "a sexy article." For several years afterward Steinem received no "hard" news assignments and was relegated to writing human interest and women's stories for magazines like *Glamour*. In 1964, she became a contributing editor to and even posed for a pictorial essay in *Glamour*. With the publication of her study on sun worshiping called *The Beach Book*, Steinem seemed far away indeed from becoming a writer on political and gender issues, and well on the road to being a well-known New York personality with an active and highly publicized social life.

While Steinem proceeded though what she remembered as "the low point of [her] writing life," world and personal events swirled around her. The assassination of her hero, John Kennedy, occurred only one year after her father had died in an automobile accident. The war in Southeast Asia continued to escalate, and the black civil rights movement grew angrier. In 1963, President Kennedy's Commission on the Status of Women, chaired by Eleanor Roosevelt, issued its report on the many inequities that American women faced. With the proceeds from *The Feminine Mystique*, Betty Friedan founded the National Organization for Women (NOW) in 1966. Its original mission statement declared "that women . . . are human beings,

Gloria Steinem (alias Marie Ochs) is photographed while on duty as a cocktail waitress in the New York City Playboy Club. She later published an exposé of the experience entitled "A Bunny's Tale."

who, like all other people in our society, must have the chance to develop their fullest human potential." The following year, NOW issued its Bill of Rights, which outlined the general demands of feminism, including an equal rights constitutional amendment, effective laws banning sexual discrimination in employment, maternity leave rights, tax deductions for child care for working parents, child-care centers, equal educational and job-training opportunities, and the right of women to control their reproductive lives. With the formation of NOW, the modern women's movement had an institutional base.

The modern feminist movement was well timed. The civil rights movement had imprinted the politics of inclusion on the public mind. President Kennedy had been receptive, and his successor, Lyndon B. Johnson, although probably not himself a feminist, was steeped in the tradition of New Deal liberalism and social activism. Following his landslide victory over Republican Barry Goldwater in 1964, Johnson unveiled a domestic program to bring forth a "great society" in the United States. Johnson had faith in the ability of government to improve society through active policies aimed at economic stimulus, equality of opportunity for all people, and a variety of social safety nets for the elderly and the underprivileged. A progressive tax cut in 1964 stimulated the economy to full employment, and thereafter Johnson set out to reform society with a goal of making the United States an example of democracy to the world. Johnson declared a War on Poverty and planned to spend a billion dollars to clean up the nation's slums and assist the poor. His administration secured passage of Medicare and Medicaid, providing federal funding for health care to the elderly and the impoverished. Johnson launched a new program of public works, sponsored research-and-development acts, and funded a greatly expanded higher education program.

Both Kennedy and Johnson indirectly aided women's rights by championing civil rights legislation. With the help of traditional women's organizations such as the League of Women Voters and the General Federation of Women's Clubs, significant measures became law. In 1963, Congress passed the Equal Pay Act (a part of the Civil Rights Act of 1964) banning gender-based discrimination in employment. In 1965 and 1967, Johnson signed executive orders that made discrimination in employment under federal contracts illegal. Meanwhile, during the mid-1960s, several state-level conferences on the status of women convened. A robust economy and a low unemployment rate contributed to the increasing sense of optimism among women's groups.

Changing social conditions were partly responsible for the acceleration of the feminist movement. So were technological breakthroughs. In addition to birth control, which lowered the birthrate and gave women new control over having children, labor-saving devices continued to proliferate, allowing women more time to join the work force. From 1950 to 1970, the female labor force doubled, most of that increase coming during the 1960s. Women were increasingly independent, marrying later, divorcing more often, and increasingly willing to participate in movements that enhanced their position in society.

Although Gloria Steinem was aware of the feminist movement, she remained on its periphery until late in the decade. Still being ignored by publishers when it came to serious news, Steinem made her living writing about traditional subjects such as fashion and cooking. Through such work, however, and through the political satire she wrote for the network television comedy series *That Was the Week That Was*, Steinem refined her writing style. Conducting interviews with authors such as James Baldwin, Dorothy Parker, and Truman Capote, she expanded her listening skills and became better at drawing out information.

Steinem, who had tried to publish material on world poverty since the mid-1950s, remained keenly interested in the social issues of the day. She served as a campaign volunteer for several liberal politicians, including Senator George McGovern of South Dakota. As the election of 1968 loomed ahead—an election inextricably tied to the Vietnam War—Steinem and her friend Clay Felker founded *New York* magazine. Steinem wrote a column titled "The City Politic" and began to cover the political topics she had so long wished to do. Steinem went on the presidential campaign trail and conducted interviews with Democrats Eugene McCarthy and Robert Kennedy, as well as a contentious interview with Pat Nixon, in which the future first lady essentially called Steinem and the generation of protesters spoiled, indulged, and coddled.

Sometimes, Steinem's political activism was costly to her writing career. She lost her position as an editorial consultant for *Seventeen* magazine for serving as treasurer of a committee to raise funds for the defense of black radical UCLA professor Angela Davis. Davis, an avowed Communist, had been charged with kidnapping and murder in connection with a 1969 courtroom jail-break by black militants in Marin County, California. Davis was later acquitted of the charges. As the Vietnam War heated up, Steinem, who had long believed the nation was involving itself in an intractable civil war, joined in the active protest. On the occasion of Neil Armstrong's walk on the moon in July 1969, Steinem commented that the United

States was "not unlike fifteenth century Spain—discovering a new world on the one hand and conducting an inquisition (Vietnam) on the other."

The feminist career of Gloria Steinem also took shape in the late 1960s. While her work up to that time in high-fashion magazines might even be called antifeminist (Steinem herself called it "schizophrenic"), she was never unsympathic to feminism. She had experienced discrimination in trying to be a writer in a male-dominated literary world, and she had been forced to adapt to make a living. Yet her journalistic interest in feminism did not arise until 1968, when she was assigned by *New York* magazine to attend a meeting of a feminist group in Manhattan called the Redstockings. Named after a nineteenth-century French radical women's group called the Bluestockings, the Redstockings were representative of groups consisting of younger people who believed in implementing more radical measures than NOW advocated. The subject of this meeting aroused emotions that Steinem had buried for more than a decade. Woman after woman arose to tell her story of obtaining illegal "back-alley" abortions in the United States. Painfully, Steinem recalled her own experience of traveling to England for an abortion in the 1950s and realized that she could no longer bury the incident in her subconscious. Without reproductive freedom, Steinem now believed, women would always be "second-class citizens." And like minorities, women were oppressed as a group. Therefore, they needed to act as a group to end oppression.

With the revelations gained from her encounters with the Redstockings and other feminist groups, Gloria Steinem began to pour her literary talents into the women's rights movement. She did this, her male editors warned, at the risk of ruining her career. In their view, her strength was that she wrote on popular subjects, and that she "wrote like a man." Why, they asked, was she taking such an interest in "those crazy women" when she had such a bright future in conventional journalism? But Steinem would not be deterred, and Clay Felker, her editor-in-chief at *New York*, endorsed her activism. Steinem's first feminist article, "After Black Power, Women's Liberation," appeared in *New York* in April 1969. The theme of the article was that American women had fought for civil rights and other causes in recent years; now it was time to fight for themselves. She pointed out how women had worked in the civil rights and antiwar movements only to be dismissed as sex objects by men. Bobby Seale had said that the position of women in the Black Power movement was "prone," and draft evaders would be rewarded in the slogan: "Girls say yes to boys who say no." Steinem exhorted women of all ages and all socioeconomic classes to join the battle to end discrimination in the workplace, at home, in education, and in financial matters. The award-winning article indicated that Steinem could have a successful career as a feminist writer and devote her energy to writing for that cause.

Like other social justice movements, the women's rights movement had turned more radical by the late 1960s. As women began to analyze their role in the civil rights movement, they drew parallels with the efforts of female abolitionists of the nineteenth century. Again, women had worked to advance the civil rights of another group while their own civil rights were limited. By the late 1960s, unmet promises, doubt in government, unrealistic expectations, and escalation of the unpopular Vietnam War began to overshadow the achievements of Lyndon Johnson's domestic activism, and to accentuate radical views. Young blacks became weary of waiting for Martin Luther King, Jr.'s peaceful protest to affect their lives; young males of all races faced service in Vietnam; and women's groups found that discrimination continued despite legislation outlawing it. Overt demonstrations for women's rights took many forms. In August 1968, for example, women held a demonstration at the Miss America Beauty Pageant. Protesting its emphasis on women's figures, smiles, and "charm," at the alternative pageant they staged the crowning of a live sheep as "Miss America." Women also made headlines by filling a "freedom trashcan" with undergarments, hair curlers, and issues of the *Ladies' Home Journal* and *Playboy*. In public demonstrations women burned the brassieres they regarded as implements of male domination. In 1969, Kate Millett published *Sexual Politics*, which characterized the organized tyranny of male-dominated culture over women by analyzing the writings of male authors such as Henry Miller, D. H. Lawrence, and Norman Mailer.

As the 1970s began, Gloria Steinem was poised to be a leader of the women's liberation movement. A talented writer, well-known personality, and political analyst, Steinem "the feminist" was now in great demand by women's groups. Yet one more obstacle had to be overcome: her lifelong fear of public speaking. Learning to live with the butterflies and nausea, Steinem accepted the challenge of speaking out for women's rights and began traveling the country on speaking tours. In 1970, she appeared prominently with 50,000 others in a "Women Strike for Equality" march in New York. She carried a grisly photograph from the 1968 My Lai massacre in Vietnam containing the caption, "The Masculine Mystique." Steinem was featured on the covers of several magazines, including *McCall's*, which named her woman of the year, and *Newsweek*, where she was identified in an accompanying article as the "New Woman." In 1971 Steinem cofounded the Women's Action Alliance, a national clearinghouse for information on women's issues, and, along with Betty Friedan and New York congresswomen Bella Abzug and Shirley Chisholm, she founded the National Women's Political Caucus. In 1972, Steinem shook off a new level of stage fright and addressed the Democratic National Convention on behalf of the National Women's Political Caucus.

Because of the strength of the new feminist movement, Gloria Steinem and other feminist writers believed it was time for the creation of a magazine devoted solely to women's issues. However, funding for a women's magazine that covered issues rather than "101 [ways to make] hamburger" was not forthcoming. Editors and publishers continued to doubt that any great interest would be generated by a feminist magazine. Finally, *New York* magazine editor Clay Felker agreed to publish a trial issue of such a magazine as a part of *New York*'s year-end double issue. In December 1971, the first issue of *Ms.* magazine appeared on newsstands as a part of *New York*. The title of the magazine reflected its prevailing egalitarian point of view: If men are "Mr." regardless of their marital status, women, too, should have such a title, rather than "Miss" or "Mrs." (Later that year, Webster's Dictionary listed *Ms.*, and in 1973 the U.S. Government Printing Office gave official recognition to the term.) As a founding editor, Gloria Steinem wrote an article entitled "Sisterhood" that set the tone for the premier issue. "Women are human beings first," she wrote, "with minor differences from men that apply largely to the single act of reproduction. We share the dreams, capabilities, and weaknesses of all human beings." Other articles ranged from an analysis of credit discrimination to a blistering protest against the Vietnam War. Despite being a magazine with an agenda, Ms. used humor to make its point, such as in its "feminist rating" of the presidential candidates in 1972. In a few weeks, every issue of Ms. was sold, and people clamored for more. The editors of Ms., including Steinem, Letty Cottin Pogrebin, Joanne Edgar, Mary Peacock, and Nina Finklestein, went on a nationwide promotion tour, only to find Ms. sold out and unavailable in most locations.

Perhaps the most controversial article appearing in the first issue of Ms. contained a list of prominent women who had had abortions. Earlier in the year, Steinem had circulated a petition to women's groups, and those who signed it agreed to go public in Ms. with their stories. The petition, which included Steinem's name, demanded that the government repeal restrictive laws against abortion. Only one year later, the U.S. Supreme Court reached a decision on a challenge to state abortion laws in Texas and Georgia in the case of *Roe v. Wade*. Determining that the Texas laws violated a woman's right to privacy, the Court ruled seven to two that choosing an abortion during the first three months of pregnancy was to be the decision of a woman and her physician. Placing the argument in the context of doctor–patient confidentiality was not the affirmation of reproductive rights that feminists wanted, but nonetheless, the states could no longer prohibit abortions in the first trimester of pregnancy. Legal abortions now existed throughout the United States, and feminist groups celebrated what they believed was the end of restrictions on women's reproductive lives.

The modern feminist movement reached its zenith during the 1970s. Powerful feminist literature such as Shulamith Firestone's *Dialectic of Sex: The Case for Feminist Revolution* (1970) bolstered the movement and shaped the thinking of many young intellectuals. A founder of the Redstockings movement, Firestone placed the feminist revolution in the context of Marxism and argued that the socialist revolution that Marx and Engels predicted would be an incomplete one. Instead, a gender-based revolution would truly change humanity. Turning the normal male–female relationship on its ear, Firestone called for an end to "the tyranny of the biological family." Simply because the biological family of nurturing mothers and bread-winning fathers was natural, she argued, it was "not necessarily human." The human race had overcome many aspects of nature; the biological family should be another. Firestone foresaw a world in which children were born in test tubes and raised by society at large, rather than by individual parents. Robin Morgan, later a coeditor of Ms., identified a host of inequities that society took for granted in *Sisterhood Is Powerful* (1970). *Male chauvinism* and *sexism* became part of the public lexicon, women entered graduate schools and were elected to public office in unprecedented numbers, and female athletes such as tennis players Billie Jean King and Chris Evert Lloyd became national celebrities. In 1971, King became the first female athlete to earn more than $100,000 in a single year. Meanwhile, slogans like "Wages for Housework," "Every Mother Is a Working Mother," and "Equal Pay for Equal Work" began to tear at the social fabric of traditional American society.

Gloria Steinem continued to advance the issues of feminism through her writing, during several national speaking tours, and through frequent appearances on television and radio. While the Vietnam War dragged on, Ms. kept up pressure for its end and averred that, if women were in power, there would have been no such war. During the Watergate crisis, the magazine was among the first to call for Richard Nixon's resignation. Ms. also advocated the passage of pending federal legislation, including Title IX of the Education Amendments of 1972 and the Equal Credit Opportunity Act of 1974. Title IX, as it came to be known, prohibited sex discrimination in education, including athletics, and the Equal Credit Opportunity Act banned discrimination against borrowers based on sex. The passage of such acts was a reflection of the strength of the women's movement, and of the growing political acumen of feminists. Women's organizations such as NOW were becoming adept at lobbying Congress. By 1978, NOW's membership had risen to 125,000, with 700 chapters in every state in the union. The organization's mouthpiece to members of Congress and people across the nation was often Ms. magazine.

The women's movement in the United States was having worldwide impact during the 1970s. The United Nations (UN) declared 1975 the International Year of the Woman. Steinem, who attended the international conference held in Mexico City, was the only Western journalist invited to this meeting for developing countries. In the same year, President Gerald Ford signed legislation authorizing the creation of a National Commission on the Observance of the International Year of the Woman, and directing the commission to organize a National Women's Conference.

The election of Democrat Jimmy Carter to the presidency in 1976 was cause for guarded optimism on the part of women's groups. Although as a born-again Southern Baptist he was morally opposed to abortion, the new president seemed sympathetic to women's rights in general. Shortly after his election, he appointed Gloria Steinem as a commissioner to the National Women's Conference to be held in Houston, Texas, in November 1977. Two thousand delegates from every state and territory in the union and more than 20,000 guests sat down at what was called a "constitutional convention" for American women. Two months before the conference, a lighted torch was passed from hand to hand on a 2,600-mile trek from Seneca Falls, New York (the birthplace of the nineteenth-century women's movement) to Houston. As the torchbearers made their way to Houston, they were joined by Olympic athletes, politicians, and conference organizers. At the conference, the torch was held jointly by Bella Abzug, the principal organizer of the conference, and first ladies Lady Bird Johnson, Betty Ford, and Rosalyn Carter.

The optimism and force of the conference resulted in the adoption of a twenty-six-plank National Plan of Action that was presented to President Carter in March 1978. Among the issues raised were the absence of women in the nation's foreign policymaking, a protest of media stereotypes of women, special attention to the plight of minority and elderly women, a plea for the absolute protection of reproductive freedom, and the elimination of discrimination against homosexuals. A compendium of the conference was published in 1979 under the title *What Women Want*. Gloria Steinem, who wrote the introductory statement in the book, stressed the unity of the diverse women who had attended the conference, and she minimized the contentiousness in the planks regarding sexuality and reproduction. "These issues of such importance to women's lives and survival," she wrote, "were brought out into the open in Houston, and recognized as fundamental to women's self-determination. . . . Houston symbolized an end to much of the split between the younger or more radical feminists . . . and . . . older, more conservative women."

Steinem's viewpoint reflected her belief that all women must be included in the movement, but her optimism veiled deep rifts developing among feminists. The "older, more conservative women" included Betty Friedan, who charged that people like Steinem were endorsing viewpoints that were "offensive" to mainstream Americans and thereby retarding the movement toward women's rights. Friedan was primarily referring to the endorsement of lesbianism, but other issues of sexuality were becoming politically charged and simmering for a later day. In the late 1970s, however, there seemed no limit to the realization of women's rights. The Pregnancy Disability Act of 1978, for example, overturned a Supreme Court ruling that upheld a company's right to deny a pregnant woman disability benefits, and it anticipated the passage of the Family Leave Act in 1993.

The centerpiece of the women's rights movement in the 1970s was the Equal Rights Amendment (ERA). First introduced by the National Woman's Party in the 1920s, the ERA stated simply, "Equality of Rights under the Law shall not be denied or abridged by the United States or any State on the basis of sex." In 1972, both houses of Congress approved the revived amendment and sent it to the states for ratification. Between 1972 and 1974, thirty-four states ratified the ERA, and only four more were needed to make it law by the ratification deadline of 1979. But thereafter state ratification bogged down, and not even the momentum of the National Women's Conference compelled more than one state, Indiana, to endorse the ERA after 1974. Gloria Steinem believed that the impasse could be attributed to a lack of "investigative report[ing] on what the ERA will and will not do." While that was certainly a factor, other causes could be identified, including a concerted effort in pivotal states like Virginia and Illinois to defeat the ERA. In both states, legislators narrowly defeated the amendment amid intense lobbying by both sides. Conservatives, who worried about the ERA destroying the American home, also feared additional federal intrusion into their private lives and formed coalitions in all states that had not ratified the amendment, knowing they needed to defeat the ERA in all but three of the remaining states. Women's groups staged a march on Washington, DC, in July 1978 to garner support for the ERA. The organizers chose the ninth of July for the march, the birthday of suffragist Alice Paul. It attracted about 100,000 enthusiastic supporters. While the march failed to break the deadlock on the ERA, its organizers were successful in their secondary goal of extending the deadline for ratification to 1982.

Another factor contributing to the impasse over the ERA was the economy of the late 1970s. The modern feminist movement had been born in the early 1960s, a time of rising economic expectations and strong public response to social and environmental issues. In the wake of the Vietnam War and the Arab oil embargo of 1973, however, "pocketbook issues" had come to dominate the public mind. The Nixon, Ford, and Carter administrations all battled inflation caused primarily by rising oil prices. At times, the inflation rate exceeded 10 percent annually, and interest rates soared to 20 percent as the Federal Reserve Board attempted to slow the inflationary spiral. Jobs became more scarce, and layoffs increased. An amendment that would grant absolute equality in the workplace now appeared to be a threat to many men.

Economic issues in general overshadowed many of the demands being made by women's groups in the late 1970s. The Carter administration also foundered in the shoals of the struggling economy. However, foreign affairs dealt the final blow to the Carter presidency. In the Middle East, Iran exploded into revolution in the late 1970s; the pro-Western shah Muhammed Reza Pahlavi was deposed, and an Islamic fundamentalist, the Ayatollah Ruholla Khomeini, came into power. In November 1979, Iranian students stormed the American embassy, took fifty-two hostages, and held them captive until 1981. The daily spectacle of Americans held hostage dominated the nightly news. Carter's moment of triumph in bringing together Egyptian president Anwar Sadat and Israeli prime minister Menachem Begin to sign the 1979 Camp David peace accords was clearly overshadowed by events in Iran. One month after the hostages had been taken in Iran, the Soviet Union invaded the central Asian nation of Afghanistan. Protesting the invasion, Carter imposed a boycott of American participation in the Olympic Games to be held in Moscow in 1980. The boycott was extremely unpopular in the United States, especially among the athletes who were to participate in the games. To make matters even worse for President Carter, Massachusetts senator Edward Kennedy challenged him for the Democratic presidential nomination in 1980. His vigorous and often abusive campaign destroyed whatever unity Carter had been able to maintain among Democrats. But questionable incidents in Kennedy's past denied him the nomination. The Democratic party reluctantly renominated Carter.

Women's groups were generally disappointed by Carter's performance. In a 1978 issue of *Ms.*, Gloria Steinem wrote an article entitled "Will Women Make Carter a One-Term President?": "If 1980 brings enough disillusionment with Carter . . . women are less likely to vote for someone else (or indeed, to have someone better on women's issues to vote for) than we are to return to our old form of protest: just staying away from the polls." Steinem criticized Carter for endorsing the ERA only to women's groups, for appointing few individuals who cared about women's rights, and for being "almost completely closed-minded" concerning abortion. For feminists, the Carter record did not improve by 1980. Carter's moral opposition to abortion continued throughout his presidency even though he did not support a proposed constitutional amendment banning it. Still, he refused to endorse federal funding for abortions, and despite his overall support of women's rights, feminists, like most Democrats, were lukewarm toward the Georgian throughout his term. Made irate by Carter's "prolife" stance (a description based on the argument that an unborn fetus is a human life), Gloria Steinem and other feminists cofounded Voters for Choice in 1979. Despite Senator Kennedy's past, they supported him over Carter because of his "prochoice" stance (a description based on the *Roe v. Wade* decision, which says that a woman can choose whether or not to terminate her pregancy during the first trimester). After Carter's renomination, their support shifted to the third-party prochoice candidate, John Anderson.

By not supporting Carter enthusiastically, Steinem and other feminists virtually ensured the election of Republican candidate Ronald Reagan. The sixty-nine-year-old former actor and former New Deal Democrat (and later a Republican governor of California) took many advantages into the 1980 election. Not only were the Democrats split and in disarray, but the moderate Republican Anderson only succeeded in taking votes away from Carter. Moreover, as a hero of western movies and a proponent of making the United States "stand tall again," Reagan appealed to a growing bipartisan conservative trend. His declaration that "government is not the solution. . . . Government is the problem," took direct aim at the regulatory and social welfare apparatus that had been built over the past few decades. In the 1980 election, Reagan trounced Carter, while Republicans reclaimed control of the Senate and slashed the huge Democratic majority in the House. Several key members of Congress who supported women's rights, including George McGovern and Birch Bayh, were swept away by conservative, anti-ERA, prolife advocates. To "get the government off the people's backs," Reagan appointed many department heads whose objectives were to reduce the activities of the agencies they administered, and to cut the social programs that had grown since the days of the Great Society.

In one area of government, however, Reagan favored broad expansion. Defense spending rose dramatically, increasing several percentage points as a total of the budget each year from 1981 to 1989. The 1988 defense budget was over $330 billion. Making the United States stand tall again was expensive. But Reagan was determined to spend the Soviet Union, which he regarded as "an evil empire," into poverty by forcing the Soviets to keep up with the U.S. military buildup. American military involvement increased all over the globe, and especially in Central America. In addition to an overt invasion of the tiny Caribbean island of Grenada to free it of "leftist thugs," in Reagan's words, the Reagan administration oversaw covert operations against socialist insurgents in El Salvador and against the Soviet-backed Sandinista government in Nicaragua. The secret mining of Nicaraguan harbors in 1984, a violation of the War Powers Act of 1973, earned the United States the condemnation of the World Court.

Reagan's election sent shock waves through the women's rights movement. It was almost inconceivable that the public favored a return to what Reagan wanted, which, in Steinem's words, was "a gun in every holster, a pregnant woman in every home." Feminists found little encouraging about First Lady Nancy Reagan either. While it would later be revealed that she had had considerable influence over her husband's decisions as president, her overt actions suggested that Nancy Reagan had been forged in the traditional mold of a Mamie Eisenhower or a Pat Nixon. The women's movement faced a severe challenge from the so-called "New Right" as well. Opposed to abortion, the ERA, social programs, and the ban on prayer in public schools, groups such as the Moral Majority led by Reverend Jerry Falwell, the "Praise the Lord" Club led by Pat Robertson, the Conservative Caucus, the National Conservative Political Action Committee (NCPAC), and the Heritage Foundation began to flex their muscles with the election of 1980. The Eagle Forum posed a female-based threat to the ERA. Its founder, Phyllis Schlafly, traveled around the country speaking out against the "antifamily" ERA, claiming it would create a "unisex society." On March 22, 1979, Schlafly hosted a victory party in Washington celebrating the "End of an ERA" when the amendment failed to be ratified by the first deadline. Schlafly's message reached both men and women who worried about the sweeping social changes taking place before them. By 1982, it was clear that the ERA would not be ratified by the new deadline.

Gloria Steinem's response to the New Right was to continue advocating women's issues. The decade she had spent as an activist had been a blur. Her speaking engagements, editorial duties, and lobbying had kept her on the road almost constantly. She still made her residence in a one-room apartment in Manhattan but was rarely at home. Her social life was more disjointed than it had been in the 1960s, when her engagement to another writer ended because neither of them could find the time to get married. During the latter part of the 1960s and into the 1970s, Steinem dated a number of well-known and often wealthy men, and her social life was a matter of public record. This became a point of contention for some radical feminists, who questioned why "the pretty one" was so often the spokesperson for a movement in part opposed to female adornment for the benefit of men. Some charged that she was in the movement only for riches and fame. Such charges hurt Steinem more than attacks from conservatives or from more traditional members of the women's movement. Yet she defiantly refused to "put on combat boots or cut off [her] hair" and denied that she had become wealthy from her activism. This was a true statement. Her income as an editor for Ms. was modest since much of the magazine's proceeds went to support the Ms. Foundation and the publication itself. And, like her father, Gloria had never managed her money well.

Anticipating the negative reaction to the women's movement so evident by the early 1980s, Steinem repeated the theme again and again: "Women's liberation will be men's liberation too." Just as the slave-and-master relationship had diminished both groups, the male-dominant patriarchal system hurt both men and women. Steinem knew that without widespread male support through "consciousness raising," the women's movement would suffer additional setbacks. She refined such arguments during a welcome one-year fellowship with the Woodrow Wilson Center for Scholars at the Smithsonian Institution in 1978. Five years later, many of her writings were published in updated form as a book entitled *Outrageous Acts and Everyday Rebellions*. According to Steinem, outrageous acts and everyday rebellions could be anything from a march on Washington to a housewife's leaving a husband's or a child's mess untouched until the husband or child cleaned it up. The subjects of the essays covered a broad spectrum of gender issues, some of which enraged radical feminists, others of which enraged conservative men and women. Steinem told of returning to a 1981 reunion at Smith College to be asked by some schoolmates why she was still thin, and of marching in a parade in which she and others who hoped to carry openly feminist signs were asked by the same classmates to remain at the back of the proceedings. She included essays on several women, including Marilyn Monroe, Jacqueline Kennedy Onassis, African-American author Alice Walker, and pornography star Linda Lovelace. In each essay, Steinem told sympathetic stories of these women that went beyond what the media had chosen to report. Another article, entitled "Ruth's Song (Because She Could Not Sing It)," was about her mother, who had died in 1981. Although Ruth had recovered considerably, she had still suffered long-term depression until her death. The story revealed as much about Gloria Steinem as it did about her mother.

Other portions of *Outrageous Acts* provided ample evidence of the raw nerve that the women's rights movement had irritated during the 1970s and early 1980s. While hardly the most radical of feminists, Steinem was a lightning rod because of her prominent role. Conservative cartoonist Al Capp, for example, called her the "Shirley Temple of the New Left" and likened her to serial killer Richard Speck. Later, Speck, who had murdered eight women in 1966, was interviewed from prison. During the course of the interview, Speck expressed regret that not all the women he had killed were "like Gloria Steinem." She told of another man who had condemned her feminism as a disloyalty to "God, Man, and Country," and of *Screw* magazine, which had pornographically portrayed a naked female body with Steinem's head.

Gloria Steinem and other feminists watched as the New Right gathered momentum for the presidential election of 1984. There was little doubt who would be renominated on the Republican side. Although Reagan had not fulfilled the New Right's goals of securing a constitutional amendment against abortion, or one in favor of mandatory prayer in public schools, he remained the favorite of conservatives. His "supply-side" economics (the creation of University of Southern California economist Arthur Laffer), which harked back to Alexander Hamilton's "trickle-down theory," had in some part precipitated a severe recession in 1982. However, a glut of oil, created partly by Carter's conservation and energy programs, had caused energy prices to drop at the same time. Reagan's probusiness and antiregulatory stance had also helped to stimulate commercial activity. As a result, Americans were experiencing an expanding economy in 1984.

Economic issues complemented what was a growing reaction against liberalism in American society. And, for many Americans, feminism and the women's rights movement were closely tied to liberalism. Moreover, a well-organized prolife movement had developed during Reagan's first term. Since the *Roe v. Wade* decision of 1973, the number of annual documented abortions in the United States had almost doubled, totaling 1.3 million in 1977. The principal forces in the prolife movement viewed this increase as a call to arms. The Catholic church, which had officially opposed abortion since the mid-nineteenth century, began to fund organized prolife movements. The church opposed abortion and birth control as actions against the will of God. Forming alliances with the church, organizations such as the Pro-Life Action Committee and Operation Rescue went on the offensive, taking their campaign to Congress and to the streets. They targeted prochoice members of Congress for defeat, began picketing and blockading clinics that performed abortions, and rallied around the prolife President Reagan as the 1984 election neared.

Aside from social and economic issues, Republicans had one additional advantage: the personality of Ronald Reagan. A majority of voters were happy to overlook the gaffes, the staged press conferences, and the "sleaze factor" (the Reagan administration had more people under indictment than any administration in history) to give their enthusiastic support to the president. Democratic officials could only hope that the polls were inaccurate as Reagan and George Bush were pitted against Jimmy Carter's vice president, Walter Mondale, and New York congresswoman Geraldine Ferraro. The day after the nomination of Mondale and Ferraro, Reagan's double-digit lead in the polls disappeared. Undoubtedly, Ferarro's nomination was an important factor in the sudden switch. But even before the euphoria of the first-ever woman on a major party presidential ticket had worn off, Republican strategists went on the offensive. Making an issue of Ferraro's husband's financial dealings in New York, they kept Ferraro and Mondale on the defensive throughout the campaign. And although a barrier had finally been overcome for women in politics, this circumstance had little impact on the outcome of the election. Reagan received 59 percent of the popular vote and carried every state except Minnesota (Mondale's home state) and the District of Columbia. Reagan also won a majority of the women's vote. As Ferraro later analyzed this phenomenon, "Women, too, were disarmed by Reagan's charm and, like men, they voted for his popular image." Despite the defeat, Gloria Steinem and Ms. celebrated Geraldine Ferraro's nomination by making her one of the magazine's women of the year in 1985.

Shortly before the election of 1984, Gloria Steinem celebrated her fiftieth birthday. In a gala event in New York, the "feminist fatale" was honored by Hollywood celebrities, consumer advocate Ralph Nader, and even Rosa Parks, the woman who had refused to give up her seat on a bus to a white man and precipitated the 1955 Montgomery bus boycott. Tributes to Steinem were numerous. Actress Marlo Thomas declared, "Gloria is the only revolutionary leader in history who could be mistaken for a [Playboy] bunny." Coincidentally, a television movie based on Steinem's 1963 "A Bunny's Tale" had been recently released. A few months later, Steinem interviewed Hugh Hefner and his daughter, Christie, who had taken over management of Playboy Enterprises, for *People Weekly*. Steinem was objective to a point in her interview and analysis, but her long-standing opposition to pornography and sexual exploitation led her to conclude that "the last person I would want to go down in history as is Hugh Hefner." As for the magazine and the enterprise, she predicted, "As long as there are men with their heads stuck in the '50s, there'll be a place for *Playboy*."

Gloria Steinem's writing career continued to evolve through the 1980s. In 1986, for example, she published *Marilyn*, a pictorial history of movie star Marilyn Monroe. Using the photographs of George Barris (who had taken some of the last pictures of Monroe before her death) to frame the story, Steinem expanded on her sympathetic study of Monroe that had appeared in *Outrageous Acts and Everyday Rebellions*. By analyzing the hardships encountered by the starlet throughout her life, Steinem underscored her commitment to casting light on oppressed and exploited women in many walks of life. While many women, ranging from radical feminists to conservatives, held little but disdain for Marilyn Monroe, Steinem saw her as a human being caught in the vortex of stardom, "treated like an object," and finally compelled through unhappiness to take her own life. Like many other Hollywood starlets, Marilyn Monroe's story included sexual abuse as a child, an adult life marked by jealousy from other women, and an acting career that made her feel "valueless except for sex." Perhaps it took a person who herself had known hardships as a child and, later, celebrity to provide a new understanding of the life and death of Monroe. Steinem donated her fees for writing the book to help start a Marilyn Monroe Children's Fund within the Ms. Foundation for Women.

The tide of national conservatism continued to rise through the mid-1980s. The personal popularity of Ronald Reagan remained strong as his conservative message reached out to many Americans who believed that liberalism had gone too far. Even when the Iran–Contra affair became public knowledge in 1986, public opinion remained strong for the president. The incident involved the sale of arms by the

The spectrum of Gloria Steinem's political activism is revealed in part in this series of photographs. In a 1975 photograph Steinem is seen with New York Congresswoman Bella Abzug and New York Lieutenant Governor Maryanne Krupsak at the International Woman's Day March in New York City. On the opposite page (above) Steinem and NOW founder Betty Friedan sign ERAgrams to send to President Carter in 1977; (below) Steinem participates in a 1984 rally against apartheid in front of the South African embassy in Washington, D.C.

National Security Council (NSC) to the Iranian government of the Ayatollah Khomeini. The proceeds of those sales went to supply the Contras ("freedom fighters," according to Reagan), who were attempting to overthrow the Soviet-backed Sandinista government in Nicaragua. Eager to secure the release of American hostages in the Middle East and supply the Contras (even though Congress had forbidden further support for them in 1984), the Reagan administration carried out the covert operation under the direction of Marine Corps lieutenant colonel Oliver North of the NSC. As the story unfolded, it soon involved a host of shady characters, including international arms merchants, money launderers, and soldiers of fortune. In the congressional hearings on the affair, conducted in the summer of 1987, North testified that he had assumed that he had Reagan's approval for the operation. But the president denied any prior knowledge of the resupply effort. When North's superior, Admiral John Poindexter, testified that he had not told the president about North's illegal activities, Reagan was cleared of malfeasance, but North and Poindexter were both later convicted—and later acquitted—of some of the charges against them.

Reagan's credibility and popularity were damaged, but not enough to prevent the election of his vice president, George Bush, and Bush's running mate, Senator Dan Quayle of Indiana, in 1988. Despite an identification with the Iran–Contra affair, an unknown running mate of questionable ability, and a reputation as a "wimp," Bush won easily in 1988. His victory only confirmed that the Democratic party remained in disarray. Steinem and most women's groups had supported Massachusetts governor Michael Dukakis and his running mate, Texas senator Lloyd Bentsen, in the election. But Dukakis's lackluster campaigning and his reluctance to make an issue of Reagan's social conservatism had given women's rights groups little occasion for enthusiastic support.

Issues packaged as "family values" arose during the 1988 campaign. The future first lady, Barbara Bush, maintained an aura as a traditional political wife, as did Dan Quayle's wife, Marilyn, even though she was an accomplished lawyer. Both the Bushes and the Quayles gave a wholehearted endorsement to the prolife movement and expressed opposition to alternative lifestyles, specifically homosexuality. Helped by such support, the family values movement became more pronounced throughout the Bush administration. Because abortions gave an additional option to postpone parenthood, prolife forces saw it as a continuing threat to traditional family structures. They also believed that abortions killed babies, although the law did not recognize an unborn fetus as a human life. Prolifers, supported by fundamentalist Protestant and Catholic organizations, began nationwide advertising campaigns and, with civil disobedience and sometimes violence, stepped up pressure on clinics and physicians who performed abortions. Antiabortion leaders in Congress, such as Illinois representative Henry Hyde, who continually fought to revoke Medicaid funds for abortion, continued to whittle away at women's accessibility to abortions. Prochoice forces fought back with marches, lobbying, and their own political targeting of prolife members of Congress. A political candidate's stance on abortion became an issue in elections ranging from the national presidency to the city council. By late in the decade, abortion had become the most divisive issue since the Vietnam War, according to the *New York Times.*

Additional evidence of the waning women's rights movement was the financial trouble of Ms. by the decade's end. The decline in subscriptions could be partly attributed to conservatism and the volatility of the issues championed by Ms., such as reproductive rights and nondiscrimation on the basis of sexual orientation. But Ms. had been instrumental in changing many other women's magazines and inspiring a variety of others that competed for subscribers. Although they remained devoted to fashion and glamour, magazines such as *Vogue, McCall's, Redbook,* and *Cosmopolitan* had been recast to include information on women's health, politics, and issues of discrimination. A new genre of magazines like *Self* and *New Woman* appealed to women who wished to take control of their lives through physical fitness and health awareness, and they also appealed to the cultural phenomenon known as the me-generation. Turning inward after the tumult of Vietnam and Watergate, many young men and women had rejected the activism of those days for what historian Christopher Lasch called "the culture of narcissism." Through the late 1970s and the 1980s, middle-class Americans filled fitness centers, yoga classes, and diet clinics; bought millions of workout videotapes; and made a major industry of the health food business in efforts to improve their physical selves. For women, this was a relatively new phenomenon, and the success of magazines that analyzed health and fitness reflected a new feeling of self-importance inspired by the modern feminist movement. Ms. had been an important factor in the development of this growing

By the late 1980s, prolife demonstrations were common. Here, members of Operation Rescue sing a hymn as they illegally block the entrance to a clinic in New Orleans in 1989.

self-confidence in women, but its success was, in part, responsible for its financial woes by the late 1980s.

Ms. responded with its own revamping. After a seven-month hiatus during a declaration of bankruptcy, Ms. returned to publication in July 1990. The new Ms. was more intellectual and, remarkably, contained no advertising. Financial analysts and consultants, who derided the idea of returning to publication at all, thought even less of resuming the periodical without advertising dollars. But the Ms. editorial staff, including Steinem, Robin Morgan, and Ruth Bower, and the publisher, Lang Communications, believed that an intellectual feminist journal free of the coercion that advertising certain products often brought would be successful. They were willing to use the magazine's remaining financial reserves in the venture. As Morgan put it, "Only she who attempts the absurd can achieve the impossible."

The new Ms. was an instant success. The first issue sold out so rapidly that a second printing was ordered, which also sold out. Robin Morgan had taken the editor-in-chief position, and Gloria Steinem, who had held the position for almost two decades, remained on the staff as consulting editor. The magazine was quick to adapt to changing times on the world political scene, appealing to subscribers in 117 countries.

The rapid changes in society and culture in the bewildering decade of the 1990s assured readers of lively discourse in the pages of Ms., and the magazine did not back away from covering the volatile social and gender issues of the day. Ms. analyzed the Senate hearings on the confirmation of Bush Supreme Court nominee Clarence Thomas, in which one of his legal assistants, Anita Hill, accused him of sexual harassment. Supporting Hill's contention that Thomas had harassed her by making unwanted sexual advances, Ms. was at odds with public opinion polls, in which a majority of those polled believed that Anita Hill was not telling the truth. Yet the issues raised by Ms. and other women's publications were more important than the outcome of the hearings that confirmed Thomas as the second African-American Supreme Court justice. The Senate Judiciary Committee had no female members, and women's groups branded it as a "good old boys' club." Certain committee members, including Pennsylvania senator Arlen Specter, supporting the prolife, conservative Bush Supreme Court nominee, attacked Hill, questioning her loyalty to her former boss, inquiring about her sexual activities, and exploring possible ulterior motives.

The Hill–Thomas hearings symbolized deep-seated emotions concerning gender issues in and out of the workplace. Sexual harassment became more broadly defined in the wake of the hearings. Beyond direct propositioning, off-color or sexual jokes, references to another person's anatomy, derogatory terminology, touching, and condescending behavior could now be regarded as sexual harassment in the workplace. Law firms specializing in sexual harassment arose to accommodate this broadened definition. Other concepts, such as date rape and spouse rape, entered the public lexicon and expanded greatly the concept of rape as opposed to consensual sex. Women's groups targeted members of the Senate Judiciary Committee who had attacked Anita Hill. In the 1992 election, Arlen Specter barely survived the challenge of Lynn Yeakel, who ran on a platform of casting Specter as an antifeminist.

Issues of sexuality had reached new levels of complexity in the 1990s. Perhaps the single most significant underlying issue of the debate, however, was not a political one, but a medical one. In 1983, the Center for Disease Control (CDC) identified the human immunodeficiency virus (HIV) and connected it to a terminal disease called acquired immune deficiency syndrome (AIDS). The CDC believes that the AIDS virus can be transferred through the exchange of bodily fluids or through the sharing of unsterilized needles. Public awareness grew, but through the 1980s most Americans believed that AIDS was a disease that affected only homosexual males and intravenous drug users. By the end of the decade statistics were revealing otherwise. The HIV virus was detected among heterosexuals in other parts of the globe, and by the early 1990s there were nearly one million cases reported worldwide. Because HIV infection usually has a long incubation period—an average, it is now thought, of seven years—before the symptoms of AIDS appear, it seems likely that the epidemic was in its early stages until the mid-1990s. The deadly virus has inexorably changed sexual mores in both heterosexuals and homosexuals. Because sexual activity greatly heightens the chances of acquiring HIV infection, the sexual freedom of the postwar era has become somewhat of an anachronism. Well before the AIDS crisis, Gloria Steinem had called attention to the negative implications of sexual freedom for women in an article entitled "The Sexual Revolution Wasn't Our War" in the premier issue of Ms. in 1972. Ms. magazine followed the AIDS crisis through the 1980s and, in the 1990s, did a series of special reports on the impact of the epidemic on women around the world.

In 1988, Gloria Steinem began reducing her editorial duties at Ms. in order to do her own writing and draw back from the hectic pace she had maintained for so many years. She celebrated the first two-week period in over twenty years in which she had not packed and gone somewhere on an airplane. Nonetheless she continued to write and speak for women's rights and social causes and, in general, against the policies of the Bush administration. Taking particular offense at George Bush and Dan Quayle's opposition to pending family leave legislation, their support of the prolife and family values movement, and the conduct of the Persian Gulf conflict of early 1991, Steinem found it easy to support the Democratic candidacy of Arkansas governor Bill Clinton and his running mate, Senator Al Gore of Tennessee. Steinem also took heart as an unprecedented number of female candidates vied for federal and state election throughout the nation in 1992.

Early handicapping in the 1992 campaign heavily favored the reelection of the Bush–Quayle administration. Despite the opposition of women's groups to the military action, the Persian Gulf conflict against Iraqi dictator Saddam Hussein had widespread approval in the United States. Working through the United Nations, Bush had issued an ultimatum to Iraq to withdraw from neighboring Kuwait after a successful invasion in the summer of 1990. Following four months of failed negotiations, the UN forces struck in Kuwait in January 1991. In less than three weeks, the Iraqi army had been smashed, and its remnants had scurried back to the heavily damaged capital of Baghdad. Kuwait had been liberated with only a few American battle casualties (as many as 150,000 Iraqis may have been killed). President Bush's approval ratings soared past 70 percent, and his reelection, like Reagan's in 1984, seemed a foregone conclusion.

Adding to Bush's popularity was the economic and social conservatism inherited from the Reagan administration. Supply-side economics, tax cuts mixed with huge defense outlays, and continued low inflation kept the economy chugging along with about 3 percent annual growth through the early part of the Bush administration. Meanwhile, the high tide of conservatism crested over social radicalism. As gay and lesbian rights activists grew more vocal in their demands for nondiscrimination against homosexuals, they sparked a negative response in far broader groups than merely the religious right. Moderates and even some liberals of both sexes balked at enthusiastic support of openly homosexual individuals and gay rights groups such as Queer Nation. When new NOW president Patricia Ireland declared that she was a lesbian despite remaining married to a man, the mainstream organization of the women's rights movement was drawn further into the volatile issue of sexual orientation. All along, feminists such as Gloria Steinem had advocated the inclusion of lesbians in the women's rights movement, but it continued to be a divisive issue.

Fear of lesbianism, gay bashing, the antiabortion movement, and opposition to "political correctness" found much common ground in the early 1990s. Decrying political correctness as government-imposed thought control, conservatives went further to define the phenomenon as a result of the "victims' revolution." All groups "victimized" by white male oppression were now getting even by punishing one generation of white males in the United States. One of the principal critics of the "victims' revolution" was radio commentator Rush Limbaugh. Politically, economically, and culturally conservative, Limbaugh began hosting a radio talk show in Sacramento, California, in the mid-1980s. In 1988, his show reached a national audience and, by 1992, was syndicated on over 600 stations around the nation. The same year saw Limbaugh with a regular television program, using the forum to denounce liberalism and ridicule its extremes. With regard to feminism, Limbaugh charged that the mainstream movement had been coopted by a small minority of "femi-Nazis," who were satisfied only with an ever-increasing number of annual abortions and with "get-even-ism," the punishment of men for the inequities of the past.

Limbaugh's immense popularity had an intellectual counterpart in the bestselling *Illiberal Education* (1991) by Dinesh D'Souza. Using largely anecdotal evidence, D'Souza, an immigrant from India, called into question the "cultural revolution" taking place in American universities, including the curricula of ethnic and gender studies programs, and affirmative action policies favoring women and minorities over white males in enrollment and faculty hiring. Exploring issues under headings such as "Tyranny of the Minority," "More Equal Than Others," and "The New Censorship," *Illiberal Education* decries an alleged double standard in the system favoring anyone but white males. For D'Souza, the university had become a prime example of the "get-even-ism" Limbaugh identified.

Into this fray of cultural warfare came feminist journalist Susan Faludi, who published *Backlash: The Undeclared War against American Women* in October 1991. Looking back at the gender battleground of the 1970s and 1980s, Faludi, also using largely anecdotal evidence, identified a systematic effort on the part of many people to discredit, slander, and distort the goals of modern feminism. This "backlash" against feminism was designed to strike fear into women and convince them that equality was undesirable and even dangerous. Citing studies in which women who had careers had only slight possibilities of marrying and having a family, Faludi argued that such studies were biased, misleading, and designed to put women back in the home. Moreover, Faludi attacked leading antifeminists such as Phyllis Schlafly and the Heritage Foundation's Connaught Marshner, both of whom are highly educated, wealthy, and influential. Without the women's rights movement, argued Faludi, Schlafly and Marshner would not be in prominent positions to attack feminism.

Despite the so-called backlash, women of the 1990s appeared to have little inclination to return to the 1950s. Even if they wanted to return to being housewives, the economic times often prohibited such a lifestyle. Since 1973, real wages—the buying power of one's income—had steadily declined. A single breadwinner was impractical for most households, and single-parent households were on the rise. Only 33 percent of American women between the ages of eighteen and sixty-four worked outside the home in 1950, but by 1992, 69 percent of women between those ages worked. Many female role models of the 1990s exhibited little in the way of tradition either. From pop star Madonna, whose music and performances were openly sexual but female-dominant, to working-class heroine Rosanne Barr, women celebrities of the 1990s were strong and confident. Popular culture crossed over into presidential politics in 1991, when Candice Bergen in her role as Murphy Brown had a child out of wedlock. When Vice President Dan Quayle criticized the CBS network and the show's producers for "mocking family values," Bergen responded that Quayle was insensitive to the problems of American working women.

The presidential election of 1992 in many ways became a referendum on what family values actually were. Bush and Quayle maintained the conservative stance that had elected Republican candidates for three straight terms, while Clinton and Gore adopted a prochoice platform that endorsed family leave legislation and other women's rights issues. Several additional factors weighed heavily in 1992. The economy, always an issue, began to stagnate after the Persian Gulf war. Just as suddenly, it seemed, the Cold War ended as the Soviet Union literally broke apart. On New Year's Eve, 1991, the Soviet Union officially disbanded. The immediate American response was euphoria, but euphoria quickly turned to desperation for the defense industry. The United States had been "downsizing" since the late 1980s, but the major reductions came after 1991. Defense-based economies, especially in southern California, which had for so long boomed with Cold-War military spending, fell into serious recession. Through most of 1992, much of the United States seemed to be at an economic standstill.

Still another factor in the election of 1992 was Texas billionaire H. Ross Perot. Forming the "Stand Up, America" political organization, Perot attracted millions to his on-again, off-again presidential candidacy. Perot's message was that the country belonged to "its owners," the taxpayers of the nation. If elected, Perot declared, he would act as chief executive officer of a corporation, because "government should operate like a business." Casting both President Bush and Governor Clinton as "career politicians" and a big part of what was wrong with the country, Perot developed a great following among Americans disgruntled with the major political parties.

A stagnant economy and the impact of Perot served to make the Bush popularity decline one of the most precipitous in American history. No president with a such a high approval rating had ever lost a reelection bid. But by mid-1992 Bush's popularity had dropped to under 30 percent. Women's groups spearheaded a second frontal attack against the Bush administration, decrying its prolife, antifeminist policies. On election day, all factors spelled defeat for Bush and Quayle. Many Republicans and conservative Democrats voted the third party, and while he carried no states, Perot received 19 percent of the popular vote. Women voters supported the Clinton candidacy strongly, giving the Democrat 47 percent of their votes. The result was a victory for forty-six-year-old Bill Clinton and forty-four-year-old Al Gore, with 43 percent of the popular vote and 357 electoral votes. The high percentage of women voters who cast their ballots for Clinton was crucial in gaining dozens of electoral votes for the Democrat in this three-way race.

Although two more white males entered the White House in 1993, women's rights advocates had much to celebrate politically in the "year of the woman." Carol Moseley Braun became the first African-American female to be elected to the U.S. Senate; California elected two women senators, Diane Feinstein and Barbara Boxer; and two other women from both parties entered the "good old boys' club." As a result of the election of 1992, 6 percent of the Senate and 3 percent of the House of Representatives was now female. In all, 117 women ran for Congress.

Bill Clinton's election brought a "liberated woman" into the White House. Hillary Rodham Clinton promised to be the most politically active first lady since Eleanor Roosevelt. During the campaign, Hillary Clinton campaigned independently for her husband rather than remaining loyally by his side. After Clinton took office, Hillary Clinton, an accomplished lawyer, took charge of the president's ambitious health care program and was given the responsibility of both plan formulation and promotion.

True to his campaign promise, Clinton appointed a cabinet and staff "that looked like America." In addition to two male African Americans and two Latinos, Clinton appointed Janet Reno as Attorney General, Donna Shalala as head of Health and Human Services, Laura d'Andrea Tyson as chief economic adviser, Hazel O'Leary as Secretary of Energy, and Carol Browner as head of the Environmental Protection Agency, and gained Senate approval of Ruth Bader Ginsberg to the U.S. Supreme Court. Gloria Steinem was impressed by Clinton, who, in contrast to George Bush, saw himself as "a catalyst of change from the bottom up." His inclusion of women and minorities gave further credence to her opinion.

The Clinton–Gore magnetism prevailed again in 1996, when the Democratic incumbent defeated long-time Kansas senator Robert Dole, and his running mate, Jack Kemp. Again the Clinton–Gore ticket enjoyed strong support from women. Presiding over the peaceful post-Cold-War era, Clinton attained high job-approval ratings based largely on a strong economy. By early 1998, the Dow Jones industrial average approached 9000 for the first time ever, inflation was virtually nonexistent, interest rates were at thirty-year lows, and national unemployment was less than 5 percent. Women again supported Clinton in about the same percentages as 1992. This was despite strong allegations of Clinton's own philandering: allegations con-

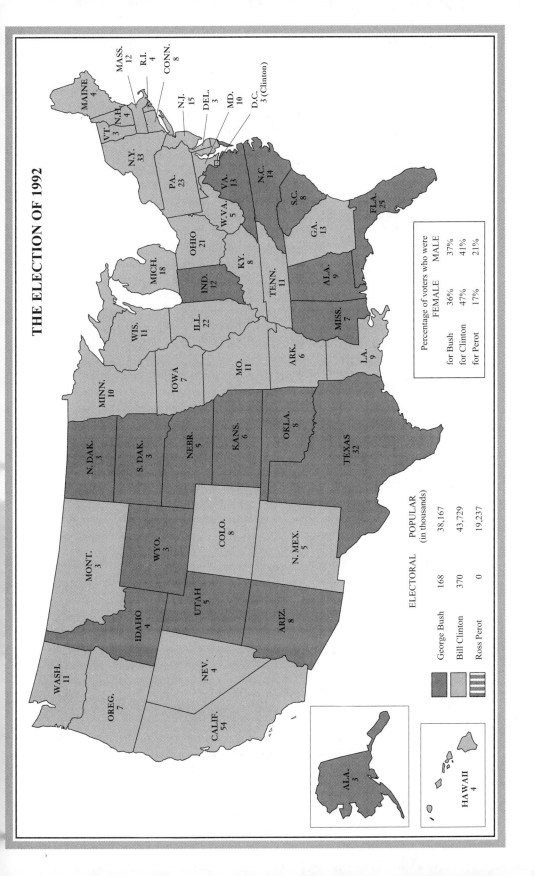

THE ELECTION OF 1992

MASS. 12
R.I. 4
CONN. 8
N.J. 15
DEL. 3
MD. 10
D.C. 3 (Clinton)

MAINE 4
VT. 3
N.H. 4
N.Y. 33
PA. 23
VA. 13
N.C. 14
S.C. 8
FLA. 25
W.VA. 5
GA. 13
OHIO 21
KY. 8
TENN. 11
ALA. 9
MICH. 18
IND. 12
ILL. 22
MISS. 7
WIS. 11
LA. 9
MINN. 10
IOWA 7
MO. 11
ARK. 6
N. DAK. 3
S. DAK. 3
NEBR. 5
KANS. 6
OKLA. 8
TEXAS 32
MONT. 3
WYO. 3
COLO. 8
N. MEX. 5
IDAHO 4
UTAH 5
ARIZ. 8
WASH. 11
OREG. 7
NEV. 4
CALIF. 54

ALA. 3
HAWAII 4

	Percentage of voters who were	
	FEMALE	MALE
for Bush	36%	37%
for Clinton	47%	41%
for Perot	17%	21%

	ELECTORAL	POPULAR (in thousands)
George Bush	168	38,167
Bill Clinton	370	43,729
Ross Perot	0	19,237

firmed with 1998 revelations concerning an affair with White House intern Monica Lewinsky. Because Clinton initially denied the existence of the affair to special prosecutor Kenneth Starr, he became the second president in U.S. history to be impeached by the House of Representatives. Clinton was spared removal from office, however, when fewer than two-thirds of the Senate voted to convict him of obstruction of justice.

Regardless of their sentiments toward President Clinton, more women gained political office again in 1996 and 1998. That a number of these women were conservatives was perhaps an indication of a "third wave of feminism." Women were firmly in the political process and could now take for granted the basic rights for which feminists had so long fought. In short, women politicians could now afford to be conservative. The "third wave" also has strong cultural ramifications. "Postfeminist" authors (the term suggests that traditional feminism is waning) have little in common with previous generations. Celebrating sexuality, authors like Camille Paglia, who published *Sexual Personae* in 1990, argue that a woman's sexual attraction is the greatest force in humanity. Throughout history, men have remained powerless because of their obsession with the female body, and therefore are actually the weaker sex. Decrying what she views as the "victimhood" promoted by traditional feminism, Paglia argues that women should instead use their sexual attraction to their best advantage. Postfeminists therefore ascribe to health, fitness, and adornment to achieve their goals, and a generation of young women follow the guidance of the sexy Spice Girls more than the nostrums of traditional feminism.

Gloria Steinem's activism continued throughout the mid-1990s, and she has proven her ability to adapt to the changing world of feminism. She devoted much of her time to producing *Revolution from Within: A Book of Self-Esteem*, released in early 1992, and *Moving Beyond Words: Age, Race, Sex, Power, Money, Muscles: Breaking Boundaries of Gender*, released in 1994. *Revolution from Within* soared to the top of the bestseller list, and while it earned acclaim from many readers and critics, some feminist leaders decried its content. Rather than a call to arms against the backlash of the times, *Revolution from Within* is a treatise on self-improvement. The message is both simple and abstract: The power of the individual is the greatest power on earth, and yet Western society has consistently suppressed individual self-esteem for several centuries. How this is done and how people can overcome it is the complex part of the book. Through subtle illustrations and careful analysis, Steinem demonstrates how childhood molds people into easily manipulated adults. She dedicated the book "to anyone who respects the unique self inside a child." Through "unlearning" and "rethinking," people can regain the powerful self, for "it's never too late for a happy childhood."

Steinem's premise drew a diversity of criticism. Existentialists called it "squishy new-age thumbsucking," while feminists wondered where Steinem's "anger" had gone. Her sympathetic analysis of abused children who become abusive men outraged women who viewed men as the enemy. And her personal accounts of relationships with men weakened her in the estimation of some feminists. But sales suggested that readers of both sexes were receptive to her message, and Steinem shrugged off the criticism. "Instead of feeling discouraged and confused," she wrote

in 1993, "I felt the strength of readers coming back to me. Instead of losing something when this book left home, I understood that I had gained the learning, comfort, and magic of community." By getting at the things that arouse people's deepest
emotions—love and hate, companionships and disunity—Gloria Steinem had
again touched a raw nerve in American society. But this time she had a solution to
the problem: self-esteem.

Moving Beyond Words is series of essays reflecting Steinem's keen understanding
of human behavior. Offering fresh perspectives on the work and impact of Sigmund
Freud, the advertising industry, wealth, women's health, and aging, Steinem weaves
a seemingly disparate group of topics into a seamless study of people. Neither stri-
dent nor preachy, her essays demonstrate that she continues to learn more about
people and why they do what they do.

Taking up the cause of feminism almost three decades ago, Gloria Steinem believed that women's rights activism would be only another phase in her career. She
found, however, that feminism was her life's blood and passion. Her writing evolved
with the evolving women's rights movement and benefited from the humanism
forged in listening to the stories of thousands of people. Gloria Steinem's concern
for all people extends from the view that society can be improved—even though
the process is often slow and beset by obstacles. "As a feminist," she once wrote,
"I've learned that lasting social change, like a house, can only be built from the bottom up."

SELECTED READINGS
The Person

Daffron, Carolyn: Gloria Steinem: Feminist (1988). Life and times biography in an illustrated
juvenile format.

Heilbrun, Carolyn G.: The Education of a Woman: The Life of Gloria Steinem (1995). The first
definitive biography.

*Hoff, Mark: Gloria Steinem: The Women's Movement (1991). Brief biography placing
Steinem's work in the context of the women's movement.

*Steinem, Gloria: Outrageous Acts and Everyday Rebellions (1983). Steinem's first full-length
book, containing autobiographical information, essays, biographies, and commentary.

*Steinem, Gloria: Revolution from Within: A Book of Self-Esteem (1992). A collection of
Steinem's observations, personal anecdotes, and overall philosophy.

*Steinem, Gloria: Moving Beyond Words: Age, Race, Sex, Power, Money, Muscles: Breaking
Boundaries of Gender (1994). Essays on diverse topics with the common theme of humanity.

Stern, Sydney: Gloria Steinem: Her Passions, Politics, and Mystique (1997). A thorough biography.

---

*Available in paperback.

The Period

*Beauvoir, Simone De: *The Second Sex* (1953). Pioneering study of how Western society is inherently unequal for women.

*Evans, Sara: *Personal Politics: The Roots of Women's Liberation in the Civil Rights Movement and the New Left* (1979). Insights into the origins of the feminist crusade in the 1960s.

*Faludi, Susan: *Backlash: The Undeclared War against American Women* (1991). An analysis of the negative reaction to modern feminism.

Ferraro, Geraldine: *Ferraro: My Story* (1985). The autobiography of the first female vice presidential candidate in one of the major political parties.

*Firestone, Shulamith: *The Dialectic of Sex: The Case for Feminist Revolution* (1970). One of the early bibles of the modern radical feminist movement advocating an end to patriarchal society.

*Friedan, Betty: *The Feminine Mystique* (1963). Both a primary document and a secondary source, the book had an important role in launching the modern women's rights movement.

Gelb, Joyce, and Marian Lief Palley: *Women and Public Policies* (1982). Scholarly assessment of the impact of women's groups on public policy since the 1960s.

Landrum, Gene N.: *Profiles of Female Genius: Thirteen Creative Women Who Changed the World* (1994). Steinem is included in these brief biographies of contemporary American women.

Lasch, Christopher: *The Culture of Narcissism: American Life in an Age of Diminishing Expectations* (1979). An essentially hostile analysis of the changes in American priorities from the 1960s to the 1970s.

*Limbaugh, Rush: *The Way Things Ought to Be* (1990). Reflections of the conservative radio commentator on liberalism in the United States.

Limbaugh, Rush: *See, I Told You So* (1993). A conservative critique of, among other things, the early Clinton administration.

Millett, Kate: *Sexual Politics* (1970). Analysis of male writing in the context of antifeminism.

Morgan, Robin: *Sisterhood Is Powerful* (1970). Study of systematic discrimination against women.

National Commission on the Observance of International Women's Year: *What Women Want* (1979). Proceedings of the Houston conference in 1977, with an introduction by Gloria Steinem.

Ryan, Mary: *Womanhood in America: From Colonial Times to the Present* (1983). Perhaps the most useful of several general surveys.

Steinem, Gloria, and George Barris: *Marilyn* (1986). Pictorial study of Marilyn Monroe from the perspective of Steinem and the last person to photograph her.

FOR CONSIDERATION

1. Once in college, Gloria Steinem was determined to succeed. Why was she perhaps more determined than most of her classmates at Smith College?

---

*Available in paperback.

2. As a graduate of Smith College, Steinem had limited career horizons. What historical factors created this condition for women of the 1950s?

3. Discuss the events leading to Steinem's interest in women's rights.

4. The mid-1970s was the zenith of the women's movement. Why was this? What were some of the landmark events of the period, and what happened to the movement in the 1980s?

5. Steinem has always been inclusive in her feminist work. How have women's issues become increasingly complex in recent years? What are some solutions offered by Gloria Steinem?

Credits

We gratefully acknowledge the use of photographs from the following sources:

Reading 1:
Page B: Brown Brothers;   Page 6: Harper's Monthly, 1858;   Page 11 (top): January 1865/Harper's New Monthly Magazine; (bottom): The Fine Arts Museum of San Francisco, Gift of Elizabeth C. Lacey;   Page 12: Nevada Historical Society, Virginia City;   Page 31: Library of Congress.

Reading 2:
Page 40: AP/Wide World Photos;   Page 54: University of Maryland, Baltimore County Library;   Page 55: Library of Congress;   Page 62 (top): Collection of Oliver Jensen; (left): University of Illinois at Chicago/Jane Addams Memorial Collection, the University Library; (right): Library of Congress.

Reading 3:
Page 74: Brown Brothers;   Page 86: Library of Congress;   Page 93 (top): The Newark News/Wisa; (bottom): Tacoma Ledger.

Reading 4:
Page 106: From the Collections of the Henry Ford Museum & Greenfield Village; Page 115: Automobile Association of America. Reproduced by permission;   Page 116 (top): Ford Archives/From the Collections of Henry Ford Museum & Greenfield Village;   Page 134: Corbis/UPI;   Page 135: AP/Wide World Photos.

Reading 5:
Page 142: Corbis;   Page 150: The Franklin D. Roosevelt Library;   Page 151 (top): AP/Wide World Photos; (bottom): Corbis;   Page 177 (top): The Franklin D. Roosevelt Library; (bottom): AP/Wide World Photos;   Page 178 (top): AP/Wide World Photos; (bottom): Corbis/UPI.

Reading 6:
Page 182: Bruce Davidson/Magnum Photos, Inc.;   Page 198 (top): AP/Wide World Photos;   Page 199 (bottom): AP/Wide World Photos;   Pages 205 and 206: AP/Wide World Photos.

Index

Note: Italicized page numbers indicate illustrations

Birth control, 153, 299
Bixby, Horace, 5, 8
Black, Bill, 269, 277, 285
Black, Hugo, 162
Black, Lillie Devereaux "Tiger Lillie," 62
Black Americans
  blues music of, 267
  demography of, 205
  Eleanor Roosevelt and, 158–160, 164
  election of 1936, 192
  election of 1940, 164
  New Deal, of Franklin D. Roosevelt and, 159
  Progressive Party and, 60–61
  racial pride, 190–191
Blackboard Jungle (1955), 276
Black Cabinet, 192
Blackman, Joan, 279
Black Muslims, 198, 204
Black Panther Party for Self-Defense, 205, 209, 210, 246
Black Power advocates, 190, 206–207, 209, 300
Black Star Steamship Line, 190
Black Thursday, 132
Black Tuesday, 132
Blaine, James G., 26, 30
Bland-Allison Act (1878), 28
Blue-collar radicalism, 59
Blue Moon Boys (band), 271
Blue Moon of Kentucky, 269
Blues, 266–267
Bonaparte, Napoleon, 75
Bonus Army, march on Washington, 135–136
Boone, Daniel, 1
Boone and Crockett Club, 87
Bootleggers, 126
Boston Manufacturing Company, 112
Boston University, 195
Bower, Ruth, 314
Boxer, Barbara, 318
Boycotts
  Montgomery bus boycott, 196–197
  Olympic Games boycott (1980), 305
Boy Scouts (1910), 94–95, 155
Brady, Tom, 196
Brandeis, Louis D., 57, 61, 97
Brandeis University, 176
Brando, Marlon, 274
Braun, Carol Moseley, 318
Bread lines, in the Great Depression, *134*
Bridger, Jim, 10, *24*
Brisbane, Albert, 53
Brister, Owen, 176
Britain, Battle of, 165
British invasion, of rock music, 281
Brooke, Edward, 210

Brook Farm, 53
Brooklyn, New York, immigration into, 45
Brotherhood of Pullman Porters, 193
Brown, Edmund G., 242
Brown, H. Rap, 205, 206–207
Brown, James, 276
Browner, Carol, 318
Brown v. Board of Education of Topeka (1954), 195–196, 211
Bryan, William Jennings, 52, 59, 63, 95, 119
Bryant, William Cullen, 81
Bryce, Cornelia. See Pinchot, Cornelia Bryce
Buchanan, James, 8
Buddy Holly and the Crickets, 276
Buffalo, hunting of, 23, 25
Buffalo Springfield, 282
Bulgaria, 168
Bull Moose Party. *See* Progressive Party
Bull Run, Battle of (1861), 9
Bunche, Ralph, 193, 195
A Bunny's Tale (Steinem), 297
Bureau of Forestry, 89–90
Burns, Lucy, 152
Burroughs, Edgar Rice, 95
Burroughs, John, *117*, 124
Burton, James, 286
Bush, Barbara, 312
Bush, George, 308, 312, 315–316, 317–318
Business and corporations, 112
  in the 1920's, 132
  anti-trust suits and corporate regulation, 88
  diversity of General Motors, 133
  government regulation of, 28
  gross national product, in World War II, 167
  growth of, in late 1800's, 19–20
  horizontal integration of, 20
  monopolistic, 88
  muckraking of, 87
  New Deal, dislike of, 221
  probusiness attitude of Harding and Hoover, 129
  reforms of Theodore Roosevelt, 88, 89
  small business, in the 1920's, 132
  vertical integration of, 20
Busing, 211
Butterfield Overland Mail Company, 10
Byrd, William, 81
Byrnes, James, 167

Calhoun, John C., 184–185
California, 13–14
Call of the Wild (London, 1903), 95
Cambodia, 235, 246, 248
Camp David Peace Accord (1979), 305